A+
Technician's
On-the-Job
Guide to

Windows® XP

A+

Technician's
On-the-Job
Guide to

Windows® XP

Curt Simmons

McGraw-Hill/Osborne

New York • Chicago • San Francisco
Lisbon • London • Madrid • Mexico City
Milan • New Delhi • San Juan
Seoul • Singapore • Sydney • Toronto

The McGraw·Hill Companies

McGraw-Hill/Osborne
2600 Tenth Street
Berkeley, California 94710
U.S.A.

To arrange bulk purchase discounts for sales promotions, premiums, or fund-raisers, please contact **McGraw-Hill**/Osborne at the above address. For information on translations or book distributors outside the U.S.A., please see the International Contact Information page immediately following the index of this book.

A+ Technician's On-the-Job Guide to Windows® XP

1234567890 DOC DOC 019876543

ISBN 0-07-222690-0

Publisher
Brandon A. Nordin

Vice President & Associate Publisher
Scott Rogers

Acquisitions Editor
Nancy Maragioglio

Project Editor
Jody McKenzie

Acquisitions Coordinator
Jessica Wilson

Technical Editor
Kim Frank

Copy Editors
Andy Saff
Lunaea Weatherstone

Proofreader
Claire Splan

Indexer
Jack Lewis

Computer Designers
Carie Abrew
Lucie Ericksen

Illustrators
Melinda Moore Lytle
Michael Mueller
Lyssa Wald

Series Design
Carie Abrew
Kelly Stanton-Scott

Cover Series Design
Jeff Weeks

This book was composed with Corel VENTURA™ Publisher.

ABOUT THE AUTHOR

Curt Simmons (A+, MCSA, MCSE, CTT) is a technology author and trainer based in Dallas, Texas. Curt is the author of more than 20 high-level and user-level computing books on a variety of topics. When Curt is not writing about new technology, he spends his time with his wife and children. You can visit Curt on the Internet at **http://www.curtsimmons.com** or send him an e-mail at **curt_simmons@hotmail.com**.

ABOUT THE TECHNICAL EDITOR

Kim Frank (MCT, MCSE on W2K/NT4.0, MCSE+I, MCSA, MCP+I, A+) has more than 10 years experience in the global Internet technology (IT) arena. He is originally from Denmark, where he worked for a leading multinational professional services organization. Kim is now a technical trainer and cofounder of CTE Solutions, Inc., a prominent Microsoft Certified Technical Education Center (CTEC) in Ottawa, Canada, and teaches at various locations across the country. Among his specialties are .NET Server, Windows XP, and Windows 2000 Active Directory design, implementation, and migration. Kim can be reached at **kim@kimfrank.com**.

CONTENTS AT A GLANCE

CONTENTS

ACKNOWLEDGMENTS

I would like to thank several people who have made this book possible. First, thanks to Nancy Maragioglio for thinking of me for this project—it's been fun. Thanks to Kim Frank for a thorough technical review. Also thanks to Jody McKenzie and Jessica Wilson for keeping things moving in the right direction and bringing the book to completion. As always, thanks to my agent, Margot, for taking care of the details. And finally, thanks to my family for their support.

INTRODUCTION

WELCOME TO A+ TECHNICIAN'S ON-THE-JOB GUIDE TO WINDOWS XP

Windows XP is Microsoft's latest operating system, and one that has been well received by the public as well as Microsoft networking environments. It does more, works better, is easier to use, and is problem-free… right? As an A+ technician, or someone who is aspiring to be an A+ technician, you may be faced with the task of supporting Windows XP. Although Windows XP is overall a good operating system, it is a complex operating system that can present you, the problem solver, with complex problems. Why write a book about Windows XP for A+ technicians? To help you do your job!

A+ certification gives you a marketable certification in today's computer support work force. But beyond the standard exam objectives and questions (which now include a lot of Windows XP material), you'll need to support Windows XP as it makes its way into your network. You'll need to know what Windows XP can and can't do, how to configure it, and perhaps most important, how to solve a number of Windows XP problems. This is where this book becomes your help and your guide. I've written this book so that it explores the ins and outs of Windows XP and focuses on the issues you are most likely to face as an A+ technician. In fact, this book even covers all of the A+ exam objectives in light of Windows XP.

What if you are not yet an A+ technician, but you are striving to become one? This book also serves as a great study guide. Although this book is not an exam prep book, it looks at Windows XP in terms of A+ skills. If you have yet to pass your A+ exams, you should definitely study your A+ certification guides, but also study this book so that you'll have a sharper edge for any Windows XP questions that the exam might throw your way. Windows XP is a powerful, popular operating system that is here to stay, and honing your Windows XP skills can only be a help in your career.

A+ Technician's On-the-Job Guide to Windows XP is a new kind of book. It is designed to give you easy-to-use and easy-to-find information, most often in a step-by-step, task-oriented format. After all, performing tasks and solving problems is your job, so this book's format is designed to lead you through each step of those duties. You won't have to read paragraph after paragraph of dry, boring text to find information and answers; this book gives you succinct information about many different Windows XP topics as they relate to the

A+ technician's job. In fact, the idea is that you can pull this book off your shelf, find the problem or issue you are experiencing, read about it, and fix it.

You don't have to read this book in any particular order. You can read it from cover to cover if you like, or you can jump around and find answers when you need them—the choice is yours. Just use the table of contents or the book's index to find help on all important Windows XP topics quickly and easily.

This book is for the A+ audience and for those striving to become A+ certified. It assumes that you know a thing or two about computers, but not that you are already a networking expert. If you have passed your A+ certification or if you are moving in that direction, then this book is for you.

To help you along the way, I've also included a few elements that you'll find helpful:

- **Note**   Notes are little bursts of information that give you some additional information. You don't have to read these, but they can help you.

- **Secret**   Secrets are friendly, timesaving tips I have thrown in from time to time that can make your work with XP easier.

- **Tech Talk**   These sidebars provide practical insights into specific task options. These sidebars often contain additional steps, workarounds, and other tricks that you can use on the job to make your work with Windows XP easier.

- **Troubleshooting**   These sidebars explore a specific problem and solution. You'll find these scattered throughout the book, and they deal with issues and problems that you are most likely to encounter. Make sure you pay attention to these!

- **Painful Lessons I've Learned**   These sidebars point out some painful but important lessons I have learned while supporting Windows XP.

Are you ready? Then let's dive into the world of Windows XP and your job of supporting Microsoft's latest.

Thanks! Enjoy the book!

Curt Simmons
Saint Jo, Texas
Curt_Simmons@hotmail.com
www.curtsimmons.com

INSTALLING WINDOWS XP PROFESSIONAL

1

Installing Windows XP Professional is much the same as installing previous versions of Windows—you run the setup program and follow the prompts, right? Truthfully, you can install Windows XP Professional rather easily and most often without complication. However, as an A+ technician supporting Windows XP, you need to be aware of a number of potential setup issues and setup options to manage Windows XP installations effectively. The good news is we'll cover those issues and setup options in this chapter so that you'll be able to tackle any Windows XP installation problems or situations that come your way. In this chapter, you'll...

- Get ready for installation
- Perform attended installations of Windows XP
- Perform unattended installations of Windows XP
- Transfer files and settings

GETTING READY FOR INSTALLATION

Windows XP Professional provides you with two different types of installation: attended and unattended. In an attended installation of Windows XP Professional, you "attend" to the computer as installation is taking place. In this situation, you can use a CD-ROM to install Windows XP, or you can install Windows XP over the network from a network share. In either case, you physically run the installation and answer installation prompts as they occur. You can also install Windows XP Professional in several "unattended" ways, which you can learn more about later in this chapter. In an unattended installation, you use an automated method to install Windows XP so that installation occurs automatically without user input.

As with previous versions of Windows, particularly Windows 2000 Professional, the key to a successful Windows XP Professional installation is to plan carefully beforehand. Through proper planning, you can avoid problems before they occur and you can make sure your computer and applications are ready to meet the demands of Windows XP Professional. If you are armed with the correct information, installation is typically anticlimactic because you solve potential problems before they occur. In the following sections, you'll explore the important planning steps you should take before installing Windows XP Professional.

MINIMUM HARDWARE REQUIREMENTS

Sure, you've heard this before, but the simple fact remains: Your computer must be able to handle the hardware demands of Windows XP; otherwise, your installation will either fail or result in a system that is so pitifully slow that it is of no practical value. Before installing Windows XP Professional, you need to check out the computer's hardware and make sure it's powerful enough to handle the demands of Windows XP. Table 1-1 gives you the minimum as well as the recommended hardware requirements for Windows XP. As you might expect, the base, or minimum, hardware requirements are just that—what you need to install Windows XP Professional and to ensure that it will actually run. However, if you want good performance from the machine, you should meet the recommended hardware requirements, and preferably exceed them.

During setup, Windows XP Professional will check the computer's hardware as well as software applications to determine whether there are incompatibilities. However, your best bet is to check these items first so you can avoid problems during installation. You should also take inventory of the computer's hardware, such as the sound card, video card, modem, and related components, and check the Windows XP Hardware Compatibility List (HCL) found at **www.microsoft .com/hcl**. Hardware that is not explicitly listed on the HCL is not recognized as

Component	Minimum Requirement	Recommended Requirement
Processor	233 MHz Pentium	300 MHz or higher—the faster the processor, the better performance you are likely to see. Windows XP Professional also supports two processor systems.
RAM	64MB	128+MB recommended—4GB maximum
Hard disk space	2GB partition with at least 640MB free	4+GB
Monitor	VGA monitor	SVGA monitor
Mouse	Windows-compatible	Windows-compatible
CD-ROM	Windows-compatible CD or DVD-ROM drive	Windows-compatible CD or DVD-ROM drive
Network card	Compatible network card and cable if over-the-network installation is desired	Compatible network card and cable if over-the-network installation is desired

TABLE 1.1   Windows XP Professional Installation Requirements

compatible; however, this does not mean that the hardware will not work—it just has not been tested by Microsoft. If you have some questionable hardware, you should check the hardware manufacturer's web site for more information and possible driver updates or upgrade packs. You should acquire the new drivers or updates before starting the installation of Windows XP Professional.

NETWORK CONNECTIONS

If your Windows XP Professional computer will be a part of a network, then you will need to gather some information from an appropriate network administrator. If the computer is not connected to a network or is not connected to a Windows domain, you can simply choose the "workgroup" option during setup. You'll need to enter the name of your workgroup (or the name of a new workgroup if you are creating one with this installation).

Let's make sure your terminology is up to speed here. A *domain* is a logical grouping of users and computers on a Microsoft network. The domain is designed to be an administrative unit that is controlled by network administrators via Windows 2000/.NET servers. The domain is an effective way to partition a large network into manageable "chunks." The domain model has been around since the days of Windows NT, but it has been greatly simplified and made less restrictive since the days of Windows 2000. The domain model is recommended on networks with more than 10 computers (but is not required).

A *workgroup*, on the other hand, is a collection of local computers that function together in order to share data. There is no domain controller, or a computer in charge of the network, and each user typically manages his or her own computer on the network. The workgroup model does not have the overhead of a domain, but it can be more difficult to manage as it grows since it is not centrally controlled. If the computer will become a member of a domain, Windows XP Professional can join the domain during the installation of XP, but there is some information you might need to know during setup, which is described in the following bullet list:

- The name of your computer and the name of the domain.

- An appropriate IP address and subnet mask. In order for a computer to communicate on any TCP/IP network, the computer must be configured with an IP address and subnet mask that is appropriate for the particular subnet. In most Windows networks, a Dynamic Host Configuration Protocol (DHCP) Server handles this task automatically. The DHCP server automatically assigns IP addresses and subnet masks to client computers, ensuring that they have both an appropriate address and one that is unique on the network. If DHCP is not used on the network, then you'll need a unique IP address and subnet mask in order for network connectivity to work. See Chapter 10 to learn more about networking.

- Domain controller and DNS server. During the installation, at least one domain controller and DNS server must be online on the network in order for you to join the domain. The computer must have a computer account in the Active Directory (configured by a domain administrator), or your user account must have the permission to create a computer account.

- Hardware. The computer must be outfitted with a network adapter card and it must be physically connected to the network. See Chapter 5 to learn more about hardware.

NOTE As you are installing Windows XP Professional, keep in mind that you can always join a workgroup or domain once the installation is finished, if it is more convenient for you to do so at that time. Active Directory users have the default right to add up to 10 computer accounts to a domain, unless the network administrator has restricted the default right.

HARD DISK CONFIGURATION

If you are installing Windows XP Professional on a computer that has no existing operating system, and XP is the only operating system you want to use, there is nothing you need to do. The setup routine will format the drive for you and allow you to select a file system of your choice (FAT, FAT32, or NTFS). Windows XP is optimized for the NTFS file system, which provides file-level security and a number of additional security features that are not available under FAT or FAT32, such as:

- **Encryption**   NTFS drives under Windows XP support encryption. You can seamlessly encrypt user data so that only you can view it, but you can use that data without having to decrypt and reencrypt every time you want to use it.

- **Compression**   NTFS drives under Windows XP natively support compression. You can compress a drive or folder in order to save disk space, but you can continue to use the compressed drive normally.

- **Quotas**   On NTFS volumes, you can configure how much space a user is allowed to access for data storage. This feature is particularly helpful on systems where a Windows XP Professional computer is functioning as a file server.

The most important difference, however, is file- and folder-level security, which is the backbone of a Windows network. Although FAT and FAT32 are useful in some respects, they do not contain advanced management features, and for this reason, Windows XP is optimized for NTFS.

If an operating system currently exists on your computer, Windows XP can either upgrade the existing operating system or install a clean copy of Windows XP, which installs Windows XP in a different folder. Alternatively, you can install Windows XP Professional in a separate partition for a dual-boot scenario. A dual-boot scenario enables you to boot more than one operating system on the same computer. For example, you could have a system that will boot Windows 2000 Server and Windows XP Professional, or you could have a system that will boot Windows Me or Windows XP Professional. Each operating system resides in its own partition, and during boot, you are given a boot menu that enables you to choose which operating system you want to boot. Across the board, dual-boot configurations are easy to configure, but it is important to keep in mind that only Windows XP, Windows 2000, and Windows NT 4.0 with service pack 4.0 and higher can read NTFS partitions. Windows 9*x*, Me, and 95 can read only FAT or FAT32 drives. So, if you want the down-level operating system to read the Windows XP partition, you'll need to use FAT or FAT32 as the file system instead of NTFS.

If your computer has more than one partition, or you are working with a new computer for which you want to have more than one partition, you can use Windows XP's Disk Administrator tool to create new partitions as needed. If you are working with a computer that has no current operating system, you can create partitions using FDISK or a third-party tool, such as Partition Magic, or you can create the partitions during Windows XP setup. If you are partitioning a disk for installation, make sure that the partition you will use for Windows XP meets the minimum storage requirements as described in the previous section.

Though dual-boot scenarios and partitioning options are beyond the scope of this book, it is a good idea to get familiar with them, preferably by trying practice configurations on a test machine. You can learn more about dual booting by performing a search at **Microsoft.com** (try Knowledge Base articles Q153762 and Q306559) or any Internet search engine.

SERVICE PACKS

Microsoft occasionally releases service packs that contain system updates and fixes to problems. Services packs are available on CD-ROM or downloadable from **Microsoft.com** or the Windows Update web site. Also, check the Windows Update web site for any hotfixes, which are software fixes for Windows XP, that are available and install them as well. Once you install Windows XP Professional, you should also install any current service packs that may be available for the operating system.

PERFORMING A BACKUP

The best action you can take before installing Windows XP Professional as an upgrade is to back up the previous operating system and all of your data. In the event that something goes wrong during installation, you can always recover from backup. If you are installing a clean copy of Windows XP Professional or installing XP on a new computer with no operating system, such a backup is unnecessary. In an upgrade scenario, however, it is very important to protect your data by backing it up. Depending on the operating system you are currently using, your backup options may vary—you can even use third-party backup tools, so you'll need to check your current operating system for backup instructions.

APPLICATION COMPATIBILITY

Before installing Windows XP Professional, you should take a look at the applications that you want to use with the operating system. If you are moving from some earlier version of Windows, such as Windows 98, you may have applications that are not compatible with Windows XP. If you are moving from Windows 2000, you are not likely to experience any problems. The good news is that Windows XP Professional contains an application compatibility tool that will often enable you to run applications designed for previous versions of Windows. See Chapter 5 to learn more about the Program Compatibility tool.

Finally, before you begin installation, you need to check a few last minute items:

- Uninstall any antivirus programs. Setup needs full access to your computer's hard drive, and antivirus programs may interfere.

- You cannot install Windows XP Professional on any drives that are compressed. Decompress affected drives before running the installation.

- Remove any disk management software, as these programs may interfere with installation.

- This is a good time to do housecleaning; remove any programs that you no longer use, that are incompatible with Windows XP, or that are outdated.

UPGRADING TO WINDOWS XP PROFESSIONAL

In many cases, you will want to upgrade a previous operating system to Windows XP. This feature should enable you to maintain the existing settings and applications during the upgrade to Windows XP. As a general rule, upgrades are more troublesome than clean installations. Windows XP must deal with previous operating system files, possible incompatibilities, driver issues, and often hardware components that were not designed with Windows XP in mind. Because of this, you should study upgrades carefully before performing them. Careful consideration will help you ensure that the upgrade will be successful.

When you begin the installation of Windows XP, the setup routine detects any previous versions of Windows that may be present. Depending on the version, Windows XP can either upgrade the existing operating system or it can install a clean copy of Windows XP. The procedures are as follows:

- **Upgrade**   Windows XP installs in the same folder as the previous operating system, upgrading files and drivers as needed. Your existing applications and settings are preserved.

- **Clean Install**   Windows XP installs in a different folder. Once installation is complete, you must reinstall any applications that you want to use.

If you want to maintain existing settings and applications, choose the upgrade option. However, in some cases, a clean install may be desirable. For example, let's say you are upgrading Windows 98 to Windows XP. A first choice might be to perform an upgrade and keep your existing settings. However, suppose that you ran into some problems during the Windows 98 installation that you have been unable to resolve. A better choice might be the clean installation, so that you can be sure of avoiding installation problems with Windows XP. In either case, you'll have to decide which option best suits your needs and the particular computer you are installing.

TROUBLESHOOTING

Limitations of Upgrades

Notice that Windows 95 did not make the list, nor did any previous versions of Windows NT. If you want to upgrade these operating systems, your choices are a clean install (in which case, you lose all of your applications and settings) or an upgrade of the unsupported operating system to a supported version, followed by an upgrade to Windows XP. For example, you could upgrade Windows 95 to Windows 98, and then to Windows XP.

Before running these kinds of upgrade, however, you should carefully inspect the computer's hardware and make sure it can handle Windows XP. Most Windows 9x computers will need either a RAM or processor upgrade—or both—before installing Windows XP, so be sure to look at not only the operating system, but also the hardware itself before you try to run any upgrades.

All hardware requirements still apply in an upgrade scenario, so it is important to check out the computer's hardware before starting an upgrade. Also, spend a few moments checking out the applications that you are installing to see whether they are compatible with Windows XP. You can check the software vendors' web sites for upgrade information.

Windows XP Professional can directly upgrade the following operating systems:

- All versions of Windows 98
- Windows Me
- Windows NT 4.0 Workstation (with service pack 5 or later)
- Windows 2000 Professional
- Windows XP Home Edition

RUNNING AN ATTENDED INSTALLATION OF WINDOWS XP PROFESSIONAL

You can peform an attended install of Windows XP Professional by using the installation CD-ROM or over the network from a network share. In many network environments, the network installation option is often used to make installations easier and to provide one central location for the installation files. The following sections explore both types of installations.

INSTALLING FROM CD-ROM

The Windows XP installation CD is bootable, and you can start installation simply by booting from the CD if your computer supports CD booting. In an upgrade or clean install scenario, just insert the CD-ROM while you are booted into your current operating system and follow the setup instructions. If your computer has no operating system and your CD-ROM drive is not bootable, you'll need to boot into DOS using a startup disk (or even a Windows 98 startup disk). You can then start the installation by accessing your CD-ROM drive and running setup.exe.

At the Welcome to Microsoft Windows XP screen, you can launch setup, or you can have setup check your system for compatibility. The following steps walk you through the installation routine.

INSTALLING WINDOWS XP PROFESSIONAL

To install Windows XP Professional, follow these steps:

1. Launch the CD-ROM or setup.exe, as appropriate for your particular installation.

2. Setup begins and collects information about your computer. In the dialog box that appears, choose to Install Windows XP. In the Welcome to Windows Setup screen, you can use the drop-down menu to select New Installation or Upgrade. Make your decision and click Next.

3. The Licensing Agreement window appears. Read the agreement, click the I Accept This Agreement radio button, and click Next.

4. The product key window appears. Enter the 25-character product key that is found on the yellow sticker on the back of your CD case. Enter the key, and click Next.

5. The Setup Options window appears, as shown here (if you selected the New Installation option in step 2). At this point, you can change the Accessibility Options and language if desired. Click the Advanced button.

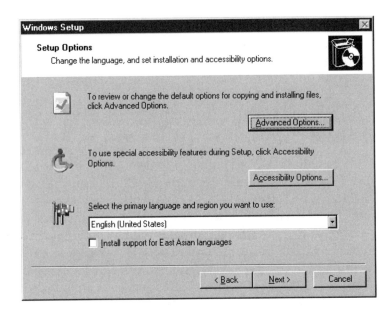

6. The Advanced Options window appears. You have the following options:

■ **Copy Installation Files from This Folder**   You can specify the location from which the setup files should be copied. This feature can be useful if you need to start setup from a CD but actually want the files copied from another location.

■ **To This Folder on My Hard Drive**   You can specify the folder name to which the files should be copied. \Windows is the default and typically what you should use.

■ **Copy All Installation Files from the Setup CD**   Use this option to copy all files to the computer's hard drive before beginning installation. This feature can be helpful if you need to install several computers but have only one CD. You can copy the files and continue with the installation without the CD-ROM so that it can be used on another machine.

■ **Choose the Install Drive Letter and Partition during Setup**   This option allows you to choose the installation drive letter and partition during setup.

Make any desired selections, click OK, and then click Next.

7. The Setup Files window appears. You can choose to connect to the Internet and check for updated files that can be downloaded and used during the installation. For this option to work, your current operating system must be configured with an Internet connection; if you have such a connection, you should use the option. Choose either Yes or No and then click Next.

8. At this point, the file copy process begins. The setup program copies necessary files to your computer's hard drive, and then automatically reboots your computer (make sure there is no floppy disk in the disk drive).

9. Once the computer reboots, the MS-DOS portion of setup begins. The Setup Notification window appears. Press ENTER to continue.

10. In the Welcome to Setup window, you can choose to install Windows XP Professional by pressing ENTER, repair an existing installation by pressing R, or quit setup by pressing F3. Press ENTER to continue with Setup.

11. Depending on your upgrade or clean install choices, you may see a partition window where you can choose the partition in which you want to install Windows XP Professional and format that partition as well. Follow the prompts that appear for selecting a desired partition, creating a partition from unpartitioned space, and formatting that partition.

12. Once the partition is established and formatted with a file system, the file copy process begins. This may take some time and requires no intervention from you.

13. Once the file copy process is complete, the computer automatically reboots. At this point, you see the Windows XP setup screen and the installation continues. This screen displays the approximate amount of time that setup will require. It is not unusual for the screen to flicker several times during this phase of setup.

14. During the installation of Windows XP Professional, the Regional and Language Options window appears. You can click the Customize button to choose a different language or region, or you can click the Details button to view information about your current regional configuration. Click Next to continue.

15. In the Personalize Your Software window, enter your name and organization. Click Next.

16. In the Computer Name and Administrator Password dialog box, enter a name for the computer (or accept the default) and an administrator password. The password will be used in conjunction with the Windows XP

Professional administrator account and should be kept private. Typically, for the best security, the local administrator password should be at least seven characters long and should contain both letters and numbers.

17. In the Modem Dialing Information window, choose your country and enter your area code and outside line number (if necessary). This window does not appear if your computer does not have a modem attached. Click Next.

18. In the Date and Time Settings window, use the drop-down menus to choose the correct time, date, and time zone. Click Next.

19. Setup continues, and a Networking Settings window appears if a network adapter card is installed on the computer. You can choose Typical Settings (which installs TCP/IP), Client for Microsoft Networks, or File and Printer Sharing for Microsoft Networks. If you want to select the services and IP address that you will configure, choose the Custom Settings option and click Next to complete the information.

20. The Choose Workgroup or Computer Domain window appears. Choose a desired work or domain name and click Next. If you are creating a new workgroup, enter the desired name in the provided dialog box.

Setup continues and may require another 30 minutes or longer before the computer reboots. Once the computer reboots, Windows XP Professional boots for the first time.

INSTALLING FROM A NETWORK SHARE

You can easily install Windows XP on client computers via the network by using a network installation. The actual installation steps and procedures remain the same when installing over a network share, but the installation is started by connecting to the network share and launching setup.exe.

In order to install Windows XP Professional over the network, you must first set up a server that will function as a "distribution server." This server holds a shared folder that contains all of the contents of the Windows XP Professional installation CD-ROM. The distribution server can even be another workstation— the requirement is that client computers have access to the server, whether it is an actual server or another client computer. To use a distribution server, create a shared folder on the desired computer, then copy the contents from the Windows XP installation CD-ROM to this folder.

For client computers to access the shared folder, the client computer must be configured with a network card and connection cabling. In most cases, the use of a distribution server is helpful for upgrades, where IT support personnel or even end users themselves use the existing operating system to connect to the shared folder and begin installation. If a computer has no current operating system, then you need a network boot disk to install Windows XP in this manner.

To begin the installation, the client computer simply connects to the distribution server's shared folder and launches setup.exe. For example, if the distribution server's name is ServerSet and the shared folder's name is XP, then you can start the installation by connecting to \\ServerSet\XP\setup.exe. When setup.exe is launched, the files are copied from the distribution server to client computer, and installation proceeds as it typically would.

NOTE   Prior to starting a network installation, you must create a partition in which Windows XP can be installed.

USING WINNT32.EXE

You can modify the setup program using Winnt32.exe. Winnt32.exe is a setup program used to start a Windows XP installation using a variety of setup switches. Windows XP Professional, like previous versions of Windows, supports Winnt32.exe, and you can use this program for an upgrade of supported versions of Windows. Using the provided setup switches, you can make the installation of Windows XP easier by invoking different needs or setup options automatically. Also, if you want to use an unattended installation of Windows XP Professional, you can start the unattended installation using Winnt32.exe as well, which you can learn more about later in this chapter. The syntax of Winnt32.exe is as follows:

```
winnt32 [/checkupgradeonly] [/cmd:command_line] [/cmdcons]
[/copydir:i386\folder_name] [/copysource:folder_name]
[/debug[level]:[filename]] [/dudisable] [/duprepare:pathname]
[/dushare:pathname] [/m:folder_name] [/makelocalsource] [/noreboot]
[/s:sourcepath] [/syspart:drive_letter] [/tempdrive:drive_letter]
[/udf:id [,UDB_file]][/unattend[num]:[answer_file]]
```

Table 1-2 explains the available command-line switches.

Switch	Explanation
/checkupgradeonly	Checks your computer for upgrade compatibility with Windows XP. If you use this option with /unattend, no user input is required. Otherwise, the results are displayed on the screen, and you can save them under the filename you specify. The default filename is Upgrade.txt in the systemroot folder.
/cmd:command_line	Tells the setup program to carry out a specific command before the final phase of setup. This occurs after your computer has restarted and after setup has collected the necessary configuration information, but before setup is complete.

TABLE 1.2   Winnt32.exe Command-Line Parameters

Switch	Explanation
/cmdcons	Installs the Recovery Console as a startup option on a functioning computer. You can use the /cmdcons option only after the normal setup process is finished.
/copydir:i386\folder_name	Creates an additional folder within the folder in which the Windows XP files are installed. You can use /copydir to create as many additional folders as you want.
/copysource:folder_name	Creates a temporary additional folder within the folder in which the Windows XP files are installed. You can use /copysource to create as many additional folders as you want, but the folders that /copydir creates, /copysource folders, are deleted after the setup program completes.
/debug[level]:[filename]	Creates a debug log at the level specified, for example, /debug4:Debug.log. The default log file is C:\systemroot\Winnt32.log, and the default debug level is 2. The log levels are as follows: 0 represents severe errors, 1 represents errors, 2 represents warnings, 3 represents information, and 4 represents detailed information for debugging. Each level includes the levels below it.
/dudisable	Stops Dynamic Update from running. This option will disable Dynamic Update even if you use an answer file and specify Dynamic Update options in that file.
/duprepare:pathname	Carries out preparations on an installation share so that it can be used with Dynamic Update files that you downloaded from the Windows Update web site. You can then use this share to install Windows XP for multiple clients.
/dushare:pathname	Specifies a share on which you previously downloaded Dynamic Update from the Windows Update web site and on which you previously ran /duprepare:pathname. When run on a client, specifies that the client installation will use the updated files on the share specified in pathname.
/m:folder_name	Specifies that the setup program copies replacement files from an alternate location. Instructs the setup program to look in the alternate location first and, if files are present, to use them instead of the files from the default location.
/makelocalsource	Tells the setup program to copy all installation source files to the local hard disk. Use /makelocalsource when installing from a CD to provide installation files when the CD is not available later in the installation.
/noreboot	Instructs the setup program not to restart the computer after the file copy phase of setup is completed, so that you can execute another command.
/s:sourcepath	Specifies the source location of the Windows XP files. To simultaneously copy files from multiple servers, type the /s:sourcepath option multiple times (up to a maximum of eight). If you type the option multiple times, the first server specified must be available, or Setup will fail.
/syspart:drive_letter	Specifies that you can copy setup startup files to a hard disk, mark the disk as active, and then install the disk into another computer. When you start that computer, it automatically starts with the next phase of setup. You must always use the /tempdrive parameter with the /syspart parameter. See Chapter 3 to learn more about the System Preparation tool.
/tempdrive:drive_letter	Directs the setup program to place temporary files on the specified partition. For a new installation, Windows XP will also be installed on the specified partition. For an upgrade, the /tempdrive option affects the placement of temporary files only; the operating system will be upgraded in the partition from which you run winnt32.

TABLE 1.2   Winnt32.exe Command-Line Parameters *(continued)*

Switch	Explanation
/udf:id [,UDB_file]	Uses an identifier (id) for the setup program to specify how a Uniqueness Database (UDB) file modifies an answer file (see the /unattend entry).
/unattend	Runs an upgrade using the previous operating system (if supported). All user settings are taken from the previous installation, so no user intervention is required during the setup process.
/unattend[num]:[answer_file]	Performs a fresh installation in unattended setup mode. The specified answer_file provides the setup program with your custom specifications. num is the number of seconds between the time that the setup program finishes copying the files and when it restarts your computer. You can use num on any computer running Windows 98, Windows Me, Windows NT, Windows 2000, or Windows XP.

TABLE 1.2   Winnt32.exe Command-Line Parameters *(continued)*

ACTIVATING WINDOWS XP

Windows XP Home and Professional editions use a new feature from Microsoft called product activation. Due to software piracy, product activation is now used to enforce the end-user license agreement that stipulates that the end user can install one copy of Windows XP on one computer only. This feature prevents the copying of installation CDs, otherwise known as "softlifting."

During installation, the product key found on the back of the CD-ROM case is combined with a generated hardware identifier number, taken from information about the computer system on which the software is being installed. Taken together, the two numbers create a unique installation ID that is uploaded to Microsoft servers via the Internet, or manually through a call to Microsoft customer support. Once the product is activated, the CD cannot be used to

PAINFUL
LESSONS

I'VE LEARNED

Command Line Confusion

The command line installation switches provide you with a number of options for installing Windows XP. Those options can be very helpful in a number of circumstances, but it is important to use only the switches you really need. I have seen techs get really excited about using command line switches for installations, but typically problems occurred because too many switches were used without thinking through all of the effects of those switches. The moral of the story is to use the command line switches you need, think carefully about their impact, but don't make things more complicated than necessary.

install another computer with Windows XP Professional, which enforces the end-user license agreement of one CD per one computer. In large environments where a large number of computers are configured with Windows XP Professional, activation may work differently or not be necessary at all, depending on the licensing agreement between Microsoft and the corporation or organization.

In a typical activation scenario, the user is prompted to activate Windows XP once an installation completes, if a modem is detected on the computer. If one is not detected or a connection cannot be made, the user is prompted to contact Microsoft to activate the product manually. Users can skip this step and activate Windows later because there is a 30-day grace period in which to activate. From an IT professional's perspective, however, users should activate as soon as installation is completed in order to avoid further problems. If Windows XP is not activated immediately after setup, then an Activate icon appears in the Notification Area; to start the activation process, you can click this icon or you can simply click Start | All Programs | Activate Windows.

PERFORMING UNATTENDED INSTALLATIONS

Windows XP Professional's unattended installation methods fall into two broad categories: scripted installations and image installations. The first category, scripted installations, uses an answer file to answer setup prompts so that once installation begins, the process is completely automated. The second category can be thought of as an imaging process. A computer with no operating system and with similar hardware receives a complete installation image that is copied to the hard drive. Remote installation services and System Preparation tools are both used for image-based installations. As you will see in the following sections, all of these installation options have unique advantages in a number of scenarios.

USING SETUP MANAGER

Windows XP Professional contains a program called Setup Manager that can help you generate answer files for a Windows XP Professional unattended installation. Before getting into answer file creation, let's back up a bit and talk about unattended installations and answer files. In an unattended installation, you typically start setup using Winnt32.exe, using an unattended switch, and then pointing to an answer file. An answer file is simply a text file that setup can read to find the "answers" to setup prompts. For example, setup always asks whether you want to check for Dynamic Updates on the Web. You can answer the question one time using an answer file. Subsequently, setup will simply read the file and will not require any direct input from you. The advantages are obvious—you can start the installation routine on hundreds of computers at one time and never have to return to them in order to babysit the setup program. You can find a sample of an answer file, called Unattended.txt, in the I386 folder on your Windows XP Professional CD-ROM. As you can see in Figure 1-1, Unattended.txt is a simple text file that you can read.

In the past, answer files were somewhat difficult because you had to write them from scratch. With Setup Manager, a wizard guides you through the process and helps you create the answer file, which makes unattended setups a lot easier.

Setup Manager and the other deployment tools explored in this chapter are not available directly from Windows XP Professional after installation. Instead, you must copy from them from cabinet file (compressed) from the Windows XP Professional CD-ROM. The following steps walk you through this process.

EXTRACTING THE DEPLOY.CAB FILES

1. On the desired computer, log on as the administrator and create a folder in which to place the deployment tools, then name the folder as desired.

2. Insert the Windows XP Professional installation CD-ROM. Close the installation window that appears.

3. Open My Computer, right-click the CD-ROM drive, and click Explore.

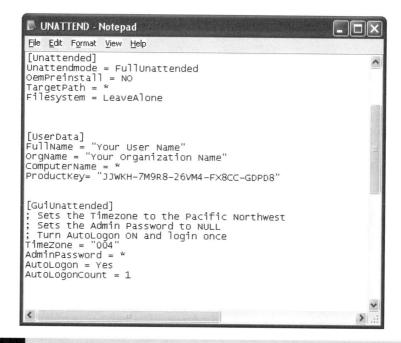

FIGURE 1.1   Unattended.txt sample answer file found in the I386 folder on the installation CD-ROM

4. Open the Support folder, and then open the Tools folder. You'll see the Deploy.cab file, as shown here.

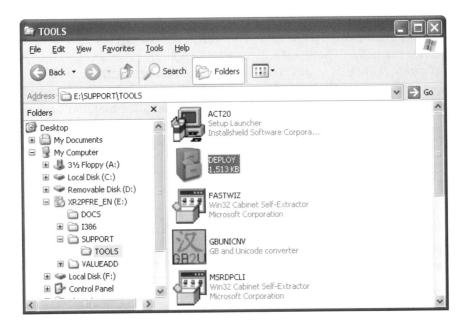

5. Double-click the Deploy.cab file to open it. Several different tools will appear, including Setup Manager (setupmgr).

6. Click Edit | Select All, and then right-click the files and click Extract.

7. In the Select a Destination dialog box that appears, browse for the folder you created, select it, and then click the Extract button. The tools are copied from the CD-ROM to the desired folder.

Now that you have copied the Deployment tools to the desired computer, you can create an answer file to use for an unattended installation. Remember that an answer file simply answers the questions that the setup routine typically poses to you during an attended setup. With this automated method, an IT technician can start an installation and not have to wait for each prompt the setup routine poses. Instead, the answer file contains the answers that you want provided, and it can even provide setup with information about hardware, such as sound cards, modems, and so on.

Windows XP Professional's setup routine is designed to continue, even if certain pieces of hardware, such as modems and sound cards, do not install properly. This feature prevents setup from stopping due to a single hardware problem.

Of course, the Windows XP Professional CD-ROM gives you unattend.txt, which you can use for unattended installations. This text file provides basic setup options, but you may need to customize your own setup file. Using Setup Manager, you can easily create this file, as shown in the following steps.

USING SETUP MANAGER TO CREATE AN ANSWER FILE

1. Launch the setupmgr program in your deployment folder.

2. Click Next on the Welcome screen.

3. In the New or Existing Answer File window, you can choose to create a new answer file, or you can modify an existing answer file by selecting the option and browsing for the file. For this exercise, you will create a new answer file. Click the radio button option and then click Next.

4. In the Product to Install window, you can create the answer file for a Windows Unattended Installation, Sysprep Install, or Remote Installation Services installation. For this exercise, you will create an answer file for a Windows unattended installation (you will learn about the other two options later in this chapter). Select the unattended option and click Next.

5. In the Select the Platform That This File Installs window, choose the Windows XP Professional radio button and click Next.

6. The User Interaction Level window appears, as shown here.

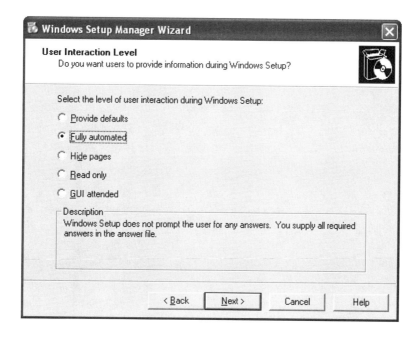

You have five different options, which are:

- **Provide Defaults**   This option provides an unattended setup where the answers you provide are considered the defaults. When the installation is run, the user can see the answer defaults and interrupt setup to change them if desired. As you can see, this option is not fully automated, but does enable the user to review the answers before beginning the installation.
- **Fully Automated**   Using this method, the user is never prompted to answer any questions. All answers are taken from the answer file and the user cannot interrupt setup or change any of the options.
- **Hide Pages**   If you provide all of the answers for the Windows Setup wizard page, the wizard page is hidden from the user.
- **Read Only**   If the Windows Setup wizard page is not hidden from the user, you can use this option so that the page is read only. The user can make no changes to the setup wizard.
- **GUI Attended**   Only the text-mode portion of Windows setup is automated.

Make your selection based on the level of user input/automation that you want and click Next.

7. The Distribution Folder window appears, as shown next. When using an answer file, you can choose to install Windows XP Professional from the CD or from a distribution folder. A network distribution folder holds the Windows XP Professional installation files so you can connect to this folder over the network.

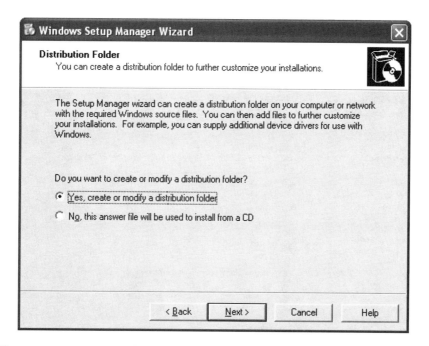

If you use an answer file, you can roll out any number of installations at one time. Choose the desired radio button; for this exercise, you will create a distribution folder. Click Next.

8. If you chose to create a distribution folder, you can copy the files from CD or from another location. Make your selection and click Next.

9. In the Distribution Folder Name window, you can choose to create a new distribution folder or modify an existing one. If you choose to create a new distribution folder, select the location and the share name for the folder, and then click Next.

10. The License Agreement window appears, if you choose a fully automated installation. Read the basic End User License Agreement (EULA) and click the I Accept check box. Click Next.

11. The Customize window appears, as shown here. At this point, you can click each setting in the left window and enter your answer in the right pane. Setup will use the answers provided here to configure the answer file, which automates setup. Simply respond to the answer prompts and click Next for the entire list of settings.

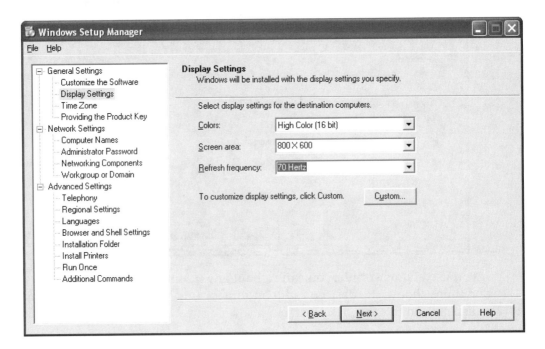

12. After you answer the final prompt, a dialog box appears telling you that Setup Manager has successfully created an answer file and prompting you for the location to save the file. Choose the desired location and click OK. Click Finish when prompted.

Once the answer file is created, you can begin running unattended setups with the answer file. Before doing so, however, you should open the unattended file you created and scan through it; look for any errors or other issues that might be a problem. If there are any mistakes, you can directly edit the unattended text file as needed.

Once you are ready to run setup, you can use Winnt32 to begin the unattended installation of Windows XP Professional. The syntax for running the unattended setup is:

```
Winnt32 /s:d:\i386 /u:c:\unattend\unattend.txt
```

where:

- **/s:d:\i386**   Specifies the location of the Windows XP Professional installation files; this can be your I386 folder on the CD-ROM or a network distribution folder.

- **/u:c:\unattend\unattend.txt**   Specifies that this is an unattended installation and that the answer file is unattend.txt and is located in the Unattend folder on the C drive. Of course, your location will probably be different, so just enter the correct UNC path to the answer file.

REMOTE INSTALLATION SERVICES

Although unattended installations can be extremely helpful if you are installing numerous machines, Windows XP Professional also supports Remote Installation Services, which uses the Active Directory to run setup automatically on computers that connect to the Remote Installation Server. Remote Installation Services (RIS) is technically a service that runs on Windows 2000 Server—it is simply supported by Windows XP Professional and not something you can configure on the Professional computer. For that reason, we'll not go into a lot detail about using RIS, since you need to be a server administrator to do so, but I do want to give you a quick overview of the feature.

Remote Installation Services was first introduced with Windows 2000 as a way to roll out massive installations of Windows 2000 Professional. A former criticism of Windows workstations was how difficult it was to perform mass installations. Providing Setup Manager and RIS, Microsoft has tried to answer that complaint by making mass installations of Windows 2000, and now Windows XP, much easier. RIS meets that challenge—to a point, anyway.

RIS is a server-based networking product that is designed to use the power of the Active Directory, Dynamic Host Configuration Protocol (DHCP), and Domain Name Service (DNS) to install Windows XP Professional software over the network to machines that support the Pre-Execution Environment (PXE) ROM. PXE enables a computer to boot over the network. In order to support PXE, your computer must be outfitted with a network adapter card that is PXE-compliant. Windows 2000 Server supports only PCI network adapter cards that are PXE-enabled. The good news is that if your computers do not support the PXE boot ROM, you can use an RIS boot disk instead of the PXE network adapter card.

When you start a computer using a PXE boot ROM or an RIS boot disk, the computer queries the network for a DHCP server using a BootP message. The DHCP server must be configured to allocate IP addresses to the BootP client. Boot Information Negotiation Layer (BINL) extensions are used on the DHCP server to redirect the RIS client to the RIS server, so that the installation of Windows XP Professional can begin. Depending on network configuration, the user may need to log on to continue the installations. The server installation is image-based, which means the installation is completely automated. This type of installation is especially helpful in networks that are upgrading all computers at one time, or in new networks where new machines with no operating systems are awaiting installation. When installation begins, the Trivial File Transfer Protocol (TFTP) is used to transfer the image files to the RIS client. Once the installation is completed, the client simply reboots as a normal network client.

NOTE You can manage RIS through a Group Policy. You can also make use of answer files in order to customize installations as needed.

USING SYSTEM PREPARATION

The second type of disk imaging deployment that is supported by Windows XP Professional is System Preparation. System Preparation is also available once you copy the Deploy.cab file from the Windows XP installation CD-ROM to your hard drive. This file enables you to prepare a disk image of a particular computer. This image can then be used to install hundreds or thousands of computers. System Preparation is a useful tool for organizations that are rolling out many new computers with the same configuration.

TECH TALK

RIS Safety Controls

Any Windows 2000 Server administrator can install and configure the RIS service on the server. However, as a control and management measure, Windows 2000 requires that a domain administrator who is logged on as an enterprise administrator or a domain administrator of the root domain "authorize" the RIS server with the Active Directory before it can function on the network as an RIS server. The same authorization process occurs with DHCP servers on a Windows 2000 network. Unless the Active Directory authorizes a DHCP server to do so, the server cannot lease IP addresses to clients. The same is true for RIS servers. You do not want someone to create and run a RIS server on the network without Active Directory authorization. Because this authorization scheme requires you to have domain administrator rights in order to authorize an RIS or DHCP server in the Active Directory, the scheme prevents the appearance of "rogue" servers. In a nutshell, authorization is simply a security feature of the Active Directory, but one that is required in order for the RIS server to function.

The System Preparation tool, called SysPrep, which is included in your deployment tools, is used to create an image from a desired Windows XP Professional computer. This image includes all configurations, applications, and virtually everything else on the computer. The computer becomes the master computer and is imaged so that other computers are exactly the same. Windows XP actually only prepares a computer for imaging; you must use a third-party imaging tool to create the image and deploy that image on the network. The use of SysPrep also imposes some additional rules and issues:

- SysPrep images are designed to be used on computers that have the same hardware. The image is not actually installed, but it is burned on the computer's hard drive. Therefore, the hardware must be the same. The exception is minor plug-and-play devices, such as sound cards, modems, and so on. These can be redetected and installed, but the hard drives, controllers, and Hardware Abstraction Layer (HAL) must be the same. Press F5 during boot to view and select the HAL.

- Sysprep is used for clean installations only. You cannot upgrade a computer using a Sysprep image.

- Sysprep creates the image only. Windows XP or Windows 2000 Server does not provide a way to burn images onto other computers. You'll need to use a third-party tool, such as Symantec's Norton Ghost or PowerQuest's DriveImage software.

- The master computer must be thoroughly tested before Sysprep is run. Otherwise, any problems or errors will be copied to the image as well.

- You must have a volume licensing agreement with Microsoft to comply with the EULA.

Sysprep is a great tool that enables you to generate an image of a Windows XP Professional installation, then copy that complete and configured installation to other computers as necessary. Original Equipment Manufacturers (OEMs) often use this type of imaging. For example, suppose that you own a small computer company that has just sold 8,000 of its new desktop computers to a startup company. All of the hardware is the same, and the operating systems are sold bundled with certain applications. You can use Sysprep to copy a configured system, then generate an image of that system for all of the other computers. When end users boot the computer, they see the mini-setup program running. If you have bought an OEM computer before, such as a Compaq, HP, Dell, or other popular brand, you have seen a type of mini-setup run that completes the imaging that was done at the factory. The end result is that with just a few keystrokes, you can generate an image of an operating system, configuration parameters, and applications for thousands of computers.

MIGRATING FILES AND SETTINGS TO WINDOWS XP

While we are on the subject of installations and upgrades, I would like to point out a new feature that Windows XP Professional brings to the table. One of the big problems with implementing a new computer system involves migrating documents and settings to that new computer. Windows XP Professional addresses this problem by providing a new File and Settings Transfer Wizard.

The File and Settings Transfer Wizard enables you to copy files and settings from a previous version of Windows. With the wizard's help, you can save these files and settings on a removable media or network connection and then transfer them to a new computer. Keep in mind that this feature works for moving data from one computer to another and is not necessary when upgrading the operating system on the same computer. For example, suppose that you have an old Windows 98 computer and then purchase a new computer with Windows XP. You can use the File and Settings Transfer Wizard to move all of your information and settings to the new computer quickly and easily. You can transfer files and settings from any of the following operating systems:

- Windows 95
- Windows 98
- Windows 98 SE
- Windows Me
- Windows NT 4.0
- Windows 2000
- Windows XP (32 bit only)

The File and Settings Transfer Wizard can transfer settings and properties affecting accessibility, the command prompt, the display, Internet Explorer, Microsoft Messenger, NetMeeting, the mouse, the keyboard, MSN Explorer, network printers and drivers, Outlook Express, sounds and multimedia, the taskbar, Windows Media Player, and Windows Movie Maker, as well as regional settings. You may also be able to transfer settings from other software programs, such as Microsoft Outlook. The wizard can also transfer specific folders, such as

Desktop, Fonts, My Documents, My Pictures, Shared Desktop, and Shared Documents. Additionally, the wizard can transfer most other multimedia files not found in these folders.

To transfer settings from an older version of Windows, you can use the Windows XP Professional installation CD. The following steps walk you through the process.

TRANSFERRING SETTINGS FROM A DOWN-LEVEL OPERATING SYSTEM

1. On the down-level computer, insert the Windows XP Professional CD-ROM. At the Windows XP startup screen, click Perform Additional Tasks and then click Transfer Files and Settings.

2. The File and Settings Transfer Wizard appears. Click Next.

3. A message may appear asking whether you are at the old or new computer. Choose the old option. The system is scanned and the Select a Transfer Method window appears, as shown here. You can choose to use a direct cable connection, network connection, removable media connection, or another type of connection (such as saving the settings to disk drive or network folder). Make your selection and click Next.

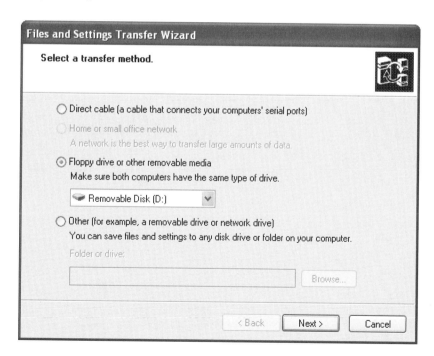

4. In the What Do You Want to Transfer window, you can choose to transfer settings only, files only, or both. You can click the Let Me Choose check box to specifically select what you want to transfer, as shown here. Make your selection and click Next.

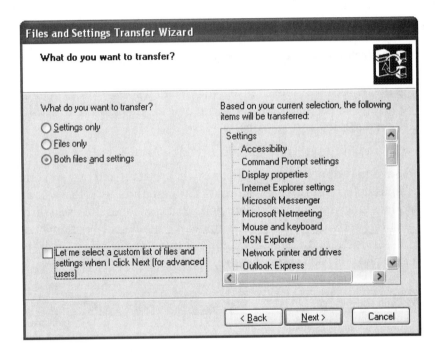

5. If you chose the Let Me Choose check box option in step 4, the Select Custom Files and Settings window appears, shown next. From this window, you can add and remove settings and files, file types, and folders as desired. When you are done, click Next.

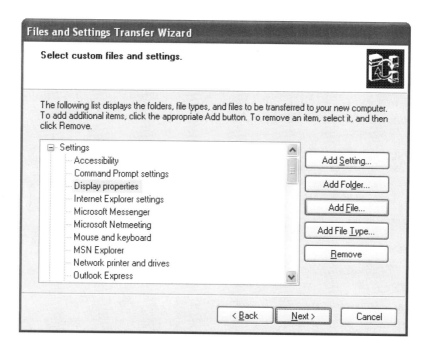

6. The wizard collects the data that you specified. This may take some time, depending on how much information you want to transfer. When the wizard is done, click Finish.

Once you have completed the collection portion of the File and Settings Transfer Wizard, you can now run the wizard on your Windows XP computer so that the settings can be migrated and configured. Once again, the File and Settings Transfer Wizard walks you through this process.

MIGRATING SETTINGS AND FILES TO WINDOWS XP

1. Click Start | All Programs | Accessories | System Tools | Files and Settings Transfer Wizard.

2. Click Next on the Welcome screen.

3. On the Which Computer Is This? screen, click the New Computer radio button and click Next.

4. The wizard then provides a screen asking whether you have a Windows XP CD and telling you that you need to run the wizard on the old computer. Notice here that the wizard can create a wizard disk for you if you are missing the CD-ROM. Since you have already collected your settings in the previous exercise, click the I Don't Need the Wizard Disk radio button option, shown here, and then click Next.

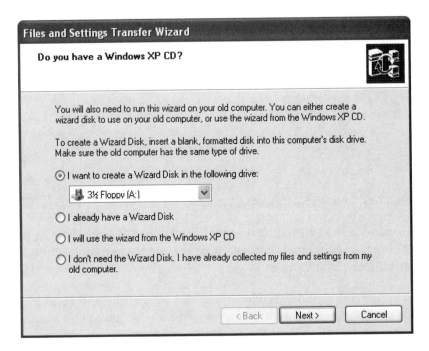

5. Choose where the files should be collected (for instance, direct cable connection, removable media, or network folder). Make your selection and click Next.

6. The wizard locates the files and transfers them to the new computer. Click Finish. You will be prompted to log off and log back on in order for the settings to take effect.

TROUBLESHOOTING FAILED INSTALLATIONS

Although the Windows XP Professional installation is generally easy and problem free, there is always a possibility that something may go wrong during installation. Typically, if you follow the hardware guidelines and setup procedures, you are unlikely to experience installation problems, but, as an IT professional, you should be aware of potential problems and troubleshooting areas.

In a typical Windows XP Professional installation scenario, the most common causes of installation problems or failure are as follows:

- Hardware incompatibilities, or hardware that does not meet the minimum hardware requirements. Typically, Windows XP will tell you if the hardware in the PC is not compatible or does not meet minimum standards; however, in a failed installation, you should always start by making sure that there are no compatibility problems.

- Some CD-ROM drives, particularly older drives, may not work well with Windows XP. Make sure the CD-ROM drive is compatible. Also, make sure you do not have a faulty CD.

- During hardware detection and driver installation, your computer can lock up. Although this typically does not happen with Windows XP, you can simply restart the computer, and installation should continue where it left off.

- Make sure your video card is up to date and is supported by Windows XP Professional. Installation problems can occur due to faulty video cards.

If you are having extensive problems with setup and you have checked the previous bullet points, you can also access a setup log to determine what problems may have occurred. This assumes that you can actually install the operating system. The log is called setupact.txt and is located in C:\Winnt (if you installed in a different drive, just substitute the correct drive letter for C).

WRAPPING UP

Windows XP installation is typically easy and problem free. Before installing or upgrading any computer to Windows XP, make sure the computer meets the hardware requirements; this can save you a world of trouble before installation ever begins. In larger environment deployments, Windows XP gives you some tools—such as unattended installations, RIS, and SysPrep—that can make Windows XP Professional rollouts automatic and completely unattended. As you are working with installations in your environment, make sure you consider all of the possible setup issues and problems before starting any installation; this approach will make your work with Windows XP installations much easier.

In Chapter 2, we'll turn our attention to some operating system fundamentals that Windows XP brings to the table.

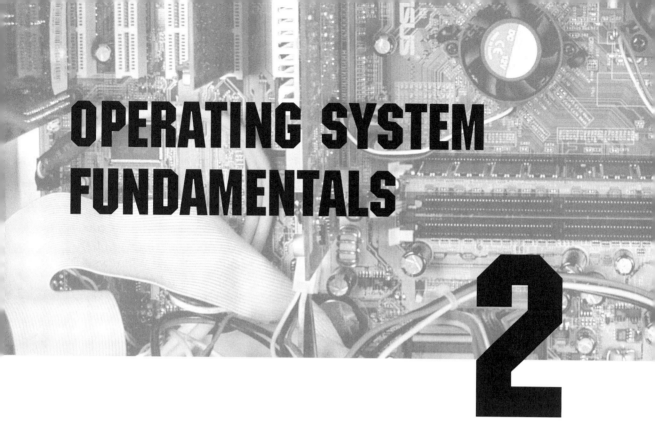

OPERATING SYSTEM FUNDAMENTALS

2

Perhaps you have been using Windows XP for some time, and perhaps Windows XP made its way into your networking environment during the early days of its release. Or, perhaps you have had Windows XP thrust upon you recently, which has sent you running to the bookstore for a book just like this one. If you need to support Windows XP but the operating system is fairly new to you, this chapter will cover just what you need. However, even if you have been using XP for a while, you should read this chapter, because you might learn a thing or two about Windows XP. In fact, you may find quite a bit of information in this chapter that will make Windows XP easier to use and easier to support. In this chapter, you'll...

- Explore the desktop, Start Menu, and taskbar
- Take a look at Control Panel
- Configure Display and Power Options
- Learn how to use the Microsoft Management Console

EXPLORING THE DESKTOP, START MENU, AND TASKBAR

When users new to Windows XP first boot the operating system, they are often in for a shock, especially if they have used previous versions of Windows. The interface looks quite different. After all, where is My Computer? Where is My Network Places? In fact, in a typical XP installation, the only thing that appears on the desktop is the Recycle Bin. A+ technicians often receive interface support calls from users reporting a faulty installation. Most likely the installation is fine, but the differences between Windows XP and previous versions of Windows often confuse new users. For this reason, you need be very familiar with the Windows XP interface. The good news is that Microsoft has attempted to streamline the design of Windows XP to reduce desktop clutter and make the operating system easier to use. Whether or not Microsoft succeeded is ultimately up to you and the users you support. In either case, Windows XP is here to stay and has become the most popular operating system since Windows 95.

Although your job as an A+ technician typically involves more complicated problem-solving and configuration issues than the Start Menu and the taskbar, you need to know how to configure these two items to help users in your environment. In fact, if Windows XP is new in your environment, you must spend quite a bit of time helping users reduce the learning curve.

CONFIGURING THE START MENU

The XP Start Menu, shown in Figure 2-1, gives you an easy place to access the most common Windows configuration items as well as other items that you might decide to put on the menu.

The new Windows XP Start Menu consists of two primary parts. The left side of the Start Menu lists programs, and the right side of the Start Menu provides access to common Windows folders, as well as the Help, Search, and Run commands. The Start Menu lists items that you use most frequently. So, if you open a program, Windows XP will remember it and place an icon in the Start Menu so you can more easily open the program next time. As you can see in Figure 2-1, I use Microsoft Word a lot, so Windows XP has put Word on the Start Menu so I can more easily access the program. Typically, I have to click Start | All Programs | Microsoft Word. Once I open Word for the first time, Windows XP adds the Word icon to my Start Menu. The next time I want to use Word, all I have to do is click Start and then click the Word icon. In a nutshell, the Start Menu simply adds shortcuts to itself on your behalf. You can easily manage these icons by right-clicking on them. This action gives you typical menu

FIGURE 2.1   Windows XP Start Menu

options, such as Open, Send To, Copy, Remove from This List, Rename, and Properties for the shortcut. If you want to remove the shortcut from the Start Menu, just click the Remove from This List option. This action only removes the shortcut from the Start Menu.

When you right-click an item, you also see an option called Pin to Start Menu. This action simply moves the item to the top-left portion of the window, where it will always be visible. You'll notice that Internet Explorer and Outlook Express are available in the Start Menu by default, but you can remove them by right-clicking the items and clicking Remove from This List.

Why should you use pinning? Over time, Windows XP will remove from the Start Menu items that the user no longer uses frequently. For example, if you stop using Microsoft Word, XP will remove it from the Start Menu after a period of inactivity. If you want Word always to be available, whether you have used it recently or not, you can simply pin it to the Start Menu to keep it there. Below the pinned items (separated by a line), you see a list of most frequently used

Diffuse Start Menu Confusion

Users are often worried about deleting items from the Start Menu. Instruct users that everything on the Start Menu—including all programs and even documents that users store on the Start Menu—is simply a link. Deleting an item from the Start Menu never deletes the item from the operating system, it only deletes the shortcut. However, some icons, such as My Documents and My Computer, cannot be deleted from the Start Menu. You can drag and drop them to the desktop, though, if you want to access those items directly from the desktop.

items. When you open a program, Windows XP will place the program link to this list for quick reference in the future. If you no longer use the program, Windows XP will eventually remove the link from the Start Menu.

Finally, you can also click All Programs to access typical Windows menus and installed applications.

NOTE If you want to use Internet Explorer (IE) and Outlook Express from the Start Menu, you can right-click the icons to find easy access options. For example, you can choose to read e-mail, browse the Internet, or even access Internet properties. See Chapter 9 for more information about configuring Internet properties.

On the right side of the Start Menu, you see common Windows items that you will need to access. The included items are as follows:

- **My Documents, My Pictures, and My Music**   The My Documents folder is the default storage location for files of all kinds, including pictures, music, and movies. My Documents contains default subfolders of My Music and My Pictures, and may also contain My Videos and Remote Desktops. You can learn more about My Documents and folder management in Chapter 3.

- **My Computer**   This default folder stores information about drives connected to your computer.

- **My Network Places**   This folder contains information about other computers and shared folders on your network. You can learn more about My Network Places in Chapter 8.

- **Control Panel**   This is the default location for managing all kinds of programs and services on your XP computer. You will explore Control Panel later in this chapter.

- **Network Connections**   This folder contains your dial-up and broadband connections as well as local area network connections. You can learn more about networking in Chapter 8.

- **Help and Support**   Windows XP includes a Help and Support feature that can answer your questions and even locate answers on the Internet.

- **Search**   The Search feature enables you to find items on your computer or items on the Internet.

- **Run**   You can use the Run dialog box to start programs quickly or connect to network shares.

- **Log Off / Turn Off Computer**   These standard icons enable you to log off, shut down, or restart the computer.

CUSTOMIZING THE START MENU

To customize the Start Menu, you need to access the Start Menu's Properties menu. To access this menu, open Control Panel and double-click the Taskbar and Start Menu icon, then click the Start Menu tab. If you don't see a Taskbar and Start Menu icon, switch Control Panel to Classic view using the Control Panel link on the left side of the window.

NOTE   You can also access the Start Menu's properties in two other quick ways. First, you can right-click any empty area of the taskbar, click Properties, then click the Start Menu tab, or better yet, just right-click the Start button and click Properties.

Regardless of which of these methods you use, you will arrive at a simple Start Menu properties page, shown in Figure 2-2.

The Start Menu properties page offers two options: You can click the Start Menu option to use the current Windows XP version of the Start Menu, or you can click the Classic Start Menu option to use the Start Menu familiar in previous versions of Windows. The following two sections explore the configuration of each of these different options.

USING THE XP START MENU

To continue using the XP Start Menu, just click the Customize button. This takes you to a Customize Start Menu dialog box that includes General and

FIGURE 2.2 Start Menu properties page

Advanced tabs. The General tab, shown in Figure 2-3, offers three different customization options:

- **Icon Size**   You can choose to use large or small icons in the Start Menu. Small icons may be harder to see, but you can put more shortcut icons directly on the Start Menu. Large icons are selected by default.

- **Programs**   By default, your Start Menu will place five program shortcut icons in viewing range when you click Start. You can change this number by using the drop-down menu. The Start Menu can display up to nine icons. This setting just makes your Start Menu larger so it can display all of nine program icons you place on it.

- **Show on Start Menu**   This panel allows you to display Internet and e-mail options on the Start Menu, then provides you a drop-down menu to select the application (Internet Explorer and Outlook Express by default). If you have other browser or e-mail clients installed on your computer, you can use the drop-down menu and select a different browser or e-mail client, or just clear the check boxes if you don't want to display these items at all.

FIGURE 2.3   The Customize Start Menu dialog box's General tab

The Advanced tab, shown in Figure 2-4, presents some additional options that you may find very useful.

First, you see the Start Menu Settings panel, which provides two check box options:

- **Open Submenus on Hover When I Pause on Them with My Mouse**   By default, the Start Menu stores folders such as My Documents and My Computer as a link. You can click them to open the folders in a different window. However, you can use a menu option so that a menu appears where you can choose subfolders. For example, suppose that you have a folder called My Files in My Documents. Without using the menu option, you have to click My Documents, then open My Files. Using the menu option, if you point to My Documents on the Start Menu, a pop-out menu appears showing your other folders, such as My Folders, and you can just click on My Folders to open it directly. This check box simply asks whether you want the pop-out menu to appear when you put your mouse cursor over the item, or if you want to have to click the item to see the pop-out menu. You will see how to use the menu option later in this section.

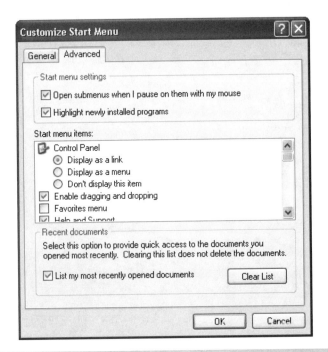

FIGURE 2.4 The Customize Start Menu dialog box's Advanced tab

- **Highlight Newly Installed Programs**   When applications are first installed on your XP computer, the Start Menu highlights them until you use them for the first time. This highlighting serves as a simple reminder that you have new stuff that you haven't used. If this feature gets on your nerves, just clear the check box.

The next part of the Advanced tab is a scroll box where you can select the folder and Windows items that appear on the Start Menu. The scroll box also

PAINFUL LESSONS

I'VE LEARNED

"Windows XP Keeps Popping Out Menus at Me!"

Have you heard this support call? You might! Windows XP provides easy access to submenus through pop-out menus, if the Open Submenus on Hover When I Pause on Them with My Mouse option is selected on the Advanced tab. Although many users find this feature handy, others simply find it disturbing. If you get a support call about out-of-control pop-out menus, this setting is probably the culprit.

enables you to control how the Start Menu displays those items. For example, by default, the Start Menu displays Control Panel as a link. You can change this behavior so that Control Panel is shown as a menu, or not at all. Simply scroll through the list and click the desired check boxes and radio buttons to determine what Windows items you want to include and how those items are presented (link or menu). You may want to experiment with these settings until you find the combination that is right for you. And remember, you can change these settings as often as you like.

On the last panel of this configuration window, you can configure the Start Menu to list recently used documents. For example, suppose that you're writing your life story. Once you open the document and then close it, the Start Menu will put your manuscript in Recent Documents, which is a folder that will now appear on the Start Menu. Then you can easily access the document from the Start Menu the next time you need it.

TROUBLESHOOTING

Users Have No Control over the Start Menu

If you are using Windows XP Professional in a domain environment, you may receive help requests from users who state that they cannot configure any items on the Start Menu, or even on the taskbar for that matter. If this happens, you usually need to address one of two issues:

- There is a local Group Policy. The local computer administrator on the Windows XP Professional computer can configure a local Group Policy that prevents limited users from making changes to the Start Menu and taskbar.

- There is a network Group Policy. In a Windows domain, a site, domain, or organizational unit policy can prevent users from making Start Menu and taskbar changes.

If the user really needs to make some kind of configuration change, you'll need to check with the administrator of the local computer concerning any local Group Policy. You'll also need to check with a domain administrator about corporate Group Policies that may be in place.

USING THE CLASSIC START MENU

To use the Classic Start Menu, select the Classic Start Menu option on the Start Menu tab of Taskbar and Start Menu Properties dialog box. This option allows you to use the Start Menu that previous versions of Windows provided. If you want to use the Classic Start Menu, select the radio button and click the Advanced button, which displays the Customize Classic Start Menu dialog box shown in Figure 2-5.

This interface offers the same basic Start Menu options, just in a different format. If you want to add items to the Classic Start Menu, click the Add button; a wizard will then help you select items on your computer to add to the Start Menu. Click the Remove button to remove items and the Advanced button to open Windows Explorer so you can manually add and remove any items you want. You can also sort the items and clear recent documents, programs, Web sites, and so on. The Advanced button enables you to display a number of Windows items, use expandable (menu) folders, and more. These items are self-explanatory; feel free to experiment and try new configurations.

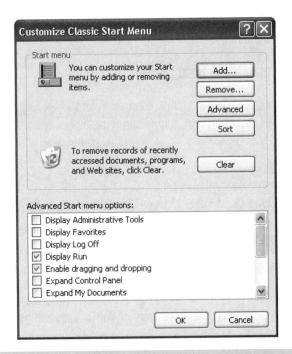

FIGURE 2.5 The Customize Classic Start Menu dialog box

CUSTOMIZING THE TASKBAR

You can also customize your taskbar just as you customize your Start Menu. You can access the taskbar and Start Menu properties by double-clicking on the icon in Control Panel. Or, just right-click any empty area of the taskbar, click Properties, then click the Taskbar tab. The Taskbar configuration page then appears as shown in Figure 2-6.

The tab has two basic customization panels: Taskbar Appearance and Notification Area. The Taskbar Appearance panel includes a few check box options that enable certain features:

- **Lock the Taskbar**   You can drag the taskbar to different places on your desktop. For example, if you want the taskbar at the top of the screen instead of the bottom, just drag it to the top. If you use the Lock the Taskbar check box, then the taskbar will be locked on the bottom of the screen and you will not be able to move it.

- **Auto-Hide the Taskbar**   This feature keeps the taskbar out of your way. When you are not using the taskbar, it disappears below your screen view.

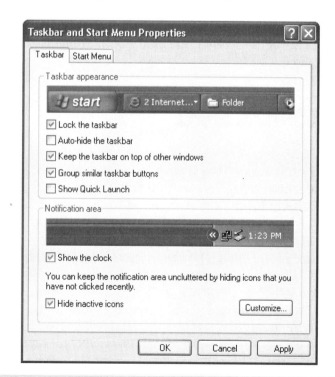

| FIGURE 2.6 | The Taskbar tab |

When you need it, just point your mouse to the location of the taskbar and it will reappear. Some users like this setting, so experiment with it.

- **Keep the Taskbar on Top of Other Windows**   As you are using various windows, they may cover up portions of the taskbar. This setting always keeps the taskbar on top.

- **Group Similar Taskbar Buttons**   This feature keeps similar items together. For example, if you open two Web pages, then minimize them both, they will appear next to each other on the taskbar. Also, if you have several items opened by the same program (such as three Word documents), they are collapsed into one menu when the taskbar becomes too crowded.

- **Show Quick Launch**   This option shows the Quick Launch option on the toolbar, if selected.

The Notification Area, formerly called the System Tray, is the small icon area on the right side of your taskbar. It tells you which functions are running on your computer and can notify you of certain application functions. The Notification Area panel offers two simple check box options. You can choose the Show the Clock option to display the time in the Notification Area, and you can choose the Hide Inactive Icons option, which simply "cleans up" the Notification Area so that it displays only active icons. You can try both of these settings to see whether you like them.

USING THE CONTROL PANEL

You can access Control Panel in three major ways. First, you can click the Start Menu and click Control Panel. This is probably the most common and easiest way of accessing Control Panel. Second, you can access Control Panel from within any other XP window by simply typing **Control Panel** in the Address dialog box found on the window. This will cause the current window to change to Control Panel. Finally, if a folder is using the XP view, it may have a link to Control Panel in the See Also dialog box, found in the left column of the folder. For example, if you are in My Computer, just click the Control Panel link in the Other Places box to switch to Control Panel. When you use any of these methods, Control Panel opens and you get your first look at the XP Control Panel, as shown in Figure 2-7.

If you've used any previous version of Windows, you will first notice that Control Panel in Windows XP looks a little different. The Windows XP Control

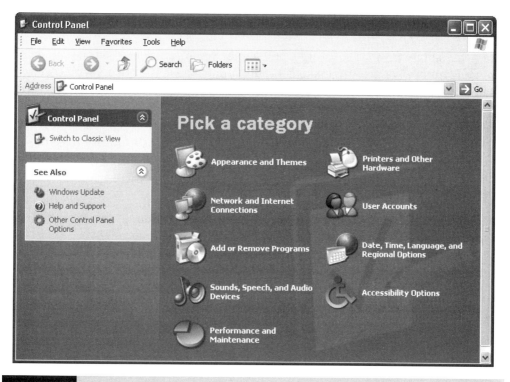

FIGURE 2.7   The Windows XP Control Panel

Panel is divided into categories. If you click on a category, the window changes and enables you to pick a task that you want to perform, or to choose a related Control Panel icon. Windows XP groups Control Panel icons in these different categories to make them easier to locate. However, you need to know two important things. First, the category view does not provide you access to every Control Panel tool that is available. The view provides you access only to the tools that Microsoft considers the most commonly used tools. To see all of your Control Panel options, you can click the Switch to Classic View icon found on the left side of your Control Panel. This setting will give you the typical icon list found in previous versions of Windows.

Now that you have taken a look at XP's Control Panel views, let's now turn our attention to the programs that Control Panel offers. The following sections explore all of the Control Panel icons, and you will learn what you can do and configure with each. To see all of the Control Panel icons, you need to use the Classic view, so just click the Switch to Classic View icon in Control Panel to switch to that view.

ACCESSIBILITY OPTIONS

The Accessibility Options category icon enables you to configure your computer's input and output behavior to make computing much easier for users with certain disabilities. Windows XP provides excellent support for accessibility configuration, and you click this icon in Control Panel to configure most of the settings.

If you double-click Accessibility Options in Control Panel, a Properties window appears with several different tabs that you can configure for your needs. The following sections describe each of these.

KEYBOARD

The Keyboard tab, shown in Figure 2-8, enables you to change the way your keyboard inputs information to the Windows XP operating system.

The Keyboard tab provides you with several options to make using your keyboard easier. First, you can enable StickyKeys. With this feature enabled,

FIGURE 2.8 Use the Keyboard tab to change your keyboard's behavior

you do not have to hold down several keys at one time on the keyboard. For example, suppose that you want to press CTRL-ALT-DEL at the same time (which opens the Close Program window). Normally, you would press these keys at the same time, but with the StickyKeys feature enabled, the keys "stick" so that you can press CTRL, then press ALT, then press DEL, one key at a time. This is an excellent feature for people who can use only one hand on the keyboard. To enable StickyKeys, just click the Use StickyKeys check box and then click the Settings button.

When you click Settings, a new Window appears with a few check boxes. First, you can enable the StickyKeys shortcut, which enables you to turn on StickyKeys by pressing the SHIFT key five times in a row. You can also select or deselect these options:

- Press modifier key twice to lock. This option specifies that CTRL, SHIFT, or ALT remains active if you press it twice. (Press the key a third time to unlock it.)

- Turn StickyKeys off if two keys are pressed at the same time.

- Make a sound when modifier key is pressed (CTRL, SHIFT, or ALT).

- Show StickyKeys status on screen.

Once you enable or disable these options as desired, you can then use StickyKeys by pressing SHIFT five times in a row. A message appears on your screen telling you that the StickyKeys feature is enabled, and a StickyKey icon appears in your Notification Area. Once you play around with StickyKeys, you'll see they are easy to use and very helpful.

Windows XP provides FilterKeys to help your operating system "filter" keystrokes. If a user has difficulty using the keyboard, you can activate FilterKeys so that XP will ignore brief or repeated keystrokes. To use FilterKeys, just click the Use FilterKeys check box on the Keyboard tab, then click the Settings button.

In the window that appears after you click the Settings button, click the Use Shortcut check box so that you can turn on FilterKeys by pressing the right SHIFT key for eight seconds. You can use the remainder of this window to determine how the FilterKeys feature behaves by selecting (or not selecting) the following options:

- **Ignore Repeated Keystrokes**   For example, if a user presses **t** twice quickly, XP will filter the keypresses so that only one *t* appears on the screen. Click the Settings button to adjust the rate as desired.

- **Ignore Quick Keystrokes and Slow Down the Repeat Rate** This option ignores quick keystroke repeats.

- **Beep When Keys Are Pressed or Accepted** This option plays a tone when keys are pressed.

- **Show FilterKey Status on Screen** This option displays a status icon.

As with StickyKeys, the FilterKeys feature is easy to use. Play around with the settings to meet your specific needs.

The ToggleKeys feature simply tells the operating system to play a tone when you press CAPS LOCK, NUM LOCK, or SCROLL LOCK on your keyboard. To turn on this feature, just click the Use ToggleKeys check box. If you click the Settings button, a simple dialog box appears in which you can specify a shortcut to turn on ToggleKeys by pressing and holding down NUM LOCK for five seconds.

Beneath the ToggleKeys settings on the Keyboard tab is the Show Extra Keyboard Help in Programs check box. This feature turns on keyboard help pointers that some applications that you use may support.

SOUND

The Sound tab of the Accessibility Options category gives you two quick options to enable Windows sounds to help you. The first option is the SoundSentry. Depending on what happens with Windows XP (or what you do), certain warning or notice sounds are made, such as when you close programs or when error messages appear. The SoundSentry option enables these warnings to appear on your screen instead of as a sound. This feature is obviously helpful to hearing-impaired Windows XP users. To use the SoundSentry, just click the Use SoundSentry check box. If you click the drop-down menu, you can decide what the screen should do to give you the warning (such as flash the active title bar, and so on).

The tab's second option is to use ShowSounds. ShowSounds tells your programs to display text for any sounds or verbal speech cues they might give you. You enable this option simply by clicking the Use ShowSounds check box.

DISPLAY

The Display tab enables you to use highly contrasting colors on your display that may be easier to read. To enable it, just click the Use High Contrast check box. If you click the Settings button, you can enable the shortcut, which is LEFT ALT-LEFT SHIFT-PRINT SCREEN, by clicking the check box to enable the shortcut. You can also use this window to determine how high contrast should be used, such as white on black, black on white, or a custom combination. You can experiment with these settings to find which one works best for you.

Also notice on the Display tab that you can adjust the cursor settings. Use the slider bars to adjust cursor's blink rate and its width. These settings can make the cursor easier to see.

MOUSE

The Mouse tab provides you with a simple check box that enables you to control the mouse pointer on your screen with the numeric keypad on your keyboard so that you do not actually have to use the mouse. Click the Settings button to enable the shortcut to this option, which is LEFT ALT-LEFT SHIFT-NUM LOCK. You also use the Settings page to control how fast the mouse pointer moves and configure related settings, which are self-explanatory.

GENERAL

Finally, the General tab provides some basic control options for accessibility. You have the following options:

- **Turn Off Accessibility Features If Idle**   This feature enables a timeout period where accessibility features are turned off if the computer is idle for a certain period of time. Use the drop-down menu to select the desired idle time.

- **Give Warning Message When Turning a Feature On**   This feature makes a warning message appear when you turn a feature on.

- **Make a Sound When Turning a Feature On/Off**   This option makes a sound when you turn a feature on or off.

- **Support SerialKey Devices**   SerialKey devices are additional input devices (also called augmentative communication devices) attached to the computer. Users who cannot use a standard keyboard and mouse may benefit from these devices. This setting tells Windows XP to support such devices.

- **Administrative Options**   If you are an administrator for the computer, you can choose to apply all Accessibility Options that you have configured to the logon desktop (the area in which you select your user account and enter your password) and for all new users. This way, the Accessibility Options are available and configured for each person who uses the XP computer.

ADD NEW HARDWARE

The Add New Hardware icon that appears in Control Panel is actually a wizard that you can use to help you install troublesome devices on your computer and solve problems with hardware. Chapter 4 explains this wizard in detail.

ADD OR REMOVE PROGRAMS

The Add or Remove Programs icon enables you to install new programs, remove programs, and install and remove Windows components. These features are explored in Chapter 5, so refer to that chapter for step-by-step instructions.

ADMINISTRATIVE TOOLS

Windows XP includes a folder called Administrative Tools. In this folder, you will find several different tools that can help you manage the Windows XP computer, including the Computer Management tool and a Performance Monitor. Because of the complexity of these tools, you will explore and use them in several chapters throughout the book.

DATE, TIME

The Date, Time icon in Control Panel enables you to set your operating system's clock. When you double-click the icon, Windows XP displays a simple interface

TROUBLESHOOTING

Adding Hardware in Windows XP

Although Chapter 4 explores hardware exclusively, I do want to point out that plug and play hardware is typically installed automatically in Windows XP. Generally, you simply plug the device into the computer and Windows XP installs it. The Add Hardware wizard is used to troubleshoot problematic hardware or install hardware that Windows XP does not readily detect. As a general rule, however, you don't need to use the Add Hardware wizard to install hardware on Windows XP.

that contains a calendar noting the current date. You can change the date simply by using the drop-down menus. Likewise, you see a clock with a drop-down menu in which you can change the current time as well as the time zone. The options here are self-explanatory.

If you need to adjust your computer's date and time, you don't have to use the Control Panel icon. Just right-click the time in the Notification Area and click Properties. This action opens the same Date/Time window. You'll also see an Internet Time option that enables you to synchronize the computer's time with an Internet time server. However, if the Windows XP Professional operating system resides in a Windows domain, this feature is disabled.

DISPLAY

The Display icon in Control Panel enables you to configure your desktop and other display settings so that your computer looks the way you want. The numerous settings enable you to define your display in a variety of ways. You will learn all about using the Display settings later in this chapter.

FOLDER OPTIONS

Windows XP enables you to configure the appearance of your folders. You can completely change the appearance of your folders and customize them to meet specific needs that you or your users might have. Several options are available, and you can learn all about them in Chapter 3.

FONTS

The Fonts folder in Control Panel simply houses all of the possible fonts that your computer can use. When you open the Fonts folder, you see a listing of all of the fonts available. The folder does not enable you to configure the fonts, although you can remove fonts from the folder or add them to the folder. However, usually you will not need to do so, since Windows XP and your applications handle the fonts that are used. You can determine which fonts you want Windows XP and your applications to use by using the Display icon or configuring a specific application's properties. You can, however, double-click any font in the Fonts folder to learn more about the font, such as the creator, and to see a sample of how the font looks.

GAME CONTROLLERS

The Game Controllers icon in Control Panel enables you to manage any gaming devices attached to your computer, such as joysticks and other playing devices.

INTERNET OPTIONS

The Internet Options category icon in Control Panel enables you to configure, as you might guess, Internet Explorer. You can access this same property sheet from within Internet Explorer itself.

KEYBOARD

The Keyboard icon in Control Panel enables you to configure how your keyboard operates. When you double-click this icon, you see two tabs. The Speed tab enables you to configure how fast your keyboard responds to keystrokes. The Speed tab gives you a few simple options for adjusting your keyboard's speed. First you see two slider bars for character repeat. The first, Repeat Delay, determines how much time passes before a character repeats when you hold down a key. If you are a fast typist, you will probably want to move this slider bar's setting to a shorter duration.

You also see a Repeat Rate slider bar. The Repeat Rate slider bar determines how fast a character repeats when you hold it down. The Repeat Delay slider determines how fast the initial repeat begins, whereas the Repeat Rate slider determines how fast the characters are actually repeated. A medium setting (between slow and fast) is typically all you need.

At the bottom of the window, you see the cursor Repeat Rate slider. When you use the slider bar to change the rate, you can see the cursor blinking on the tab for test purposes. The best setting is typically toward the fast end of the slider bar.

The Hardware tab simply lists the type of keyboard that is attached to your computer. Two buttons are available that allow you to troubleshoot the keyboard if you are having problems, or you can click the Properties button to access the device's properties sheets. You can learn more about configuring devices for your system in Chapter 4.

MOUSE

The mouse is a universal input device that lets you point and click your way around Windows. The mouse itself is a simple device, but surprisingly, you can access a number of configuration options for the mouse by double-clicking the Mouse icon in Control Panel. You can configure how fast or slow the mouse operates and even adjust the buttons. The options are self-explanatory.

If you want to use different mouse pointers for your own custom configuration, you can use one of two types of files. First, you can use a standard cursor file, which ends with the .cur extension. Also, you can use an animated cursor file, whose filename ends with an .ani extension. When you browse for a different pointer file, Windows XP looks only for files with either a .cur or .ani extension.

NETWORK CONNECTIONS

The Network Connections icon in Control Panel enables you to configure networking components so that Windows XP can participate on a local, remote, or wide area network. You can learn all about networking with Windows XP in Chapter 8.

PHONE AND MODEM OPTIONS

The Modems icon in Control Panel provides a place where you manage modems attached to your computer. In the past, modems were painfully difficult to set up and troubleshoot, but Windows XP makes modem configuration much easier. You can learn more about modem setup and configuration in Chapter 4.

POWER OPTIONS

Windows XP is equipped to save energy by using power schemes that you can configure. These options can automatically turn off your monitor or hard drive after a certain period of inactivity. The Power Options in Control Panel are also available within the Display Properties dialog box, which you'll explore later in this chapter.

PRINTERS AND FAXES

The Printers folder contains a listing of any printers or fax machines attached to your computer, and includes a helpful wizard to aid you in setting up these devices. As you can imagine, printing and faxing can be complex topics, so check out Chapter 7, which covers them.

REGIONAL AND LANGUAGE OPTIONS

The Regional and Language Options category icon in Control Panel helps you to configure your computer to use different language symbols, currencies, and other specific regional options. For example, suppose that you are using

Windows XP in France and you want Windows XP to calculate money in French currency. You can enable this option by using Regional and Language Options. When you open Regional and Language Options, you see a standard Regional Options tab, a Languages tab, and an Advanced tab. Each tab contains drop-down menus so you can select the desired regional settings.

SCANNERS AND CAMERA

Because of the popularity of scanners and digital cameras, Windows XP includes a Control Panel icon to help you manage these hardware devices. You can learn about installing and managing scanners and cameras in Chapter 4.

SCHEDULED TASKS

The Scheduled Tasks folder in Control Panel contains several wizards you can use to help you set up a variety of PC maintenance utilities to run in the background. Chapter 9 covers all these options.

SOUNDS, SPEECH, AND AUDIO DEVICES

The Sounds, Speech, and Audio Devices icon in Control Panel enables you to make some basic configuration changes. By resetting the available options, you can change the way your Windows XP computer handles default Windows sounds and multimedia, as well as sound devices attached to your computer. If you double-click the Sounds, Speech, and Audio Devices icon in Control Panel, the properties page appears with five tabs that enable you to configure such sound options as volume, event sounds, and audio.

SPEECH

The Speech icon in Control Panel allows you to configure text-to-speech translation. This means that Windows XP can read to you any text in Windows that you want read. By default, the Microsoft Sam voice is selected for you, which is the only voice option available in the default XP installation. You can use the Preview Voice buttons and the Audio Output buttons to hear the voice and to select the device that you want to use for voice playback (which is typically your computer's sound card). You can also use the slider bar to slow down or speed up the rate at which the computer reads information to you.

SYSTEM

The System icon in Control Panel contains seven different tabs, such as Hardware, System Restore, Automatic Updates, Remote, and others. These tabs manage different components of your Windows XP system, and they are explored in several other chapters throughout this book.

TASKBAR AND START MENU

As mentioned earlier, the Taskbar and Start Menu icon enables you to configure these Windows elements to suit your needs.

USER ACCOUNTS

Finally, the last icon in Control Panel is the User Accounts icon. This icon gives you an interface where you can create new user accounts and manage existing user accounts so that different people can log on to your Windows XP computer. Without a valid username and a password, different users cannot log on, so you use this window to create these accounts. Chapter 6 explores user account management in depth.

CONFIGURING DISPLAY AND POWER OPTIONS

One of the major ways to configure your Windows XP system's appearance is by using your Display Properties dialog box. Display is an icon in Control Panel that you can click to display a tab on which you can configure various settings that affect the appearance of your Windows XP display. Just click Start, point to Settings, click Control Panel, then double-click the Display icon to open the Display Properties dialog box. Or, right-click an empty area of the desktop and click Properties. Once you open the Display Properties dialog box, you see several tabs, all of which are explored in the following sections.

THEMES

A theme is a group of settings that are applied to Windows XP under a single name. The settings usually relate to each other, thus creating a theme of some kind. If you've used Windows before, you are familiar with the concept of themes, but you are not used to seeing a Themes tab, shown in Figure 2-9, on the Display Properties dialog box. Microsoft placed the Themes option in this

FIGURE 2.9   The Themes tab

dialog box in Windows XP because the default Windows XP interface is simply a theme. You can use the XP interface, or you can change to a different theme, or even use a "Windows Classic" theme, which basically gives you the plain Windows interface you saw in Windows 9x, Me, and 2000. Simply use the drop-down menu to select a desired theme and click Apply to see all of the settings that the theme has to offer. You can also modify any theme (including the default XP interface theme) by making changes to the other tabs available on the Display Properties dialog box.

SECRET

If you modify the XP theme, it will appear on the themes tab as Windows XP (Modified).

DESKTOP

The second tab you see on the Display Properties dialog box is the Desktop tab (formerly called Background), shown in Figure 2-10. The Desktop tab lets you decide how your Windows XP desktop area should look. In other words, the Desktop tab lets you decide what color, style, or even picture appears on your desktop.

In the Background scroll box of the Desktop tab, Windows XP gives you several built-in options that you can choose for your background. Some files give your desktop a pattern, whereas others give your desktop a picture.

In the Background scroll box of the Desktop tab, each file has a name and an icon picture next to it. The background patterns and pictures are simply .JPEG, .BMP, .GIF, and related picture file formats that you commonly see on the Internet, as well as HTML files.

On the Desktop tab, when you can select one of the files, it appears in the test monitor window on the Desktop tab. By default, Window XP stretches pictures

FIGURE 2.10   The Desktop tab lets you choose a desired desktop background

across your screen so that they take up the entire desktop area, and sets patterns to tile so that they repeat until the entire desktop area is used. This causes the pattern to fill the entire test screen so you can see how it looks before you decide to use it. You can also use the Center option in the Background scroll box to center the pattern in the middle of the test screen, which will give you a different look. If you like what you have selected, click the Apply button at the bottom of the window. Windows XP will then apply the new pattern to your desktop. If you don't like it, just pick something else from the Desktop tab's Background scroll box. You can look at all of the patterns and even reapply different patterns until you find the one you want.

When you choose to center a picture or pattern, Windows XP leaves an area of your desktop showing. You can use a color to alter the remaining desktop area. For example, suppose that you choose a wallpaper pattern from the Background scroll box on the Display tab and you center the picture. You will have additional leftover background space. You can use the color drop-down menu to select a color for the remaining portion of the desktop area. Once you have finished your background pattern and selected anything else from the Background scroll box on the Display tab that you want to use for the main pattern, just click Apply and then click OK.

Finally, a Customize Desktop button appears near the bottom of the Desktop tab. If you click this button, you are taken to the Desktop Items dialog box, which contains a General and Web tab. On the General tab, shown in Figure 2-11, you can choose which desktop icons you want to display, such as My Documents, My Computer, My Network Places, and Internet Explorer. All of these items are selected by default. You also see a window showing the default icons that are used for each of these items. If you want to use different icons, just click the Change Icon button and select different icons from the provided list. If you manage to foul up your configuration, just click the Restore Default button to return to XP's default icon settings.

At the bottom of the tab, you see the option Run the Desktop Cleanup Wizard Every 60 Days. The Cleanup Wizard is configured to run every 60 days by default, but you can run it at any other time by clicking the Clean Desktop Now button. This wizard simply removes old shortcuts (ones not used in the last 60 days) and puts them in a folder called Unused Shortcuts. If you create many shortcuts but use them infrequently, this wizard can help keep your desktop free of clutter.

The Desktop Items dialog box's Web tab, shown in Figure 2-12, allows you to place a complete Web page on your desktop.

You can use the wallpaper feature to place an HTML file on your desktop, but if you choose the Web option, you can place on your desktop a Web page that you can synchronize with the Web page that appears on the Internet. To place a

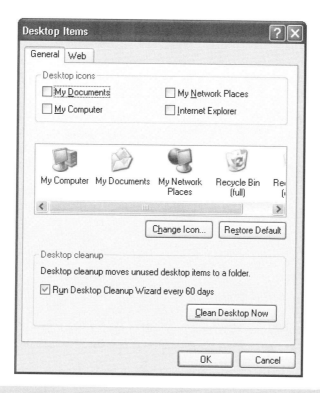

FIGURE 2.11 The Desktop Items dialog box's General tab

Web page on your desktop, just click the New button and enter the URL in the New Desktop Item dialog box, as shown in Figure 2-13. You'll need an Internet connection to finish adding the Web page.

Once you click OK, a confirmation message appears. If the Web site requires you to enter a password, click the Customize button and enter your password; otherwise, just click OK. When you choose the Web page option, the entire Web site is downloaded and stored on your computer so that you can use the site just as if you were actually using a browser.

SCREEN SAVER

The Screen Saver tab of the Display Properties dialog box provides two functions: It enables you to configure a screen saver for your computer and to configure power management options. A screen saver is a simple program that runs after your computer has been idle for a certain period of time. In the past,

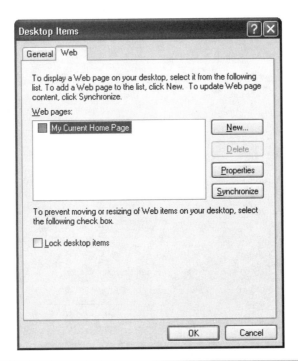

FIGURE 2.12 The Desktop Items dialog box's Web tab

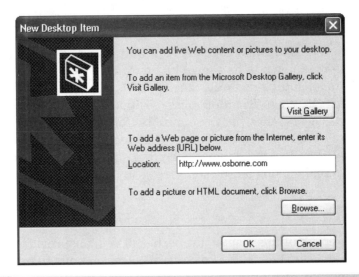

FIGURE 2.13 The New Desktop Item dialog box

the screen savers protected monitors from "screen burn." When you left a monitor unattended for too long with one continuous picture or window displayed, the image could burn itself onto the monitor and always be vaguely visible in the background. Monitors today are less susceptible to this problem, so screen savers are used mostly for decoration. However, you can also use the On Resume, Password Protect option so that your password has to be entered to regain the desktop when a screen saver is in use. This is an additional security feature.

You can also access Windows XP's power management options from the Screen Saver tab. If you press the Power button, the Power Options Properties dialog box appears, opening to the Power Schemes tab, shown in Figure 2-14.

The Power Schemes tab offers a few options to manage how your computer conserves energy when it is idle. First, you see a drop-down menu called Power

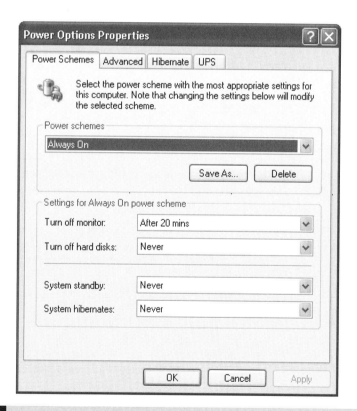

FIGURE 2.14   Use the Power Options Properties dialog box's Power Schemes tab to manage the power used by your computer

Schemes. There are a few basic schemes, which will vary slightly if you are using a laptop computer:

- **Home/Office Desk**   When you select this scheme, Windows XP automatically turns off your monitor after 15 minutes of inactivity, shuts down hard disks after 30 minutes, and places your system on standby after 20 minutes.

- **Portable/Laptop**   This scheme uses the same settings as Home/Office Desk.

- **Presentation**   This scheme is used for laptops or computers used for teaching or presentations. Essentially, the power options are turned off and the system never goes on standby.

- **Always On**   This scheme automatically turns off your monitor after 30 minutes of inactivity and your hard drives after one hour. However, your system never goes on standby.

- **Minimal Power Management**   This scheme simply turns off your monitor after 15 minutes, but never shuts down the hard drive.

- **Max Battery**   This scheme contains the same settings as Minimal Power Management.

You can use a particular scheme and change any of the settings you want simply by using the drop-down menus. For example, suppose that you want to use the Home/Office Desk scheme, but do not want your monitor to turn off until 30 minutes of inactivity. To accomplish this, just use the drop-down menu for the monitor and change its setting to 30 minutes. You can also change all of the settings and click Save As to create your own scheme. Just give the scheme a name and it will appear in your scheme list. To bring the computer out of standby mode, just press SPACEBAR or ENTER.

Keep in mind that the default power options that you see are simply suggestions for power conservation when the computer is used in a particular way. The options, however, can easily be edited so that you can make custom power schemes, which may meet the needs of your users more accurately than the default options.

The Power Options Properties dialog box also has an Advanced tab (which really isn't that advanced). It offers only two check box options that you can select:

- **Always Show Icon on the Taskbar**   This option puts a power icon on your taskbar.

- **Prompt for Password When Computer Goes Off Standby**   This option requires you to reenter your password when your computer goes off standby before you can use the system again. This helps prevent someone from gaining access to your system when you are away from it.

On the Hibernate tab, you can simply click the check box to enable the hibernate feature. Hibernation allows Windows XP to store information that is in memory on your hard disk before the operating system shuts down. When the computer is brought back online, XP can remember its previous state so that you do not lose any data. The computer's BIOS (Basic Input/Output System), however, must support hibernation. Computers that support the ACPI (Advanced Configuration Power Interface) standard support the hibernation feature. If the computer does not support ACPI, the feature will not be available. Check your computer's BIOS to see whether it supports ACPI. To return the computer from hibernation, simply turn on the computer.

For laptop computers, you'll see button options to sleep, hibernate, or shut down after a period of time has passed while running on batteries.

The APM (Advanced Power Management) tab is for computers that support the APM standard. APM allows your computer to use less power and gives you information about battery life if you are using a battery (such as with a laptop). The tab has no settings to configure; if this tab tells you that your computer supports APM, you can enable the feature by clicking the single check box option.

The final tab is UPS, which stands for Uninterruptible Power Supply. UPS devices are basically batteries that give your desktop computer enough power to remain online in the event of a power failure. This gives you enough time to shut down your system properly. A UPS is typically used with server systems and rarely used with desktop systems, but if you have a UPS, you can enable the feature on this tab. Be sure to follow the UPS manufacturer's suggestions for configuration and settings.

APPEARANCE

The Appearance tab, shown in Figure 2-15, enables you to pick an appearance scheme for your Windows XP computer.

This tab offers a few standard options:

- **Windows and Buttons**   You can use the drop-down menu either to choose XP style or Windows Classic style.

- **Color Scheme**   A number of color schemes are available. Use this drop-down menu to select one you like. You can experiment with this setting and change it at any time.

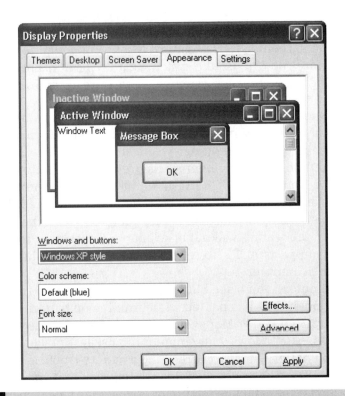

FIGURE 2.15   Use the Appearance tab to pick an appearance scheme

- **Font Size**   You can choose normal, large, and extra large from the drop-down menu.

- **Effects**   Click the Effects button to open the Effects window, which gives you some basic check box options such as fade, shadows under menus, and so on.

- **Advanced**   If you click the Advanced button, you can make specific font and color changes to different window components, such as menus, buttons, the active title bar, and a host of others. Usually you will not want to edit all of the settings. However, if you want to change a specific window component, just select it using the drop-down menu and configure its available options.

SETTINGS

The final Display Properties tab is the Settings tab. You use this tab to manage the actual video card hardware that resides within your computer. As you can see in Figure 2-16, the tab presents a few basic options.

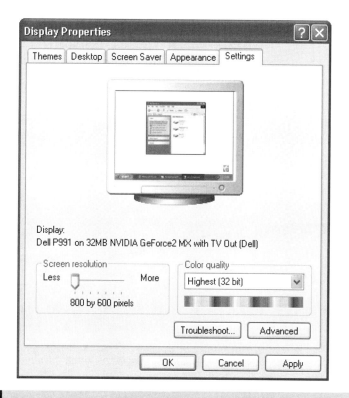

FIGURE 2.16   Use the Settings tab to configure your video adapter card

First, you see the Color Quality drop-down menu. This menu enables you to select the number of colors that Windows XP can use to generate all of the graphics and pictures that appear on your monitor. You can select a different color quality, depending on the option supported by your video card (such as 24-bit and 32-bit color).

The Settings tab also offers the Screen Resolution slider bar. Using this control, you can adjust the screen area to suit your needs. As you adjust it, your desktop area (including your icons) will become either larger or smaller depending on the option that you select.

The tab also has an Advanced button. This option opens the properties pages for your video card. For most systems, the default settings should suffice, but these pages offer a few options that can help you solve particular problems:

- On the General tab, you can change the dots per inch (DPI) setting, which by default is typically set around 96. Increasing this value can increase the size of the items found on the screen. However, this setting increases all items. If you want to change only the font size, use the Appearance tab on the Display Properties dialog box to change the font.

- On the Monitor tab, you can adjust the screen refresh rate. If the screen seems to respond slowly to keyboard strokes, increasing this rate may improve performance, depending on the quality of your monitor. Again, as a general rule, the default setting is best.

- On the Troubleshoot tab, you can change the rate of hardware acceleration for the video card. If you are having no problems, you should leave this setting at Full. However, if you are having performance problems, you can try to resolve the problem by reducing the acceleration value in slight increments.

TECH TALK

Video Cards and Problems

Configuring video cards can be problematic for A+ technicians. If your environment is starting out with new computers that meet all of the Windows XP standards, you may not experience any problems. However, in the case of upgrades, video card compatibility and performance can become an issue. As you are working with video cards in your Windows environment, keep the following points in mind:

- Video card compatibility is a must. Visit the Hardware Compatibility List at http://www.microsoft.com/hcl for an up-to-date list of video cards that are compatible with Windows XP.

- In the case of upgrades, make sure you have the correct driver. Visit the manufacturer's Web site and look for any updated drivers designed for Windows XP. If you need help installing a new driver, see Chapter 4 for details.

- If the Settings tab of the Display Properties dialog box does not give you many color options or resolution options, again, the problem is the driver. To fix the problem, you'll need a driver that is compatible with Windows XP. If one does not exist, try using a driver written for Windows 2000.

- You can adjust the Advanced settings from the Settings tab if necessary, but in most cases, these fixes really do not solve all of the problems. Again, compatibility is the key.

WORKING WITH THE MICROSOFT MANAGEMENT CONSOLE

Like Windows 2000, Windows XP makes heavy use of the Microsoft Management Console, or MMC. The MMC is a stripped-down graphical user interface (GUI) that provides a way for all tools within Windows XP to have the same look and feel. Instead of providing one disk management tool with its own interface and other Group Policy tools with their own interface, the MMC provides a common interface to all tools. This helps reduce your learning curve so that Windows XP is easier to use.

Windows XP provides several default consoles that you can use. For example, if you open Administrative Tools in Control Panel, you see icons for IIS, Performance, and Computer Management. Each of these consoles is an MMC console that uses snap-ins. A snap-in is simply a program that works within the MMC. For example, if you click Start | Run, you can type **MMC** and click OK to open an empty MMC, as shown in Figure 2-17.

As you can see, you cannot do much with the MMC alone. This is because the MMC is designed to house snap-ins. The MMC gives you a way to manage the snap-ins, which allow you to perform specific tasks in Windows XP. So, if Windows XP provides the MMC for snap-ins, which make your work with Windows XP easier, where exactly do you, the A+ technician, come in?

Although Windows XP provides a number of default consoles, you can open your own MMC consoles and load the snap-ins that you want to use. You can even create custom consoles so that you can configure Windows XP more easily. The good news is that working with the MMC is rather intuitive—you can use the menu commands as you would any folder in Windows XP, and you can right-

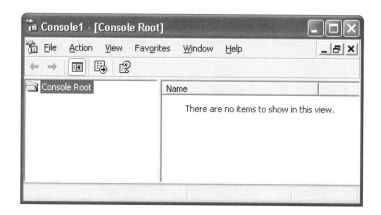

FIGURE 2.17   An empty MMC console

click just about any item in the console for menu options. However, the following sections will sharpen your MMC skills and show you how to make the best use of the console.

OPENING SNAP-INS

You can easily open any MMC snap-in from within an MMC console. This allows you the flexibility to open a snap-in that you need to use and even combine snap-ins so that they appear in one MMC console. The process is simple and easy, using the following steps:

1. Click Start | Run. Type **MMC** and click OK.

2. In the empty MMC console, click File | Add/Remove Snap-In.

3. In the Add/Remove Snap-In window that appears, shown in Figure 2-18, click the Add button.

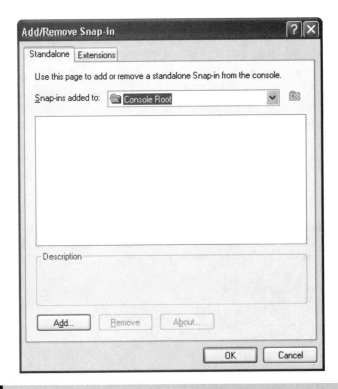

FIGURE 2.18   Click Add to add a snap-in

4. The Add Standalone Snap-In dialog box appears, as shown in Figure 2-19. Select the snap-in that you want to add and click Add. Another window may appear asking you which computer you want to manage, depending on the snap-in. If you want to add other snap-ins, select the next snap-in and click Add. Click Close when you are done.

5. Click OK on the Add/Remove Snap-In dialog box. The snap-in now appears in the console, as shown in Figure 2-20.

6. To save the console so that it will be available for future use, click File | Save As, and give the console a name.

NOTE   You can put the MMC console that you have created anywhere on your computer for easy access. You can even drag and drop it to the Start Menu.

USING THE MMC

All MMCs work the same way. As you can see in Figure 2-20, the MMC console window has a left console pane and a right console pane. In the left console pane,

FIGURE 2.19   Select the snap-in you want to use and click Add

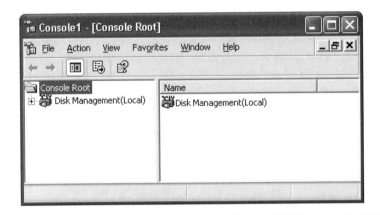

FIGURE 2.20   The snap-in appears in the window

you see the snap-in. If you click the snap-in, it expands to include subcategories available for the snap-in. For example, the Local Users and Groups snap-in has subcategories of Users and Groups. If you select a subcategory, information about the category appears in the right console pane. For example, if you are using Local Users and Groups, the subcategory of Users contains user accounts that will appear in the right console pane. If you right-click any subcategory or icon in the console, menu options related to that subcategory will appear. For example, if you right-click Users, the option to create new user accounts appears. If you right-click a user account, you can delete it, rename it, access its properties, and so on. The Action menu also gives you the same menu options as right-clicking.

CREATING CUSTOM MMCS

When you open a snap-in and save the console, you have created a custom MMC—it's that simple. However, you can create other custom MMCs that will make your work with Windows XP easier. For example, suppose that you frequently use local Group Policy on a particular Windows 2000 Professional computer, but you also use the local Users and Groups console. Rather than having to open two different consoles each time, you can simply create a console that has these two snap-ins available and then save the console. Then all you have to do it open your saved console each time you want to access Group Policy or the disk administrator program. As you can see, the snap-ins do not have to be related to each other, but you can store everything that you commonly use under one console so that you can do all your work using only one interface. As a busy technician, this can save you a lot of time.

Custom MMC consoles are also a great way to help users perform tasks. For example, if users in your environment frequently need to use tools such as Disk Defragmenter, you can create a console containing the tools and place the console on the Start Menu. This makes the tools easier for the users to locate and use. The MMC is designed to help you, so if you need to make users' work easier, always consider the possibilities that the MMC sends your way.

NOTE If you need more skills to get you started with the MMC, open an empty MMC and click the Help menu to get more help from Windows XP. Also note that you can move consoles from one Windows XP computer to another. You can create one console and copy it to other computers for ease of use.

WRAPPING UP

Windows XP is designed to be an easy operating system to use, but it is quite different from previous versions of Windows. As an A+ technician, you are likely to run into use questions and problems relating to Windows XP's basic operations and appearance. The good news is that Windows XP is rather flexible and you can easily address most appearance and display issues that users encounter. Remember, though, that user training is of utmost importance. As you are working with users in your environment, try to help users understand how XP works and how it is different from previous versions of Windows. This gives you the opportunity to support users' technical needs, but also teach them something new.

Now that you've taken a look at Windows XP's operating system fundamentals, let's now turn our attention to file, folder, and disk management in Chapter 3.

MANAGING FOLDERS AND FILES

3

Folder and file management is a major part of computing, since all data is stored in a file format, which is then stored in a folder. The good news is that file and folder management will not consume a lot of your time as an A+ technician. However, users in your environment may be unfamiliar with a number of folder and file management features that you will end up supporting. Fortunately, folder and file management is easier in Windows XP than in previous versions of Windows. Windows XP includes some additional management features that you can use to save disk space and provide greater security. In this chapter, you'll…

- Configure and manage files and folders
- Use folder and file compression
- Manage folder and file encryption
- Work with offline files

MANAGING FOLDER OPTIONS

Windows XP gives you more folder configuration flexibility than ever before. However, this same flexibility can lead to more help desk support calls, in which case you'll need to both help and educate the users you support. For folder configuration, one of your primary places to configure folders is Folder Options. You can configure Folder Options from either one of two places. You can double-click the Folder Options icon in Control Panel, or you can configure Folder Options from within any Windows folder. For example, you can open My Documents, click the Tools drop-down menu, then click Folder Options. This opens the same Folder Options you see when you open the Control Panel icon. You can use the Tools menu to access Folder Options from any folder in Windows XP.

NOTE Folder Options apply to all folders. In other words, you cannot configure Folder Options individually for each folder —one setting applies to all folders in Windows. Folder Options do not affect folder toolbars, but you can change folder toolbars, which you learn about later in this chapter.

Once you open Folder Options (regardless of where you open it), you see a simple interface with four tabs. You can configure several items on each tab, and you'll take a look at those in the following sections.

GENERAL TAB

The major changes that you can make to folders' appearance are performed on the General tab, which presents you with a list of radio buttons, shown in Figure 3-1.

As you can see in Figure 3-1, you have four different categories from which you can choose a radio button option. The following list explains these options:

- **Tasks** This option enables you to display web content in your folders. This includes the blue links you have seen in the left side of your folders (which jump to another location when you click them). Web content also enables your folders to display HTML documents and graphics files, such as thumbnails. To use the web view, just click the Show Common Tasks in Folder radio button. My Computer and the Control Panel are always displayed with the web page view, even if you do not select this option. If you want to use the old Windows look, click Use Windows Classic Folders.

- **Browse Folders** This option enables you to choose how your folders are displayed when you are browsing through a folder structure. For example,

FIGURE 3.1   Most folder configuration options are found on the General tab

suppose that you open My Computer, and then open Control Panel. You can have My Computer open in a window and Control Panel open in a separate window. Or, you can choose to use the same window so that you open My Computer, then when you open Control Panel, it replaces what you see in My Computer.

■ **Click Items as Follows**   You can have your mouse clicks act as though your Windows XP interface is the Internet. On the Internet, you simply click your left mouse key to open any item because all Internet movement is performed through hyperlinks that connect web pages and Internet sites together. You can have your computer act this way as well so that you only have to point to an item to select it and left-click it one time to open it.

VIEW TAB

The View tab contains a number of check boxes that enable you to make a number of different decisions about files and folders, as shown in Figure 3-2.

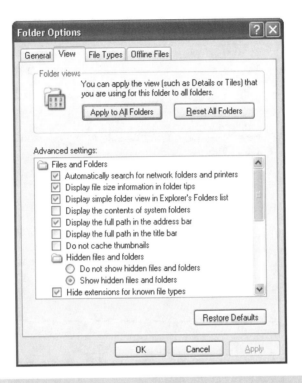

View tab

The options found here control the display of certain file types, folder views, and other lower-level settings. Windows XP does a good job of configuring the common settings for you, but users may decide to change these settings, so you need to be familiar with them. The following list points out some of the more common options and whether those options are enabled by default.

- **Do Not Show Hidden Files and Folders** and **Hide Protected Operating System Files**   These two separate options, both of which are enabled by default, do not show hidden files and folders in Windows XP. Windows XP hides many of the files and folders that hold operating system files that make Windows XP run. Obviously, you don't need to do anything with these files, and Windows XP hides them to help prevent tampering or accidental deletion.

- **Hide Extensions for Known File Types**   This option hides file extensions. For example, let's say you type a Microsoft Word document called Development. The document's official name is Development.doc. The Hide Extensions option hides the .doc extension and all other extensions for files that Windows recognizes. This makes your folder files cleaner and easier to read. This option is enabled by default.

■ **Remember Each Folder's View Settings**   You can use the View menu in a particular folder to determine how the folder appears and what you can view (you can learn about these options later in this chapter). This setting tells Windows to remember each folder's view settings. This option is enabled by default and you should keep it enabled.

FILE TYPES TAB

This File Types tab provides you with a window that lists every type of file supported in Windows XP. Your operating system and applications do a great job of managing this list, so you do not need to perform any configuration here unless an application explicitly instructs you to do so. Removing file types from this list can prevent certain application files from functioning in Windows XP, however.

OFFLINE FILES TAB

Offline files allow Windows XP to store network files locally on your computer, then synchronize your local copy with the network copy. For example, let's say that a document resides on a network server, but you need to take that document home on your laptop one evening and make some changes to it. With offline files, Windows XP stores the document on your local computer instead of always saving changes to the network file; then, when you reconnect to the network, the local file can be synchronized with the network file. The Offline Files tab enables you to turn on offline file support and configure some basic functions for offline files. You can learn more about using offline files later in this chapter.

CONFIGURING FOLDER VIEWS AND TOOLBARS

Once you make some decisions about how you want your folders to appear using the Folder Options, you can also make some decisions about your folder views and toolbars. When you open a folder, you see a View menu, shown in Figure 3-3.

Most of the options you see on this menu are self-explanatory, and you can try the different setting options to determine what you like best. The following sections explore your major options.

FIGURE 3.3 Use the View menu to make changes to your window's appearance

TOOLBARS

When you hold your mouse over the Toolbars item, a submenu pops up. This submenu allows you to select the toolbar items you would like to use. Some of these are enabled by default, but you can enable or disable then by just clicking them with your mouse. You have these options:

■ **Standard Buttons** Enabled by default, this option provides you with the standard toolbar buttons, such as Back, Forward, Up One Level, Search, and so forth. You need these, so keep this option enabled.

■ **Address Bar** Enabled by default, this gives you the address bar so you can move to different areas of your computer or even the Internet. For example, you could access a folder on your computer by simply typing the path to the folder (such as C:\My Documents) or an Internet address.

■ **Links** This option, which is enabled by default, gives you a Links button on your toolbar so you can add links, which are resource locations that you commonly access.

Aside from these standard options, you can also lock the toolbars and you can click Customize. This option opens a Customization toolbar, as shown in Figure 3-4, which is a window in which you can add and remove various toolbar buttons and options. To create a customized toolbar, use the following steps.

CREATE A CUSTOMIZED TOOLBAR

1. In a desired folder, click View, point to Toolbars, then click Customize.

2. In the Customization Toolbar window, select any item in the left portion of the window that you want to add to your toolbar, then click the Add button. Continue this process until you have moved all options that you want.

3. In the right portion of the window, select any item that you do not want to use on your toolbar, then click Remove. Continue this process until you have removed any options you do not want.

4. In the right portion of the window, select a desired option and use the Move Up or Move Down buttons to adjust the order of the toolbar as desired.

5. Click Close when you are done.

STATUS BAR

The status bar is the small bar that runs along the bottom of your window. It tells you about the connection status when you are trying to use or connect to

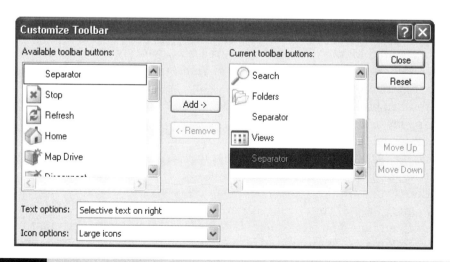

FIGURE 3.4   Use the Customization options to create custom toolbars

other resources. This bar works just like the status bar in Internet Explorer, and you can choose to use it or not by clicking Status on the View menu.

EXPLORER BAR

This option has an additional pop-out menu that lists various Internet Explorer items you can select, such as Search, Favorites, and so forth. If you select one of these items, an additional pane appears in your window to provide the Explorer option. For example, if you select the Search option, the window provides a search section. You can experiment with these settings to find ones that are useful to you.

ICON APPEARANCE

The remainder of the View menu contains a number of different icon and list options to configure the display of a folder's contents. For example, you can use tiles, thumbnails, icons, list, and so forth. Just click these options to experiment with them until you find the appearance that you like best.

CREATING, RENAMING, AND DELETING FOLDERS

You use folders in Windows XP to store data, such as documents, pictures, spreadsheets—you name it. Any type of file or application can be stored in a folder. Depending on your needs, you may not require additional folders. After all, Windows XP automatically tries to place files in your My Documents folder or one of its subfolders, such as My Pictures. However, you may need to create your own folders to manage data. Users in your environment may also need to manage folders on their computers by creating specific folders to meet their needs. You can create folders within folders, and folders within those folders, to as many levels as you want or need.

To create a new folder, open the folder in which you want to create the new folder, such as My Documents or simply your C drive. Click the File menu, point to New, and then click Folder. A new folder appears. Type a desired name for the new folder. If you want to create a new folder directly on your desktop, just right-click an empty area of your desktop, point to New, and click Folder.

At any given time, you can rename a folder by simply right-clicking the folder and clicking Rename. Then press BACKSPACE, type a new name, then press ENTER. This feature makes it easy to keep your folders organized and to move your folders from place to place as needed.

Finally, you can delete any folder by right-clicking the folder and clicking Delete. This moves the folder to the Recycle Bin. Keep in mind that this action deletes everything in the folder as well. This includes files, applications, and any subfolders. If you just want to delete the folder, hold down SHIFT while deleting the folder. This action deletes the folder, but not the files.

NOTE You can share any folder on a network so that other users can access the data in the shared folder. See Chapter 9 to learn more about Windows XP networking.

USING FOLDER AND FILE COMPRESSION

Windows XP includes a built-in folder compression feature that can help users conserve disk space. Compression shrinks the normal size of a folder and its contents in order to free up more disk space that you can use for other purposes. Compression in Windows XP is quick and easy to use, and you can even compress files individually. Windows XP supports both NTFS compression as well as standard Zip compression technology.

USING NTFS COMPRESSION

NTFS compression gives you the freedom to compress individual files or folders, as well as entire drives. Of course, to use NTFS compression, you must have an NTFS drive. The good thing about NTFS compression is that it is fast and easy—and it gives you a lot of compression options. Consider the following points:

- NTFS compression enables you to compress a single file, a folder, or an entire NTFS drive.

- All compressed items remain in a compressed state unless you move the contents to a FAT volume. FAT does not support NTFS compression, so compression is lost when the file or folder is moved. If you move the files to a different NTFS volume, the files inherit the state of the destination folder.

- If you want to work with a compressed file, Windows XP automatically decompresses it for you while the file is in use. When you close the file, Windows XP automatically compresses the file again.

- If you move or copy a file into a compressed folder, it is compressed automatically. If you move a file from a different NTFS drive to a compressed folder, it is also compressed. However, if you move a file from the same NTFS drive into a compressed folder, it retains its original state, either compressed or uncompressed.

■ You cannot encrypt an NTFS compressed file.

As you can see, these are fairly straightforward rules, but it important that you keep them in mind as you are working with NTFS compression. Otherwise, compression is very easy to use, and the following steps show you how.

NOTE Typically, NTFS compression reduces drive, file, and folder size by about 50 percent. Applications are reduced by about 30 percent.

COMPRESSING A DRIVE, FOLDER, OR FILE

1. Click Start | My Computer.

2. In My Computer, right-click the desired NTFS drive and click Properties.

3. On the General tab, shown here, click the Compress Drive to Save Disk Space check box in order to compress the entire drive. Then click OK.

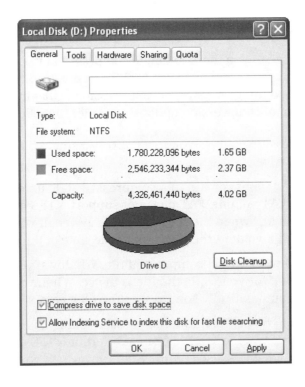

4. To compress a folder or specific file, browse to the desired file or folder that you want to compress. Remember that the file or folder has to reside on an NTFS drive in order for compression to be available.

5. Right-click the desired file or folder and click Properties.

6. On the General tab, click the Advanced button.

7. In the Advanced Attributes window, click the Compress Contents to Save Disk Space check box and click OK.

Aside from the Windows XP interface options, you can also use a command-line utility called Compact.exe to manage compressed files and volumes in Windows XP. Using Compact.exe, you can compress, decompress, and view the compression attributes of a folder, file, or drive. The syntax for Compact.exe is:

```
Compact.exe [/c] [/u] [/s[:dir]] [/a] [/i] [/f] [/q] [filename […]]
```

Table 3-1 defines each of the command switches.

COMPRESSED (ZIPPED) FOLDERS

Windows XP also contains a built-in compression feature, first introduced in Windows Me, that enables you to compress folders on either FAT or NTFS partitions. Folder compression, which is built on WinZip technology, gives you

TECH TALK

Using Color on Compressed Items

If you want to be able to easily keep track of what items are compressed and what items are not compressed, Windows XP gives you an easy option to make compressed items appear in a different color. This setting also applies to encrypted files and folders as well. To configure color for compressed folders, just follow these steps:

1. Open Control Panel and double-click Folder Options.

2. Click the View tab.

3. Scroll and locate the Show Encrypted or Compressed NTFS Files in Color check box. Select the check box, and then click OK.

Switch	Explanation
C	Compresses the specified file
U	Uncompresses the specified file
S	Performs the specified operation on the files in the given folder and all subfolders
A	Displays the file with hidden or system attributes
I	Continues performing the specified operation even after errors have occurred
F	Forces the compress operation on all specified files, including currently compressed files
Q	Reports only the most essential information
Filename	Specifies a pattern, file, or folder

TABLE 3.1   Compact.exe Switches

a quick and easy way to copy files to a compressed folder, which can then be e-mailed or stored. At first glance, Zipped folders may seem unnecessary since NTFS compression is available, but there are several advantages and issues to keep in mind:

- Compressed folders can reside on either NTFS or FAT volumes, unlike NTFS compression, which works only on NTFS volumes.

- Files that reside in a compressed folder can be directly opened without unzipping them, and some applications can also run in a Zipped state.

- Zipped folders can be moved to any drive or folder on your computer or another computer, moved to the Internet, or sent via e-mail, After being moved or sent, the folders remain in their compressed state.

- Files cannot be individually compressed using the Zip feature. You must place them in a compressed folder in order to compress the files.

- Compressed folders can be password-protected.

Using the Compressed Folder feature is very easy. If you have a folder that you want to compress, simply right-click the folder and click Send To | Compressed Folder. This will create the Zipped folder with all of the original folder's contents compressed, but the original folder remains. In other words, you'll see your original folder and a copied, compressed folder with the same contents. If you want to create an empty compressed folder to which you can copy items, simply click File | New | Compressed Folder from within the desired folder or Windows Explorer. If you want to create the new compressed folder on

TECH TALK

Selecting Default Programs to Open Files

Users may complain about opening certain files with certain programs. For example, let's say that a user opens a number of JPEG images, but those images always open with Windows Picture and Fax Viewer. However, the user needs Internet Explorer to open the JPEG images by default. How can you change this setting?

Different file types have different applications associated with them. However, you can easily change the association by following these steps:

1. Right-click the desired file and click Properties.

2. On the General tab, click the Change button.

3. In the Open With dialog box, select the program that you want to use to open the file. If you want to always open this kind of file with the selected program, click the check box for this option. Click OK.

your desktop, simply right-click an empty area of the desktop and click New | Compressed Folder. Any items you store in the folder will be compressed.

USING ENCRYPTION

Like Windows 2000 systems, Windows XP Professional also provides built-in encryption so that users can encrypt files. Once files are encrypted, other users cannot read them. For example, if several different people use a Windows XP Professional computer, each user can encrypt his or her own private data so that other users cannot read it. Encryption is seamless and easy to use, and it is a feature of the NTFS file system. The user does not have to be aware of any keys or the underlying encryption technology. The user simply selects to encrypt data, but can open the data and use it seamlessly without any kind of manual decryption. If another user attempts to access the encrypted data, that user's key will not decrypt the data and he or she will still be unable to read it.

There are a couple of important issues to consider when working with Encrypting File System (EFS). First, EFS is a feature of NTFS and only works on NTFS drives. However, encryption and compression are not compatible—you can either encrypt a file or folder or compress it, but you cannot do both. Also, encryption tends to slow access down—using encrypted files is slower than using regular files because Windows XP Professional must encrypt and decrypt files as they are opened or closed. A new encryption feature in Windows XP, however, enables you to give several users access to the same encrypted file or folder.

To use encryption, simply right-click the file or folder that you want to encrypt, click Properties, and then click the Advanced button on the General tab. The Advanced Attributes window, shown here, gives you a simple encryption check box that you can use to turn on EFS.

NOTE You cannot encrypt any files that have the system attribute or any files located in %SystemRoot% or any of its subfolders. You also cannot encrypt any files or folders in a roaming user profile.

As you can see, encrypting data is rather easy. At any point, you can permanently decrypt the file or folder by returning to the Advanced Attributes window and clearing the check box. However, what if you need to access your encrypted data over the network via several different workstations? You can do so in a couple of different ways. First, if you set up a roaming user profile, then the key will be available no matter where you log on. If not, you can copy your key and carry it with you on a floppy disk. Then, you can use the key to open your encrypted data. This export process is rather easy, and the following exercise walks you through the steps.

EXPORTING A PRIVATE KEY

1. Click Start | Run. Type **MMC** and click OK.

2. In the MMC, click File | Add/Remove Snap-In.

3. In the Add/Remove Snap-In window, click Add. In the snap-in list that appears, click Certificates and click Add.

4. In the Certificates snap-in window, select My User Account and click Finish. Then click Close on the Snap-in window, and then click OK on the Add/Remove Snap-In window.

5. In the MMC, expand Certificates – Current User, as shown here.

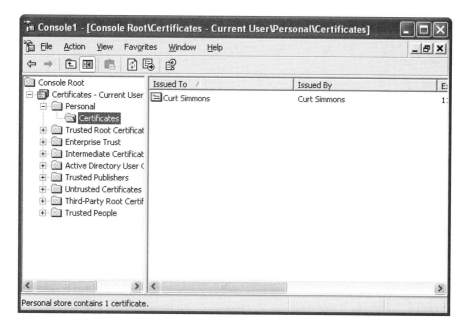

6. Expand the Personal folder, and then select the Certificates folder. In the right pane, select the desired certificate.

7. Click Action | All Tasks | Export, which will start the Export Certificate Wizard.

8. Follow the wizard's simple steps. Make sure that you select to send your private key with your digital certificate. If you are moving to another Windows XP or 2000 system, choose the Enable Strong Encryption option.

9. Choose a password, which you will need to import the certificate in the new location.

10. The wizard saves your certificate and private key to a file (*.pfx, which is a Personal Information Exchange file). You can now copy this file to a floppy disk and move it to a new computer.

11. Once you have copied your certificate and private key, you can import the certificate and private key to another computer. Open the Certificates MMC.

12. Open Certificates – Current User. Expand the Personal folder and select the Certificates folder.

13. Click Action | All Tasks | Import. This will launch the Import Wizard.

14. Use the Browse option to select the file that you want to import, then complete the wizard steps. You will need to provide the password that you assigned to the file when you were exporting it.

Although using encryption is rather easy for end users, many difficulties that you will face as an A+ technician will involve data recovery. Aside from using the private key to encrypt/decrypt data, Windows XP Professional also provides Recovery Agents for this purpose. Consider this example: A certain user knows just enough to be dangerous, and accidentally deletes his private key. The computer is full of company-sensitive encrypted data that no one can read without the user's private key. What can you do? The answer is to use the Recovery Agent. In same manner, what if a user leaves the company and leaves important data encrypted? Again, the answer is to use the Recovery Agent.

The Recovery Agent can be assigned so that the data can be recovered if the user's private key is lost or corrupted, or if the user suddenly decides to never return to work. To prevent data from being hopelessly lost in encryption, a Recovery Agent can decrypt the data. It is important to note that the agent can only decrypt data, not reencrypt it.

To configure a Recovery Agent, you must be logged on to Windows XP Professional as an administrator and you need to know the location of the certificate of the person who will become the Recovery Agent. If you are part of a domain, a network administrator will need to assist in this process since certificates are most often stored in the Active Directory in Windows domain networks. To configure a Recovery Agent, follow the steps described in the next section.

CONFIGURING A RECOVERY AGENT

1. Click Start | Run. Type **MMC** and click OK.

2. In the console window, click File | Add/ Remove Snap-In.

3. In the snap-in window, click Add. In the Add Standalone snap-in window, click Group Policy, then click Add.

4. In the Group Policy Object window, leave the Local Computer option selected, as shown here, and click Finish.

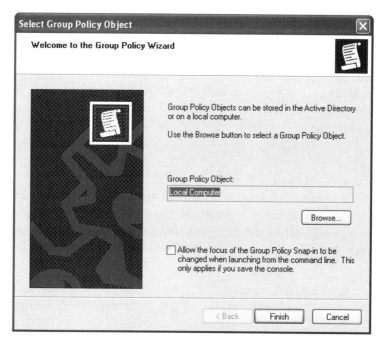

5. Click Close on the Add Standalone snap-in window, then click OK on the Snap-In window. You now see the Local Computer Policy in the MMC. Expand Local Computer Policy | Computer Configuration | Windows Settings | Security Settings | Public Key Policies | Encrypting File System.

6. Right-click the Encrypting File System folder and click Add Data Recovery Agent. This starts the Add Recovery Agent Wizard. Click Next on the Welcome screen.

7. Using the wizard, locate the desired user certificate. You can select the certificate from the Active Directory. If the certificate is not located in the Active Directory, you need to choose a local *.cer file. The certificate must be saved as a *.cer file.

Switch	Explanation
/e	Encrypts the specified file or folders
/d	Decrypts the specified file or folders
/s: dir	Performs the selected operation on all folders and subfolders in the specified directory
/a	Performs the selected operation on all files with the specified name
/l	Continues the selected operation even if errors occur
/f	Forces the encryption operation on all specified files, including currently encrypted files
/q	Reports only the most essential information
/h	Performs the selected operation on hidden files

TABLE 3.2 Cipher Command Switches

Aside from the using the Windows XP GUI interface for encrypting and decrypting data, you can also use the Cipher command-line tool. The command-line syntax and switches for the tool are as follows:

```
cipher [/e] [/d] [/s[:dir]] [/a] [/i] [/f] [/q] [/h] [pathname [...]]
```

Table 3-2 defines each of the command switches.

You can also allow other users to access an encrypted file. This feature, which is new in Windows XP, provides a great way to secure a file that only a few people need to access. To give other users access to an encrypted file, follow the steps in the next section.

NOTE You can give access only to individual encrypted files, not folders. Also, if you want to give access, you must first encrypt the file and close the Advanced Attributes dialog box before following these steps.

GIVING OTHER USERS ACCESS TO AN ENCRYPTED FILE

1. Right-click an encrypted file and click Properties.
2. On the General tab, click the Advanced button.
3. On the Advanced Attributes dialog box, click the Details button.
4. In the Encryption Details dialog box, shown next, use the Add and Remove buttons to manage the users that can access the encrypted file.

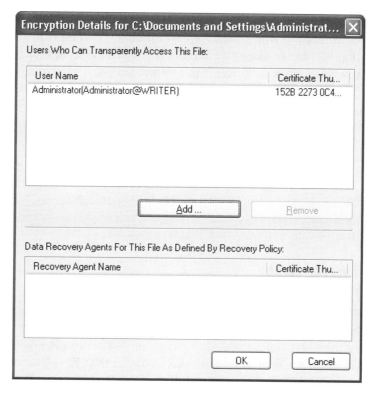

Only users who have an EFS certificate on the computer appear as selection options. If a user does not appear that you need to give access, have the user log on to the computer and encrypt a file. This will create the needed certificate. The user will then appear in the Encryption Details dialog box as a selection option.

USING OFFLINE FILES

Consider this scenario: A certain document is stored on a Windows 2000 file server. During the day, four users access the file and make editorial changes to it. One user needs to work on the file in the evening using a laptop computer that will not be connected to the network. She simply downloads the file, makes any desired changes, and synchronizes with the server when she returns to work. The changes are recognized and incorporated. When other users access the file, they see the new changes. Offline Files is quick and easy and a great tool for collaborative work. Users do not have to keep up with which file is new and what changes have been made. Windows XP Professional can easily synchronize with the server without any input from the user. Virtually any type of file, from documents to web pages, can be made available offline.

First of all, files shared or stored on Windows 2000 or Windows XP Professional computers must be made available offline before you can use them as offline files. You can set this on the server by using the Caching Options feature on the file's Properties pages. Windows XP Professional makes setting up offline files easy using a wizard tool that helps the user connect with the desired network file. The following steps show you how.

Although typically easy to use, offline files are incompatible with Fast User Switching (which you can disable in the Users applet in Control Panel). Offline files are also not available when Remote Desktop is configured to allow multiple connections. See Chapter 11 to learn more about Remote Desktop.

SETTING UP OFFLINE FILES

1. Log on as a local computer administrator.

2. Open Control Panel and open Folder Options. Click the Offline Files tab. If you see a message telling you that Fast User Switching is enabled, you'll need to change the option in User Accounts so that Fast User Switching is disabled. Offline files are not compatible with Fast User Switching.

3. On the Offline Files tab, click the Enable Offline Files check box, shown in Figure 3-5. You can then set some other offline file options:

   ■ Synchronize all offline files when logging on.
   ■ Synchronize all offline files before logging on.
   ■ Display a reminder every few minutes. You specify the number of minutes.
   ■ Create an Offline Files shortcut on the desktop.
   ■ Encrypt offline files to secure data.

   By default, offline files use 10 percent of your hard drive's disk space for storage. You can raise or lower this amount as desired by moving the slider bar.

   Using the Delete Files button, you can delete previously stored offline files. Using the View files button, you can view any currently stored offline files.

4. If you click the Advanced button, you see an Advanced Settings window. This option tells Windows XP to notify you when a network connection has been lost so that you can begin working offline. A radio button option

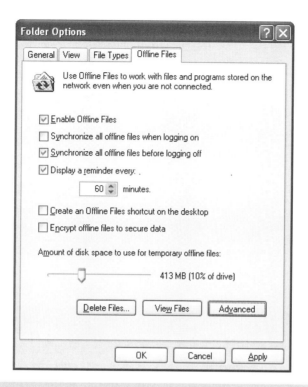

FIGURE 3.5   Offline Files tab

in this window enables you to specify that you will never go offline. You can also generate an exception list. For example, let's say that you always want your computer to go offline if a network connection is lost, unless you are working with a particular computer. You can add that computer to your list so that you do not begin working offline in that particular case. Make any desired configuration changes and click OK.

5. Now that Offline Files are enabled, you can now choose what file or folder you want to make available offline. Using My Network Places or any desired window, simply browse to the network resource, right-click it, and click Make Available Offline.

6. The Offline Files Wizard appears. Click Next on the Welcome screen.

7. The Synchronization window appears. If you want to synchronize an existing offline file automatically when you log off and log on, leave the check box selected and click Next. If not, clear the check box and click Next.

8. In the final window, you can choose to enable reminders and create a shortcut to the desktop. Click Finish. The files are copied to your computer, as shown here.

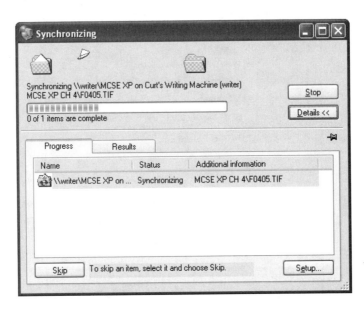

Once you set up offline files, you simply use the file as desired. Depending on your settings, the file is automatically synchronized with the original file. You can manually enforce synchronization at any time simply by right-clicking the file or folder and clicking Synchronize. You can also further manage offline files by accessing the Synchronization tool.

USING THE SYNCHRONIZATION TOOL

To manage offline files using the Synchronization tool, follow these steps:

1. Log on as an administrator.

2. Click Start | All Programs | Accessories | Synchronize.

3. The Items to Synchronize window appears, as shown next. As you can see, any current offline files or folders appear here. You can select any items that you want to synchronize manually and click the Synchronize button.

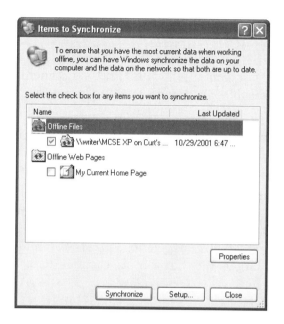

4. You can also click the Setup button to display the Synchronization Settings window. You can change these settings at any time. As you can see in the image shown here, the window presents a Logon/Logoff tab, an On Idle tab, and a Scheduled tab. These tabs are self-explanatory, and you can use them to determine how and when synchronization occurs. Make any desired changes and click OK.

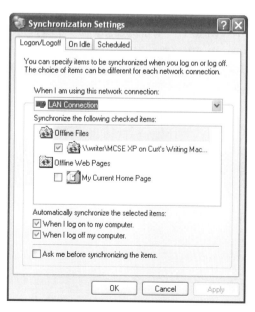

As you can see, offline files are easy to configure and use. Just remember the following:

- Offline files are not compatible with Fast User Switching. To use offline files, you must disable Fast User Switching in the Users applet found in Control Panel.

- The Synchronization tool only allows you to synchronize items and configure how they are synchronized; you cannot add new items from this location—that must be done with Windows Explorer or My Network Places.

- You can cache data, such as web pages, from the Internet. Just add the desired site to your Favorites folder in Internet Explorer, then right-click the web page in Favorites and choose to make the page available offline. However, files with a .db?, .pst, .mdb, .ldb, .slm, or .mde extension cannot be cached. The largest file that you can cache is 2GB.

WRAPPING UP

Windows XP file and folder management is rather easy. Keep in mind that the most important configurations take place in Folder Options. You can find Folder Options in Control Panel or in the Tools menu when you are in any folder. You can easily make changes to the default appearance of file and folders, and you can even create customized toolbars.

You can use Windows XP's compression, encryption, and offline folder options, all available in Windows XP Professional. These features give you more file and folder management and security flexibility.

Now that you have taken a look at file and folder management, let's turn our attention to Windows XP hardware in Chapter 4.

MANAGING WINDOWS XP HARDWARE

4

Installing and managing hardware is one of those gory topics that often cause A+ technicians to pull their hair out. After all, by definition, A+ technicians are proficient in installing and managing computer hardware, regardless of the operating system. Of course, the operating system has a lot to do with whether the hardware will work and whether it will work the way it is supposed to. Windows XP does a good job of managing hardware, and due to advancements in plug and play technology, hardware management is easier in Windows XP than it has been in previous versions of Windows. However, this does not mean that hardware management is a piece of cake, either. Think of this chapter as your hardware reference guide to Windows XP. In this chapter, you'll…

- Install and remove hardware
- Use Device Manager
- Manage drivers
- Use hardware profiles
- Manage multiple monitors and processors
- Configure devices

INSTALLING AND REMOVING HARDWARE

Windows XP is a fully compliant plug and play system. Simply put, Windows XP can detect new hardware that is added to the system and automatically install it for you. As an A+ technician, you can save yourself much time and configuration aggravation by using plug and play systems. These systems also make hardware management easier for the end user. In short, if the hardware is compatible with Windows XP, then Windows XP can usually install the hardware automatically without any intervention from you or the user.

Windows XP has the most extensive device driver database to date, and Windows can usually locate a basic driver to work with most plug and play devices. The trick is to use hardware that is compatible with Windows XP. When purchasing and installing new hardware, check for compatibility and also check the hardware compatibility list (HCL) at **http://www.microsoft.com/hcl** for a list of compatible devices. For troublesome hardware, Windows XP provides the Add Hardware Wizard so that you can attempt to install the hardware manually.

If a hardware device is not listed in the HCL, that does not necessarily mean that the device will not work with Windows XP—it simply means that "official" testing for that device has not been performed. You can also check the hardware vendor's web site for more information about compatibility.

If you need to install a hardware device on Windows XP manually, you can use the Add Hardware Wizard in Control Panel, which will help you install the device. Before installing a device manually, you'll probably need the driver for the device. A driver is a piece of software that allows Windows XP and the hardware device to communicate with each other. Windows XP has a large database of generic drivers that will often work, but often your best choice is the specific driver that the hardware vendor created for the hardware device. If Windows XP is having problems installing the device automatically through plug and play, then you will probably need the device driver. The driver often accompanies the hardware device on floppy disk or CD-ROM; you can also usually find it on the device manufacturer's web site. The Add/Remove Hardware Wizard is easy to use and can walk you through the installation process. The following steps show you how to use the wizard.

USING THE ADD HARDWARE WIZARD

1. Click Start | Control Panel | Add Hardware.

2. Click Next on the Welcome screen.

3. The wizard searches for any hardware that has been connected to the computer. If the wizard fails to find the hardware component, then a window appears that asks whether the hardware is connected. Make the correct selection and click Next.

4. You can use the Add Hardware Wizard to troubleshoot a device that is not working or add a new hardware device. In the provided window, make a selection. Select the Add a New Hardware Device option as shown here.

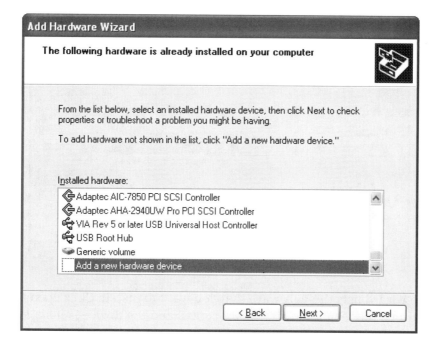

5. The wizard prompts you either to install the hardware by selecting it from a list or have Windows search again. Since Windows so far has failed to detect the hardware, it is usually best to choose the Install the Hardware That I Manually Select from a List radio button. Click Next.

6. A hardware type window appears that allows you to choose the kind of hardware device that you want to install. Choose a desired category and click Next.

7. Windows XP generates a list of hardware from the category that you selected. In the selection window, shown here, choose the manufacturer and the model of the hardware that you want to install. If you have an installation disk for the hardware, you can click the Have Disk button and run the hardware installation routine from the disk. Make a selection and click Next.

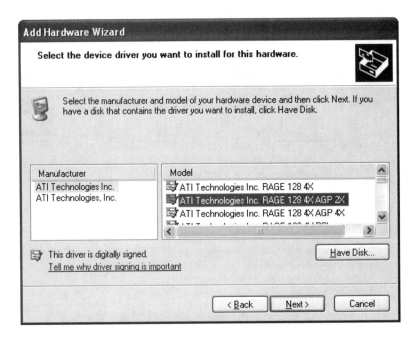

8. The wizard lists the hardware that you want to install. Click Next to continue the installation. Files are copied and the device is installed. Click Finish to complete the installation.

As mentioned in the previous exercise, you can also use the Add Hardware Wizard to troubleshoot problematic devices. This option essentially provides you with a look at the device's properties and attempts to help you discover what is causing the problem so that you can fix it. The following steps show you how to use this feature.

USING THE ADD HARDWARE WIZARD TO TROUBLESHOOT A DEVICE

1. Click Start | Control Panel | Add Hardware.

2. Click Next on the Welcome screen.

3. Windows XP searches for new hardware. If it doesn't find any, it displays a list of devices currently installed on the computer. Devices that are not functioning properly appear with a yellow exclamation point beside them, as you can see in the illustration shown here. Select the problematic device and click Next.

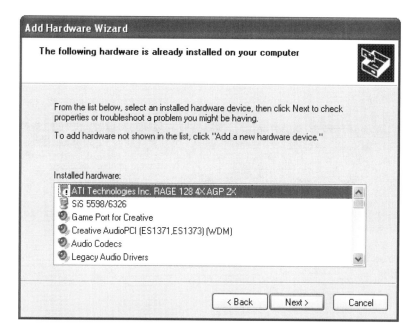

4. The final screen appears with a status message for the device. Click Finish. The troubleshooter for the device begins. You can then use the troubleshooter or attempt to solve the problem on your own.

USING DEVICE MANAGER

A helpful tool that you can use to explore the configuration of hardware devices and make changes to that configuration is Device Manager. Device Manager has been around for several releases of Windows, and its importance in Windows XP continues. You can access Device Manager via the Computer Management console, or you can simply click the Device Manager option on the Hardware tab of System Properties.

The Device Manager interface, shown in Figure 4-1, gives you a listing of hardware categories. If you expand the category, you can see the hardware devices installed under that category. Notice that any hardware that is not functioning correctly appears with a yellow exclamation point beside it. Using Device Manager, you can easily scan hardware categories and the hardware installed. If you right-click a hardware device, you can update the driver, disable the device, uninstall it, scan for hardware changes, or access the device's properties.

NOTE If you click the View menu, you'll see some options to view devices by type (the default option) or by connection, or you can view resources by type and connection. Simply changing views may make hardware information easier to view and explore when using Device Manager. Also, the View menu has an option to "show hidden devices," which can allow you to see any devices that are hidden on the system.

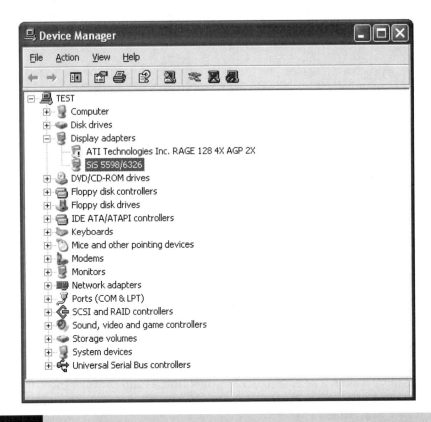

FIGURE 4.1   Device Manager

If you right-click the desired device and click Properties, you'll see a few different tabs. As a standard, most devices have a General, Driver, and Resources tab. Some devices may have additional tabs specific to those devices. For example, a standard Mouse Properties page usually has an Advanced Settings tab where you can configure how the wheel operates. Since the General, Driver, and Resources tabs are available on most devices, let's consider the available options on each.

The General tab, shown in Figure 4-2, offers a few basic items. First, you see the device name, type, manufacturer, and the physical location of the device on the system. In the Device Status window, you can see any error messages or problems that apply to the device. If there are problems, you can start the hardware troubleshooter by clicking the Troubleshoot button. The Device Usage drop-down list presents enable or disable device options. To disable the device, simply choose the disable device option from the drop-down list.

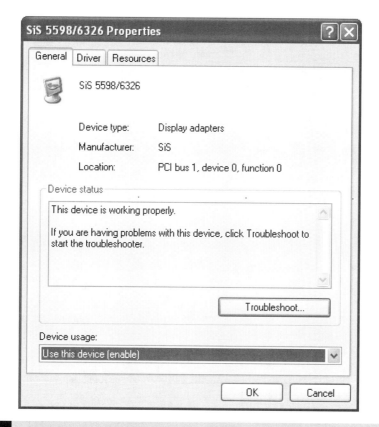

FIGURE 4.2   General tab for device properties

NOTE   When you disable a device, the device cannot work on the system; however, the device's driver and related software are not uninstalled. At any time, you can return to this tab and enable the device again. The "on the fly" enable and disable feature can be very helpful when troubleshooting hardware problems.

The Driver tab provides you an easy way to manage a device driver. Driver management is a big part of hardware management, so you'll learn about the device drivers and the information on this tab in much greater detail in the next section.

On the Resources tab, shown in Figure 4-3, you'll see the memory ranges, I/O range, and IRQ setting. You also see the related hardware resource configuration that has been configured automatically by Windows XP. Note that the settings cannot be changed unless there is a conflict. If there is a conflict, the conflicting device will be listed in the dialog box, and the option to change the setting

| **FIGURE 4.3** | Resources tab |

manually will not be grayed out. You can then try to adjust the resource settings so that the devices do not conflict with each other.

MANAGING DEVICE DRIVERS

A device driver is simply software that allows Windows XP to interact with a hardware device. The driver determines communication parameters, and essentially acts as a bridge between the operating system code and the device driver. The driver then allows the operating system to "drive" the device so that the operating system can control the hardware device, which you then control through the operating system interface.

Hardware vendors develop drivers, and from Microsoft's point of view, how well a driver operates with Windows XP is solely the responsibility of the hardware vendor. When Microsoft releases a new operating system, a vendor generally must update its device driver so that the vendor's device can communicate with the new operating system. This is the primary reason that some devices fail to operate after an upgrade: The driver is incompatible with the new operating system.

Even though device drivers are the responsibility of hardware manufacturers, Windows XP still maintains a generic database of drivers so that hardware can function with Windows XP, even if a manufacturer's driver is not available. Under most circumstances, the manufacturer's driver should be used if possible since it is specifically developed for the hardware device's interaction with Windows XP. So, in short, you should simply use hardware that is compatible with Windows XP and make sure you are using the most current driver designed by the hardware's manufacturer if possible.

Because driver configuration and management can be difficult, Windows XP provides you with the Driver tab, found on each device's Properties pages, which you can access from Device Manager. The Driver tab, as you can see in Figure 4-4, gives you a few different button options that you can use to manage the device's driver.

If you click the Driver Details button, you see information about the driver, such as the location, provider, file version, copyright, and digital signer information, as shown in Figure 4-5. This data can be helpful when you simply want to gain basic information about the driver.

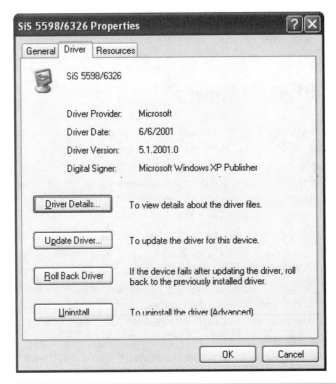

FIGURE 4.4 Driver tab

Since drivers are updated periodically, you should strive always to use the most current driver. To help with this process, Windows XP provides the Hardware Update Wizard, which enables you to replace an older driver with a newer one. The following steps show you how to update a driver.

UPDATING A DRIVER

1. In Device Manager, right-click the desired device and click Properties. Then click the Driver tab.

2. On the Driver tab, click the Update Driver button.

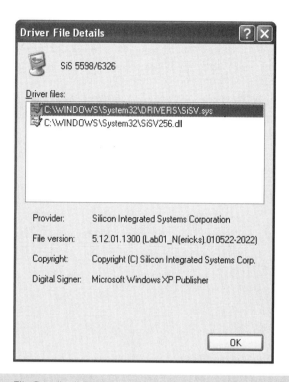

FIGURE 4.5   Driver File Details dialog box

3. The Hardware Update Wizard appears. Notice that the Welcome screen presents two radio buttons: You can have Windows XP install the new driver automatically from a disk or CD, or you can install from a list of specific drivers or locations. If you choose the automatic option, Windows XP searches your CD and floppy drives for a new driver, then installs the driver that it finds. If you want to update the driver manually, choose the manual option on the Welcome screen and click Next.

4. The Search and Installation options window appears. You can choose to have Windows XP search for the driver in specific locations, such as the floppy and CD-ROM drives, or you can specify the path to the driver. If you want to specifically choose the driver, choose the Don't Search radio button option. Click Next.

5. The next window gives you a selection list, as you can see here. You can choose the kind of device that you are using and allow Windows to try and match the device with a driver from its database.

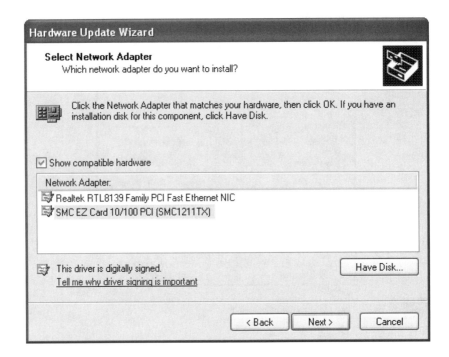

If you have an installation disk, you can also use the disk here. However, even if you have an installation disk, keep in mind that you can use the automatic installation method on the Welcome screen of the wizard (which is faster and easier). Make the desired selection and click Next.

6. The files for the driver are copied and install. Click Finish.

Microsoft keeps a large database of drivers, so some drivers can also be updated through Windows Update. For this reason, it is a good idea to use the Windows Update feature regularly.

On the Driver tab, you also see buttons for Roll Back Device Driver and Uninstall. If you install a new driver for a device and the new driver does not function well, you can use the Roll Back feature to use the old driver. This feature pulls the old driver out of a backup file and reinstalls it. However, you have to be an Administrator to roll back the driver, and you can only roll back the driver to one level. By default, drivers are stored in %systemroot%\ system32\reinstallbackups.

If you want to remove a driver completely, simply use the Uninstall button. A warning message then alerts you that you are about to remove the device from your system. When you uninstall the driver, the device is uninstalled as well. At this point, Windows XP plug and play will detect the uninstalled hardware device as new hardware and attempt to reinstall it. In some cases, this can help you uninstall and reinstall a problematic device, especially if you are having driver problems.

In addition to configuring the driver management options found on the Driver tab, you can also manage driver signing in Windows XP. Driver signing, first introduced in Windows 2000 systems, enables you to make certain that you are installing and using only drivers that have been "signed," or certified, by Microsoft. This feature makes certain that the drivers have been tested and will work with specified hardware on Windows XP. This certification, however, certainly does not mean that unsigned drivers are damaging to your system or will not work—it just means that Microsoft has not approved or tested them and that you are on your own in terms of testing, compatibility, and troubleshooting.

Signed drivers have a digital signature stamp that cannot be altered without altering the entire driver package. This feature tells you that a signed driver is, in fact, a signed driver, and that you can feel safe when using the driver on your system.

NOTE   Another advantage of signed drivers, especially concerning Internet download, is that a signed driver tells you that the package is actually a verified driver—not a virus or other malicious code acting like a driver. When you are downloading software, the signed driver feature can certainly give you a measure of protection.

The basic rule to follow is to use signed drivers if at all possible. With the signed driver, you can ensure that the driver has been tested and has received Microsoft's seal of approval. Of course, in some cases, it may not be possible to use a signed driver. This is certainly fine, but it leaves you to do your own homework to determine whether the driver will work and if the driver is safe to use.

You can manage how Windows XP handles driver signatures so that they work for you and your environment. If you open System Properties and click the Hardware tab, shown in Figure 4-6, you see a Driver Signing button.

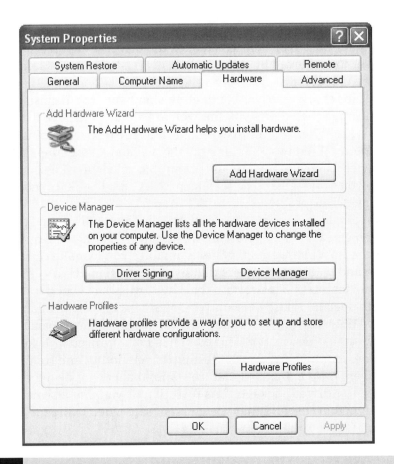

FIGURE 4.6   Hardware tab of System Properties

If you click the Driver Signing button, you see a Driver Signing Options window, shown in Figure 4-7. You can invoke the following options to determine how Windows XP handles driver signing:

- **Ignore**   If the driver is not digitally signed, this option tells Windows to ignore that the software is not signed and to install the software anyway. You will receive no warning messages or prompts when using this setting.

- **Warn**   If the driver is not digitally signed, a warning dialog box appears so you can choose to install the driver or not. This is the default setting.

- **Block**   If the driver is not digitally signed, the operating system will not install it.

FIGURE 4.7   Driver Signing Options window

- **Administrator Option**   This check box option enables you to make your choice of Ignore, Warn, or Block the default setting for all users on this particular Windows XP computer. You must be an administrator on the local machine to enable or disable this option.

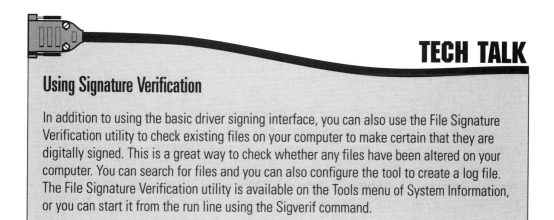

TECH TALK

Using Signature Verification

In addition to using the basic driver signing interface, you can also use the File Signature Verification utility to check existing files on your computer to make certain that they are digitally signed. This is a great way to check whether any files have been altered on your computer. You can search for files and you can also configure the tool to create a log file. The File Signature Verification utility is available on the Tools menu of System Information, or you can start it from the run line using the Sigverif command.

(continued)

To use File Signature Verification, just follow these steps:

1. Click Start | Run. Type **sigverif** and click OK.

2. The File Signature Verification utility appears. You can immediately start the utility by clicking the Start button, or you can click the Advanced button to configure options for the utility. Click Advanced.

3. The Advanced Search window presents two basic options: You can search the entire system for files that are not digitally signed, or you can look for specific types of files in specific locations for signatures. This second option is helpful if you are suspicious about a particular file or group of files. You can quickly verify them without checking the entire system.

4. Click the Logging tab. You can choose to save the results of the File Signature Verification utility to a log file, which is named sigverif.txt by default. You can choose to append the scan to the existing log or overwrite the existing log (which is the default option). Make any desired changes and click OK.

5. Click the Start button to begin the utility. When the utility begins, it builds a file list and presents a status bar as files are verified. Once the utility completes, it displays a completion window. If any files are not digitally signed, they will appear in the dialog box.

6. Once the scan is complete, you can also easily view the log file by clicking the Advanced button, then clicking the Logging tab. Click the View Log button, and the log file appears in a simple text format.

USING HARDWARE PROFILES

Hardware profiles are used to configure a computer to use, or not use, certain hardware devices in certain situations. The purpose of hardware profiles is to enable a laptop computer to have different hardware configurations, without requiring the user to install and uninstall hardware every time the computer is in use.

Let's consider an example. Suppose that you use a laptop computer in an office setting. While connected to the local area network at the physical office, you use a mouse, keyboard, and desktop monitor with the laptop. You also have a local printer. However, when you are on the road, you do not use the external keyboard, mouse, monitor, and printer. Using hardware profiles in this situation, you could configure a "docked" and "undocked" profile so that Windows XP knows what hardware to use when you are connected to the physical network and when you are traveling. The result is that you save system resources when you are on the road by not loading additional hardware configuration data that is not needed, and your applications do not get confused about what device is available or not. You can easily configure hardware profiles for a computer as needed, which you can read about in the following steps.

In addition to providing convenience, hardware profiles can also help you conserve battery power on laptop computers. If a device is not in use at the moment, that does not necessarily mean that the PC cards installed on the laptop are not pulling battery power. If mobile users are not using a device when traveling, they can use a hardware profile to disable the device and save battery power!

CREATING A HARDWARE PROFILE

1. Open Control Panel and open System Properties.

2. Click the Hardware tab and click the Hardware Profiles button. The Hardware Profiles window appears as shown here.

3. The window displays the current default profile. If you click the Properties button, you can see the basic properties of the default profile, shown here. You have two basic options: You can identify the profile as a profile for a portable computer, and you can choose always to include the profile as an option when Windows starts. Click OK to return to the main window.

4. To create a new profile, click the Copy button. A Copy Profile dialog box appears. Enter a desired name for the new profile and click OK. The current configuration from default profile is copied to the new profile. At this point, you have two profiles that are the same.

5. You can now select the new profile and click Properties. In the Profile Properties dialog box you can choose the portable computer option and always to include the profile option when Windows starts. Click OK when you're done.

6. When you restart the computer, a boot menu appears from which you can select the profile that you want. Click OK on the Hardware Profiles dialog box and restart Windows XP.

7. During bootup, a hardware profile menu appears. Select the new hardware profile that you want to use and allow Windows XP to boot using that hardware profile. Log on to the computer.

8. Open System in Control Panel, click the Hardware tab, then click the Device Manager option.

9. Now that you are in Device Manager, access the Properties pages for the devices that you do not want to use under the new profile. On the General tab of those devices, choose the Do Not Use This Device in the Current Hardware Profile (Disable) option. Continue this process until you have disabled any devices that should not be part of the portable hardware profile configuration.

10. Close the Properties pages for the device. Notice that the devices you have disabled now appear in Device Manager with a red X over them, indicating that the device is disabled, as shown here.

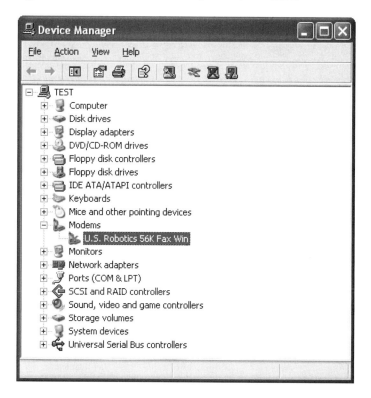

11. At any time, you can create additional hardware profiles by following these steps, or you can delete any hardware profiles by returning to the Hardware Profile dialog box.

TECH TALK

Understanding Advanced Configuration and Power Interface (ACPI)

Advanced Configuration and Power Interface (ACPI) is an industry standard designed to save power on computer operating systems. Developed by a number of companies, such as Microsoft, Intel, Compaq, and several others, ACPI enables a computer to power down system components automatically when they are not in use, then power up system components automatically as they are needed.

To understand ACPI completely, you first need to consider Advanced Power Management (APM), an older power management scheme that was supported under Windows 95 and the older computer Basic Input/Output System (BIOS). The idea behind APM is the same as that of ACPI, but it simply did not work as well. The computer could not make accurate inactivity assessments, and as such, the hardware sometimes shut down at inopportune times, such as during a long file download. Also, APM could not detect when a device connected to the computer needed to be used. For example, suppose that your network printer is attached to your computer using APM. Once APM shut the hardware down, the system could not detect that a network user needed the printer—it remained in sleep state until someone physically moved the mouse or touched the keyboard—and even then it sometimes would not wake up.

ACPI is a much better specification and gives the operating system more control over hardware power-down states and greater ability to power up hardware as needed. For example, suppose that you use ACPI on 100 Windows XP computers. The computers power down during the night, but you want to run disk defragmenter once a month during the middle of the night. Under ACPI, this configuration is no problem because the system can power up the hard drive when it is needed, such as when disk defragmenter needs to run. Once the utility has run, the system can power down again. This configuration is not possible under APM because manual mouse and keyboard strokes are required to wake the computer.

In an ACPI-compliant system, power management is handled throughout the entire computer system, which includes computer hardware, software, and the operating system itself. ACPI works in Windows XP through operating system management and through the BIOS. For ACPI to work, the computer's BIOS must support ACPI. In today's computer market, this typically is not a problem since almost all newer computers support ACPI.

(continued)

If the computer does not seem to support ACPI, you can check the computer's CMOS settings and make sure that "operating system control" is turned on; this setting ensures that Windows XP can control power management throughout the system. Check your computer documentation for details about accessing CMOS setup and configuring the CMOS settings on your PC.

USING MULTIPLE MONITORS

Windows XP continues to support multiple monitors, a feature first introduced in Windows 98. With more than one monitor, you can run different applications on different screens and increase work productivity. Multiple monitors are useful to many different people, especially those working with multiple documents and graphics files. With Windows XP and the right hardware, you can connect as many as 10 individual monitors to a single PC.

When using multiple monitors, you can place different applications or files on different monitors, then stretch items between monitors. For example, suppose that you have a spreadsheet with many columns. You could use two monitors to stretch the file so that all columns are visible across the two monitors.

When using multiple monitors, one monitor serves as the primary monitor where older applications and the Windows logon screen will appear. You can use multiple video cards with different settings, or you can use a single video card that has multiple outputs where you can connect the monitors. Regardless of the configuration you choose, you use Display properties to adjust the appearance of each monitor. When setting up multiple monitors, there are a few basic rules you should keep in mind:

- If the computer has a video adapter built into the motherboard, then the built-in adapter must be used as the Video Graphics Array (VGA) device.

- Monitors in the multiple monitor setup must use either Peripheral Component Interconnect (PCI) or AGP slots.

- The PCI and Advanced Graphics Peripheral (AGP) cards cannot use any VGA resources.

- Only Windows XP–compatible drivers can be used on the monitors.

To set up multiple monitors, follow the steps in the following section.

SETTING UP MULTIPLE MONITORS

1. Turn off the computer. Follow the manufacturer's instructions to install the new PCI or AGP video card.

2. Attach a monitor to the new card and boot the computer.

3. Windows XP plug and play will detect the new card and install it.

4. Right-click an empty area of the desktop and click Properties. Click the Settings tab, which includes two monitor icons. Select the monitor that you want to use as the secondary monitor.

5. Click the Extend My Windows Desktop onto This Monitor check box.

6. Adjust the resolution and color scheme settings as desired for the monitor. Click OK.

7. To add additional monitors to the configuration, repeat steps 1–6.

USING MULTIPLE PROCESSORS

Like Windows 2000, Windows XP supports multiprocessor computers. The use of multiple processors on one computer increases the computer's ability to handle tasks and is particularly useful for Windows XP computers that function as network file and print servers. Simply put, the greater the processor speed and the more processors available to Windows XP, the faster it can work and meet the needs of local and network processes.

Essentially, Windows XP must be able to divide the workload between the processors into even pieces in order to utilize the processors. This process, which is called *multitasking,* enables the operating system to juggle processor requests between the two processors. Windows XP Professional is a true multitasking operating system that uses a type of multitasking called *preemptive multitasking.* Preemptive multitasking systems have the ability to manage and control applications and processor cycles. Because the Windows XP kernel remains in control of all resources, the operating system can halt applications or make them wait, or *preempt* them. With this kind of power and control, Windows XP can divide tasks between processors and determine what processor performs which task.

NOTE You may also be familiar with cooperative multitasking. Found in older versions of Windows, this feature simply enables applications to share the processor and wait on each other for processor cycles. The difference with preemptive multitasking is that Windows XP can manage the entire process and direct which task is handled by which processor. For this reason, Windows XP Professional is a true multitasking operating system.

Windows XP Professional can support two Intel-based processors. Windows XP does not support other processor types, such as Alpha or MIPS, so in order for multiprocessor functionality to work, two Intel-based processors must be used. If you install Windows XP Professional on a computer with two Intel-based processors, the processors should be detected and installed during Windows XP setup.

CONFIGURING WINDOWS XP DEVICES

Now that you have taken a look at hardware installation and removal issues, let's turn our attention to specific devices in this section. Exploring every possible device that you could install on Windows XP is beyond the scope of this section, but you need to be aware of some specific categories of devices that have a number of configuration issues or potential setup problems.

CONFIGURING KEYBOARDS AND MICE

Windows XP makes keyboard and mice configuration easy. Under most circumstances, you simply plug in the device and boot the computer, then plug and play automatically detects and sets up the device for you—it's that simple. In today's marketplace, there are many keyboard and mouse styles and models from which choose, and a number of connection options, including serial, Universal Serial Bus (USB), and even wireless.

For installation of these devices, follow the manufacturer's instructions. You'll need to make sure that the device is attached to the correct port and that your driver is appropriate for Windows XP. For standard keyboards and mice, Windows can assign one of its own drivers.

Once these devices are installed, you can access Control Panel icons for the keyboard and mouse in order to configure them. The following two sections take a look at configuring the keyboard and the mouse.

KEYBOARD CONFIGURATION

Keyboard configuration is performed with the Keyboard icon in Control Panel. When you click the icon, two different tabs are available. On the Speed tab, shown in the Figure 4-8, you can adjust the keyboard repeat speed. As you can see in the figure, the tab has settings for Repeat Delay and Repeat Rate. The Repeat Delay slider bar determines how fast multiple characters are generated when you press a single key. A short delay means that characters occur quickly when you hold down a single key. The Repeat Rate slider controls how fast characters are repeated when you hold down a single key. The Repeat Delay control sets how much time passes before the repeat begins, whereas the Repeat Rate determines how quickly characters are repeated. Finally, the Cursor Blink rate at the bottom of the tab configures how fast the cursor blinks.

The Hardware tab simply provides information about the installed hardware, such as the keyboard manufacturer and the port into which the keyboard is

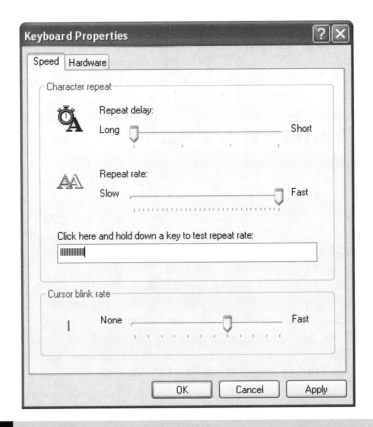

| FIGURE 4.8 | Speed tab |

plugged. If you click Troubleshoot, the Windows troubleshooter opens to help you solve problems. The Properties button opens the device's General and Driver tabs from Device Manager.

CONFIGURING THE MOUSE

Control Panel also provides several mouse configuration tabs that enable you to control how the mouse operates. As with the keyboard settings, the settings here are straightforward, but you should be familiar with them so that you can solve any problems that users bring your way.

The Buttons tab contains three different options, which are as follows:

- **Button Configuration** By default, the right mouse button gives you menu options whereas the left mouse button performs actions. You can switch this behavior by clicking the Switch Primary and Secondary Buttons check box.

- **Double-Click Speed** Use the slider bar to adjust how fast double-clicking occurs.

- **ClickLock** ClickLock allows you to highlight or drag an item without holding down the mouse key. Using ClickLock, you can press the button once to lock it, then press it again to unlock it. If you turn on ClickLock, you can click the Setting button and adjust how long you need to hold down the mouse button for ClickLock to turn on.

On the Pointers tab, shown in Figure 4-9, you can determine what pointers and what pointer scheme you want to use. As you can see in Figure 4-9, the Windows Default scheme is typically used, which gives you the normal select, hourglass busy, and other pointers. However, if you click the Scheme drop-down menu, you'll see many other schemes from which you can choose, including animated schemes.

The Pointer Options tab presents three different setting categories that you can configure:

- **Motion** Use the slider bar to select pointer speed movement. You can also use the Enhance Pointer Precision check box, which gives you more control over the pointer when moving short distances.

- **Snap To** If you select this check box, the pointer automatically moves to the default button in any given dialog box.

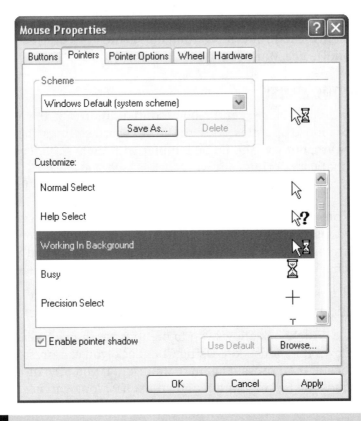

Pointers tab

- **Visibility** You can configure effects here, such as Show Pointer Trail, Hide the Pointer While You Are Typing, and Show the Location of the Pointer When You Press CTRL.

The Wheel tab, which is used for mice that have wheel controls, enables you to control the scrolling when using the wheel. The default setting is typically three lines per wheel notch. You can increase the value, however, and you can also choose to scroll one screen per notch.

Finally, the Hardware tab gives you the make and manufacturer of the mouse. You can access the Windows troubleshooter from this tab and the Device Manager properties for the mouse. You should also be familiar with the Device Manager's Advanced Settings tab. This tab gives you some basic settings that determine how Windows XP interacts with the mouse. By default, the mouse is sampled 100 times per second. This means the operating system is constantly checking the mouse to determine its position. The default setting is 100, but you can increase the speed to increase mouse tracking. Typically, however, you don't need to change this setting unless mouse operations seem sluggish.

Under Wheel Detection, the default setting assumes that a wheel is present on the mouse. You can change this setting so that the system does not try to detect the mouse wheel, which effectively disables the wheel, and so that the operating system always checks for the wheel. If the mouse has a wheel and it works correctly, you can leave the default setting configured.

Finally, the input buffer length, which is set to 100 by default, is the size of the input buffer that stores information about the position of your mouse. If the mouse seems to behave erratically, try increasing the input buffer length in order to fix the problem.

MANAGING MULTIMEDIA HARDWARE

Multimedia hardware covers a number of different hardware devices, such as scanners, digital cameras, digital camcorders, and even handheld devices such as Palm and BlackBerry. These hardware devices generally fall under the category of multimedia, and for the most part, they are all managed and installed in the same way. You typically connect the device to a correct port and install software on Windows XP that allows XP to operate with the device. For example, if you want to use a digital camera, the camera typically plugs into a serial or USB port, and you install software that enables Windows XP to interact with the camera and download picture files from it.

If the multimedia device does not have a setup program, access the manufacturer's web site and follow instructions for setup. For cameras and scanners, you can also use Windows XP Scanner and Camera Installation Wizard, which is explored in the following steps.

INSTALLING A CAMERA OR SCANNER

1. Open the Scanners and Cameras folder in Control Panel.

2. In the left pane, click the Add an Imaging Device link.

3. The Scanner and Camera Installation Wizard appears. Click Next to continue.

4. In the Scanner and Camera Installation window, shown next, you can choose the manufacturer and model of the camera or scanner that

you want to install. If you have an installation disk, you can click the Have
Disk button. Make your selection and click Next.

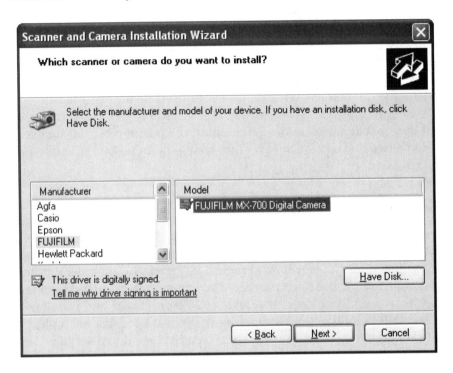

5. The Connection window appears. Connect the camera to the correct port
   on your computer and make a selection on the Available Ports window.
   Notice that you can choose to have Windows automatically detect the port
   as well. Click Next.

6. Click Next again. Then Click Finish.

Once you have installed the scanner or camera, the icons for the devices
appear in the Scanners and Cameras folder. You can then access configuration
properties by right-clicking the icon and clicking Properties. The properties for
the device are device-specific, and you will probably use manufacturer's software
to manage the device rather than use the configuration options presented in
this section. However, you can use the icons for specific actions, such as Get
Pictures or Start Scan. Again, the trick with multimedia hardware is to follow
the manufacturer's instructions for setup and use.

CONFIGURING MODEMS

Modems have been around since the early days of Windows, and in the past, modem configuration was a big pain. You had to know some things about IRQ settings, port data, and even scripting. Modems continue to be a big part of any computer system today, and are used for access to the Internet as well as for corporate dial-up connections. The good news is that modem installation and configuration is rather easy these days, and as with all hardware, if you are using modems and modem drivers that are compatible with Windows XP, you are not likely to have problems.

Windows XP automatically detects and installs plug and play modems. However, if you are having problems installing a modem, Windows XP provides the Add Hardware Wizard/Install New Modem feature that can help you install the modem. The installation wizard works just like any other installation wizard. The wizard scans for hardware changes. If it finds the modem, the wizard installs it. If not, you have the option of accessing the familiar selection list to select the manufacturer and model of the modem, or you can click the Have Disk button. Once the modem is installed, it appears on the Modems tab of Phone and Modem Options dialog box in Control Panel, as shown in Figure 4-10.

As you can see, installation is generally easy. However, the Phone and Modems Options dialog box in Control Panel gives you a number of configuration options that determine how the modem operates. The rest of this section explores modem configuration. If you open the Phone and Modems Options dialog box in Control Panel, you'll see three tabs. The following sections explore these tabs individually.

DIALING RULES TAB

The Dialing Rules tab enables you to configure dialing locations. For laptop users, the configuration on this tab can be very important for the modem to dial access numbers correctly. Any existing dialing rules are found on the Dialing Rules tab. You can click the Edit button to make changes to the existing rule, or you can create a new rule by clicking the New button. The following steps walk you through the process of creating a new dialing rule.

CREATING A NEW DIALING RULE

1. Open Phone and Modem Options in Control Panel. On the Dialing Rules tab, click New.

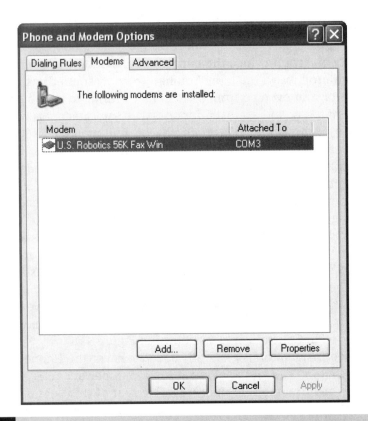

FIGURE 4.10 Modems tab

2. The New Location dialog box appears, presenting the three tabs. On the General tab, shown Figure 4-11, enter a location name. Location names typically work well as calling locations (such as Home, Office, and so on). Enter the country or region and current area code. Then enter any desired rules, such as line number carrier codes, and so on. Also, use the check box at the bottom of the window to disable call waiting while you are using the line.

3. Click the Area Code Rules tab. You see an empty window with no current area code rules. To create an area code rule, click the New button.

4. In the New Area Code Rule dialog box, enter the area code you are calling. Then you can specify prefixes to include in the area code. Once you have added the prefixes that belong, you can then determine whether or not to dial a 1 when making the call and whether or not the area code should be used. Once you are done, click OK.

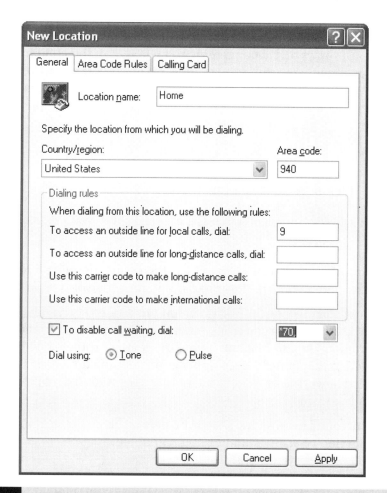

FIGURE 4.11   General tab of the New Location dialog box

5. Now the new location appears in the Area Code Rules tab. At any time, you can edit the connection or delete it from this window.

6. On the Calling Card tab, you can configure a calling card type that should be used when calling from the location. Select an existing type and enter your account and PIN numbers to use the calling card. If the calling card is not listed, click the New button to enter the card and name and information so that it can be used. When you're done, click OK.

7. The new location now appears in the Dialing Rules tab. You can edit or delete the location at any time from this interface.

CONFIGURING THE MODEMS

The Modems tab shows all modems that are installed on the computer. You can add and remove modems from the computer from this tab, and you can also click the Properties button to access the Properties sheets for the modem. The following sections outline many of the important configuration options available on the Modem Properties tabs.

GENERAL TAB   The General tab gives you the same information you find on any general device tab when accessed from Device Manager. You can see the device status and disable the device from this window.

MODEM TAB   The Modem tab, shown in Figure 4-12, gives you three important settings:

- **Speaker Volume**   If you want to hear the connection noise, leave the volume turned up on the slider bar; if not, turn the volume down.

- **Maximum Port Speed**   The maximum port speed setting determines how quickly programs can transmit data to the modem, not the line speed from modem to modem. If you are having problems with a device connected to the modem or an application sending data over the modem, you can try lowering or raising the port speed value. The default setting is typically 115,200 Kbps.

- **Dial Control**   The Wait for Dial Tone before Dialing check box is enabled by default and typically should remain enabled.

DIAGNOSTICS TAB   The Diagnostics tab gives you a Query Modem option. The query performs several command tests to see whether the modem is working correctly. Once the test is complete, the window displays a list of commands that were issued and the responses. You can also click View Log in order to see test data from a log file.

ADVANCED TAB   The Advanced tab provides you a place to enter additional initialization commands. Although unnecessary on most modems today, initialization commands can control the functions of the modem and can be used to adjust modems that work too slowly or that are subject to frequent hang-ups. The initialization commands vary from modem manufacturer to manufacturer.

You can also access Advanced Port settings here by clicking the Advanced Port Settings button. The Advanced Settings window enables you to determine the FIFO buffer usage. The FIFO (first in, first out) buffer setting uses the Universal Asynchronous Receiver/Transmitter (UART) chipset, which is the

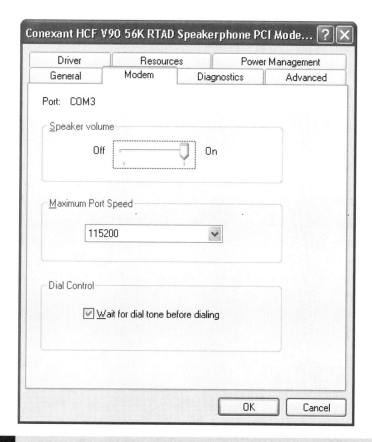

FIGURE 4.12   Modem tab

primary component that buffers incoming information to the modem until it is transferred to the computer. The default settings for the Receive and Transmit buffers on this tab are High, but you can lower them to correct performance problems. However, the higher the setting, the higher the performance.

You can also choose to change default preferences on the Advanced tab, which features a few important configuration options. First, you see a General tab. The following settings are available:

- **Disconnect Call If Idle**   This setting, when enabled, disconnects a call if it is idle for more than the specified number of minutes. If a user is getting disconnected during idle times, this is the setting to check.

- **Cancel Call If Not Connected**   You can configure a value for this setting, which is 60 seconds by default. If the call does not complete during this period of time, the call is disconnected and can be reinitiated.

- **Port Speed** This is the same Port Speed setting option seen on the Modem tab.

- **Data Protocol** This option controls data error correction. The common setting is StandardEC. However, if you are connecting with a modem that uses a different type of error correction, you can also choose to disable the option or try to force error correction, as provided on the drop-down menu.

- **Compression** Compression reduces the number of kilobytes of data for transmission purposes. A standard configuration uses the Enabled option here, but you can disable it if your specific connection calls for it.

- **Flow Control** This setting specifies whether hardware or software flow control is used to manage the flow of data between the modem and the computer. RTS/CTS is hardware flow control, while XON/XOFF is software flow control. Flow control is used to manage data between the modem and the computer.

TROUBLESHOOTING

Modem Hang-Ups

An aggravating issue that many modem users face is random modem hang-ups, or disconnects. Users in your environment may complain that their modem works for a period of time, and then they are disconnected from the Internet. A couple of problems can cause modem disconnects. First, check the Advanced tab and make sure that the modem is not configured to disconnect automatically after a certain period of idle time. The modem might automatically disconnect from the ISP while the user is taking a break from the Internet, or even during some downloads where the computer thinks there is no connection activity.

A second problem concerns the ISP itself. Some ISP modems automatically disconnect users after a certain period of time, although many ISPs are reluctant to admit that this practice is in place. If modem disconnects are a common problem, first check the modem settings and make sure the problem does not exist on the local machine. If all seems to be in order locally, it is probably time to contact the ISP.

If you click the Advanced tab, you see the option to manage hardware settings. The options are as follows:

- **Data Bits**   This setting determines the number of data bits that are used for each character that is sent and received. The default setting is 8, and the modem you are communicating with must have the same setting.

- **Parity**   This setting configures the type of error checking that is used for the port. The usual setting is None, but if parity is used, the modem you are communicating with must have the same setting.

- **Stop Bits**   This setting tells the system that a packet of information has been set. The standard setting here is 1.

- **Modulation**   The modulation type must be compatible with the modem with which you are communicating. Most modems use standard modulation, but if you are having problems communicating with a particular modem, you can try the nonstandard setting here.

DRIVER AND RESOURCES TAB   Finally, the Driver and Resources tab found on the modem's Properties sheets is the same as the Driver and Resources tabs you see when accessing any device's properties from Device Manager.

CONFIGURING ADVANCED MODEM SETTINGS

The Advanced tab of the Phone and Modem Options dialog box lists the telephony providers that are installed on the computer. Telephony providers are applications that enable your modem to communicate with specific types of applications or even hardware. For example, one of the providers listed in the Advanced tab is the Microsoft H.323 telephony service provider. H.323 is a protocol used by NetMeeting and related multimedia applications. If you select the provider and click the Properties button, you can configure the service provider so that your modem can connect with the appropriate server. Of course, if you are not using any of these specific providers, there is nothing you need to configure in this tab.

MANAGING USB DEVICES

Only a few years ago, computer users were limited by the number of physical ports available for peripherals. This limitation wasn't such a big deal since the primary peripheral hardware consisted of keyboards, mice, and printers. Today, however, computer users hook up multiple peripherals and hardware devices to their computers, such as scanners, external modems, hard drives, Zip drives, digital cameras, game controllers, and so on. Yet, until recently, PC users remained limited by the number of physical connection ports and the same slow serial bus that had been used for years.

Enter the USB, or Universal Serial Bus. USB is a faster serial bus technology that enables multiple USB devices to connect to a single port. In fact, you can connect as many as 127 individual peripherals to a single interface to the computer using USB hubs. The idea is to make using a peripheral as easy as plugging a lamp into a wall socket—you don't have to worry about configuration and setup, you simply plug in the peripheral and use it. When you install USB hardware, you simply plug the hardware into the USB port. Windows XP automatically detects and installs it with no interaction from you and no rebooting. Most peripherals sold today are available in the USB format, and in the future you can expect even PCs to be primarily USB machines.

Overall, USB usage is easy and problem-free, but there are a few facts and features you should know about USB. First, let's consider USB hub configuration. The USB port found on the front or back of the PC is referred to as the USB root hub. It is the hub that connects directly to the internal computer's motherboard. The USB root hub may have multiple USB ports available, and in many cases, USB devices will even have their own ports so you can daisy-chain peripherals together off one port. These devices, called *compound devices,* also form an additional hub. For example, a typical USB keyboard may plug directly into the USB root hub, but provide a USB port for the mouse to plug into the keyboard. This compound device acts as a hub.

From the USB root hub, you can connect several different devices, but you can also connect another external hub. USB hubs typically support as many as seven additional connections, including another hub. For this reason, the USB has a tiered star topology. One hub feeds from the root hub, then the next hub feeds from the first hub, and so forth. Using this tiered star topology approach, you can combine enough hubs to support as many as 127 devices. Of course, hardly anyone will ever need to connect 127 devices to a single PC. The point is that by chaining together additional USB hubs, you can easily extend USB connections as you need them.

Both bus-powered and self-powered USB hubs are available. Bus-powered hubs draw their power from the USB bus, or essentially the power flowing into the computer system from the AC/DC outlet. For most USB peripherals, such as keyboards and mice, the power available from a bus-powered hub is all you need. However, some USB devices may require more power. For example, suppose that you have a USB bus-powered hub. You purchase a USB external hard drive, but it does not work when you plug it into the USB hub. The problem is that the external hard drive needs more power to operate than the USB bus-powered

Self-powered Hubs

Let's say that most users in your environment use laptop computers. Many computers use bus-powered USB hubs. However, many of those users complain about battery power—the laptop batteries simply do not last long enough. The problem? The bus-powered hubs are draining the batteries.

The importance of self-powered hubs cannot be understated in the case of a laptop computer using batteries. Since the bus-powered hub draws power from the system, the USB bus can drain laptop batteries when peripherals, especially those using a lot of power, are in use.

hub can provide. In this case, you need a USB self-powered hub, which connects to its own AC/DC connection. Of course, most peripherals that need their own power supply have their own AC/DC connection. But you can see the need for self-powered hubs, especially in situations where you are chaining several hubs together and attaching multiple peripherals. As a general rule, a bus-powered hub can support as many as 100 mA per port whereas a self-powered hub can support as many as 500 mA per port.

As I mentioned, installing a USB device is as easy as plugging it in. Windows XP can automatically detect and install the USB without any help and without a reboot. When a device needs to be removed, simply unplug it. Windows XP can detect that the device is no longer available and remove it from the operating system.

You can gain a lot of helpful information about USB devices and USB configuration on a particular computer system by using Device Manager. If you open Device Manager, you can see a category for Universal Serial Bus Controllers, and if you expand that category, you see device options for the USB Root Hub and the USB Universal Host Controller.

If you right-click the USB Universal Host Controller and click Properties, you see the standard Device Manager Properties sheets, containing the General, Driver, and Resources tabs. However, you also see an Advanced tab, as shown in Figure 4-13. The Advanced tab shows you how much bandwidth each USB controller is using. Since each device attached to the controller has to share the bandwidth, this is a good tab to check to see whether a system is running low on USB bandwidth due to the number of devices attached to the USB port. You can also check the Don't Tell Me about USB Errors check box, which will stop

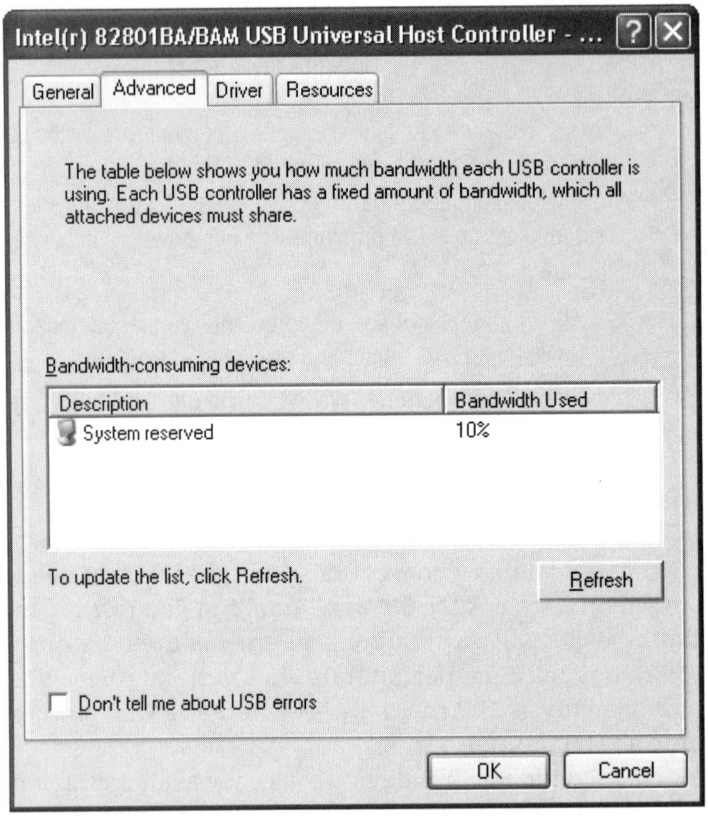

Intel(r) 82801BA/BAM USB Universal Host Controller - ...

General | **Advanced** | Driver | Resources

The table below shows you how much bandwidth each USB controller is using. Each USB controller has a fixed amount of bandwidth, which all attached devices must share.

Bandwidth-consuming devices:

Description	Bandwidth Used
System reserved	10%

To update the list, click Refresh.   Refresh

☐ Don't tell me about USB errors

OK   Cancel

FIGURE 4.13 USB Host Controller Advanced tab

the reporting of any bandwidth, power, and USB device errors. However, you should typically leave this box unchecked.

If you right-click the USB root hub option in Device Manager and click Properties, you also see the standard Device Manager tabs, with two additional tabs specific to the hub. The first is Power, which you can see in Figure 4-14. The Power tab tells you information about the hub type and power available per port. In Figure 4-14, Device Manager is reporting that the system uses a self-powered hub that has 500 mA available per port. You can also see a list of attached devices and the power required to run those devices. Again, this is a good place to gain overall information about the USB root hub and how power is being used on the hub.

The second tab is Power Management, which includes two check box options. First, you can choose to allow the computer to turn off the device in order to

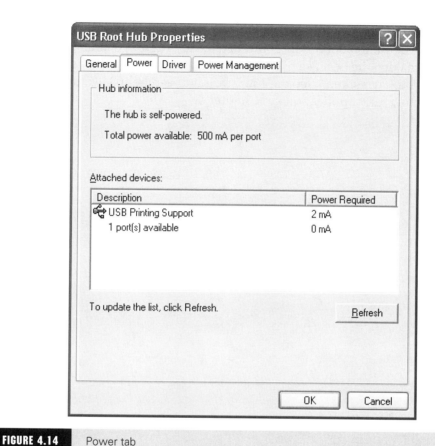

FIGURE 4.14   Power tab

save power, which is typically selected by default. Second, you can have the device bring the computer out of standby if standby is configured.

WRAPPING UP

In this chapter, you explored hardware installation and configuration in Windows XP. Windows XP's plug and play system, as well as the Add/Remove Hardware Wizard, gives you an easy environment in which to install and configure hardware. The most important point you can remember is simply to use hardware that is compatible with Windows XP. While you may be able to get hardware to work with XP that is not specifically compatible, you may experience more operation problems as well as problems with the driver. Keep in mind that hardware devices, such as modems, scanners, cameras, and even USB devices, often have configuration options in Control Panel and in Device Manager, so make sure you are making the best use of the tools that Windows XP provides you.

Now that you have taken a look at hardware management, let's turn our attention to managing applications in Chapter 5.

MANAGING APPLICATIONS

5

As an A+ technician, your job not only revolves around computer hardwareand operating systems; you may find yourself dealing with software on a regular basis as well. Software provides the rich computing environment that users need in order to do their jobs, and perhaps even to enjoy using their computers. After all, applications are often the main reason for owning a computer in the first place. In your network environment, you may be required to support applications that users have installed on Windows XP, and you may be called on to troubleshoot applications, and more specifically, to try to get them to work with Windows XP. In this chapter, you'll...

- Install and remove applications
- Use program compatibility mode
- Adjust Windows XP for application performance
- Manage and control applications
- Run 16-bit and MS-DOS applications
- Manage automatic updates
- Control user program installation and removal

INSTALLING AND REMOVING APPLICATIONS

Windows XP supports numerous applications, from word processing applications to spreadsheets, presentation software, antivirus software, and even games. In fact, you can find software for just about anything you might want to do with Windows XP. However, the greatest mistake users and even corporate decisions makers make is assuming that all software applications will work with Windows XP. Just because a software package says "compatible with Windows" on the box, that does not mean that the software is actually compatible with Windows XP. Software written for Windows 9x simply may not work with Windows XP at all, or if it does work, it may work intermittently. So, the number one rule of using applications on Windows XP, or any operating system for that matter, is to use applications that are written for Windows XP. This almost guarantees that you will have few if any problems, and your help desk calls will be minimized.

NOTE When you upgrade to Windows XP from a previous version of Windows, the previous operating system's applications and programs are kept in place. However, this does not mean that they will work once the upgrade is complete.

Unfortunately, software purchasing and distribution decisions in your networking environment may not be up to you, and you may have to support what is already deployed or being deployed. The good news is that Windows XP gives you a few tools and options that can help you manage software, even if that software is not explicitly written for Windows XP.

NOTE Windows XP is built on Windows 2000 code, and like Windows 2000, Windows XP does not allow programs to alter operating system files, which are kept in a separate folder. This feature greatly reduces system lock-ups that occurred so frequently in Windows 9x.

INSTALLING SOFTWARE

Software is installed by launching a setup.exe program. The setup program copies the software's files from a source to a folder on the computer's hard drive. The setup program can be launched from an Internet download or from an installation CD. Most software sold today has an autostart feature on the CD that walks the user through the installation process. If an installation CD does not automatically start the installation, you can simply browse the CD and locate the setup program, as in the example shown in Figure 5-1.

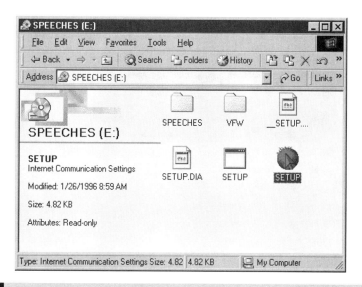

FIGURE 5.1 You can manually launch a program installation by double-clicking Setup.exe

NOTE In Windows XP, new programs that you have not yet opened are displayed in yellow when you look at them in Start | All Programs. Once you open a program, this "highlighting" feature is removed so you can keep track of which programs you have explored and which ones you have not. If you don't like the highlight feature, you can remove it by accessing the Start Menu properties and removing the feature.

As you might guess, you can also use Add/Remove Programs in Control Panel to install a program. You'll see an Add New Programs button on the left side of the screen, shown in Figure 5-2. Once you click the button, you can click the CD or Floppy button to begin an installation from a floppy disk or CD-ROM. You can also install programs that are available from a network share as well. If you want to download something from the Windows Update site, then click the Windows Update button. Essentially, the Install option found here just looks for Setup.exe on the floppy disk or CD. To use this option, see the following step-by-step instructions.

INSTALLING A PROGRAM USING ADD/REMOVE

1. Click Start | Control Panel.
2. Click the Add/Remove Programs icon.

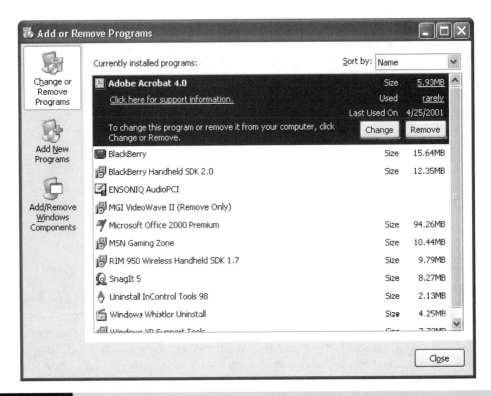

FIGURE 5.2 Use the Install button to let Windows XP help you install a program

3. In the Add or Remove Programs window, click the Add New Programs button.

4. In the window that appears, click the CD or Floppy button.

5. The Install from Floppy Disk or CD-ROM Window wizard appears. Click the Next button.

6. Windows searches your floppy and CD-ROM drives for the Setup.exe program and gives you the location, as shown here. If this is not correct, click the Browse button to browse to the correct location.

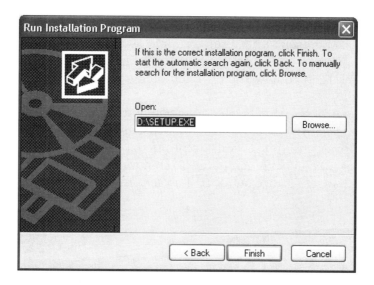

7. Click Finish, and installation begins. You may need to respond to other prompts, depending on the setup routine.

NOTE Users are often worried about how they should install a program. Should you install a program using its setup icon or use the Add/Remove Programs icon? In truth, there is no difference. Add/Remove Programs just launches the setup program for you so you do not have to start it yourself. Most programs today have an autostart file, so all you have to do is put the CD-ROM into your computer and the disk will tell you what to do next. If this does not happen, you can start setup yourself by double-clicking Setup.exe or by using the Install option in Add/Remove Programs. As you will find, Windows XP often provides more than one way to accomplish a task—it's just a matter of preference.

Just as you can install a program on Windows XP, you can uninstall the program as well. For example, suppose that you use a particular application, and at a future date, you purchase a different application to replace your older one. If the application you purchase is not an upgrade to the old one, you may want to remove the old application from Windows XP so that it does not take up space. Keep in mind, however, that any files created by the application cannot be used once the application is removed.

There are two ways to remove a program from your computer. Some programs come with their own uninstall option. You can just put the CD-ROM into the CD-ROM drive, and let it automatically begin. A window then appears that allows you to install additional components or remove existing components—or the entire program. Microsoft Office is an example of a program that utilizes this feature. Some programs also have a built-in uninstall routine. You can click Start | Programs, then point to the program's folder; a menu pops out with an uninstall option.

If you have a program that doesn't help you with the uninstall process, you can, once again, use Add/Remove Programs in Control Panel. When you open Add/Remove Programs, you see a list of programs. The programs listed on this window are installed on your computer. To remove one of them, simply select it and click the Change/Remove button. Follow any additional prompts that appear.

TECH TALK

Manually Removing a Program

Sometimes, you end up with programs that really like you and do not want to leave your computer: There is no uninstall option on the CD-ROM, and the program is not listed in Add/Remove Programs as an option you can uninstall. Although this normally does not happen, you can still remove the program by deleting its folder. This is not a recommended action since you may experience problems by forcing an application to delete itself. For example, if other applications use the application files, those other applications may have problems after you delete the files. However, you can use this option when absolutely necessary.

1. Open My Computer, then double-click your C drive icon.

2. Locate a folder called Program Files, then double-click it. You may need to click the View All Contents link as prompted.

3. Look through the folders and find the one that has the program you want to uninstall. Typically, the name of the folder will indicate the program's name or the manufacturer's name.

4. When you have found the folder, right-click it and click Delete to remove it from your computer. Make sure you are deleting the correct folder before completing the action.

NOTE Some programs give you a Change button and a Remove button, while some only give you a Change/Remove button. If you have programs that can be upgraded or if additional parts of the program can be installed, you'll see both Change and Remove. This allows you to install additional portions of the program, or simply remove the program from your computer.

USING PROGRAM COMPATIBILITY MODE

Windows XP includes a new feature, called compatibility mode, that allows Windows XP to act like a previous version of Windows, specifically Windows 95, 98, Me, NT, or 2000. The purpose of compatibility mode is to allow you to use older applications that might not work with Windows XP. When in compatibility mode, Windows XP acts like the previous version of Windows (which you select) so that the application is tricked into thinking it is installed on the correct operating system. This feature allows you to use older applications that are not 100 percent compatible with XP.

It is important to note that compatibility mode is intended for standard applications and even games. However, compatibility mode is not designed for use with programs that run portions of your system configuration. For example, you should not use this mode with antivirus programs that are not compatible with Windows XP because they may damage your system. The same is true for disk management utilities and backup software. In other words, if the application is used to manage the operating system or some portion of the operating system, it should not be used with compatibility mode—you need to upgrade and get the compatible version of the software.

Windows XP's compatibility functions use application database files that interact with programs that you install. Because programs are outside of the operating system kernel, the application database files are used as a translator for the program and the operating system. There are four main application database files, which are

■ **MigDB.inf** This database file is used for migration of applications from Windows 9x and Me. The database file is able to identify and flag programs that are incompatible or require an upgrade. This file is responsible for the message that may appear during installation telling the user that a certain application may not work correctly under Windows XP.

■ **NTCompat.inf** This database file is used for upgrades from Windows NT and Windows 2000. It also provides incompatibility information concerning applications.

- **SysMain.sdb**   This database file contains matching information and compatibility fixes.

- **AppHelp.sdb**   This help file that can give the user clues about compatibility and how to resolve problems.

The SysMain.sdb is the primary database file that pulls the information from the MigDB.inf and NTCompat.inf files. It then looks for "matches" that can fix the incompatibility problems. These matches are often simple changes that allow Windows XP to give the program what it needs to function properly. The fixes, which are also called "shims," are held in this database file, which contained about 200 at the time of XP's release. Any application can use shims, but third-party developers cannot write new shims for Windows XP. This a security protection feature implemented by Microsoft. What you get out of the box is all you get.

With shims, Windows XP can invoke several compatibility modes. Essentially, a compatibility mode enables XP to use the identified shims for that category and possibly fix the application compatibility problems that the program has with Windows XP. These shims emulate the operating system that is needed by the program. For example, if an application is written for Windows 98, the shims can emulate the structure of the Windows 98 Registry, the location of certain system and user folders, file paths, and related changes in the operating system that the application would not be able to handle. The compatibility modes available in Windows XP are as follows:

- **Windows 95**   This mode emulates the Windows 95 environment.

- **Windows 98/Me**   This mode emulates the Windows 98/Me environment.

- **Windows NT 4.0**   This mode emulates the Windows NT 4.0 environment.

- **Windows 2000**   This mode emulates the Windows 2000 environment.

- **256 Colors**   This mode reduces video card color to 256 colors for applications that can handle only 256 colors.

- **640 × 480 Screen Resolution**   This mode restricts screen resolution to 640 by 480 for applications that can handle only that screen resolution.

Compatibility Modes and Shims

The compatibility modes and shims provided with Windows XP support around 100 of the most popular programs so they can work with Windows XP. However, they do not support everything and they certainly do not support any custom applications. However, you can still try to use one of these applications with compatibility mode and perhaps achieve good results. Be sure to use Windows XP's dynamic update and Windows update from time to time to ensure that your XP system has all of the available shims in its database. The main lesson to keep in mind here is that compatibility mode is not a fix for all problems—it can help you in some circumstances and with some applications, so don't assume that compatibility mode will come to your rescue every time.

- **System Modes**   A few other modes are available that most power users and administrators can invoke. These modes are used to limit or manage security and profiles for the user in order to run programs that require a limited security context. There is a Limited User Account mode available as well as a Profiles mode. You can invoke Profiles mode by using the QfixApp or CompatAdmin tools, which I'll describe later in this section.

- **Custom Modes**   You can create a custom mode for a particular application, based on the applications needs, using the CompatAdmin tool, which I explore later in this section.

USING THE PROGRAM COMPATIBILITY MODE WIZARD

You can easily configure a program to run in Program Compatibility mode with the help of the Program Compatibility Mode Wizard. The following steps show you how to use the wizard:

1. Click Start | All Programs | Accessories | Program Compatibility Wizard.
2. The Program Compatibility wizard appears. Click Next on the Welcome screen.

3. In the next window, shown here, choose the desired radio button to locate the program. Make your selection and click Next.

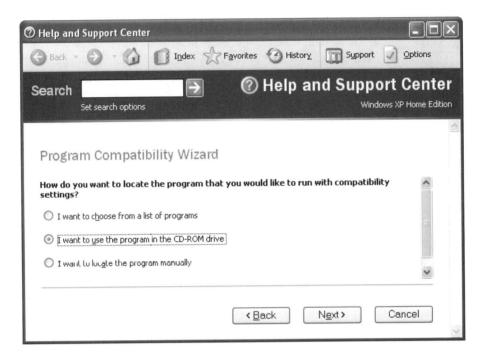

4. In the next window, choose the operating system that you want to emulate, such as Windows 95, NT 4.0, Windows 98/Me, and so on.

5. In the next window, you can choose the screen resolution that the program works best under, or you can choose to disable Windows visual themes, which can interfere with some older programs. However, the settings here typically apply to games and educational programs that use a lot of graphics. If you do not want to use any of the settings, simply click Next without selecting any items.

6. In the next window, click Next to test the compatibility settings with the program.

7. The program opens and runs. Use the program for a few minutes to see whether the program works correctly. Then, close the program in order to return to the wizard.

8. The wizard asks you if the program works correctly. If so, click Yes to continue, or No to try different compatibility settings. Click Next.

9. The Program Compatibility Wizard collects information about your program and provides you a dialog box so that you can send compatibility information to Microsoft. Click Yes or No, then click Next.

10. Click Finish. To change settings at a later time, simply rerun the wizard. You can now open the program and use it.

You can also avoid using the Program Compatibility Wizard and more easily apply a compatibility mode to a program. Just right-click the program's executable file and click Properties. You see a Compatibility tab, shown in Figure 5-3. Simply choose to run the program in compatibility mode, choose an operating system to emulate, and apply any display settings as needed.

ADVANCED COMPATIBILITY SETTINGS

Aside from using the basic program compatibility settings to run an application, you can also configure some custom settings, or at least attempt to use a few compatibility tools that perhaps can make an application or program work with

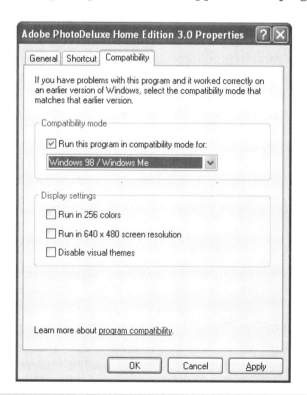

FIGURE 5.3   Choose compatibility settings

Windows XP. Keep in mind that the tools explored in the following sections are designed for administrators, and they can be complicated. However, with a little work, you may be able to solve the compatibility problems with that troublesome program.

USING QFIXAPP

QFixApp is a utility you can use to manually solve compatibility problems with applications by applying shims from an available database. QFixApp is not directly available from within Windows XP, but it is available in the Application Compatibility Toolkit, which is downloadable from http://msdn.microsoft.com.

Once you download and install the toolkit, you'll see an HTML page that outlines the documents and tools in the toolkit. If you scroll to tools, you'll see both the QFixApp and Compatibility Administration Tool. The QFixApp tool gives you control over an executable file by allowing you to examine the actual SysMain.sdb file and apply any shim to the executable. The Program Compatibility Wizard basically does this, but it applies the fixes based on one of the modes you select. With the QFixApp, you can apply a mode that you want, and you can manually overlay any additional fix that you want. This feature is quite helpful if you have applied a mode to an application, but you are still having a particular problem. If you can isolate the likely cause of the problem, then you can use QFixApp to apply that single fix while keeping the original mode application intact.

In short, you have total control over how the fixes are applied. The reverse is also true: If a fix is applied within a mode, you can individually remove fixes out of the mode for that application that may be giving you problems. Once you find the fix that works, you can apply it to the application, and you can also use a secondary tool, called the CompatAdmin.exe, so that you can apply the fix to other computers. The following steps show you how to use QFixApp.

USING THE QFIXAPP TOOL

1. In the Application Compatibility toolkit, click the open link next to QFixApp.

2. The QFixApp window appears, as shown in Figure 5-4. Browse for the executable file for the program you want to try to fix. If there are any existing fixes in the database for this application, you can choose to disable them by clicking the check box.

3. On the Layers tab, you can choose to apply one of the existing modes to the application. For example, you can choose 256 color, Disable themes, NT 4 with Service Pack 5, Windows 98, and so on. If you don't want to use an existing layer, just click the Fixes tab.

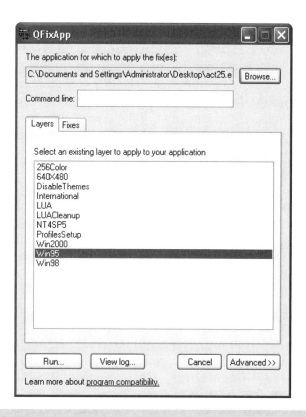

FIGURE 5.4   Select the executable file

4. In the Fixes tab, you see each individual fix that is available. If you click a fix, you can see a fix description toward the bottom of the window, describing what the fix should correct with the application. Work through the list, selecting the fixes that you want to apply.

5. When you are ready to test the applications with the fixes you have applied, click the Run button. The application will open and you can use it as desired. Make note of what problems still exist and what problems were solved. You can then add or remove fixes as needed until you find the right combination for the application.

USING THE COMPATIBILITY ADMINISTRATION TOOL (COMPATADMIN.EXE)

The Compatibility Administration Tool (CompatAdmin.exe) is also a part of the Application Compatibility Toolkit, and as you'll see, it performs many of the same functions as QFixApp. CompatAdmin.exe enables you to browse the database of fixes provided for applications in Windows XP. Then, you can assign fixes to those applications as necessary. Once you have applied the fixes to the application and the application is in good working order, you can then create a package with those fixes and deploy them to other Windows XP computers.

The CompatAdmin tool gives you a window interface, as you can see in Figure 5-5. The left pane lists all of the applications that are supported by fixes in Windows XP. As you scroll through the list, you can see there are quite a number of them. In the right pane, you can select one of the applications and see the executable file to which the fix applies and the actual compatibility fixes that are applied to this application by default. You also see the file matching results ensuring that the executable is the correct one for the application.

As you can see, there are a number of applications to view, and often a number of fixes for each specific application. If you are having a hard time browsing the applications and fixes, you can control how much information is displayed using the View menu. By default, the interface displays compatibility fixes, compatibility modes, Apphelp entries, and application patches. If you just want to see how patches are applied, you can clear the check next to the other items and the view will be a lot easier to work with.

You can perform several important actions with CompatAdmin. First, you can disable fixes. Keep in mind that the application databases provide information

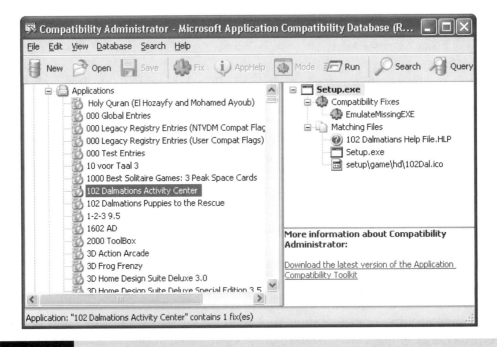

FIGURE 5.5   CompatAdmin.exe

about applications for which Microsoft has determined fixes, as well as the fixes that should be applied. When a user invokes the Application Compatibility Wizard, the wizard attempts to match that application under the desired Windows version. However, you may need to change this behavior for a particular application. As you saw with the QFixApp tool, you can use the default fixes assigned by a database and overlayed with the chosen operating system, remove them and apply your own, or simply add to the existing one. With the CompatAdmin tool, you disable the default database fix for an application, and then use QFixApp or the CompatAdmin tool to create your own fix. Then that fix can be run or even deployed. Disabling a fix disables it on the local system and only disables it—it does not delete the fix so that you can easily reenable it later. The following steps walk you through this process.

DISABLING AN APPLICATION USING THE COMPATIBILITY TOOLKIT

1. In the Application Compatibility toolkit, open the CompatAdmin tool.

2. In the CompatAdmin tool, browse the application list and select the application.

3. In the right pane, right-click the executable (or actually any portion of the fix) and click Disable Entry. A red exclamation point now appears over the fix.

4. You can reenable the fix at any time by right-clicking it and click Enable Entry.

One of the most powerful options that CompatAdmin provides is that you can create custom databases and custom fixes for the applications as needed. When you first open CompatAdmin, the tool creates a new database that appears in the lower-right portion of the screen. By default, this database is named New database(1).sdb. You can use the Database menu to rename the database as desired. You can also use the Database menu to perform a few additional actions that specifically allow you to create custom fixes for your new database, and you can even define your own compatibility mode.

To do this, select the database name in the lower-left corner, then open the Database menu. You see the option to create an application fix. The following steps show you how to use CompatAdmin to create custom fixes.

USING COMPATADMIN TO CREATE CUSTOM FIXES

1. In the Application Compatibility toolkit, click the link to open the CompatAdmin tool.

2. Select the database name in the lower-left corner and click Database | Create New | Application Fix.

3. In the Program Information window, give the fix a name and browse to select the program you want to fix. Click Next.

4. The Compatibility Modes window appears, as you can see in the image shown next. If you choose the Apply Compatibility mode, you simply select the desired executable and assign one of the preconfigured modes, such as Windows 98, 256 colors, and so on. Essentially, this option performs the same actions as the Program Compatibility Wizard. To assign custom fixes to an application, choose the desired check boxes. You can choose to perform a Test Run, or simply click Next to continue.

5. Select the desired fixes in the provided list, shown next. Click Next when you have selected all fixes that you want to apply.

6. In the identification window, browse and select the files that identify the application. You can also click the Auto-Generate option, which tells the wizard to perform this action for you; this option is recommended. Make your selections and click Next.

7. Perform a test run of the application by clicking the provided button, then click Finish when you're done.

Aside from creating custom fixes from this window, you can also create your own compatibility mode. For example, suppose that your environment has several custom applications. You could create a custom fix for those applications by creating your own custom compatibility mode. Then you can more easily apply the mode to the desired applications. The following steps walk you through creating a custom compatibility mode.

CREATING A CUSTOM COMPATIBILITY MODE

1. In the Application Compatibility toolkit, click the open link next to CompatAdmin.exe.

2. Select the database name in the lower-left corner and click Database | Create New | Compatibility Mode.

3. In the custom mode window, shown here, give the mode a name in the Name of the Compatibility Mode text box provided, then move any of the fixes you want for the mode to the Shims and Patches window to the Compatibility Fixes Available window. If necessary, you can click the Copy Mode button and select one of the existing modes (such as Windows 98, Windows 2000, 256 colors, and so on), then you can modify that mode as desired. Once you are finished, click Done.

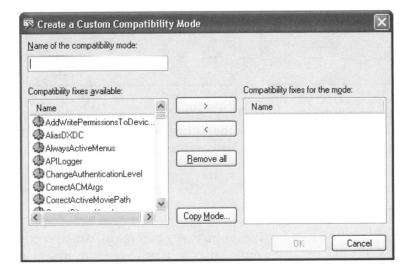

Once you have created the custom fixes and/or compatibility modes for your custom database, you can then deploy that database to other Windows XP machines. Keep in mind, however, that the console doesn't actually help you deploy the .sdb database file that you created. You save it in the console, and then simply copy the .sdb database file to the desired Windows XP computers. You can deploy the file using a simple network share, floppy disk, or whatever works best for you. The point is that the console doesn't provide a delivery method. Once the file is located on the other XP machines, simply run the .sdb file on those machines and Windows XP will register the new database.

ADJUSTING WINDOWS XP FOR APPLICATION PERFORMANCE

Aside from getting applications to work with Windows XP, perhaps one of the greatest program issues you are likely to encounter as an A+ technician is performance. Users may complain that certain applications run slowly on Windows XP, or more generally that all applications run slowly. As a technician, your job then is to take the information you have been given and see whether you can find the problem in Windows XP. The good news is that the potential performance problems are usually easy to spot. However, solving them can be another story because there are only a few actions that you can take.

CHECK REQUIREMENTS AND COMPATIBILITY

At the very core of application performance are hardware requirements. As is the case with most other things in the computing world, you can't run software on a computer that does not have the required system hardware, or at least you can't run software effectively. Today, many applications and even games require fast processors and plenty of RAM. This is especially true of the photo and video production applications that have become so popular in the past few years. The simple fact is that the computer should exceed any minimum hardware requirements posted by the software manufacturer. If a computer does not meet the hardware requirements, the application may run, but it may run very slowly. In this scenario, your only option is to upgrade the computer's hardware.

Another issue concerning performance comes back to compatibility. You may be able to get an incompatible application to run using the Program Compatibility mode, but that application still may not run as fast or perform as well as you would like. This is simply a compatibility problem for which there is no direct workaround, except to upgrade to a compatible application.

PAINFUL LESSONS I'VE LEARNED

Dealing with the Application Junkie

Users often expect that any application should work on Windows XP, but this simply is not true. Have you met an "application junkie" who downloads any and all applications from the Internet and tries to install them? This practice can certainly create problems that usually end up in your lap! For this reason, many networking environments have strict policies about application installation and Internet downloads.

USING PERFORMANCE OPTIONS

Aside from applying basic common sense about using applications, you can try a couple of Windows XP settings to make sure the environment is optimized for applications. The correct settings are actually configured by default, but if you are having a lot of performance problems with programs, you should check these settings. Right-click My Computer, click Properties, then click the Advanced tab. Click the Settings button under Performance, and the Performance Options dialog box appears. Click the Advanced tab, shown in Figure 5-6. The Processor Scheduling and Memory Usage settings should both be set to Programs. If they are not, select the Programs buttons and click OK.

NOTE The Background Services options should never be selected unless the Windows XP Professional computer is being used as a file server, print server, or Web server on the network. If users who run applications access the computer, as is normally the case, then you should configure these settings to Programs.

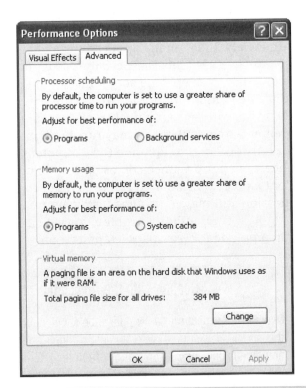

| FIGURE 5.6 | Performance options should be set to Programs |

TECH TALK

Video Cards and Performance

One issue with application performance is video cards. Surprised? Depending on the program or application, especially if the program or game is graphics-intensive, the video card may appear to slow down the program. Actually, the video card is unable to keep up with the demands of the program, which makes the system appear to run more slowly. Thus, the video card becomes the system bottleneck, rather than the application itself. So, if the computer meets the hardware requirements for the application, but there still seem to be performance problems, check the video card. Make sure the video card is optimized for the kinds of programs that you need to run, and make sure you are using the latest driver available for that particular video card. Again, when all else fails, you may need a video card upgrade. See Chapter 4 to learn more about hardware drivers and hardware management.

MANAGING AND CONTROLLING APPLICATIONS

If you used Windows 9x, you are probably familiar with the common application lockups and crashes that happened frequently. Unfortunately, Windows XP is not immune from this behavior, but it happens much less frequently. Once again, if you are using applications that are not quite compatible with Windows XP, you are more likely to experience problems than you would be if you were using applications that are designed for Windows 2000/XP.

As with previous versions of Windows, your main tool for controlling applications and getting control of the operating system when something goes wrong is Task Manager. To use Task Manager, press CTRL-ALT-DEL. Task Manager may appear immediately; if it does not, click the Task Manager button. You'll see the Windows Task Manager, shown in Figure 5-7. On the Applications tab, you see all applications that are currently open, as well as their status (running, failed, and so on). To stop an application from running, simply select the application in the list and click End Task.

You can also use Task Manager's Processes tab to end application processes or set application priority. If you click the Processes tab, you can right-click an

Use Task Manager to end tasks

executable that is running and point to Set Priority, then select a different priority for the application. The priorities available are

- **Realtime** The Realtime priority gives an application total control over all system resources. This can make the process run much faster. However, because this priority can cause your system to crash, you usually should avoid this setting.

- **High** The High priority gives the processes priority over all other applications. This may make the process run faster, but it may interfere with other processes running on your computer. Use this setting with caution.

- **AboveNormal** This option gives a process slightly more priority than other processes. This can help speed up an application, but it can slow other applications down.

- **Normal** This is the default setting.

- **Belownormal**   This setting causes the process to run more slowly than other applications that are open.

- **Low**   This option gives other processes more priority than the currently selected process.

So, should you adjust the priority settings for applications? As a general rule, the answer is no. Windows XP does a good job of managing application priority. However, if you have several applications running and you want to make one run a bit faster than the others, try giving the application an AboveNormal priority to see whether this helps performance.

NOTE   Keep in mind that the priority settings may work differently with various applications, so you'll need to experiment with them a bit to see whether you improve performance significantly.

RUNNING 16-BIT AND MS-DOS APPLICATIONS

Windows XP has the capability to run old 16-bit applications and MS-DOS applications (which are also 16-bit applications) that were originally developed for Windows 3.x. Basically, all programs sold today are 32-bit applications. However, your environment may have a custom application that was developed years ago that management still wants to use on Windows XP. To run 16-bit applications, Windows XP starts a virtual machine, which is a subsystem designed to mimic the Windows 3.x environment so that these applications can run. The subsystem places the 16-bit application in its own virtual machine, or memory space, so that the application theoretically can run without interfering with other applications on Windows XP.

If you need to use a 16-bit application, keep in mind that most do not support long filenames and most will not run as fast as 32-bit applications, due to the translation process necessary to make the programs run under Windows XP. Also, some 16-bit applications simply do not run well under Windows XP because of the way they try to access hardware. So, keeping in mind all of these caveats, Windows XP can run most 16-bit applications using the virtual machine. When you run several 16-bit applications, Windows XP places each in its own virtual machine, so that the 16-bit applications cannot interfere with each other. Keep in mind, however, that virtual machines consume more system resources, so try to keep their use to a minimum.

NOTE If you are not sure whether an application is a 16-bit application or not, open Task Manager and inspect the executable on the Processes tab. You'll see an entry for NTVDM.exe in the Image Name column. You'll also see the Wowexec.exe processes running; this executable is the virtual machine.

MANAGING AUTOMATIC UPDATES

Windows XP supports the Automatic Updates feature, which allows Windows XP to check the Windows Update Web site periodically for updates to Windows XP. Depending on your configuration, Windows XP can automatically download and install updates without an intervention from the user. However, you may not want Windows XP performing this task automatically, in which case you can manage the updates manually.

If you open System Properties and access the Automatic Updates tab, shown in Figure 5-8, you can choose one of three options:

- Download the updates automatically and notify me when they are ready to be installed. This option automatically downloads the updates and prompts you that they are ready to be installed. At this time, you can choose to install the updates or decline the install.

- Notify me before downloading any updates and notify me again before installing them on my computer. This option lets you know when an update is available. You can then choose to download and install it.

- Turn off automatic updating. I want to update my computer manually. If you do not want Windows XP checking for updates automatically, use this option. You can then manually check for updates when convenient by clicking Start | All Programs | Windows Update. Note that you also have the option to restore declined updates that you have previously declined.

If you are using a modem connection, Windows XP will automatically attempt to dial the connection to check for updates. Again, if you do not want the system to check for updates automatically and make random dial-up connections, simply turn off automatic updating.

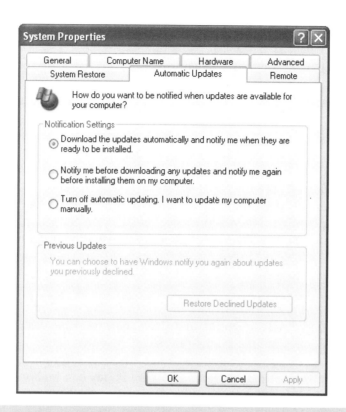

FIGURE 5.8 Automatic Updates option

CONTROLLING USER PROGRAM INSTALLATION AND REMOVAL

In many cases, you may not want users in your environment installing and removing programs. As I have mentioned before, user installations and removals can become a problem for help desk technicians, so many environments choose to control users and limit what users can and cannot do with programs. There are a few different issues to consider.

XP USER ACCOUNTS

Windows XP provides local user accounts as Administrator accounts and Limited accounts. Limited accounts cannot make changes to hardware or system configuration changes. They are also limited when installing programs. Depending on your network, you should consider giving users only limited accounts locally on Windows XP, with only certain users having administrative accounts on the computer. This can greatly cut down on problems since Windows XP prevents limited accounts from doing anything drastic, including program management. However, some older programs may not work well when users are logged on with limited accounts, so keep this in mind as you experiment with older programs. If you are in a domain environment, domain administrators may manage domain user accounts in such a way that users are limited from installing programs as well.

DOMAIN GROUP POLICY

In a domain environment, domain administrators may use domain Group Policy, configured on Windows 2000 Server, in order to control users and software. Using domain Group Policy, domain administrators can even install and remove software automatically from users' computers without any user interaction at all, which is a great management technique. Domain Group Policy can be applied at the site, domain, and organizational unit levels.

LOCAL GROUP POLICY

On Windows XP Professional, a local computer administrator can also enforce local Group Policy on other users who log on to the computer. This is yet another way to control what users can and cannot do on the computer, including software installation and removal. Using local Group Policy, you can invoke a setting that removes Add/Remove Programs from Control Panel that will further limit what users can do. The following steps walk you through this process.

ENFORCING LOCAL GROUP POLICY

1. Log on to a Windows XP Professional computer with a local administrator account.

2. Click Start | Run. Type MMC and click OK.

3. In the MMC window, click File | Add/Remove Snap-in.

4. In the Snap-in window, click Add.

5. In the Snap-in dialog box, select Group Policy and click Add. A window appears asking whether you are using local Group Policy. Click OK and click Close.

6. The Group Policy console is now available, as shown here.

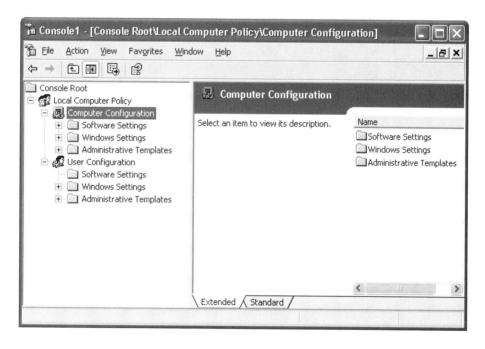

7. Expand User Configuration, Administrative Templates, Control Panel, Add/Remove Programs. Open the Remove Add/Remove Programs policy and enable it, as shown here.

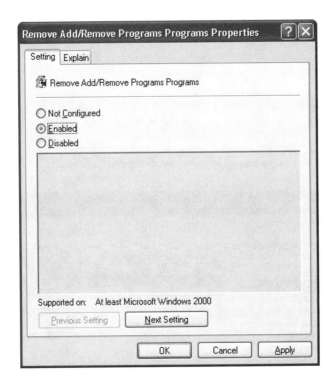

8. Click OK and close the Group Policy console.

WRAPPING UP

The trick to using applications with Windows XP is simply compatibility. Applications that were written for older versions of Windows may work fine with Windows XP, and if they do not, you can use the Program Compatibility Wizard to try to get the program to operate. However, even this option is not foolproof, so as you are installing applications on Windows XP computers, always think about compatibility.

In the next chapter, we'll turn our attention to user accounts and permissions.

MANAGING USER ACCOUNTS AND PERMISSIONS

6

User account and permissions management is an ongoing task that many A+ technicians face in their networking environments, depending on your job title and current responsibilities. Account and permissions management does not have to be terribly complicated, but it can certainly be aggravating, and depending on how accounts and permissions are used in your network, the task at hand can be confusing. Windows XP brings more local account configuration options to the table, with easier but more flexible account management strategies in Windows XP Professional. Windows XP supports folder permissions as well as NTFS permissions, which gives both local and shared folders more permission flexibility. In this chapter, we'll take a practical approach to account and permissions configuration and management, and stay focused on the issues and problems you are likely to encounter in your job. In this chapter, you'll…

- Configure and manage local user and group accounts
- Work with simple file sharing
- Configure and use NTFS permissions

CONFIGURING LOCAL WINDOWS XP ACCOUNTS

Windows XP Professional, in an attempt to be all things to all people, provides flexible account management, but account management that is also powerful at the local level. When I say "local level" or "local machine," I am taking about local computer accounts configured at a local Windows XP Professional computer—not domain accounts that are configured on a Windows 2000 Server and stored in the Active Directory. In many cases, only domain accounts are used, and the configuration of local accounts is not necessary. However, depending on the setup of your environment, you may very well use local computer accounts to control what users can and cannot do at the local machine.

You can configure local user accounts in two different places—the User Accounts applet in Control Panel, and the Local Users and Groups option in Computer Management. The following sections explore the options that Windows XP Professional gives you and shows you how to configure and manage accounts.

UNDERSTANDING USER ACCOUNTS

To make account management easier for end users, Windows XP provides three different types of accounts: Administrator, Limited User, and Guest. By default, Administrator and Guest accounts are created when Windows XP is first installed. The following bullets give you a quick overview of these account types:

- **Administrator** The Administrator account has complete control over the computer and access to all portions of the operating system. The Administrator can configure all system components, and install and remove hardware and all programs. In short, the Administrator account has full control. The Administrator can add, remove, or modify all existing user accounts. You can configure multiple Administrator accounts, or assign administrative privileges to multiple accounts if necessary, although local users should not have an Administrator account unless absolutely necessary.

- **Limited** The Limited account, formerly called a user account, should be used for most users. The Limited account gives the user full access to using the computer, but the Limited user cannot make hardware or system configuration changes. The Limited user also cannot install programs, but the user can use programs already installed. The Limited account cannot make any changes to existing accounts or add other accounts.

- **Guest**   The Guest account is designed for someone who does not have an account on the computer. The guest can log on, but not make any changes to the computer or install software, although the guest can launch programs currently installed. The guest account can access the Internet, check e-mail, and perform other basic tasks. The guest account can also be disabled if it is not needed.

You may also see an "unknown" account type if you open and browse User accounts in Control Panel. The unknown account appears if you upgraded to Windows XP from a previous version of Windows. The accounts that existed at the time of the upgrade are considered "unknown" accounts.

One of the best features of accounts in Windows XP is that accounts control what users can and cannot do, but accounts keep one user's data separate from that of another user. For example, when an account is created, you'll find a folder for that account in C:\Documents and Settings. The user's specific files and settings are stored in this user's folder, which is not accessible by other users, except the Administrator, who can browse any user's folder. If four different users access the same computer, then each user can log on with his or her account, and see his or her own desktop settings (assuming Group Policy allows the user to do so) and his or her own documents and files. To the user, it appears that he or she is the only one that uses the computer.

WORKING WITH USER ACCOUNTS IN CONTROL PANEL

You can easily configure user accounts using the User Accounts applet in Control Panel. This interface, designed for local accounts and created for easy account management by end users, gives you an easy way to create, modify, and delete local user accounts on Windows XP. When you first open the User Accounts applet in Control Panel, you see the existing accounts and the option to pick a task, shown in Figure 6-1. The following steps show you how to create a new account.

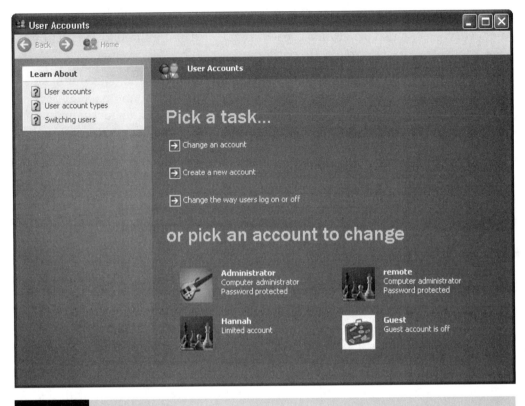

FIGURE 6.1 User Accounts

CREATING A NEW ACCOUNT

1. Log on with an administrator account and open User Accounts in Control Panel.

2. Click the Create a New Account option under Pick a Task.

3. In the Name the New Account dialog box, shown next, assign a name for the account. This is the name that will appear on Windows XP's Welcome screen and the Start Menu, so this account name is the "username" that the user will use to log on to the system. Enter the desired name and click Next.

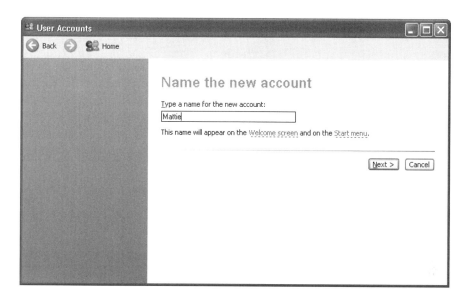

NOTE Usernames must be unique and can contain up to 20 characters, including numbers. However, user accounts cannot contain any of the following characters: " ? \ [ ] : ; | = + * / < >.

4. In the Pick an Account Type dialog box, shown here, choose whether you want the account to be an Administrator account or a Limited account by selecting the desired radio button. Click Create Account.

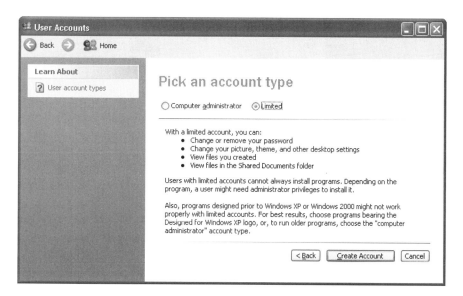

The new account is created and is now ready for use.

CHANGING AN ACCOUNT

A computer administrator can make changes to any account at any time. A Limited user, on the other hand, can change only his or her password or the account picture that appears. In other words, a Limited user cannot change other accounts, delete accounts, or change his or her account from Limited to Administrator. If you need to change an account, simply open User Accounts in Control Panel, then select the option to Change an Account under Pick a Task. In the next dialog box, select the account that you want to change. As you can see in Figure 6-2, you can change the account's name, password, picture, or account type, or you can delete the account. Simply select a desired action and follow the prompts.

WORKING WITH PASSWORDS

Windows XP gives you complete password flexibility; in fact, you don't even have to use passwords. If this seems odd, remember that Windows XP Professional is designed for both domains and small environment use. In

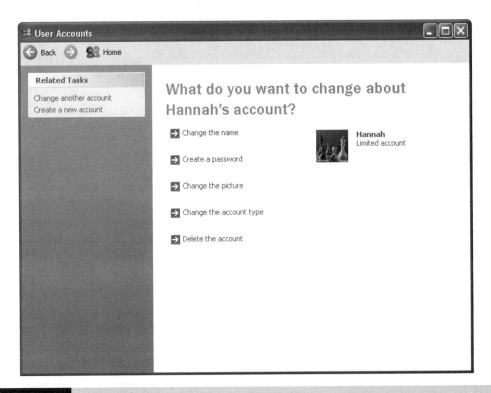

FIGURE 6.2   Choose an action in the User Accounts window

TROUBLESHOOTING

The Problem with Multiple Administrators

As you are aware, the administrator on the local Windows XP computer has complete control over the system—including the other user accounts. You might wonder if you can have more than one administrator. Yes, in fact, you can create as many administrative user accounts as you want. Actually, all accounts on the computer can be administrator accounts. Before handing out administrative privileges, however, you should always stop and think about this decision. Since administrators can make system-wide changes, including software and hardware changes, the administrator account should be treated with care. The best rule of practice is to give administrative accounts only to those people who should be making system-wide changes and who have the technical knowledge to make wise choices. Failure to do so can result in a number of problems as users make configuration changes they should not have made. So, although the trouble here is simply user error, it is a problem that can be avoided by carefully determining who should, and should not, get an administrator account.

a small office or even a home office setting, several users may need their own account in order to keep settings and files separate, but security may not be a concern. In this case, a user can simply log on at the Welcome screen by clicking his or her username. The option of having no password just keeps things simple.

However, in most cases, passwords are very important and keep only valid users logging on to the computer, instead of anyone who simply wants to. For this reason, users can create a password for themselves, and as a computer administrator, you can change users' passwords as needed.

For passwords to be effective, they should combine letters and numbers and be at least seven characters long. Passwords are case-sensitive, so passwords that use both upper- and lowercase letters are stronger. Also, passwords should not be common items, such as a name, children's names, and so on. The more random you can make them, the stronger they are.

To change your password, both Administrators and Limited users need only open the User Accounts applet in Control Panel, choose the Change an Account option, then click your account. Choose Change My Password from the list. Enter your existing password, the new password, and a hint that can remind you of your password, as shown in Figure 6-3. You can leave the hint option blank if you do not want to use it.

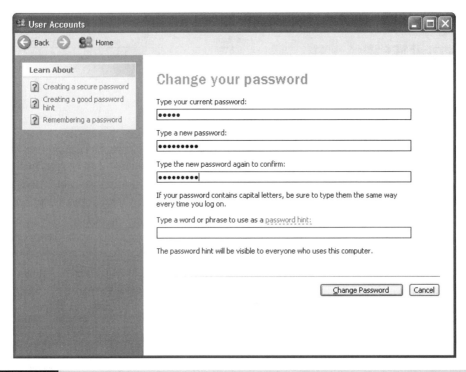

FIGURE 6.3   Change your password

As a local administrator, you can also use the User Accounts applet to change a user's password. This simply gives you a way to create and enforce a new password for a particular user, in the event that user forgets his or her password. The problem, however, is that the user will lose all Encrypting File System (EFS) encrypted files, certificates, and stored passwords for Web sites and network connections. Because of these problems, your best solution is to have users create a password reset disk. The password reset disk allows you to change your account's password without having to know the old password. It is a good practice to have users create a reset password disk and store the disk in a secure location (since the disk would also allow anyone else access to the account). To create a password reset disk, follow the steps described in the following subsection.

NOTE   You only need to create the password reset disk one time—not each time you change the password.

CREATING A PASSWORD RESET DISK

1. Log on with your desired account.

2. Open User Accounts in Control Panel.

3. Click the Change an Account option.

4. Click your account.

5. In the Related Tasks box in the left pane, click the Prevent a Forgotten Password option, shown here.

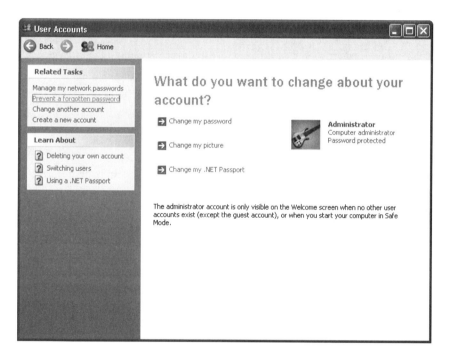

6. The Forgotten Password Wizard appears. Click Next on the Welcome screen.

7. Choose to create a password reset disk and store it on a floppy disk or other removable disk. Click Next.

8. Enter the current user account password and click Next.

9. The necessary data is copied to the disk. Click Next, then click Finish.

NOTE   If you are using a laptop computer that has no floppy disk drive, the password reset data is stored in the C drive.

TECH TALK

Using a .NET Passport

In an effort to integrate local computing more closely with the Internet, Windows XP also supports the linking of your user account to a .NET Passport. A .NET Passport gives you a single sign-on to a number of secured Microsoft sites and other Web sites that support the .NET Passport initiative. You can access bank records, pay bills online, check e-mail, and perform other online options.

When you associate a user account with a .NET passport, you are automatically logged on to Passport when you log on to Windows XP. Essentially, this gives users a one-stop logon process to access both the local computer and the Internet sites requiring a Passport. To associate a Passport with your user account, simply open User Accounts in Control Panel, then click Change an Account. Select your account from the list and choose to Set Up My Account to Use a .NET Passport. Then the .NET Passport Wizard appears. Then follow the instructions to set up the Passport.

MANAGING THE WAY USERS LOG ON

If the computers you manage are part of a Windows domain, a typical domain logon dialog box appears. To log on, users must enter their domain user account and password in this dialog box. If the computer is a stand-alone computer or a member of a workgroup, then you can either use the classic logon, where the user presses CTRL-ALT-DEL and enters the username and password, or you can use the Welcome screen, which is typically enabled by default. The Welcome screen shows you all of the current user accounts, except for the administrator account, which is hidden. Then the user simply clicks the user account that he or she wishes to use when logging on. If a password is required, a password dialog box appears and the user enters the password.

The administrator account is hidden, but not unavailable. When you see the logon screen, simply press CTRL-ALT-DEL. This will give you a standard Windows logon dialog box where you can enter your administrator account and password.

You can easily enable or disable the Welcome screen with User Accounts in Control Panel. Log on with an Administrator account, then open User Accounts. Click the Change the Way Users Log On or Log Off option. In the dialog box that appears, shown in Figure 6-4, you can choose to use the Welcome screen by clicking the Use the Welcome Screen check box option.

Also notice that you can choose to use Fast User Switching. This feature, which is new in Windows XP, allows multiple users to be logged on to the computer at the same time. One user can use the computer, then another user can switch to his or her account, keeping the existing applications and files open that the other user was accessing. This feature allows different people to use the computer quickly and easily without having to close programs and stop processes, while keeping individual files and information secure.

However, Fast User Switching does have some restrictions. To use this feature, you have to enable the Welcome screen and you must never join the computer to a domain. Also, Fast User Switching does not work when offline files are enabled as well as some networking services, such as Client for NetWare networks.

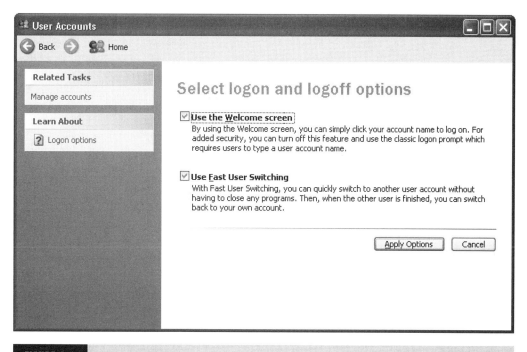

FIGURE 6.4   Logon and logoff options

TECH TALK

Fast User Switching in the Real World

Fast User Switching is a cool Windows feature designed for computers that have multiple users, particularly if those users access the computer several times each during the same day. With Fast User Switching, multiple users can have different programs open, working on different projects, and then simply trade off using the computer among themselves as needed—without closing programs or losing work. It is a great workgroup feature; however, do keep in mind that Fast User Switching does not work when a computer is configured to access a Windows domain and it does not work with offline files. However, Fast User Switching does work well with most Windows services, including Windows XP's remote desktop feature.

If you are using Fast User Switching, you can simply click Start | Log Off | Switch User to switch between users. This opens the Welcome screen, and the next user can simply log on.

NOTE You can also simply press the Windows logo key + L. This brings up the Welcome screen more quickly for Fast User Switching.

WORKING WITH COMPUTER MANAGEMENT

If you open the Computer Management console, which is found in Administrative Tools in Control Panel, you see a Local Users and Groups node in the left console pane. If you expand Local Users and Groups, you'll see the Users and Groups Container. If you open the Users container, you can see the current local users that are configured, as shown in Figure 6-5.

If you have to manage a number of local users, you may find the Local Users and Groups console easier to work with. You can easily create a new user by following the steps described in the following subsection.

CREATING A NEW USER

1. In the Computer Management console, expand Local Users and Groups. Right-click the Users container and click New User.

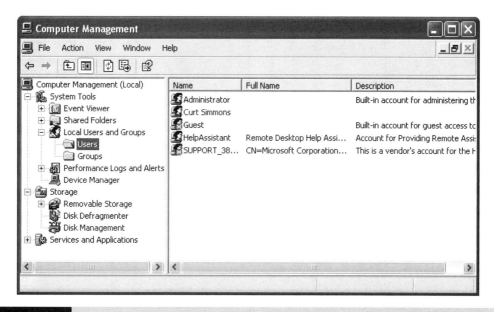

2. In the New User dialog box, shown in Figure 6-6, enter a username, full description, and password, then confirm the password. Then, you can choose to:

   ■ Change password at next logon
   ■ Restrict the user from changing the password
   ■ Ensure that the password never expires
   ■ Disable the account

3. After making your selections, click the Create button. The new account appears in the Local Users container.

Once you have created a new user account, you can manage it from within the Users container simply by right-clicking on the user account. From the menu that pops up, you can reset the user's password, rename the account, delete it, or access its properties. If a user forgets his or her password, you can reset the password using the Set Password option. This is the same feature that you can use in User Accounts. Again, the user will lose personal data tied to the account, so a password reset disk is always your best option.

On the User Account Properties sheet, shown in Figure 6-7, you can manage the password restrictions. You can disable the account on the General tab, and

FIGURE 6.6 Account creation

FIGURE 6.7 User Account Properties sheet

using the Member Of tab, you can add the user to desired local groups. Finally, on the Profile tab, you can configure a local or roaming user profile, which is described in the next section.

You have more options when configuring user accounts in Computer Management than in Users in the Control Panel. For example, you can force a user to change his or her password, you can configure the password to never expire, and you can even disable the account quickly and easily. These options are not available in Users in the Control Panel.

CONFIGURING USER PROFILES

Once a user account is created, a Documents and Settings folder is created. This folder stores any settings configured by the user as well as any personal documents. Users cannot access each other's folders, with the exception of the administrator, who can access any folder as needed. Once users are created, they can be grouped as needed for organizational purposes and rights assignment. Each local user account is given a folder, which is found in \Documents and Settings*username*. (If the computer was upgraded to Windows XP, the user's profile could be stored in \\%windir%\profiles.) The Documents and Settings folder is the default location where all user profiles are stored. You can change this location if you like and configure some additional profile options. To make changes to the default profile path, you must access the user account's properties via the Computer Management console. Expand Local Users and Groups, and in the right pane, right-click the desired user account. Then click Properties. Click the Profile tab, as shown in Figure 6-8.

As you can see, the Profile path is empty, which means the default of \ Documents and Settings*username* is being used. If you want to store the profile in a different location, just enter a new path. You may want to store the profile a more secure location or even on a different disk. If a logon script is used, you can enter the script path in the Logon Script text box.

You use the Home Folder panel to establish a local home folder. By default, My Documents is used, but you can specify a different home folder in which to store the user's files by entering a local path in the Local Path text box.

You can also configure a roaming user profile in the Profile tab. This feature is beneficial to users who access several different computers each day, but want the same documents and settings regardless of where they log on. You can configure the profile on a server, such as in a domain environment, and then configure the profile path as a network address, such as \\server1\profile1. The following steps show you how to set up a roaming user profile.

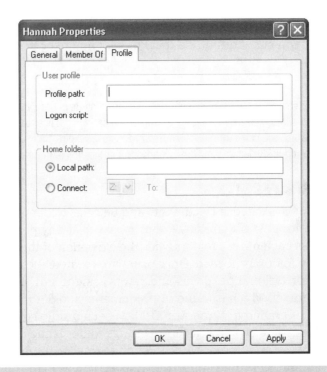

FIGURE 6.8 Profile tab

SETTING UP A ROAMING USER PROFILE

1. On the primary computer that the user accesses, configure a shared Home folder with a desired network path. For example, suppose that a user, JohnM, has an account on a computer, XP49, and a Home folder stored in Documents and Settings\JohnM. Configure the system as desired for JohnM. Or, create a shared folder that can store the profile, and place the folder on a server in the domain environment.

2. Go to the next machine that JohnM will use and create a user account with the same name and password for the user.

3. Access the User Account Properties sheet and click the Profile tab. Choose a desired drive letter, and then enter the Universal Naming Convention (UNC) path to the profile that you originally created. In this example, the profile would be \\XP49\Documents and Settings\JohnM. The user should receive the same settings on the remote computer.

WORKING WITH GROUP ACCOUNTS

Group accounts are used on the local computer to assign certain rights and permissions to certain users. Group configuration is an easy way to manage group rights and permissions. Although not as complicated at the local level, Windows 2000 groups are extremely important in domain environments, where thousands of users may need different types of rights and access. The group account is the preferred method of managing these users.

Windows XP Professional has several built-in groups that you can use. These are

- **Administrators**   Administrators have complete and unrestricted access to the computer.

- **Backup Operators**   Backup Operators can override security restrictions in order to back up and restore data.

- **Users**   Users are restricted to their own individual folders in terms of system configuration. This setting thus restricts users from making systemwide changes. The Users group is more restrictive, as you can see. In fact, a Users group cannot run a number of legacy applications.

- **Guests**   A Guests group has the same permissions as the Users group by default. However, additionally, the Guests group is denied access to the application and system event logs.

- **Network Configuration Operators**   Members of this group have some administrative features that enable them to manage and configure networking.

- **Power Users**   Power Users have most administrative rights, with certain restrictions. They can run most applications, including legacy applications.

- **Remote Desktop Users**   Group members have the right to log on remotely.

As with user accounts, you can easily create a new group by right-clicking on the Group container, then clicking New Group. Enter the group name and a description if desired, and then add members to the group. You can manage the membership of the group by accessing the group's properties.

SIMPLE FILE SHARING AND NTFS PERMISSIONS

Windows XP Professional introduces a new file-sharing feature called Simple File Sharing. This feature is also used in Windows XP Home edition as well. Simple File Sharing is a simplistic way to manage file-sharing permissions, and is designed for home and small office networks. When Simple File Sharing is in use, you simply click a check box to share a folder or printer. Users then basically have read access to the share. You can also assign Modify rights by clicking the Allow Network Users to Change My Files check box. As you can see in Figure 6-9, you can access Simple File Sharing by accessing the Sharing tab, found on a folder's Properties sheets.

So, why Simple File Sharing? As you might guess, the process is, well, simple. Simple File Sharing gives end users in a home or small office network an easy way to share files and folders without the complications of folder and New Technology File System (NTFS) permissions. The problem, though, is that Simple File Sharing does not give you much flexibility—the folder is either

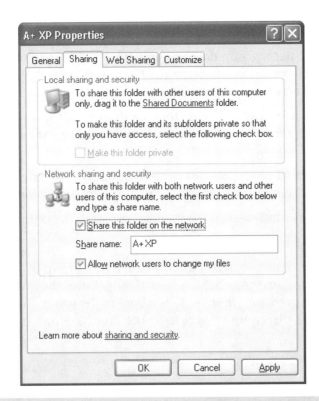

FIGURE 6.9   Simple File Sharing options

shared or not, and full control is either granted or not. You cannot individually assign access control permissions to users. If you are in a home or small office environment that uses Windows XP Home edition, you are unfortunately stuck—simple file sharing is in use and it cannot be disabled. However, if you are using Windows XP Professional, you can disable file sharing so that you can use classic sharing, which uses NTFS and folder permissions. To disable Simple File Sharing on a Windows XP Professional computer, follow the steps described in the following subsection.

DISABLING SIMPLE FILE SHARING

1. On Windows XP Professional, log on as administrator.
2. Open Control Panel, then open the Folder Options applet.
3. Click the View tab.
4. Under Advanced Settings, scroll to the bottom of the list and clear the Use Simple File Sharing check box, shown in Figure 6-10.

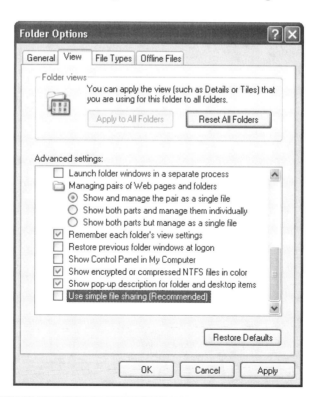

FIGURE 6.10   Disable Simple File Sharing

When you now access the Sharing tab of a folder's properties, you see the classic sharing options and the Security tab so that NTFS permission can be configured.

EXPLORING FILE AND FOLDER PERMISSIONS

File and folder permissions are set on the Security tab found on the Properties sheet of the file or folder. Simply right-click the desired file or folder and click Properties, and then click the Security tab, shown in Figure 6-11. As you can see, you can select a desired group or individual user and configure the desired file-level permissions for that file.

The standard permissions are Full Control, Modify, Read & Execute, Read, Write and Special Permissions. Each of these permissions is actually a

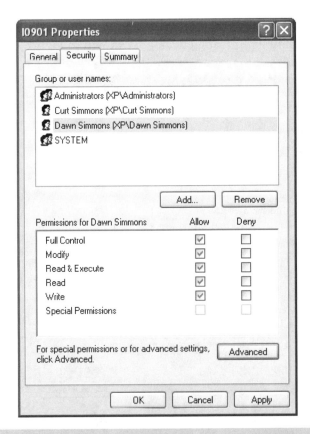

FIGURE 6.11 Security tab found on an individual file

combination of certain special permissions. Before looking at what special permissions make up these standard permissions, let's first consider the special permissions and their definitions, which are described in Table 6-1.

When configuring permissions, keep in mind that if a permission is grayed out, the permission has been inherited from a parent folder. Since the permission is inherited from the parent folder, you can't directly configure permissions at the child folder level.

Now that you have taken a look at the special permissions, let's return standard permissions mentioned previously. Standard permissions are combinations of special permissions that give users or groups certain rights. The following bulleted list tells you which special permissions are included in which standard permissions.

Special Permission	Explanation
Traverse Folder, Execute File	Allows or denies browsing through folders to reach other subfolders. Also allows or denies executing a file.
List Folder, Read Data	List Folder allows or denies viewing file/subfolder names. Read Data allows or denies reading data in a file.
Read Attributes	Allows or denies the reading of attributes of a file or folder.
Read Extended Attributes	Allows or denies the reading of extended attributes of a file or folder.
Create Files, Write Data	Create Files allows or denies the right to create a file in a particular folder. Write Data allows or denies the creation of new data to a file or the overwriting of existing information.
Create Folders, Append Data	Create Files allows or denies the ability to create subfolders in a folder. Append Data allows or denies the appending of data to an existing file. (It does not allow the changing of existing data in the file.)
Write Attributes	Allows or denies the editing of attributes in a file or folder.
Write Extended Attributes	Allows or denies the writing of extended attributes for a file or folder.
Delete Subfolders and Files	Allows or denies the power to delete subfolders and files within a folder.
Delete	Allows the deletion of a file or folder.
Read	Allows or denies reading of a file or folder.
Change Permissions	Allows or denies the ability to change permission for a file or folder.
Take Ownership	Allows or denies the power to take ownership of a file of folder.
Synchronize	Allows or denies the power to synchronize data.

TABLE 6.1   Special Permissions

- **Full Control**   Full Control permissions contains all special permissions.

- **Modify**   Modify permission contains the following special permissions:
  - Traverse Folder, Execute File
  - List Folder, Read Data
  - Read Attributes
  - Read Extended Attributes
  - Create Files, Write Data
  - Create Folders, Append Data
  - Write Attributes, Write Extended Attributes
  - Delete
  - Read
  - Synchronize

- **Read & Execute**   Read & Execute permission contains these special permissions:
  - Traverse Folder, Execute File
  - List Folder, Read Data
  - Read Attributes
  - Read Extended Attributes
  - Read Permission
  - Synchronize

- **Read**   Read permission contains these special permissions:
  - List Folder, Read Data
  - Read Attributes
  - Read Extended Attributes
  - Read
  - Synchronize

- **Write**   Write permission contains these special permissions:
  - Create Files, Write Data
  - Create Folders, Append Data
  - Write Attributes
  - Write Extended Attributes
  - Synchronize

So now that you have taken a look at the file and folder standard permissions and what special permissions make up the standard permissions, it is important for you to know how the permissions work together. You should keep two important rules in mind with NTFS permissions:

- File and folder permissions are cumulative. This means that if a user has Read permission but that same user is a member of a group that has Full Control permission, then the user's effective permission is Full Control. In situations where multiple permissions apply to the same user, then the least restrictive permission takes effect.

- Deny permission overrides all other permissions. This is an exception to the first rule. For example, suppose that a user has Full Control permission but is a member of a group that is denied access. In this case, the user's effective permission is Deny. The user has no access to the file at all.

WORKING WITH ADVANCED NTFS PERMISSIONS

Under most circumstances, the standard permissions of Full Control, Modify, Read & Execute, List Folder Contents, Read, and Write are all you need to manage user access to shared folders and files effectively. However, in some cases, you may need to customize the security settings for a particular user or group. For example, what if you wanted to give a particular group Full Control to a shared folder without the special permission of Take Ownership? You could do so through advanced permissions.

You can easily set advanced permissions for any desired file or folder and apply those advanced permissions to a desired user group. Exercise 9-6 shows you how to configure advanced settings, but before considering the exercise, you need to understand the concept of inheritance. By default, objects in Windows XP Professional as well as Windows 2000 inherit the properties of the parent object. For example, suppose that a particular folder called Docs resides in a shared folder called Company. By default, the properties and permissions of Company are enforced on the Docs folder as well. This inheritance behavior keeps administrators from having to configure folder after folder. Instead, you configure the top-level folder, and all subfolders inherit those settings. As you can guess, this is a great time-saving feature. However, there may be times when you need to override this feature, and you can do so with the advanced security settings as needed. The following steps show you how.

CONFIGURING ADVANCED PERMISSIONS

1. Log on as an administrator.

2. Right-click the desired file or folder and click Properties. Click the Security tab.

3. Choose the desired user or group from the provided list and click the Advanced button.

4. The Advanced Security Settings dialog box appears, as shown in Figure 6-12. Note that the Inherit from Parent the Permission Entries That Apply to Child Objects check box is selected by default. If you want to override inheritance for this object, remove the check from the check box. In the Permission Entries list box, select the user or group for whom you want to change permissions and click the Edit button.

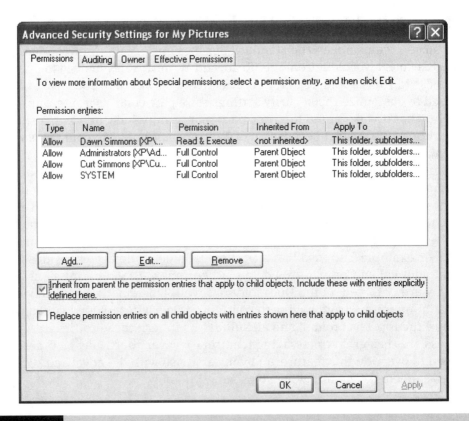

FIGURE 6.12 Advanced Security Settings dialog box

5. In the Permission Entry dialog box, shown in Figure 6-13, click the Apply Onto drop-down menu and select one of the following as applicable:

- This folder, subfolders, and files
- This folder only
- This folder and subfolders
- This folder and files
- Subfolders and files only
- Subfolders only
- Files only

Once you have made your selection, click the desired check boxes in order to configure the permissions of the user or group. Also note that at the bottom of the page, a check box enables you to apply these permissions to objects and/or containers within the existing container. Once you are done, click OK, then click OK again to leave the Advanced Security Settings dialog box.

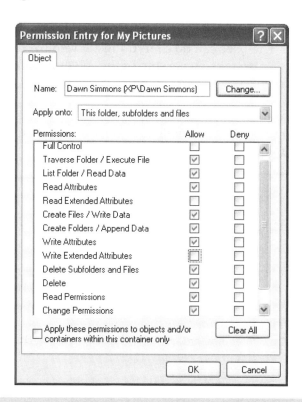

FIGURE 6.13   Select the special permissions you want to apply

WORKING WITH SHARE-LEVEL AND NTFS PERMISSIONS

As you learned in the previous section, a user's effective NTFS permission is the least restrictive permission available. For example, if a user has Read, Write, and Full Control permission based on different groups, then the user has Full Control permission because it is the least restrictive.

Now let's muddy the waters a bit. Windows XP Professional, like Windows 2000, also supports share-level permissions. Share-level permissions are the only permissions available for shared folders that reside on non-NTFS volumes, such as FAT or FAT32. They are a weaker form of permission without all of the advanced options found in NTFS permissions. There are three types of share-level permissions:

- **Read**   The user can view a list of what resides in the shared folder and subfolders, to view data and run applications in the shared folder.

- **Change**   The user can do everything allowed by Read permissions, but the user can also create files and subfolders and edit existing files. The user can also delete files and subfolders in the share.

- **Full Control**   The user can do everything allowed by Read and Change, but the user can also take ownership of the folder and change any existing NTFS permissions.

You can configure share-level permissions by clicking the Permissions button on the Sharing tab for the folder. This opens the Share Permissions tab of the Permissions for My Documents dialog box, where you can configure the permissions based on user or group, as you can see in Figure 6-14.

Like NTFS permissions, a user's cumulative share-level permissions determine the user's effective permission level. For example, if a user has Read permission due to one group membership and Full Control from another group membership, then the user has Full Control over that folder.

This all sounds simple enough. However, what happens when Share and NTFS permissions are mixed, which often happens? For example, suppose that a user belongs to a group that has the Read share-level permission of a folder but Full Control NTFS permission. Which permission does the user get? When share and NTFS permissions conflict, the most restrictive permission is applied—which in this case is Read. As you'll notice, this is the opposite of the

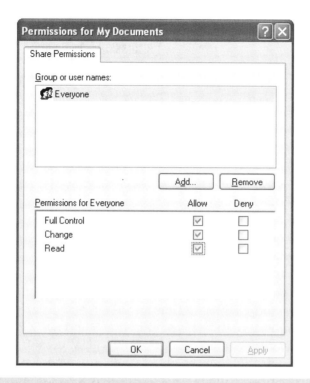

FIGURE 6.14   The Share Permissions tab

cumulative approach provided by NTFS permissions and share-level permissions. How can you keep it all straight? Here's a quick list you can memorize.

- NTFS permissions are cumulative. When a user has several different permissions for the same share, the least restrictive permission applies. The exception is Deny, which overrides all other permissions.

- Share-level permissions are cumulative. When a user has several different permissions for the same share, the least restrictive permission applies. The exception is Deny, which overrides all other permissions.

- When share-level permissions and NTFS permissions are combined, the user receives the most restrictive permission. For example, if a user has Modify NTFS permission for a share but Read share-level permission, the effective permission is Read. Again, Deny overrides everything.

Permission Confusion

As you work with share level and NTFS permissions, it is important to keep things straight. The combination of these permissions are restrictive, which often causes confusion and problems in networking environments. As you work with permissions, it is always best to be as least restrictive as possible. This requires careful consideration and planning on your part.

WRAPPING UP

Windows XP gives you flexibility and a number of configuration options when working with users and groups and permissions. As you are working with Windows XP, it is important to keep in mind that Windows XP Professional is designed for networking environments. However, Microsoft realizes that many networking environments consist of small office networks, or even home networks. For this reason, Windows XP offers easy user account configuration, but also more advanced features as they are needed. The same is true of file and folder permissions. You can use Simple File Sharing, but for greater flexibility and control, NTFS permissions are readily available in Windows XP.

In Chapter 7, we'll turn our attention to managing disks in Windows XP.

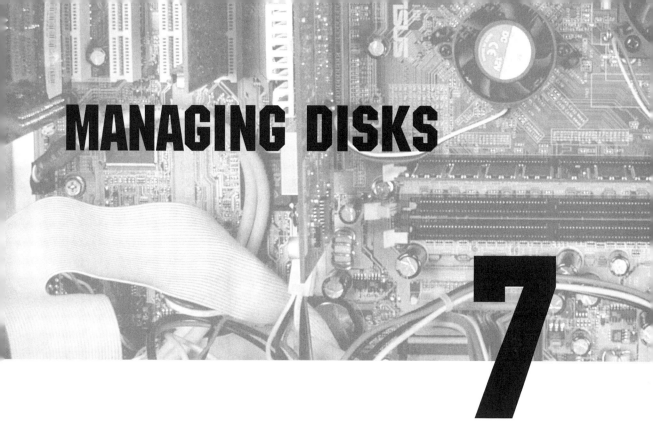

MANAGING DISKS

7

Windows XP Professional provides the same support for dynamic disks as first introduced in Windows 2000, with a few additional interfaces for managing removable disks. As an A+ technician, your job will certainly include configuring and managing hard disks on Windows XP Professional, and the operating system provides quiet a few options. In fact, managing disks can even be complex at first glance, but this chapter sorts through the important disk management topics that you need to know. Specifically, you'll…

- Format and convert drives
- Configure disks
- Use disk tools
- Manage Disk Quotas
- Manage removable disks

FORMATTING AND CONVERTING DRIVES

During the installation of Windows XP Professional, you can choose the file system that you want to use with Windows XP. However, things change, and from time to time you may need to change the file system that is used on a particular Windows XP Professional computer. Windows XP allows you to format and convert disk drives, but you should remember two simple rules about formatting and converting drives:

- You can convert a File Allocation Table (FAT) or FAT32 drive to New Technology File System (NTFS) while preserving your data. Conversion is a one-way process, however. Once you convert to NTFS, you cannot revert back to FAT.

- You cannot convert an NTFS drive to FAT or FAT32 without reformatting the drive. This means that all of your data on the hard disk will be destroyed during the formatting process. You will have to restore all of the data from backup.

If you need to convert a drive to NTFS from FAT, the process is safe and easy; however, it certainly never hurts to perform a backup just to be safe. See the "Using the Backup or Restore Wizard" section later in this chapter to learn more.

CONVERTING A FAT DRIVE TO AN NTFS DRIVE

1. Click Start | Run. Type **command** and click OK.

2. At the command prompt, you will use the Convert command to convert the FAT drive to NTFS. Keep in mind that the conversion process is completely safe and that all of your data will remain as it is. The command and syntax is convert *driveletter:* /FS:NTFS. Shown here, for example, the user is converting drive D to NTFS.

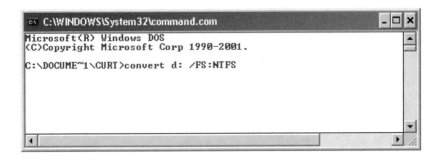

```
C:\WINDOWS\System32\command.com                              _ □ ✕
Microsoft(R) Windows DOS
(C)Copyright Microsoft Corp 1990-2001.

C:\DOCUME~1\CURT>convert d: /FS:NTFS
```

3. Conversion may take several minutes, depending on the size of the drive. When the process is complete, simply exit the command interface.

UNDERSTANDING FILE SYSTEMS

Hard drives are typically installed in a computer in an unformatted state. This means that the operating system is unable to write and read data from the hard disk. Think of an unformatted hard disk as a filing cabinet with no file folders. Without file folders, there is no way to organize and store information on the hard disk. So, to be able to read and write to the hard disk, Windows XP Professional must write a signature to hard disk and format it with a file system.

When the hard disk is formatted, magnetic rings are created on the disk, and the disk is divided into circular areas called sectors. Sectors are then grouped together in clusters. Clusters are logical areas of the disk to which the operating system writes data. Depending on how the operating system handles cluster size, the disk can hold more or less data to accommodate the loss of space resulting from the cluster size configuration.

When formatting the disk, the operating system writes a file system to the disk, which is a way to organize and manage data on that disk. The FAT file system has been around for a number of years, with later releases providing 32-bit support. FAT, or technically FAT16, is a basic file system that was designed to support small disks. Under Windows XP Professional, the FAT16 file system can grow up to 4GB. In other words, 4GB is the maximum amount of cluster storage space and management functionality that FAT16 provides.

FAT32 is significantly different from FAT16 in several ways. First available for Windows 95b, FAT32 supports larger hard drives and smaller file clusters. In other words, you can make use of a large hard drive while simultaneously conserving disk space to accommodate the small cluster size. FAT32 wastes less space on the hard disk than FAT16, and supports 32GB drives. For these reasons, FAT32 is the operating system of choice for Windows 95b, Windows 98, and Windows Me operating systems.

Another file system supported is NTFS. NTFS has been around since the earlier days of Windows NT, but the new version, first supported in Windows 2000 (NTFS5), provides additional features and functions. NTFS is the preferred operating system for Windows XP Professional. NTFS is virtually unlimited because it supports up to 2 terabytes (TB) of data, which is a theorctical number since hard disks are not yet capable of supporting so much data. Essentially, NTFS imposes no limitations on drive size (32 exabytes, theoretically), but that is only one of the advantages that the file system offers. NTFS also supports many features that are not available under the FAT (16 or 32) file system. The primary features of NTFS are

- **NTFS Security** NTFS supports both folder-level and file-level security. You can configure files and folders individually with their own security features, and configure individual security settings for users. Because of file attribute settings, you can finely control security.

- **Encryption** NTFS natively supports data encryption. You can encrypt a folder so that no one else can read it, yet you can continue to use the data in that folder as you normally would. See Chapter 3 to learn more about encryption.

- **Compression** NTFS natively supports data compression. This feature reduces the amount of disk space needed in order to store data, but allows you to continue using data as you normally would (also see Chapter 3).

- **Logging** NTFS maintains a disk log that holds information about the functioning of the NTFS file system. If a hard disk crashes, the log can be helpful in recovering and repairing data.

With these features, along with the unlimited amount of storage space available, it is easy to see why NTFS is the file system of choice for Windows XP Professional computers. The next obvious question is why anyone would ever use FAT. Although NTFS is the best file system and contains numerous features not found in FAT, FAT may still be needed for a number of reasons.

The foremost reasons concern dual-boot systems. Windows 9x and Me do not support the NTFS file system. So, if you want to dual boot between Windows Me and Windows XP Professional, the Windows Me system will not be able to read any data on the Windows XP Professional partition. In dual-boot cases, it is usually best to find the common-ground file system between the two operating systems, and in this case, that file system is FAT32.

One other reason concerns small hard drives. NTFS has a complex structure and some overhead associated with it. For this reason, drives that are 2MB or smaller are best used with FAT. NTFS consumes too much disk space in overhead on such small drives and simply does not work that well. Under most circumstances, of course, you'll use drives greater than 2GB, but it is important to remember NTFS's overhead requirements when choosing a file system.

CONFIGURING HARD DISKS

Windows 2000 introduced several new disk technologies to Windows and made the configuration and management of hard disks much easier than it had been in the past. You can configure, reconfigure, and adjust hard disk settings without rebooting, and you can make a number of changes that were once available only if you chose to reformat the disk.

The same capabilities are available in Windows XP Professional. You can access the Disk Management console through Computer Management, which is available in Start | Control Panel | Administrative Tools | Computer Management. Select Disk Management in the left console pane and you can see the disks and their configuration in the right console pane, as shown in Figure 7-1.

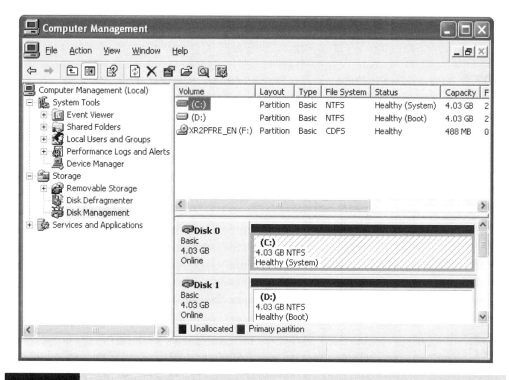

FIGURE 7.1   Disk Management

USING BASIC AND DYNAMIC DISKS

Windows XP Professional, like Windows 2000, continues to support basic and dynamic disks. It is important to define the two types of disks. A basic disk is the same kind of disk that you have always worked with in the past. It is a standard hard disk that supports standard configuration. A basic disk can have a primary partition and extended partitions that make up logical disk drives. For example, you can configure the basic disk so that it has a C drive (primary) and a D drive (extended). You can use the D drive for storage or other purposes (or to set up a dual-boot configuration). On a basic disk, you can have up to four primary partitions, or alternative configurations, such as three primary partitions and one extended partition. One of the primary partitions is considered active and is to start the computer. Basic disks behave as disks have in the past and do not provide the advanced management features supported under Windows XP Professional. Disks are always basic when first installed, but you can convert them to dynamic in order to take advantage of all that Windows XP Professional has to offer.

NOTE Keep in mind that on basic disks, extended partitions are "logical" partitions—they are a logical organization of an existing partition. For this reason, they do not contain drive letters.

A dynamic disk, which currently is supported only on Windows 2000 and XP systems, is a drive configured by the Disk Management console so that it can support volume management. In other words, the Disk Management utilities configure the drive so that it can make use of Windows XP Professional's Disk Management features, such as unlimited volumes, spanned volumes, mirrored volumes, and striped volumes. In essence, if you want to take advantage of volume management and lose the partition restrictions placed on basic disks, you need to convert the disk to a dynamic disk. Otherwise, dynamic disks offer no performance features, so there is no reason to convert. However, if you want to take advantage of volume management, then you can easily convert your existing drives to dynamic disks, as shown in the following steps.

NOTE If you are using Windows XP in a dual-boot scenario, do not convert the disk to dynamic, since previous versions of Windows (excluding Windows 2000) cannot read dynamic disks.

CONVERTING A BASIC DISK TO A DYNAMIC DISK

1. In the Disk Management console, right-click the disk number in the graphical portion of the Disk Management display, and click Convert

to Dynamic Disk. You can also click Action | All Tasks | Convert to Dynamic Disk.

2. In the Convert to Dynamic Disk dialog box, shown here, select the disk that you want to convert, then click OK.

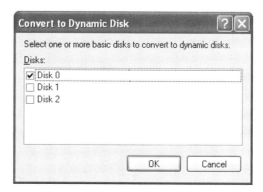

3. In the Disks to Convert dialog box, shown here, review the settings. Click Convert to continue.

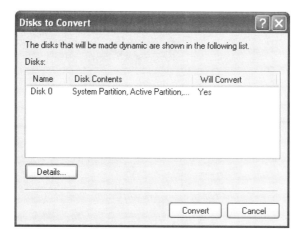

4. You will see a message telling you that other operating systems (down-level systems such as NT, 9x, and Me) will not be able to start from the disk once the conversion has taken place. Click OK to continue.

5. You may see a message telling you that you need to dimount any mounted disks. Click OK to continue.

6. The conversion process occurs, and you are prompted to reboot the computer. Once you reboot, you can see that the disk's status has changed from basic to dynamic, as shown in Figure 7-2.

Once a basic disk has been converted to a dynamic disk, you can begin taking advantage of the features of dynamic disks right away. However, you first should be able to understand and interpret many of the monitoring and management features of dynamic disks, which are explored in the next few sections.

DYNAMIC DISK STATES

Dynamic disks are capable of displaying several different states. This information tells you the current status of the disk and helps you understand problems that

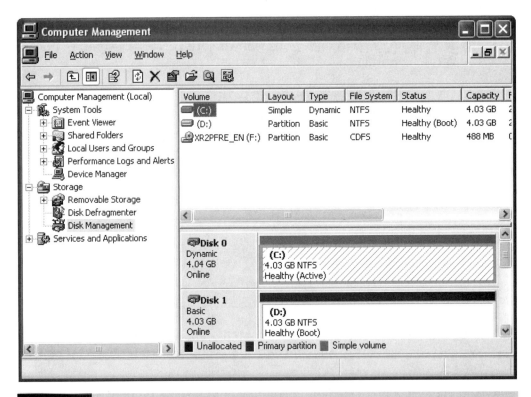

FIGURE 7.2   Check the disk's changed status in Disk Management

may exist. The following bulleted list explains the states that a dynamic disk may display:

- **Online**   The disk is online and functioning with no errors.

- **Online (Errors)**   The disk is online, but there have been some errors. These errors are usually minor. You can usually fix them by running the Error Checking tool found on the Tools menu of the disk's properties dialog box.

- **Offline**   The disk is not accessible. This problem can occur due to corruption or an input/output (I/O) problem. Try right-clicking the disk and then clicking Reactivate Disk in order to bring the disk back online.

- **Missing**   The disk is not accessible or is disconnected, or corruption has caused the disk to be unreadable. Try right-clicking the disk and then clicking Reactive Disk in order to bring the disk back online.

- **Initializing**   This message occurs when the disk is temporarily unavailable due to a conversion to dynamic state.

- **Not Initialized**   This message occurs when you are installing a new disk that does not have a valid signature. When the Disk Management utility appears, the disk appears as "Not Initialized." To write a valid signature so that you can format and begin using the disk, simply right-click the disk, then click Initialize.

- **Foreign**   This status appears when a physical, dynamic disk is moved from a Windows 2000/XP Professional computer to another Windows 2000/XP Professional computer. When this message appears, right-click the disk, then click Import Foreign Disk.

- **Unreadable**   This status appears when I/O errors keep the disk from being readable. Choose Action | Rescan Disks to fix the problem.

- **No Media**   This status appears on removable drives when no media is inserted into the drive.

CONFIGURING DRIVE LETTERS AND PATHS

Dynamic disks make drive letter and path configuration easy. You can assign a drive any alphabet letter, and you can also assign a drive to an empty NTFS folder. First, if you want to make a change to a dynamic disk volume, simply right-click the volume in the Disk Management console, then click Change

Drive Letter and Paths. A simple Change Drive Letter and Paths dialog box appears, as you can see here.

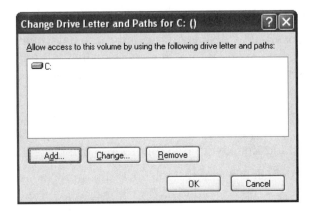

You can do the following actions:

- **Add**   If you click the Add button, a second window appears where you can mount the drive to an empty NTFS folder (which is discussed later in this section). Since a drive can only have one drive letter, you cannot assign multiple drive letters for the same drive.

- **Change**   If you click the Change button, the Change Drive Letter or Path dialog box appears, as you can see here. You can choose a different drive letter from the drop-down menu.

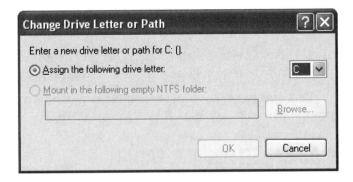

- **Remove**   You can also remove the drive letter. Dynamic disks do not require a drive letter or path to identify a drive. However, some programs may not function if you remove the drive letter.

TECH TALK

Mounting a Volume to an Empty NTFS Folder

In addition to assigning a different drive letter, you can also mount a volume to a local, empty NTFS folder. The purpose is to give you freedom and flexibility beyond the 26-letter alphabet limitation. When you mount a volume to an empty NTFS folder, a drive path is used instead of a drive number. For example, suppose that you have a local volume that is used only for storage. You could create a folder called Storage, and then mount the drive to the empty storage volume. You can then access the drive by simply accessing C:\Storage, just as you would a folder. The result is that you can have an unlimited number of drives and use them like folders rather than standard drive letters that you must keep track of. You can use both a drive letter and a mounted volume on the same drive, if you like. The following steps show you how to mount a volume to an empty NTFS folder:

1. In the Disk Management console, right-click the volume that you want to mount to an empty NTFS folder, then click Change Drive Letter and Paths.

2. In the Change Drive Letter and Paths dialog box, click the Add button.

3. In the Add Drive Letter or Path dialog box, shown here, select the Mount radio button, and then enter the path to the folder that you want to mount, or click the Browse button to select the folder.

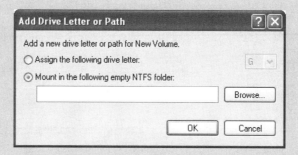

4. If you click the Browse button to browse for the folder, a browse window appears. You can locate the folder or create a new one by clicking the New Folder button. Make your selection and click OK.

5. Click OK again in the Add Drive Letter or Path dialog box. You can now open the drive by simply opening the folder to which it is mapped.

CONFIGURING DISK VOLUMES

Using dynamic disks, you open a world of management possibilities and you break free of the restrictions you often faced with standard disks. When a disk is first converted to a dynamic disk, it will appear in the disk console as unallocated space. This means that the disk has no volumes and has not been formatted. In other words, the operating system cannot use the disk in its current state. Figure 7-3 shows you the appearance of an unallocated disk.

CREATING SIMPLE VOLUMES

To use the disk, you must first create a simple volume on the disk. The following steps guide you through this process.

CREATING A SIMPLE VOLUME

1. In the Disk Management console, right-click the dynamic disk's unallocated space and click New Volume.

2. The New Volume Wizard appears. Click Next to continue.

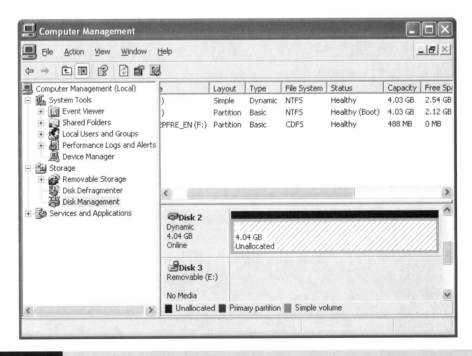

FIGURE 7.3   Dynamic disk with unallocated space

3. In the Select Volume Type window, shown here, click the Simple radio button and click Next.

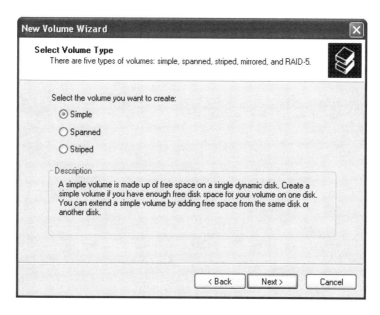

4. In the Select Disks window, shown here, select the disk that you want to configure (which is already selected for you under this wizard), then enter the size of the volume (in megabytes) that you want to create. The maximum amount of space available is listed here for you as well. Click Next.

5. In the Assign Drive Letter or Path window, choose a drive, assign an empty NTFS folder, or do not assign either. Click Next.

6. In the Format Volume window, shown here, you can choose to format the volume or not, and you can choose to use the quick format feature and enable file and folder compression for the volume. Make your selections and click Next.

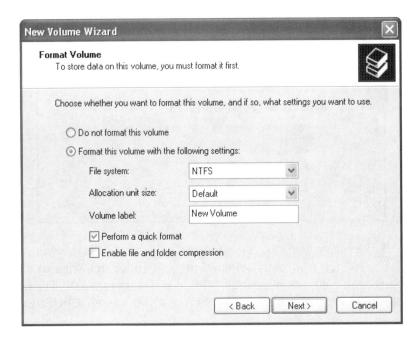

7. Click Finish. The new volume is created and appears in the Disk Management console.

Once the dynamic volume has been created and formatted, you can then begin using the volume for storage purposes. Keep in mind that you can right-click the volume in the Disk Management console to change drive letters and paths, extend the volume (adding more free space to it), format the volume (erasing all existing data), delete the volume (erasing all existing data), and access the volume's properties.

CREATING SPANNED VOLUMES

Aside from supporting the simple volume, Windows XP Professional also supports spanned volumes. A spanned volume combines areas of unallocated space on multiple disks into one logical volume. You can combine between 2 and 32 areas of unallocated space from different drives. For example, suppose that a computer has three hard drives. Each drive has about 500MB of unallocated free space. A 500MB volume is rather small and not very practical for everyday use. However, using the spanned volume option, you could combine all three 500MB areas of unallocated space to create a 1.5GB volume. You can then use the volume just as though the storage were located on a single disk. Essentially, this configuration gives you more flexibility and fewer volumes (and drive letters to maintain), and makes good use of leftover space.

After creating the spanned volume, you see it as any other volume in My Computer or the Disk Management console. It is important to note, however, that spanned volumes are storage solutions only—they do not provide any fault tolerance. If one disk in the spanned volume is lost, all data on the spanned volume is lost. However, you can back up a spanned volume just as you would any other volume.

Disk Fault Tolerance

Keep in mind that Windows XP Professional does not provide any disk fault tolerance. For example, Windows 2000 Server provides mirrored volumes and RAID-5 volumes so that you can recover data from a single disk failure. However, these features are not supported under Windows XP Professional (or even Windows 2000 Professional, for that matter). A spanned volume is a great storage solution, but it does not provide fault tolerance—if one of the disks used in the spanned volume fails, the entire volume is lost. This is why data backup is so important—you do not have any internal, disk-management options for fault tolerance, so be careful!

CREATING A SPANNED VOLUME

1. In the Disk Management console, right-click one of the areas of
   unallocated disk space on one of the disks and click New Volume.

2. The New Volume Wizard appears. Click Next to continue.

3. In the Select Volume Type window, shown here, click the Spanned
   option, and then click Next.

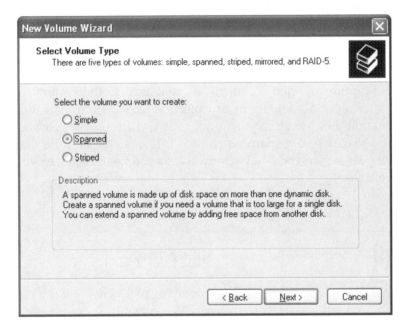

4. In the Select Disks window, the current disk appears in the Selected list
   box. Choose the free space on the desired disk(s) that appears on the
   Available list box and click the Add button. Repeat the process until all
   unallocated areas that you want to use appear in the Selected list box.
   Click Next.

5. In the Assign Drive Letter or Path window, choose a drive letter or mount
   the drive to an empty NTFS folder. You can also choose not to assign a
   drive letter or path at this time. Click Next.

6. In the Format Volume window, choose whether or not to format the
   volume at this time and whether or not to perform a quick format.
   Select the Enable File and Folder Compression check box. Click Next.

7. Click Finish. The volume is created and now appears in the Disk Management console.

 As with a simple volume, you can extend a spanned volume by adding more unallocated space to it. Simply right-click the volume in the Disk Management console and click Extend Volume. To add more unallocated space, follow the wizard steps that appear.

CREATING STRIPED VOLUMES

Striped volumes are similar to spanned volumes in that they combine areas of free disk space (between 2 and 32 areas of unallocated space on different drives) in order to create one logical volume. However, the big difference is that striped volumes write data across the disks instead of filling one portion of free space first, then the next portion, and so on. Thus you are likely to see faster read and write performance than you will with a simple spanned volume. As with a spanned volume, you can create a striped volume by right-clicking one of the areas of unallocated space and clicking Create Volume. In the Create New Volume Wizard, choose to create a striped volume.

Another important point concerning striped volumes is that the areas of unallocated free space must be the same size. For example, suppose that you want to use 500MB, 800MB, and 900MB areas of unallocated disk space to create a striped volume. Since the areas have to be the same size, Disk Management will configure 500MB from each disk, which means that you will still have some unallocated space left over. This configuration enables data to be written evenly across the disks. As with spanned volumes, striped volumes provide no fault tolerance.

NOTE You cannot extend a striped volume. Only simple and spanned volumes can be extended.

MANAGING REMOTE DISKS

Using the Disk Administrator console, you can also manage remote disks on Windows XP Professional computers. This feature enables you to manage disks on other Windows XP Professional computers in a Windows domain. To access Disk Management on other Windows XP Professional computers, you must be a member of at least the domain administrators group or the server operators group. In a workgroup environment, you can also remotely manage disks by having the same administrative account name on the computers that you wish to manage. To manage a disk remotely, follow the steps described in the following section.

MANAGING DISKS ON A REMOTE COMPUTER

1. Log on to the Windows XP Professional with the proper permissions.

2. Click Start | Run and type **MMC**. Click OK.

3. In the MMC console that appears, click Console | Add/Remove Snap-In.

4. In the Snap-Ins dialog box, click Add and select Disk Management from the selection list. Click Add.

5. In the Selection window that appears, choose a different computer, and then enter the computer's name (or browse for the name). Click Finish.

6. Click Close on the Snap-Ins dialog box and click OK to begin using the Disk Management snap-in.

USING DISK PROPERTIES

Each disk volume contains Properties pages that you can access by right-clicking the volume and clicking Properties. Using the Properties pages, you can configure several different items on the hard disk. The Properties pages are generally self-explanatory, but keep the following items in mind:

- On the General tab, you can see how much disk space has been used, and you can also enable compression and indexing.

- On the Tools tab, you can run the error-checking tool, Disk Defragmenter, and the Backup or Restore Wizard. See the "Using Disk Tools" section later in this chapter for more information.

- The Hardware tab enables you to view information and troubleshoot hardware devices. See Chapter 4 to learn more about hardware.

- The Sharing tab enables to you share an entire volume.

- You can configure Disk Quotas, a feature available on Windows XP Professional, so that users who are storing data on your computer (such as over the network) are limited by the amount of data that they can store. See the "Using Disk Quota Management" section later in this chapter for more information.

USING DISK TOOLS

Windows XP Professional provides a few built-in tools that can help you manage hard disks and data and solve problems that might come your way. Windows XP also gives you a Backup or Restore Wizard.

NOTE Windows XP Professional provides the backup utility as a part of System Tools. Oddly enough, Windows XP Home edition does not provide this tool. However, you can find the backup utility lurking on the Windows XP Home edition installation CD-ROM, from which you can install and use it. If you browse the installation CD-ROM, you'll find the backup tool in \valueadd\msft\ntbackup.

USING ERROR CHECKING AND DISK DEFRAGMENTER

The error-checking and Disk Defragmenter tools are found on the Tools tab of the disk's Properties dialog box. You'll also find Disk Defragmenter in Start | All Programs | Accessories | System Tools. The error-checking tool is a simple tool that can scan the hard disk and fix basic problems that it finds. These include file system errors and recovery of bad disk sectors. As a general rule, you do not need to run the error-checking tool unless you are experiencing disk problems, or if you needed to invoke a hard reboot of the system (by pressing CTRL-ALT-DEL). If you need to run error checking, just click the Error Checking button on the Tools tab. You'll see a simple dialog box where you can start the scan.

The next tool that you can use is Disk Defragmenter. Over time, fragmentation occurs in file systems. Fragmentation is a normal part of disk use and occurs when files are not written contiguously on the hard disk. As more and more files are fragmented, Windows XP requires more time to read and write data to the hard disk. As a general rule, you should get in the habit of running Disk Defragmenter every few months to reduce fragmentation. The telltale sign that a disk is heavily fragmented is simply slow data reading and writing.

The good news is that Windows XP's Disk Defragmenter can analyze a disk for you and perform the defragmentation if necessary. Simply open the disk defragmenter, as shown in Figure 7-4, and use the interface to analyze and defragment the disk. Note that disk defragmentation can take some time to perform—up to several hours—and you should close all programs (including any antivirus programs) because the tool needs exclusive access to the disk in order to work correctly.

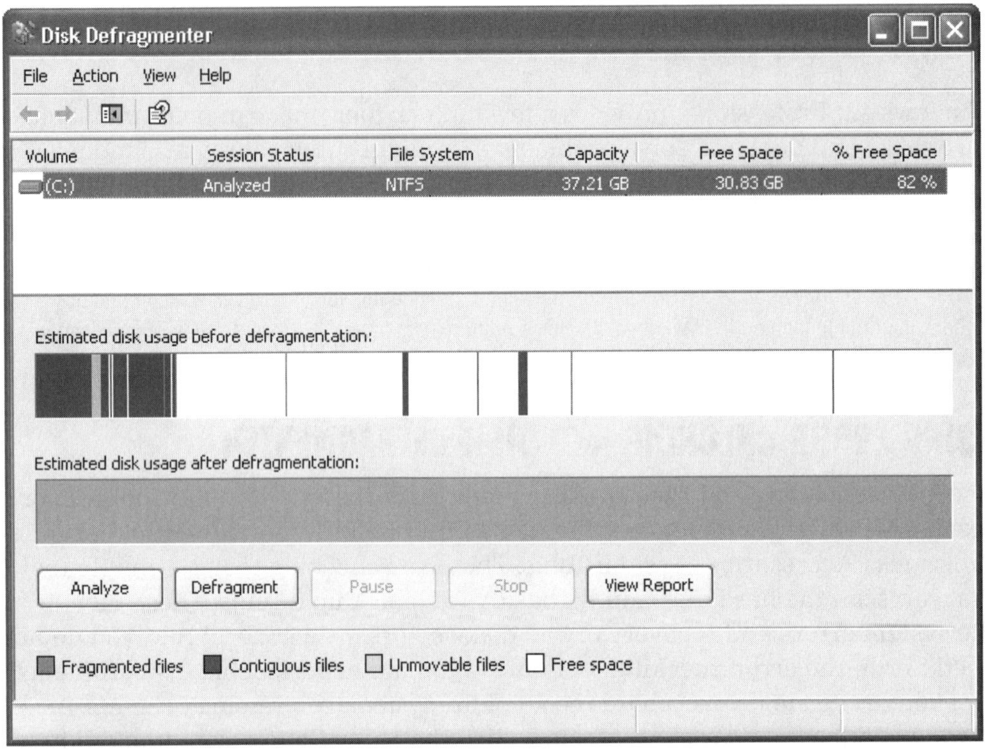

FIGURE 7.4 Disk Defragmenter

NOTE There is also a Disk Cleanup tool found in Start | All Programs | Accessories | System Tools. The Disk Cleanup tool simply helps you locate unneeded or unused files so you can delete them. A wizard guides you through the cleanup process.

USING THE BACKUP OR RESTORE WIZARD

Windows XP Professional supports the same backup and restore features that were first introduced in Windows 2000 Professional. As you can read in most technical books, the importance of an effective backup plan cannot be understated. By effectively backing up data and following an effective backup plan, you can recover a failed operating system without losing any data.

It is important to understand the different kinds of backup and restore features that are available and how to back up and restore data on a Windows XP Professional computer. The following sections explore the issues and skills you need concerning backup and restore operations.

Windows XP Professional supports several different types of backups, all of which can be performed on NTFS and FAT drives.

- **Normal**   A normal backup backs up all selected files and marks them has having been backed up. All files you select are backed up, regardless of their previous backup state. You use this type of backup, also known as a Full backup, to perform the initial backup of your data.

- **Incremental**   An incremental backup backs up all selected files that have changed since the last backup. Commonly, a normal backup is performed, followed by several incremental backups, which only back up the changes. This backup strategy reduces overall backup time and storage space.

- **Differential**   A differential backup is the same as an incremental backup, but the files backed up are not marked as having been backed up. The result is that a differential backup may re-backup files that have not changed because they are not being marked. The difference between an incremental backup and a differential backup is recovery. A differential backup takes longer than an incremental back up, but in the event of a failure, you only need to run the normal backup job for recovery with the differential backup. If you were using an incremental backup job, you would have to recover the normal backup and every incremental backup that was created since the last normal backup.

- **Copy**   A copy backup backs up selected files without marking them as having been backed up. This option is useful when you want to back up certain files between normal and incremental backups without altering the incremental backup jobs.

- **Daily**   This backup backs up all selected files that have changed during the day without marking them as having been backed up.

When you are ready to back up data, you can do so easily with Windows XP Professional's Backup or Restore Wizard. The following steps walk you through the process.

CREATING A BACKUP JOB

1. Click Start | All Programs | Accessories | System Tools | Backup.
2. The Backup or Restore Wizard appears. Click Next on the Welcome screen.
3. In the Backup or Restore window, choose the Back Up Files and Settings radio button and click Next.

TROUBLESHOOTING

Using the Right Backup

The different types of backup can certainly cause some confusion and give you backup jobs that you really don't want, if you are not careful. The trick is to make sure you understand the different types of backup and how they are used when you restore data—case in point: incremental and differential backups.

Incremental and differential backups can be confusing, but they are really about time. Incremental backups are faster, but it takes more time to restore data fully in the event of a failure because you may have to run several different incremental backup jobs. Differential backups are slower to create, but faster when recovery is needed because you only have to run the single differential backup, along with the normal backup. So, it is simply a time trade-off: You can make backups faster, but recovery slower, or you can make recovery faster, but backups slower—it's just a matter of choice.

4. In the What to Back Up window, shown here, you can choose a category to back up, or you can choose the custom option. Make a selection and click Next.

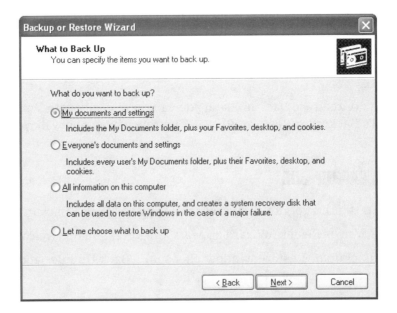

5. If you choose what to back up, the Items to Back Up window appears, as shown here. In this Explorer-based window, browse in the left pane, then select the files that you want to back up in the right pane. Click Next.

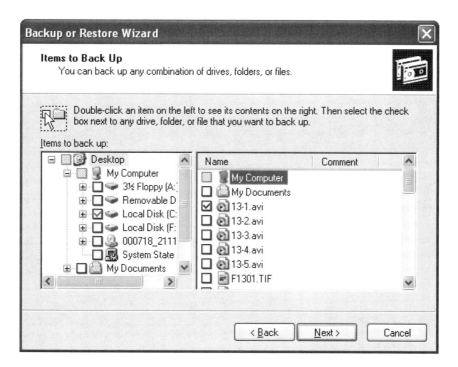

6. In the Backup Type, Destination, and Name window, choose a backup location and give the backup job a name. Click Next.

7. In the Completion window, click the Advanced button instead of clicking Finish.

8. In the Type of Backup window, use the drop-down menu and choose either a Normal, Incremental, Differential, Copy, or Daily backup.

9. In the How to Back Up window, you can choose to verify data after backup, use hardware compression (if available), and disable volume shadow copy (which allows a backup to occur, even if the file is currently being written to). Click Next.

10. In the Backup Options window, shown here, you can choose to append this backup job to an existing backup job or replace an older backup job. Also note that you can allow only the owner and administrator to have access to the backup (if you are overwriting an older job). Make your selection, then click Next.

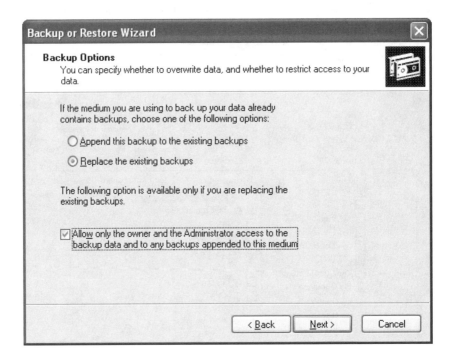

11. In the When to Back Up window, you can choose to run the backup job now or at a scheduled time. Make any desired selections and click Next.

12. Click Finish. The backup job completes. Click Close when the job is complete.

As you see in the Backup or Restore Wizard, you have basic options to back up everything on your computer, or you can back up selected files and folders. If you simply want to back up user data, choose the My Documents and Settings option or the Everyone's Documents and Settings option, or the Let Me Choose What to Back Up option in the wizard's What to Back Up window. However, you can also back up everything on the computer, including system state data, by choosing the All Information on This Computer option. System state data refers to a collection of operating system data, which includes the Registry, COM+ Class Registrations, system boot files, and related operating system data. To back up specific user data or system state data, you can simply select the Let Me Choose

What to Back Up option in the wizard, and then choose the user data or select system state data. However, you may find it easier to make the desired selections manually instead of using the Backup or Restore Wizard.

MANUALLY CREATING A BACKUP JOB

1. Click Start | All Programs | Accessories | System Tools | Backup.

2. In the Backup Utility dialog box, click the Backup tab, shown in Figure 7-5. In the left pane, select the System State check box. Note the Backup Destination and Backup Media or File Name fields at the bottom of the screen. You can change these values if desired. Click the Start Backup button.

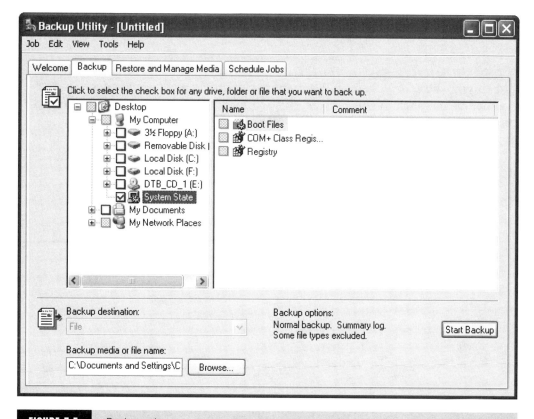

FIGURE 7.5   Backup tab

3. In the Backup Job Information dialog box, you'll see the option to enter a backup description and append or replace former backup jobs, as shown here. Make any desired changes.

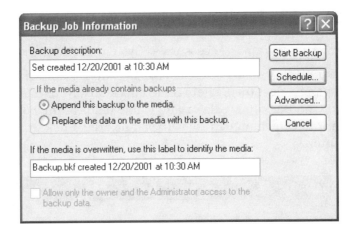

4. If you click the Schedule button, you can create a schedule specifying when the backup should start. Also note that you can click the Advanced button to display the Advanced Backup Options dialog box shown here. Here you can choose the advanced backup options, such as verification and backup type, that you saw when using the wizard. Make any desired changes and click OK.

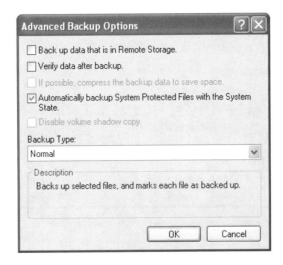

5. Click the Start Backup button to begin the backup job.

RESTORING DATA

In the event of user data, system state data, or a complete operating system failure, you can use the backup jobs that you have created to restore the data to the computer. In the event of a disk failure or operating system failure, you can reinstall Windows XP, and then use your backup jobs to restore the data or the complete operating system that has been saved in your backup jobs. As with backing up data, you can also restore data with the help of a wizard.

When you restore data, you choose the backup file that you want to restore using the Restore Wizard (or you can simply use the Restore and Manage Media tab on the Backup Utility dialog box). You can choose to restore the data to its original location or you can choose a different location.

USING DISK QUOTA MANAGEMENT

Disk Quota management, a feature introduced in Windows 2000, enables you to control user storage capabilities. Suppose that you are using Windows XP as a file server and user storage center. You want to have users store files and folders on the shared hard disk, but you do not want users storing more than 500MB of data. This restriction keeps users from wasting a lot of disk space storing items they no longer need. Using Disk Quotas, you can easily configure this restriction. When users begin running out of storage space, they will receive warning messages. Depending on your configuration, you can even prevent users from storing data until they have removed old data in order to stay below the 500MB limit.

NOTE Disk Quota management works only on NTFS volumes. Also, users cannot compress data in order to store more than their quota limits.

Disk Quotas are available on the Quota tab found on the disk's Properties dialog box, as shown in Figure 7-6. You can enable Disk Quota management on the Quota tab by clicking the Enable Quota Management check box. Once you enable Disk Quota management, you have a few configuration options available to you:

- **Deny Disk Space** You can use Disk Quota management to deny disk space to users who exceed the quota limit, or you can use it to warn users

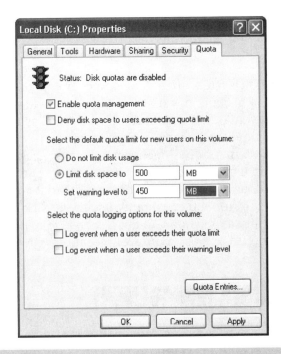

FIGURE 7.6 Quota tab

without actually denying them disk space. If you strictly want to enforce quota management, you can choose the deny option by clicking this check box.

- **Limit Disk Space** You can set the amount of disk space that a user can have in the quota, and you can also set a warning level. The warning level is generally set to an amount slightly lower than the quota.

- **Select the Quota Logging Options** You can use the final two check boxes to log events to the event log when users exceed their storage limits or reach the warning level. These options are not available by default, but you can enable them if you like.

Once quotas are enabled on a disk, they apply uniformly to all network users who store data on the disk. However, what if you need an exception? What if you need to give certain users unlimited access while giving other users even more restrictive access? In this case, you can create a quota entry for that user. A quota entry further defines the user quota and overrides any existing general settings configured on the Quota tab. To configure a quota entry, just follow these steps.

CONFIGURING A QUOTA ENTRY

1. On the Quota tab, click the Quota Entries button. This opens the Quota Entries dialog box, as shown here.

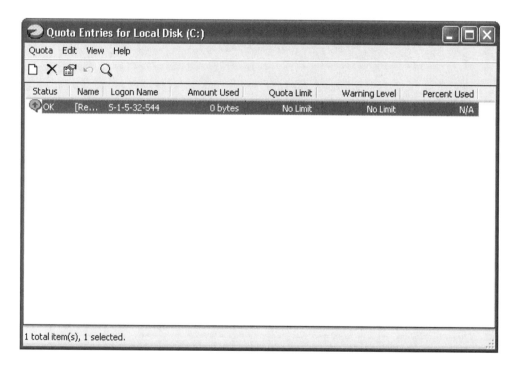

2. Choose Quota | New Quota Entry. This opens the Select Users dialog box, shown here.

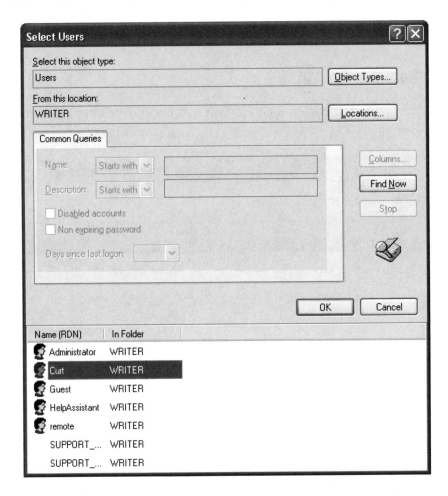

3. In the Select Users dialog box, you can search for and select the user that you want to add. When you have selected the user, click the OK button.

4. The Add New Quota Entry dialog box appears, as shown next. You can choose not to limit disk space, or you can set the quota and warning level

for the selected user. This feature allows you to have flexibility for users who need more storage space.

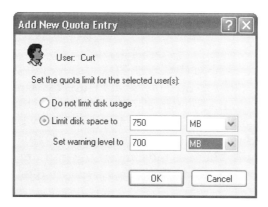

5. The new entry now appears in the Quota Entries dialog box. You can edit and change the entry, or delete it using this console.

MANAGING REMOVABLE DISKS

Aside from managing your hard disk in Windows XP, you'll also need to manage CD-ROM, DVD-ROM, Zip drives, and other types of removable storage. CD and DVD-ROM drives (or combo drives) are standard on computers today, and in many cases, computer systems now have multiple CD/DVD drives and CD read/write drives. As with any hardware device, internal CD/DVD drives must be attached to the system and detected by plug and play. You can then install the manufacturer's driver, and often you'll get additional software, such as third-party media players and CD burner software. The good news is that CD/DVD-ROM drives and CD read/write drives work better than ever before with Windows XP, and Windows XP typically identifies CD read/write drives as such. With DVD drives, you can watch movies on your Windows XP screen. Standard playback features, such as Dolby Digital, are supported and used for DVD playback. For CD-ROM drives, the CDFS file system is used. For DVD disks, the Universal Disk Format (UDF) file system is used. CDFS and UDF are industry standards natively supported in Windows XP.

As with all hardware, the trick when installing new internal or external CD-ROM devices is to use devices that are listed on the Hardware Compatibility List (HCL) and make sure you have the most recent driver. A secondary note about installation concerns audio playback. If you expand the CD/DVD category in Device Manager, you'll see your CD/DVD-ROM drives listed, as shown in Figure 7-7.

If you right-click the desired CD/DVD-ROM drive, then click Properties, you'll see a Properties tab. As you can see in Figure 7-8, you can adjust the overall CD volume here, and you can also determine whether or not the drive is allowed to play CD music. If you are having problems with a CD-ROM drive not playing music, be sure to check the setting on this tab.

You can also check the Volumes tab and see the partition setup of the CD, as well as its capacity, status, and other general information about the state of the disk.

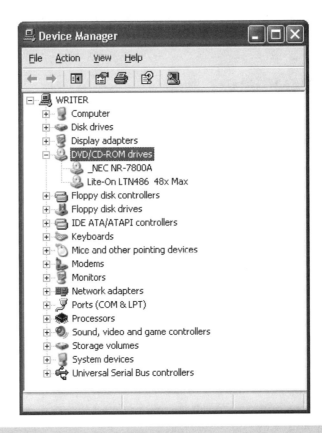

FIGURE 7.7   CD/DVD drives in Device Manager

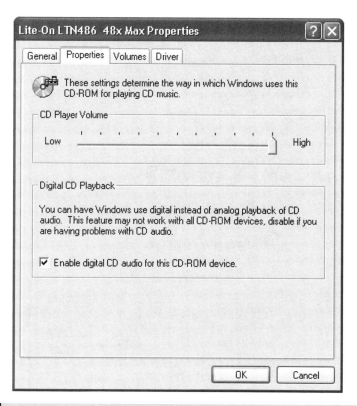

FIGURE 7.8   CD-ROM Properties tab

In addition to setting these configuration options, you can also right-click the disk in My Computer and click Properties. This gives you the same tabs you see with other hard disks. For removable disks, however, you'll also see an AutoPlay tab, shown in Figure 7-9. This tab, which is new in Windows XP, enables you to select a default action that should occur when a certain type of file is opened from the removable disk. For example, as you can see in Figure 7-9, the user is making certain that all music files are open and played with Windows Media Player. You can also use the prompt option, however, so that you can choose which action you want to take for a particular file.

Other types of removable media drives—such as Zip, jazz, or tape drives—function in the same basic way. You can install them by connecting them to an appropriate port and allowing plug and play to detect the drives. From that point, you can install an appropriate driver. Windows XP supports a number of industry standard tape drives for backup purposes, and you can support such drives by using Windows XP's Removable Storage Console found in Computer Management.

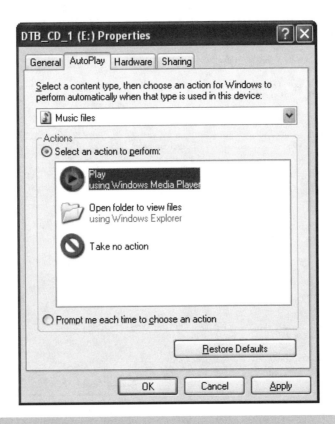

FIGURE 7.9 AutoPlay tab

WRAPPING UP

Windows XP's Disk Management console provides you the tools and features you need to configure hard disks easily. Windows XP's volume management works with dynamic disks, and you easily configure storage solutions, such as spanned and mirrored volumes. You can also use Windows XP's disk tools to solve disk problems and even implement disk quotas when Windows XP is used as a file server. Finally, you can also manage Windows XP removable drives through Device Manager. All of these features make Windows XP's disk management easy and versatile.

In the next chapter, we'll take a look at Windows XP printing.

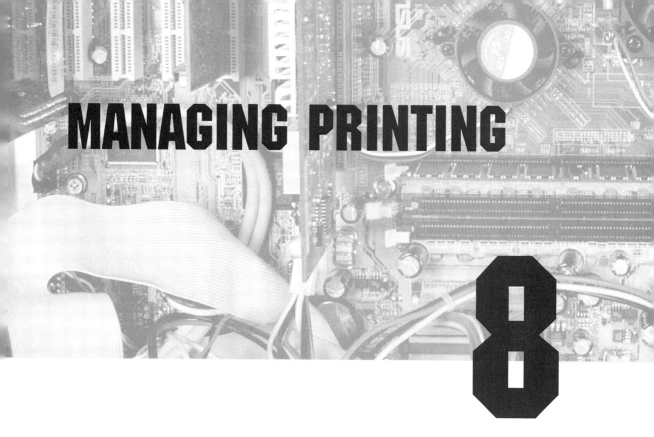

MANAGING PRINTING

8

Printing is one of those seemingly innocent topics that should be plain and simple in terms of management, but in fact, printing has often been a nightmare for both end users and technicians like you. Why? The simple reality is that printing is a complex process, and the printing needs from environment to environment vary greatly. As an A+ technician, you may be faced with the task of administering and managing printing on Windows XP Professional computers on your network. The good news is that Windows XP includes new software that makes printer management easier and typically less problematic. In this chapter, you'll take a look at all Windows XP has to offer you in terms of printing. Specifically, you'll…

- Install printers
- Connect to network printers
- Configure printer options
- Manage printer permissions
- Use the Fax Console

INSTALLING PRINTERS

Printer installation on Windows XP is generally easy, since Windows XP can automatically detect new printers that are attached to it, and the operating system gives you a printer installation wizard, in case you have problems. However, before you get into the topic of installing a printer on a Windows XP computer, you should briefly consider a few conceptual issues that will make your work with Windows XP printing easier. First, if you have been around Microsoft technology for any period of time, you are probably familiar with the basic definitions of *printer* and *print device*. If not, consider this your first lesson. A printer is the software on a Windows XP computer that drives and manages a print device, which is the physical printer sitting on the desk. In common terms, we typically refer to a printer as the device that generates the printed pages, but in Microsoft terms, this is the print device, and the printer is the software installed on Windows XP.

The printing process itself is rather complex. As an A+ technician, you don't need to know all of the software programming lingo and operating system layers that make printing work; however, it's a good idea to have a general idea of what happens when you choose to print something. Whatever application you are using sends the file you want to print as a print job to the printer driver. Commonly, a series of calls are made to the graphical device interface (GDI), which handles the printing. The print driver then converts the GDI data for the print drive into instruction-specific data for the printer. This information tells the printer what to do in order to re-create the document in print form. This information then goes to the print processor, which routes the data to the correct local or network printer. The job then goes to a spooler, which can either be local or on the network. The spooler's job is to hold the print job until the print device can actually get to the job. You can think of the spooler as a queue that holds the data until the print device is ready. When the print device is ready, the print job goes to the print monitor, which then sends the job to the print device where it is actually printed. As you can see, the process of printing an item is rather complex, but all of these actions are hidden from the user's view. To the user, it appears as though a job is simply sent and printed.

To use a printer on Windows XP, you first, of course, must install a print device, along with the correct printer software. Print devices are like all other hardware devices – you should check the Hardware Compatibility List (HCL) and use only print devices that are compatible with Windows XP. Typically, you install a print device by connecting the device to the correct port, such as the LPT port or USB port (IrDA options are also available), and then installing the printer manufacturer's software that accompanies the print device. This sets up the printer on Windows XP so that applications can use it and network users can access it, if you choose to share it for network use. If you have problems installing the printer this way, you can also use the Add a Printer Wizard, found in the Printers and Faxes folder in Control Panel. The following steps walk you through the wizard.

NOTE Manufacturers regularly update printer drivers. If you are trying to use a printer driver that is pre-Windows XP, you can probably find an updated driver on the manufacturer's Web site. Although you may be able to use an older driver, you are much more likely to experience problems if you do so. Always check the manufacturer's Web site and download the latest printer drivers that are available. Just because the print device is "new" and you have a manufacturer's installation CD, that does not mean that you will find the latest drivers on that CD.

USING THE ADD A PRINTER WIZARD

1. Attach the print device to the correct port and turn the device on. See the manufacturer's documentation for specific instructions.

2. Open the Printers and Faxes folder in Control Panel. Click the Add a Printer Wizard to start it.

3. The Welcome screen appears. Note that if you are using a USB, infrared, or IEEE 1394 print device, Windows XP can install it automatically without the help of this wizard. Click Next.

4. In the Local or Network Printer window, shown next, choose whether the printer is a local or network printer. For the exercise, assume that the printer is Local. When you choose the Local option, you can also click

the check box for plug and play detection so that Windows can automatically detect and install the printer. Click Next.

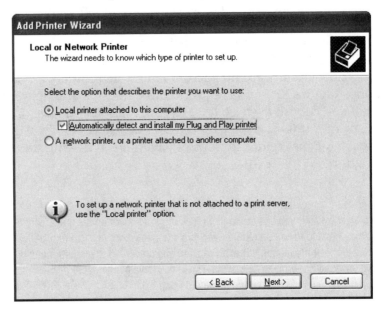

5. Windows searches for a new plug and play printer. If the printer is found, Windows installs it automatically. If not, you see a message telling you that you can install the printer manually. Click Next.

6. In the Select a Port window, you can use an existing port or create a new port type. Typically, you would use the LPT1 port, as shown next. Click Next.

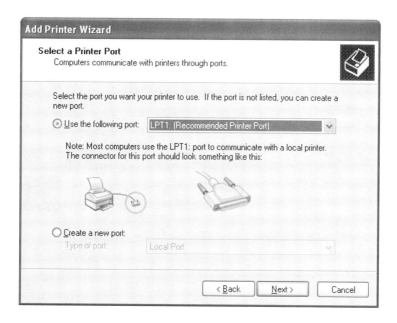

7. In the Install Printer Software window, choose the manufacturer and printer model to install, as shown here You can also click the Have Disk button to install the software from a manufacturer's disk. Make your selections and click Next.

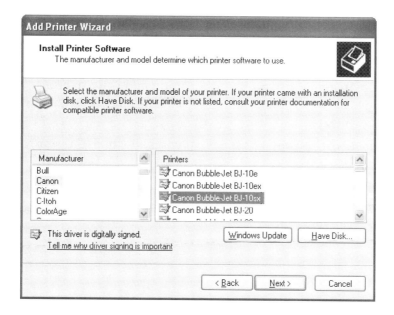

8. Enter a desired name for the printer or accept the default. If you want to use the printer as your default printer, click the Yes button; if you do not want to use it as the default, click No. Click Next.

9. You can choose to share the printer, as shown here. Choose the desired radio button. If you want to share the printer, give it a share name that network clients will recognize.

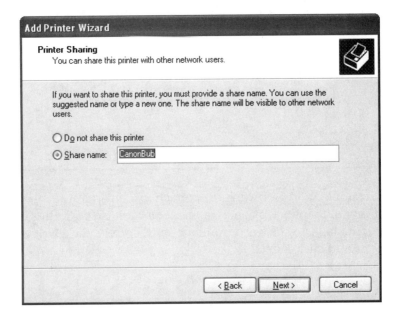

10. If you chose to share the printer, a window appears where you can enter information about the computer's location and you can add any necessary comments. Network users can read this information. Make any additions here and click Next.

11. You can choose to print a test page if you like. Choose Yes or No, then click Next.

12. Click Finish. The new printer is installed and now appears in the Printers and Faxes folder.

CONFIGURING A NETWORK PRINTER

In addition to installing a local printer on a Windows XP computer, you can also configure a printer that connects to a network or Internet print device. Keep in mind that a printer is simply the software that allows you to connect to a print device, whether that print device is local, on a network, or even on the Internet. Additionally, you can even configure several printers for the same print device that use different configurations. That may seem a little confusing, but this section will help you sort it out.

You can connect to another printer on your network and print to that printer. Typically, on Microsoft networks, a certain computer functions as a print server, and clients connect to that print server to use the printer. Windows XP Professional is quite capable of functioning as a print server. You can easily connect to a network printer by using the Add a Printer Wizard in the Printers and Faxes folder, as shown in the following steps.

CONNECTING TO A NETWORK PRINTER

1. Open the Printers and Faxes folder in Control Panel. Click the Add a Printer Wizard to start it.

2. Click Next on the Welcome screen.

3. In the Local or Network Printer window, select the Network Printer radio button. Then click Next.

4. In the Specify a Printer window, shown in Figure 8-5, you have a few different options. First, you can choose to browse for a printer. If you click this option and then click Next, you see a selection window where you can select the printer you want to use. You can select a shared network printer that you see in the window, then click Next to install it. If you know the UNC path of the printer to which you want to connect, select the radio button and enter the path. As shown next, the user is connecting to a computer named Writer and using the Epson printer attached to it. You'll

see how to connect to an Internet printer later in this section. Make your selection and click Next.

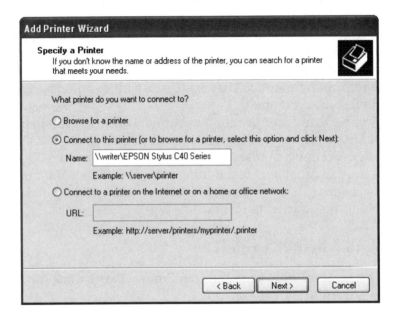

5. The wizard asks whether you want to make this the default printer. Click Yes or No.

6. The printer is installed on your computer. The Test Page window appears. If you want to print a test page, choose Yes and click Next.

7. Click Finish.

In addition to connecting to a network printer, you can also share a printer that is connected to Windows XP Professional (and Home edition, for that matter). You can share the printer when you first run the Add a Printer Wizard, or if you decide to share the printer later, once it is already installed, you can easily do so by accessing the printer's Properties pages and choosing to share the printer. The following steps show you how to share a printer.

SHARING A PRINTER

1. Open the Printers and Faxes folder in Control Panel.

2. Right-click the desired printer's icon and click Properties.

3. Click the Sharing tab, shown in Figure 8-1. To share the printer, choose the Share This Printer radio button and enter a share name. This is the name that all other clients on your network will use, so make sure it is descriptive.

4. Since some computers on your network might not run Windows XP, you also have the option to install additional drivers for down-level clients, such as Windows 2000 or Windows 9x. This feature installs the driver on the XP computer, which can then make it available for download to other clients as needed. To install additional drivers, click the Additional

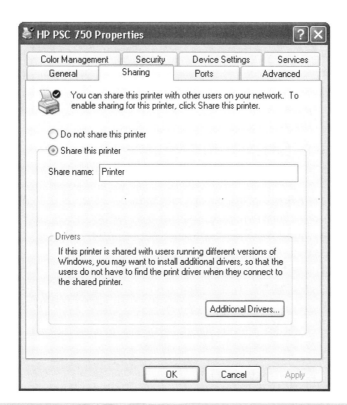

FIGURE 8.1   Sharing tab

Drivers button. In the Additional Drivers dialog box, shown here, select the drivers that you want to install and click OK.

5. You'll be prompted for the path to those additional drivers so that they can be installed. You need to have the correct drivers handy.

Windows XP also supports printing to a print device on the Internet, which Windows 2000 introduced. The idea is that networks can use the Internet as a free print transfer network. For example, suppose that you want to send a series of documents to a user in Spokane, but you are located in Dallas. You can use the Internet printing feature to print to an Internet-enabled printer in the Spokane office. (You first must configure the Internet printer to provide Internet printing, and you'll learn about that in the next section.) If you want to connect to an Internet printer, you simply use the Add a Printer Wizard again, shown in the following steps.

INSTALLING AN INTERNET PRINTER

1. Open the Printers and Faxes folder in Control Panel. Click the Add a Printer Wizard to start it.

2. Click Next on the Welcome screen.

3. In the Local or Network Printer window, select the Network Printer radio button and click Next.

4. In the Specify a Printer window, choose the option to connect to a printer on the Internet and enter the URL of the printer, as shown here.

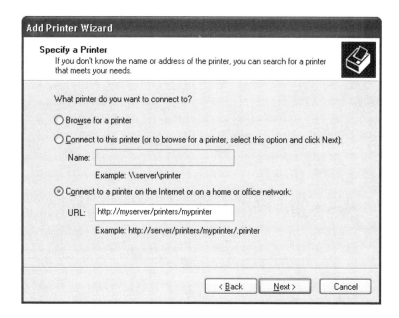

5. Click Next and click Finish.

After setting up the printers, you can then print to them as you would to a local printer. If you have more than one printer configured, you'll see a selection dialog box when you print. This dialog box allows you to choose the printer to which you want to print, as you can see in Figure 8-2.

In Windows domain environments, users can also search the Active Directory to locate printers. Printers configured and published on Windows 2000 and XP computers are automatically published in the Active Directory. Users can search the Active Directory and look for certain characteristics, called *attributes*. For example, a user could search for "laser printers" and find all laser printers on the network.

If you need to print to an Internet printer, you can follow this same format, but you can also connect to an Internet printer using a browser (IE 4.0 or later only). If you know the URL, simply enter it in the address bar in your browser. If you do not, enter the server's name followed by **/printers** to see a listing of

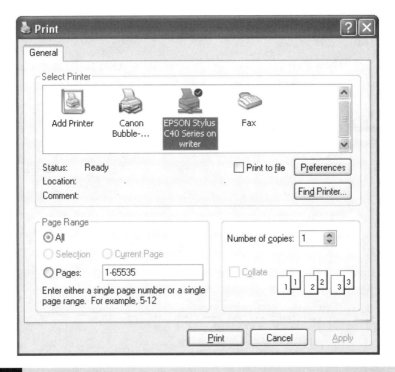

Print dialog box

Internet printers on that server. For example, suppose that you know that the server is http://myserver. If you don't know the printer name, you can type **http://myserver/printers** to see a listing of printers available on that server. If you know the name of the printer, you can simply type the server name and printer name, such as **http://myserver/internetprint**, to access the Internet printer directly. Once you locate the printer you want, you can click the Connect button. Windows XP will copy the necessary drivers, and the new printer will appear in your Printers and Faxes folder. This is a simple way to use a Web browser to access the Internet printer, rather than using the Add a Printer Wizard to set it up.

MANAGING PRINTERS

Once you have installed a local printer on a Windows XP computer, you can then configure and manage the printer's operations. This includes the functionality of the printer, as well as the print jobs sent to the printer. In

TROUBLESHOOTING

Internet Printers

There are a few troubleshooting issues that you should keep in mind when working with Internet printing:

■ If you cannot connect to the network printer, you need to verify that the printer and server are online and that the UNC path information has not changed.

■ If the network server and UNC path information is correct, check your computer's network connectivity and print server connectivity using the Ping command.

■ If you have connectivity and the server and print devices are connected and ready, you can try rebooting to restart services, or delete the printer and then re-create it using the Add a Printer Wizard.

■ For Internet printing, make sure you are using IE 4.0 or later. If you do not know the actual URL of the printer, you can access http://*servername*/printers to see what printers are available. If you know the exact URL, you can access it directly from the browser using http://*servername/printername* or you can set up the Internet printer using the Add a Printer Wizard. Either way, once the printer is recognized, you can use it as if the printer were local.

■ If you cannot connect to the Internet printer, you'll need to verify that you have Internet connectivity and that the print server and printer are online.

this section, you'll consider a number of important configuration features and issues concerning printer and print job management.

CONFIGURING A PRINTER

After installing the printer on the local Windows XP computer, you can configure how the printer operates by accessing the printer's properties. You can find the properties by right-clicking the Printer icon in the Printers and Faxes folder and clicking Properties. You'll see primary tabs of General, Sharing, Ports, Advanced, Security, and Device Settings. Depending on the printer, you may see additional tabs that are installed by the manufacturer's setup program. The following sections explore the primary tabs and show you what is available to configure.

GENERAL TAB

The General tab, shown in Figure 8-3, gives you the printer name and any location/comment information that has been configured. Under Features, you can see whether color printing is supported, what staple features are provided, the speed of the printer, and which paper types might be available.

If you click the Printing Preferences button, you can configure paper orientation (portrait or landscape), page order, paper quality, and other basic settings. Depending on the printer, you may see additional information here that is made available by the manufacturer's software, as you can see in Figure 8-4. The options provided on these tabs are self-explanatory, but you should check your print device's documentation for any additional information and printing

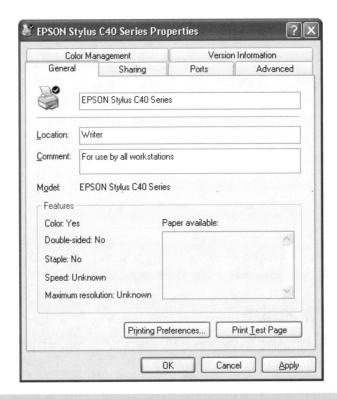

| FIGURE 8.3 | General tab |

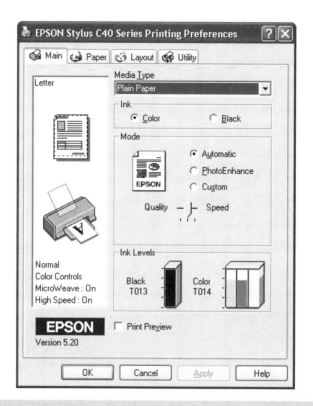

options that may be available to you. You can also send a test page to the printer for testing purposes by clicking the Print a Test Page button, if available for your printer.

SHARING TAB

The Sharing tab enables you to share the printer. See the "Sharing a Printer" steps in the previous section for more information about setting up sharing.

PORTS TAB

Windows 2000 introduced additional printing features in a number of different areas, including port configuration. These configuration options also appear in Windows XP. If you click the Ports tab of the printer properties, shown in Figure 8-5, you see several different port options and can add, delete, or configure a port. Port configuration can be a little confusing, but in this section, you can explore all you need to know about printer ports and their configuration options.

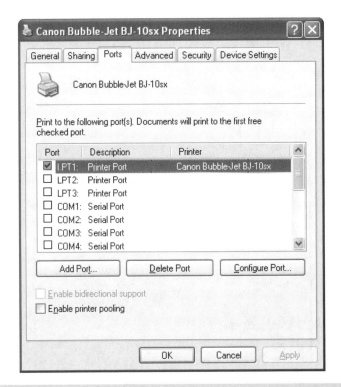

FIGURE 8.5   Ports tab

A printer port, like other kinds of ports, is a point of connection. In this case, the connection is a computer to a printer. In the past, the printer port was almost always an LPT port, but with today's new port connectivity options, such as USB and IrDA, you can use a number of different ports. You can also configure serial ports as well as TCP/IP ports on your network for printing.

When you install a local printer, the port option is configured according to the port to which the printer is attached. However, you can configure multiple ports as necessary for printer device connections.

First, you can select the existing port that is in use and click the Configure Port button. You then see a simple Configure Port dialog box, shown here.

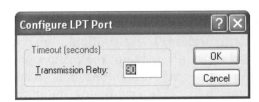

This dialog box displays the Transmission Retry value. The timeout value is the amount of time that passes before you are notified that the printer is not responding to the print request. The typical default setting here is 90 seconds. If you are using plotters on the printer port, you might need to increase this value to allow the plotter more time to buffer print data.

Also notice that at the bottom of the Ports tab are two check box options that you can enable:

■ **Enable Bidirectional Support**   If the printer supports bidirectional communication between the printer and the computer, you can enable that option here so that Windows XP can receive from the printer data about problems.

■ **Enable Printer Pooling**   You can configure a printer pool, which consists of two more identical print devices that function through one logical printer. For example, the pool acts like one printer to the user, but may actually be made up of three print devices. This feature is often used when a number of users are supported over a shared printer. To enable the feature, click the check box and select the other ports that you want to use to send printer data.

You can also add new ports. If you click the Add Port button, a window appears where you can configure a new local port or a TCP/IP port. The new local port option enables you to configure a new port type. For example, if you recently installed an IrDA device, you could configure the new port here so that IrDA-enabled printers can use the port.

You can also choose to install a standard TCP/IP port by clicking Add Port. A TCP/IP port is a logical port made up an IP address of a network printer. For example, suppose that your environment uses a network printer that has a network adapter card. The TCP/IP port feature enables your computer to print to the IP port found on the printer's network adapter, assuming you have permission to do so. The end result is that through TCP/IP, your computer can send print jobs directly to the network printer. The following steps show you how to set up a TCP/IP printer port.

CONFIGURING A TCP/IP PRINTER PORT

1. Open the Printers and Faxes folder in Control Panel. Right-click the desired printer, then click Properties.

2. Click the Ports tab and then click the Add Port button.

3. In the provided Printer Ports dialog box, shown here, select Standard TCP/IP Port, then click the New Port button.

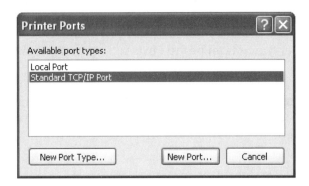

4. The TCP/IP Printer Port Wizard appears. Note that the network device must be turned on and the network must be connected and configured. Click Next.

5. In the Add Port window, enter the printer name or IP address of the printer. You can also enter the port name if necessary. Click Next.

6. If the port is found, Windows XP will install the port. Click Finish.

CONFIGURING ADVANCED SETTINGS

The Advanced tab, shown in Figure 8-6, gives you a number of different settings that impact printing availability and functionality. You should be very familiar with the options found on this tab, because they can give you a lot of printer functionality. You have several different options here, and the following bulleted list describes them:

■ **Always Available**   By default, a local printer is always available. However, you configure the printer so that it is available only for certain hours. This feature is helpful when you want to control user access to the printer.

■ **Priority**   This setting establishes a priority setting for the printer. If multiple printers print to the same print device, you can control which printer has priority by entering a value here. The lowest priority is 1, while 99 is the highest priority.

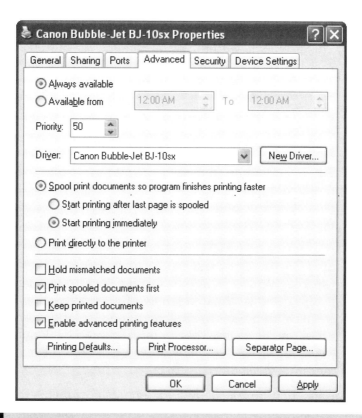

FIGURE 8.6   Advanced tab

- **Driver**   If you need to update the driver, click the New Driver button. This opens the Add Printer Driver Wizard, which will walk you through the steps of installing a new printer driver.

- **Spool Settings**   By default, documents are spooled and start printing immediately. This means that documents are held on the hard disk spooler until the printer is available to print. Essentially, this frees up the application so that the user can return to work. You can choose to hold the document until the last page is spooled, but this may slow down printing a bit.

- **Print Directly to the Printer**   This radio button option prints directly to the printer without using the spooler. The application will remain busy the entire time that the print job is running, and the user will not be able to continue working with the application. You should use this option only if you are having problems with the print spooler.

Users often think that this setting will make their jobs print faster—not so! In fact, printing directly to the printer will basically lock up the computer while printing takes place.

- **Hold Mismatched Documents** If the printer setup and the document setup formats do not match, the document is considered mismatched. Use this option to hold the document so that it will not be printed. This feature does not stop other documents from printing, and it is not selected by default. Typically, this setting is helpful for troubleshooting purposes.

- **Print Spooled Documents First** Suppose that five users have sent print jobs to the spooler. Which print job does the spooler take first? In this case, the spooler will take the first job that finishes spooling. If none of the print jobs have finished spooling, then the printer chooses the larger documents over smaller ones. This option is chosen by default and should remain selected for printer efficiency. If you clear the setting, document printing order is based solely on priority.

- **Keep Printed Documents** This setting holds documents that print correctly in this spooler so that a user can resubmit the documents for printing. This option is not selected by default.

- **Enable Advanced Printing Features** Advanced printing features enable metafile spooling, which allows different kinds of print options, such as page ordering, booklet printing, and other types, depending on your printer. This option is selected by default and should remain enabled, unless you are having computer/printer compatibility problems, in which case turning off this setting may help.

- **Printing Defaults** This option enables you to control paper orientation and related settings. These are the same settings you see under Printing Defaults on the General tab.

- **Print Processor** If you click Print Processor, you see a window that shows the print processor used and the default data type. The default data type is typically RAW, but you may choose a different data type if your printer documentation tells you to do so.

- **Separator Page** Use this option if you want a separator page to print between print jobs.

CONFIGURING SECURITY

The Security tab enables you to determine what users or groups have access to the printer and what they can do with the printer. See the "Managing Printer Permissions" section later in this chapter for details. If you are using Simple File Sharing, the Security tab does not appear.

CONFIGURING DEVICE SETTINGS

The Device Settings tab contains basic settings for the device, such as paper feed and envelope usage. This tab may not be available on all printer models.

MANAGING PRINT QUEUES

The process of printer configuration and setup is typically a one-time event, assuming everything works like you want it to. However, you may have to manage the print queue from time to time in order to manage and control documents. The queue refers to the holding area—documents that are either currently printing or are waiting to be printed. Assuming you have permissions to access the print queue on a Windows XP computer, you can do so by double-clicking the Printer icon in the Printers and Faxes folders, or you can click the Printer icon that appears in the Notification Area when items are being printed.

NOTE You must have permission to open, view, and modify the print queue. If you do not, then an "access denied" message appears if you try to open the printer in the Printers and Faxes folder, and you will not see a Printer icon in the Notification Area.

The print queue, as you can see here, gives you a listing of documents that are printing or are waiting to be printed.

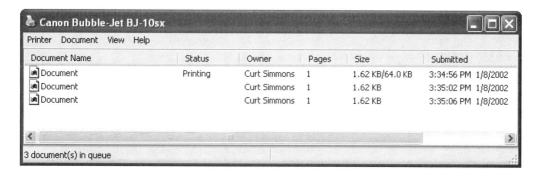

You can manage the print queue in a few different ways. First, you can click the Printer menu and choose Pause Printing or Cancel All Documents. The pause feature is useful if you need to perform maintenance on the printer without deleting everything that is waiting in the queue. You can use the Document menu to manage individual documents. For example, you can select a document and click the Document menu, where you can pause, resume, restart, or cancel the document's print. These features can be helpful if a document seems to be stuck in the queue; you can cancel it and the other documents should resume printing. You can also easily perform these same actions simply by right-clicking on the Document icon in the print queue.

You can also make a few adjustments to a document's printing by right-clicking the document and clicking Properties. As you can see in Figure 8-7, you have a standard Properties sheet with several tabs. The noteworthy items are found on the General tab. As shown in Figure 8-7, you can change the priority of the document in the queue. Under most circumstances, documents are set to a priority

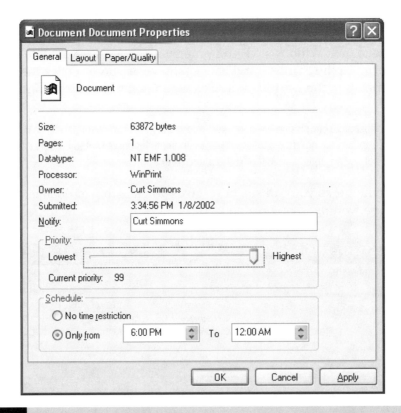

FIGURE 8.7   Document Properties dialog box

Printers and Permissions

Users who have permission to print to a network printer also have permission to manage their documents in the print queue. For example, suppose that a user prints a document, then changes his or her mind. The user can open the print queue and delete the document. However, the user cannot manage other documents in the print queue without the proper permission. Don't be surprised if users request permission to manage other documents in the queue besides their own! This permission, which is called Manage Documents, should be granted sparingly, however, since you do not want users deleting each other's print jobs. See the next section "Managing Printer Permissions," to learn more about printer permissions.

of 1. What if there are 15 documents in the print queue, but one particular document needs to be printed first? No problem, just access the document's properties and change the Priority setting to Highest—this will ensure that the document prints first, assuming no other documents have a Highest setting.

Also notice that you can configure a schedule for a particular print job. Suppose that someone in the research group has sent a 300-page research paper to the printer during peak printing hours. You can access the document's properties and change the time restriction so that the job is held in the queue until after hours. As you can see, you have a lot of power when you have rights to manage the print queue, and it is a task that should be assigned to only a few people.

MANAGING PRINTER PERMISSIONS

The preferred method for managing any network resource in a Windows 2000 environment is through NTFS permissions, and the same rule holds true for shared printers. Depending on your network needs, you may have several print devices that you want to make available to all users at all times. Or, you may have certain print devices that should be available to some users some of the time and others at other times—or not at all. The possible permission scenarios with any shared resource are many, and printer sharing is certainly no exception.

To modify the permissions of a shared printer, you first must be the administrator/owner of that printer on the local machine. If you needed to configure the permissions from a different computer through the Active Directory, you will need to be at least a member of the Server Operator or Print Operator group.

To modify the permissions of a printer, you need to access the Security tab of the printer's Properties pages. There are three primary permissions that you can assign concerning printing:

- **Print**   This permission allows a user to print to the printer.

- **Manage Printers**   This permission allows a user to open the printer's Properties pages and configure options.

- **Manage Documents**   This permission allows a user to open the print queue and manage documents.

In Windows XP, local administrators are given all three permissions. The Creator/Owner is given the Manage Documents permission, Everyone is given the Read permission, and Power Users are given all three permissions. Most users in your environment will have Print permission for the printer, while only a select few will be given the Manage Printers and Manage Documents permissions.

As with all permission features, you can also click the Advanced button to view a listing of permission entries for particular groups. You can select a desired group, click the Edit button, and reconfigure the default permissions for that group if necessary. You can also set up auditing, view the owner, and view the effective permissions for a group by using the Effective Permissions tab. The tabs you see here are standard, and they work for printer permissions as they do for any other shared object. It is important to note here that if no permission is expressly applied to the group, the group can inherit its permission from the Active Directory. If there is no inheritable permission, the group is simply denied any access.

NOTE   If you do not see a Security tab, then Simple File Sharing is in use. See Chapter 6 for details.

PERMISSIONS, PRIORITIES, AND PRINTING

As you can see, printing permissions are rather straightforward. However, in most cases, your permission problems will not be so cut and dried. For example, suppose that two different groups, Marketing and Accounting, use a certain shared printer. You want to make certain that the Marketing group can access the printer only from 3:00 P.M. until 10:00 P.M., but Accounting has full access. Also, when the printer is available to both groups, how can you ensure that the Accounting group's jobs are given preferential treatment? In such cases, you use a combination of multiple printers, different priorities, and different availability options in order to make the configuration work. Keep in mind that you cannot single out a group for certain time access through the security permissions available; that has to be done using multiple printers for the same print device.

Let's consider an example. In your network, a certain printer is accessed by the Management group and by the Research group. Although the Research group technically uses the printer more often, it frequently prints documents over 100 pages long that are not critical hard copy needs. The Management group needs the printer all of the time, and the group's documents should be printed first. You would like to configure the printer so that the Research group's print jobs do not print until after 2:00 P.M. each day, keeping open the morning hours, when the printer is most busy. Also, if a user in the Management group needs the printer in the late afternoon, that user's print job should be favored over any jobs from the Research group. How can you configure this? Follow these steps:

1. Create the first printer. You can label the printer "Management." Then access the Security tab.

2. On the Security tab, give the Management group Allow permission for Print. Make sure that you deny any other group permission to print.

3. Click the Advanced tab. Ensure that the printer is always available and that the Priority is set to 50. Click OK.

To configure a printer for the Research group, follow these steps:

1. Create the second printer. You can label the printer "Research." Then click the Security tab.

2. On the Security tab, give the Research group Print permission. Make sure that you deny Print permission for any other groups.

3. Click the Advanced tab. Change the schedule so that the printer is available only from 2:00 P.M. to 12:00 A.M. Under Priority, leave the value configured as 1.

Printer management functions like another other resource that you need to manage in a Windows 2000/.NET network. Once you establish the shared resource, you then determine who can access the shared resource and under what conditions. As a general rule, you should make certain that printer permission assignment is as simple as possible. This rule holds true for any kind of shared resource.

The more complex the permissions and the more crossgroup memberships you have in your environment, the more likely you are to have problems. As with a shared folder, NTFS permissions are cumulative, with the exception of deny. If a user is a member of one group that has Print permissions but a member of another group that also has the Manage Documents permission, the user effectively has the Manage Documents and Print permissions. In contrast, if the user is a member of one group that is given Print permission to the printer but another group that is denied access, the user effectively has no access. For this reason, Windows networking groups should be clearly and carefully defined, and then permissions to resources, including printers, should be based on those groups. Careful and logical permission assignment makes your life as an administrator much easier and simpler.

MANAGING THE FAX CONSOLE

Windows XP Professional includes a new Fax Console that can make the use of Windows XP as a fax server much easier than it has been able to in the past. With the new Fax Console, you can manage incoming and outgoing faxes in much the same way you handle e-mail in an e-mail client. This feature makes fax sending, receiving, and archiving much easier and streamlined. The new Fax Console is not installed by default when you install Windows XP, so you'll need to install it using Add/Remove Windows Components, as shown in the following steps.

INSTALLING THE FAX CONSOLE

1. Open Control Panel and double-click Add/Remove Programs.

2. In the Add/Remove Programs window, click the Add/Remove Windows Components button.

3. Windows XP Setup appears. In the Windows Components window, shown next, select Fax Services and click Next.

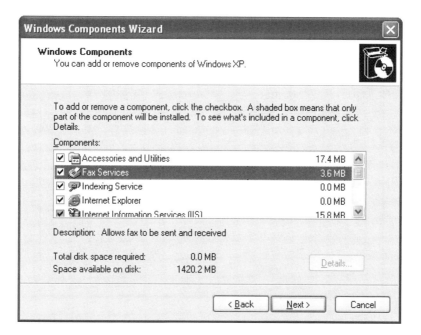

4. The fax services are installed (you may be prompted for your Windows XP installation CD-ROM). Click Finish.

Once the installation of the Fax Console is complete, you see an icon appear in your Printers and Faxes folder. If you double-click the icon, a wizard appears that helps you set up the Fax Console. The following steps walk you through the process.

CONFIGURING THE FAX CONSOLE

1. Double-click the Fax Console in the Printers and Faxes folder.

2. The Fax Configuration Wizard appears. Click Next.

3. In the Sender Information window, shown next, enter any information that is desired. Keep in mind that any information entered here will appear on the fax cover page when you send a fax.

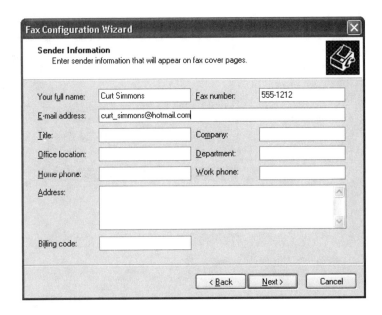

4. In the Select Device window, shown here, use the drop-down menu to select the device that you want to use for faxing, such as a fax modem. Notice that by default, the device is only set to send faxes; if you want the device to receive faxes, select the check box option and determine whether you want manual or automatic answering. Click Next.

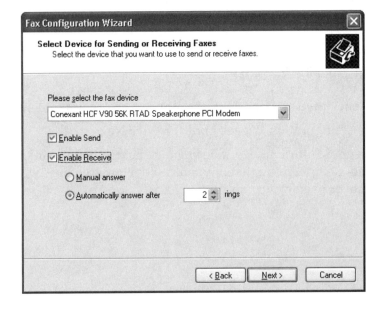

5. In the Transmitting Subscriber Identification (TSID) window, enter a business name and/or your fax number. This information will be transmitted to recipients when you send a fax. Click Next.

6. In the Called Subscriber Identification (CSID) window, enter a name or number to identify your computer. This information is transmitted back to the sender when you receive a fax in order to identify you. Click Next.

7. In the Routing Options window, you can choose to print the fax when it arrives, and you can also choose to save the fax to a specified folder. Note that received faxes are automatically archived in the Inbox folder of the Fax Console, but this option enables you to save an additional copy to a different folder. Make your selections and click Next.

8. Click Finish to complete the wizard.

USING THE FAX CONSOLE

Once installation is complete, you see the Fax Console, which contains Incoming, Inbox, Outbox, and Sent Items, as shown in Figure 8-8. As you

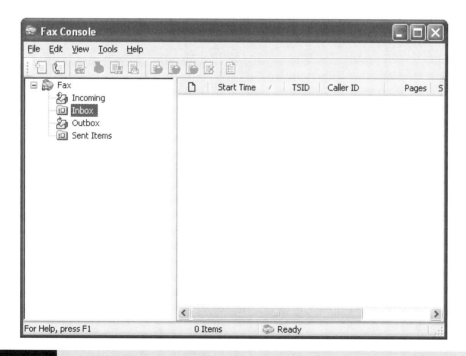

FIGURE 8.8   Fax Console

can see, the console looks like a typical e-mail client, such as Outlook or Outlook Express.

At this point, you can begin using the Fax Console. Overall, the Fax Console is very intuitive and easy to use. As you practice using the Fax Console, keep the following points in mind:

- To send a fax, use the File menu. A wizard will help you set up the fax you want to send and apply a cover sheet. You can also choose to send the fax later and assign a higher priority so that the fax will be sent before other faxes in the queue.

- If you want to import older faxes into the console, use the Import/Export feature on the File menu.

- As with an e-mail client, you can right-click faxes in your Inbox, Outbox, and Sent Items folders and perform actions such as printing, mail to, save as, delete, and so forth.

- On the Tools menu, you'll find a number of helpful features. You can configure Sender Information, which provides more information about you to the recipients. You can also configure personal cover pages. You can click the Fax Printer Status option to determine whether the fax is online or if there are problems.

- Also found on the Tools menu is the Fax Monitor, shown in Figure 8-9. The Fax Monitor tells you the current status of the fax, and enables you to answer calls and find out about transmission problems.

CONFIGURING THE FAX CONSOLE

Once you have initially set up the Fax Console, you can perform additional configuration options as necessary by using the Tools menu. If you click Tools | Configure Fax, the same Fax Configuration Wizard appears. However, if you click Tools | Fax Printer Configuration, you see a standard Properties page with a number of important configuration tabs.

GENERAL TAB

The General tab contains basic information about the fax. You can click the Printing Preferences button here and configure portrait or landscape printing when faxes are printed.

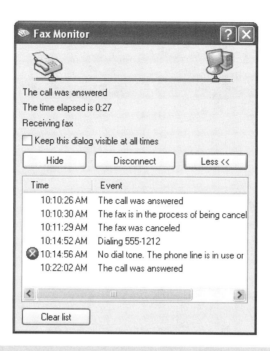

FIGURE 8.9   Fax Monitor

SHARING TAB

You may see a Sharing tab, which simply tells you that sharing of the Fax Console is not supported.

SECURITY AND FAX SECURITY TABS

You'll see Security and Fax Security tabs that govern how printers can use the fax printer. The Security tab lists basic printing permissions, discussed previously in this chapter, and the Fax Security tab, shown in Figure 8-10, lists the fax permissions. As you can see, they are essentially the same as printer permissions in that groups can fax, manage fax configuration, and manage fax documents, depending on how you plan to assign permissions. You manage permissions for the Fax Console in the same way as you would for a printer.

DEVICES TAB

On the Devices tab, you see the fax device that is used for the console. If you click the Properties button, a few important additional tabs appear.

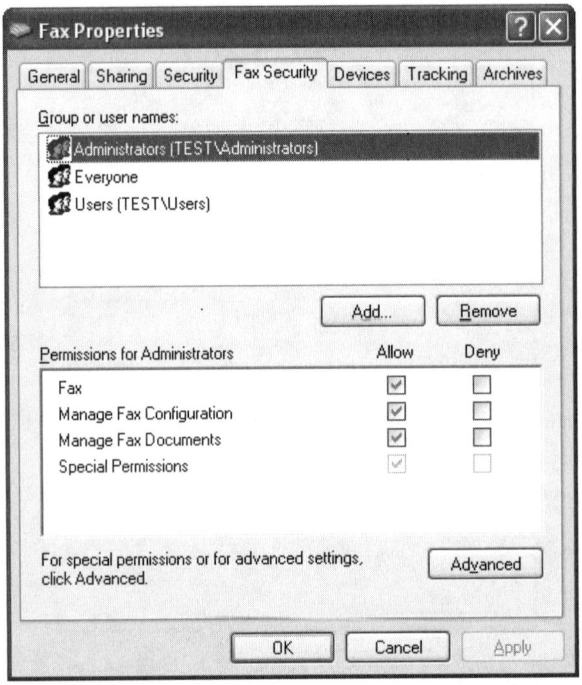

FIGURE 8.10 Fax Security tab

First, the Send tab, which you can see in Figure 8-11, enables the device for fax sending. You can configure the number of retries, the retry interval, and the discount rate start and stop if discount rates are used for faxing.

On the Receive tab, you see the same basic configuration you made when you used the Fax Configuration Wizard. You make changes here as desired.

Finally, the Cleanup tab enables you to determine how long to keep failed faxes before deleting them.

TRACKING TAB

On the Tracking tab, you can configure a few different options that keep you informed about fax activity. First, you can have the Notification Area show progress of sent faxes and status information about incoming faxes. You can also have the Fax Monitor automatically open when a fax is sent or received, and you can also configure sound events that alert you to fax activity.

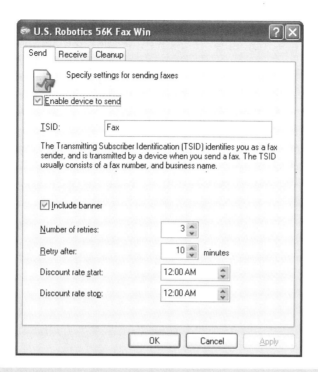

FIGURE 8.11   Send tab

ARCHIVES TAB

The Archives tab tells you the default archive locations for sent and received faxes, which are held in the Sent Items and Inbox folders by default.

WRAPPING UP

Printing can be a complex topic, but Windows XP includes the tools and features that you need for effective printing. Using Windows XP, you can easily install a local or shared network printer, and you can even access print servers over the Internet. Printer properties give you a number of options for managing printers, and print permissions are easy and straightforward. As you work with printing in your environment as an A+ technician, you may find yourself in charge of print servers running on Windows XP. Just keep in mind that all documents can be controlled through the print queue. Also, when configuring shared printer access, remember to keep things as simple and straightforward as possible.

In the next chapter, we'll turn our attention to networking with Windows XP.

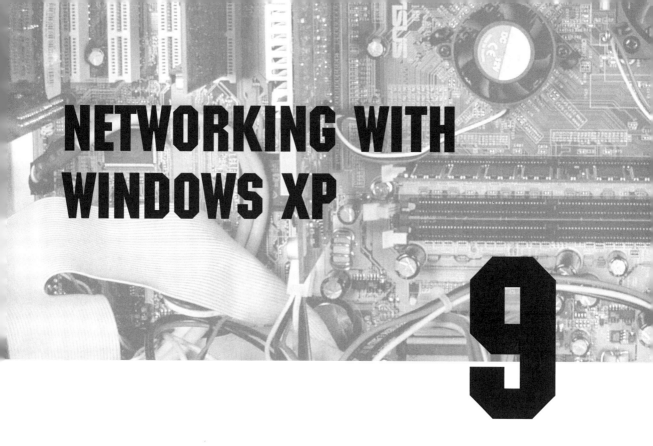

NETWORKING WITH WINDOWS XP

9

As an A+ technician, a major task that you frequently encounter, aside from hardware and software configuration, is working with Windows XP's networking features. In fact, I've devoted several chapters in this book to networking issues, such as Remote Desktop, Remote Assistance, Internet Connection Sharing, and Internet Connection Firewall. Before these features, however, are the standard networking options and functions that Windows XP brings to the networking table. If you have worked at all with Windows 2000, you will certainly see many similarities, with a few new tricks Windows XP provides to give you more networking flexibility as well as more functionality. In this chapter, you'll take a look at Windows XP networking, covering a variety of issues and configurations you are likely to run across in your job. In this chapter, you'll…

- Configure network interface cards
- Manage local area connections
- Work with TCP/IP
- Set up a home or small office network

- Configure network bridges
- Connect to a Windows domain
- Manage other network connections
- Use wireless networking

INSTALLING NETWORK INTERFACE CARDS

In order for a computer to function in a network, it has to have two items: hardware and networking software. The hardware needed is, of course, a network interface card (NIC). NICs are developed and configured to function on specific types of networks, such as Ethernet, Token Ring, and even home/office networks such as HomePNA. The NIC handles data flow and communication over the network cable and functions as your computer's interface to the network. Most NICs are installed in internal slots, such as PCI, but there are also external NIC options that can connect to a USB port.

Installing NICs in Windows XP is just like installing any other type of hardware. You simply insert the NIC, or in the case of an external NIC, attach it to the USB port. NICs sold today follow the same plug and play specification, and Windows XP can automatically detect new NICs that are installed on the computer. When the NIC is installed, Windows XP automatically binds the NIC to TCP/IP with DHCP selected by default. You should not need to reboot the computer for any of this to take place. You can install multiple NICs that can be used to connect to different network segments, or even different networks if necessary, and you can adjust and completely change the protocols and services that are bound to the NIC.

NOTE If you are installing an internal NIC, make sure you turn the power off on the computer!

If you have problems installing a plug and play NIC, you can use the Add Hardware Wizard to help you, just as you would for any hardware device. Make sure you are using a driver that is compatible with Windows XP (as well as a NIC that is compatible with Windows XP). As with any device, you can use Device Manager to manage the NIC and troubleshoot it, as well as update its driver when necessary. See Chapter 4 to learn more about managing hardware in Windows XP.

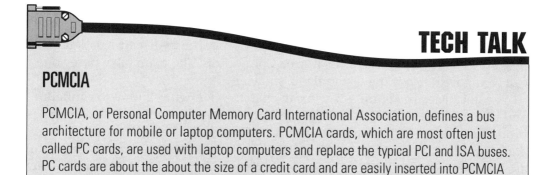

TECH TALK

PCMCIA

PCMCIA, or Personal Computer Memory Card International Association, defines a bus architecture for mobile or laptop computers. PCMCIA cards, which are most often just called PC cards, are used with laptop computers and replace the typical PCI and ISA buses. PC cards are about the about the size of a credit card and are easily inserted into PCMCIA slots on laptop computers. The installation routines and functionality of these cards are the same as the NICs you would use in a desktop system, and you can find PC cards for all types of network architectures, such as Ethernet, Token Ring, wireless networks, and even HomePNA.

MANAGING NIC BINDINGS

Once the NIC is installed, it appears in the Network Connections folder, shown in Figure 9-1, as a Local Area Connection. You'll also see any other connections

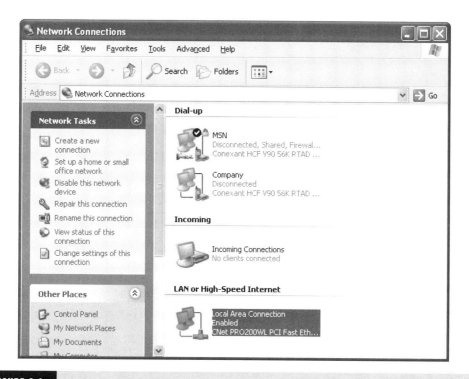

FIGURE 9.1   Local Area Connection

that are currently configured on the computer, such as dial-up and broadband connections.

If you right-click the connection and select Properties, you can access the properties dialog box for the Local Area Connection. The main tab where you can configure items is the General tab, shown in Figure 9-2.

As you can see in Figure 9-2, you can click the Configure button to configure and troubleshoot the NIC itself. This feature simply opens Device Manager properties for the NIC. In the middle of the window, you see a list of services and protocols that are bound to the NIC. Common examples you might see here are Internet Protocol (TCP/IP), Client for Microsoft Networks, and File and Printer Sharing for Microsoft Networks. These services and protocols are "bound" to the NIC, which means the NIC uses these protocols and services for communication on your network. However, depending on the needs of the network, you may need to bind other protocols and/or services as well. For example, let's say that NetWare is in use in your network. In this case, you may need to add the NWLink protocol or Services for NetWare. In small networks, you might also need the NetBEUI protocol (although use of NetBEUI has been widely replaced by TCP/IP). If you do in fact need to add a service or protocol, you can easily do so. Just follow the steps in the next subsection.

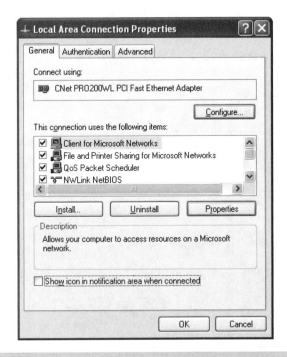

General tab

ADDING A SERVICE OR PROTOCOL

1. To add a protocol or service, click the Install button on the General tab.

2. In the Select Network Component Type dialog box, shown here, choose Client, Service, or Protocol. In this example, I'm going to install a protocol. Click Add.

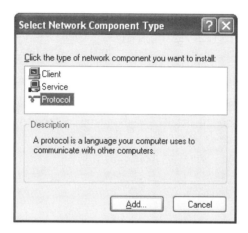

3. In the Selection List that appears, select the client, service, or protocol that you want to install. If you have an installation disk for the client, service, or protocol, click the Have Disk button and follow the instructions that appear. Otherwise, click OK.

4. The new client, service, or protocol is installed.

NOTE   You can also easily uninstall any client, service, or protocol by simply selecting it and clicking the Uninstall button.

MANAGING THE LOCAL AREA CONNECTION

Windows XP gives you more graphical interfaces than any previous version of Windows, and the same is true with networking components. You can gain more information and do more through the graphical Windows XP environment.

First of all, simply double-click the Local Area Connection icon to get immediate information about the connection. This opens the Local Area Connection Status dialog box, shown in Figure 9-3, where you can see if the connection is actually connected, the duration of the connection, the speed, and the activity. You can also access the properties dialog box and disable the connection.

TROUBLESHOOTING

Slow Network Connection

Troubleshooting slow network connections can be a complicated task, mainly because there are so many different problems that can affect the speed of the connection. From network bottlenecks to various hardware problems, slow connections arc a common difficulty in any networking environment. However, slow connections can also be caused by the clients, services, and protocols that are installed on the local NIC. The more clients, services, and protocols that you have installed, the more work the NIC must do to filter through these items to determine which one needs to be used at any given time. The key point here is simply this: Install what you need, but do not install services, clients, or protocols that you are not using. Having these items available when they are not needed does nothing but increase the odds that your network connectivity will work more slowly.

If you click the Support tab, shown in Figure 9-4, you can immediately gain information about the connection, such as the IP address, subnet mask, and default gateway, rather than having to use Ipconfig.exe. Notice that you have

| **FIGURE 9.3** | Local Area Connection Status |

FIGURE 9.4   Support tab

an option to repair the connection. If the connection is not working or seems to be misconfigured, you can click the Repair button, and Windows XP performs a few different actions. Windows XP tries to obtain a new IP address from the DHCP server. It also flushes the Address Resolution Protocol (ARP), NetBIOS, and Domain Name System (DNS) caches. Then, the computer tries to re-register with WINS and DNS servers on the network.

If you click the Details button, the Network Connect Details window appears, shown in Figure 9-5. Here you can gain additional information, such as the physical address of the NIC and the addresses of the WINS and DNS servers on the network.

You can easily manage the local area connection in the same manner by right-clicking the Local Area Connection icon and selecting from different choices that appear, such as:

- **Disable**   This stops the connection from working; however, it does not uninstall the NIC or remove any drivers. This feature is a great way to stop network connectivity while a computer is being configured or for troubleshooting purposes.

- **Status**   This gives you the same Status dialog box that appears if you double-click the connection.

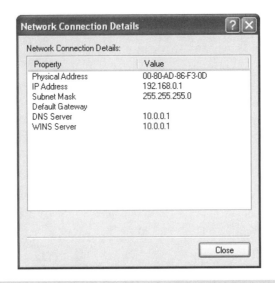

FIGURE 9.5 Network Connection Details

- **Repair** This is the same repair option that appears in the Status dialog box.

- **Bridge Connections** Windows XP provides a new bridge feature where Windows XP can act as a network bridge between two different networks. We'll explore this feature in more detail later in this chapter.

MANAGING TCP/IP

Transmission Control Protocol/Internet Protocol (TCP/IP) is the de facto standard for wide area networking today. In fact, it has even become the standard for home and small office networks since it is so reliable and much easier to configure than in times past. First things first: this section is not designed to be a tutorial on the ins and outs of TCP/IP, or figuring subnet masks. There are entire books devoted to these subjects alone, so if you are needing to work on your TCP/IP skills, I would recommend you refer to a book that is devoted to this subject. For our purposes, we'll look at Windows XP's support of TCP/IP and how to configure it. Basically, TCP/IP is made up of three primary components:

- **IP address** Each computer on the network must have a unique IP address. The IP address identifies the computer on the network. The IP address is made up of four octets, representing the binary value of the address, such as 131.107.2.200. IP addresses are divided into classes and address ranges.

- **Subnet mask**   The subnet mask hides, or masks, the network address from the host address. Since each IP address is made up of both the network address and the host address, the subnet mask is used to determine the two. At least a default subnet mask is required.

- **Default gateway**   A default gateway is the IP address of a computer or router that connects the subnet to a different subnet. Computers use the default gateway to send IP data from one subnet to another. If there is no more than one subnet, a default gateway is not required.

USING APIPA OR DHCP

As you are working with Windows XP Professional, it's important to remember that all of the old TCP/IP rules apply. Each client on your network needs a unique IP address, an appropriate subnet mask, and possibly a default gateway if the client's requests must travel to a different subnet. The good news is that Windows XP Professional can configure this addressing automatically if you are

- On a home or small office network with no DHCP servers

- On a Windows 2000 network that has DHCP up and running

Let's consider the first option. Windows XP Professional is designed to use TCP/IP in a small workgroup or office setting. Because the users in this type of setting are typically not IP professionals who can configure TCP/IP, Windows XP Professional can configure it automatically through Automatic Private IP Addressing (APIPA). When APIPA is used, Windows XP Professional first checks the network for the presence of a Dynamic Host Configuration Protocol (DHCP) server that can lease an IP address to it. If a DHCP server is not available, then Windows XP Professional uses APIPA. When APIPA is used, an IP address from the 169.254.0.0 to 169.254.255.255 address range is used, along with a subnet mask of 255.255.0.0. Windows XP Professional automatically assigns itself an IP address from this range so that it can participate on the network. Before assigning itself a random IP address from this range, the client broadcasts a network message to see if another APIPA client is already using that same IP address. Of course, if a different range of IP addresses or subnet masks are used on the network, the client still may not have IP connectivity with other clients. The point here is that Windows XP Professional can use APIPA in environments where no DHCP server is used and where static IP address configurations are not used. The end result is that a user can have a home network running TCP/IP without even knowing what TCP/IP is or that it even exists, which is the primary purpose of APIPA.

NOTE APIPA only assigns the IP address and subnet mask, not a default gateway. APIPA assume that communication is limited to the local subnet. Again, this feature is great in home or small office networks or in the case of a DHCP server failure, but it is not designed as a large networking solution.

In the same way that Windows XP Professional can automatically assign itself an IP address, Windows XP Professional is configured to search for a DHCP server so it can lease an IP address. DHCP server is a Windows 2000 Server service. Administrators can configure DHCP with a pool of IP addresses that can be leased to network clients. The client receives a unique IP lease and keeps that lease for a specified period of time, after which the lease must be renewed. If the lease cannot be renewed, the client can receive a new IP address. The end result is a system that is relatively easy to configure, all clients receive unique IP addresses, and administrators do not have to worry about unique IP addresses.

By default, Windows XP Professional configures itself for APIPA if a network adapter card is present in the computer. The same default setting is also used if a DHCP server is used. So you don't have to do anything to configure TCP/IP when APIPA or DHCP is used, which is most of the time. The only time you need to configure an IP address and subnet mask is if you want the computer to have a static configuration. The following steps show you the configuration for APIPA or DHCP.

USING APIPA OR DHCP

1. Click Start | Control Panel | Network Connections.

2. Right-click the Local Area Connection icon and select Properties.

3. On the General properties tab, select Internet Protocol (TCP/IP) in the list and click the Properties button.

4. On the Internet Protocol (TCP/IP) Properties General tab, ensure that the Obtain an IP Address Automatically and Obtain DNS Server Address Automatically radio buttons are selected, as shown in Figure 9-6. Once these are selected, Windows XP Professional looks for a DHCP server. If no DHCP server is found, an APIPA address is configured.

CONFIGURING A STATIC IP ADDRESS

APIPA and DHCP are designed to provide automatic IP addressing so that configuration never needs to be static. By static, I mean that you manually enter an IP address, subnet mask, and a default gateway if necessary. In the past, this manual form of IP addressing was required, and a simple keystroke error could

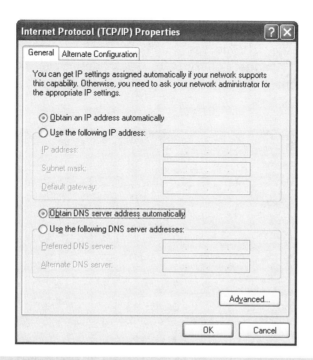

FIGURE 9.6   TCP/IP Properties General tab

cause a number of connectivity errors. As you can see, for this reason, TCP/IP was known as a "high overhead" protocol. With automatic addressing mechanisms, you will typically not perform manual assignment. However, there are cases where clients may want a workgroup to have a certain IP address range and subnet masks. When a handful of computers are used (or even up to 100), you can reasonably perform a manual assignment if necessary. Keep in mind that in order for a client computer to find its way off the local subnet, a default gateway must be configured. Also, you might consider manually entering the IP addresses of DNS servers on your network, since this information is typically provided by the DHCP server. Just walk through the following steps to manually configure TCP/IP settings.

MANUALLY CONFIGURING TCP/IP

1. Click Start | Control Panel | Network Connections.
2. Right-click the Local Area Connection icon and select Properties.
3. In the Local Area Connection Properties window, select Internet Protocol (TCP/IP) in the list and click Properties.

4. In the Internet Protocol (TCP/IP) Properties window, shown here, click the Use The Following IP Address radio button and manually enter the desired values for the IP address, subnet mask, and default gateway. If desired, you can also enter a preferred and alternate DNS server IP address in the provided boxes.

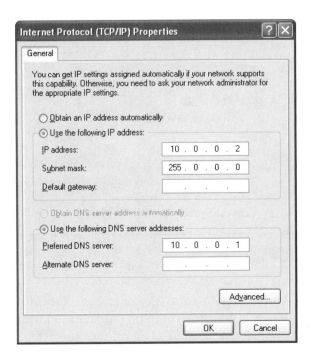

5. If you click the Advanced button, you can configure some additional TCP/IP settings. On the IP settings tab, you can add, edit, and remove IP addresses and default gateways for the computer. This feature enables you to use multiple IP addresses and default gateways on the same computer. This feature may be especially helpful in the case of a laptop computer that you move from one network to the next.

6. On the DNS tab, you can enter the additional addresses of other DNS servers that can be used. You can also determine how DNS handles names that are unqualified. The default settings are typically all you need here.

7. On the WINS tab, you can add the names of WINS servers, if they are still in use on your network and you can enable LMHOSTS lookups.

8. On the Options tab, shown next, you have a TCP/IP filtering feature. If you select TCP/IP Filtering on this tab and click Properties, you see a simple TCP/IP Filtering window. TCP/IP filtering functions like a miniature firewall

where you can allow or deny traffic on desired TCP and UDP ports, or on a protocol basis. This setting is not needed in a network environment where a firewall is in use, but it can be helpful in a workgroup setting if you want to place some IP restrictions on the computer's network adapters. Click OK and OK again once you have configured these options.

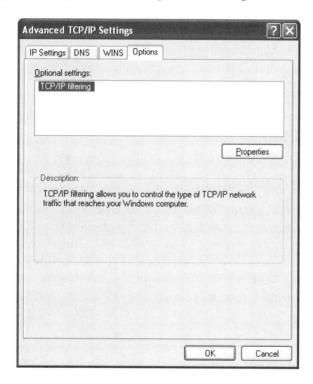

TCP/IP TROUBLESHOOTING TOOLS

Although troubleshooting TCP/IP connectivity and problems can be a difficult task, there are several command line tools that can help you. The following sections explore these troubleshooting tools, which you can use when you find yourself experiencing IP difficulties on your job.

PING

Ping is a network connectivity tool that allows you to test network connectivity against another computer, or even your computer's local network adapter card. Ping sends an ICMP echo request to the desired IP address or name and provides you with a response as to whether the ping was successful or the host was unreachable. At the Windows XP Professional command prompt, simply type **ping** *ipaddress*, such as **ping 10.0.0.1** or you can ping via name, such as **ping** computer7. You can also perform a loopback test against your computer's network adapter card by typing **ping 127.0.0.1**. To see all of ping's options, type **ping -?** at the command prompt. Figure 9-7 shows you an example of a successful ping test.

IPCONFIG

Ipconfig reports the IP configuration of your computer. At the command prompt, simply type **Ipconfig** and press ENTER. You'll see the IP address, subnet mask, and the default gateway for the local area connection. If you type **Ipconfig /all**, you can see a more detailed list of the computer's IP configuration, shown in Figure 9-8. Ipconfig also gives you some additional command line parameters, which you can review by typing **Ipconfig /?**.

NETSTAT AND NBTSTAT

Netstat is a connectivity tool that displays all connections and protocol statistics for TCP/IP. You can use a number of switches with Netstat, which you can view by typing **netstat ?**. Using the different switches, you can view the protocol local address, foreign address, and the current state of the connection.

Similarly, Nbtstat is helpful in cases where you need to troubleshoot NetBIOS naming and connectivity problems. This tool checks the status of NetBIOS over TCP/IP connections, and can give you information about the NetBIOS caches, the current sessions, and statistics. There are a number of switches, which you can view by simply typing **nbtstat** at the command line. The -RR switch (ReleaseRefresh) was first introduced in Windows 2000 to send name release packets to WINS and to then perform a refresh.

```
D:\WINDOWS\System32\cmd.exe                                    _ □ X

Microsoft Windows XP [Version 5.1.2526]
(C) Copyright 1985-2001 Microsoft Corp.

D:\Documents and Settings\Curt Simmons>ping 10.0.0.10

Pinging 10.0.0.10 with 32 bytes of data:

Reply from 10.0.0.10: bytes=32 time<1ms TTL=128
Reply from 10.0.0.10: bytes=32 time<1ms TTL=128
Reply from 10.0.0.10: bytes=32 time<1ms TTL=128
Reply from 10.0.0.10: bytes=32 time<1ms TTL=128

Ping statistics for 10.0.0.10:
    Packets: Sent = 4, Received = 4, Lost = 0 (0% loss),
Approximate round trip times in milli-seconds:
    Minimum = 0ms, Maximum = 0ms, Average = 0ms

D:\Documents and Settings\Curt Simmons>
```

FIGURE 9.7   A successful ping test

```
D:\WINDOWS\System32\cmd.exe                                    _ □ ✕

D:\Documents and Settings\Curt Simmons>ipconfig /all

Windows IP Configuration

        Host Name . . . . . . . . . . . . : xp
        Primary Dns Suffix  . . . . . . . :
        Node Type . . . . . . . . . . . . : Unknown
        IP Routing Enabled. . . . . . . . : No
        WINS Proxy Enabled. . . . . . . . : No

Ethernet adapter Local Area Connection:

        Connection-specific DNS Suffix  . :
        Description . . . . . . . . . . . : SMC EZ Card 10/100 PCI (SMC1211TX)
        Physical Address. . . . . . . . . : 00-E0-29-4F-9D-61
        Dhcp Enabled. . . . . . . . . . . : No
        IP Address. . . . . . . . . . . . : 10.0.0.1
        Subnet Mask . . . . . . . . . . . : 255.255.0.0
        Default Gateway . . . . . . . . . :

D:\Documents and Settings\Curt Simmons>
```

FIGURE 9.8   Ipconfig /all

TRACERT

Tracert is a simple utility that traces the route from one host to another.
You can trace routes over the local network, or even to a Web site, such as
www.osborne.com, shown in Figure 9-9. You can also view a listing of tracert
switches by simply typing **tracert** at the command line.

PATHPING

First appearing in Windows 2000, pathping combines the functionality of ping
and tracert. You can ping an address or DNS name and see the actual route of the
ping, including percentage information on the packets lost. This troubleshooting
tool can be useful in a large network environment where there are connectivity
problems. The pathping can help you isolate where the connectivity problem
resides so that it can be repaired.

ROUTE

The Route command can be used to view local routing tables and change them
if there are errors in the routing tables. This troubleshooting tool can be used
to verify correct routing information and correct IP routing data in the host's
routing table. You can view all the switches available for Route by typing **route**
at the command prompt.

```
C:\WINDOWS\System32\command.com                                    _ □ ✕

C:\DOCUME~1\CURT>tracert www.osborne.com

Tracing route to www.osborne.com [198.45.24.130]
over a maximum of 30 hops:

  1    175 ms    181 ms    192 ms   tnt1.denton.tx.da.uu.net [206.115.151.193]
  2    183 ms    169 ms    159 ms   207.76.35.233
  3    235 ms    203 ms    159 ms   119.ATM6-0.XR1.DFW4.ALTER.NET [152.63.99.170]
  4    211 ms    171 ms    157 ms   295.at-2-0-0.XR1.DFW9.ALTER.NET [152.63.96.150]

  5    234 ms    181 ms    169 ms   185.ATM5-0.BR3.DFW9.ALTER.NET [152.63.100.161]
  6    246 ms    169 ms    171 ms   sl-bb2-nyc-1-0-0.sprintlink.net [144.232.18.29]

  7    164 ms    169 ms    159 ms   sl-bb21-fw-13-0.sprintlink.net [144.232.11.245]

  8    327 ms    218 ms    222 ms   sl-bb21-chi-6-0.sprintlink.net [144.232.8.53]
  9    225 ms    212 ms    243 ms   144.232.10.14
 10    224 ms    212 ms    202 ms   sl-split-13-0.sprintlink.net [144.232.189.62]
 11    225 ms    224 ms    212 ms   zzz-064199022033.splitrock.net [64.199.22.33]
 12    255 ms    281 ms    230 ms   zzz-216043064006.splitrock.net [216.43.64.6]
 13    265 ms    308 ms    255 ms   zzz-209255255070.splitrock.net [209.255.255.70]

 14    268 ms    286 ms    277 ms   198.45.24.244
 15    270 ms    255 ms    267 ms   198.45.24.130

Trace complete.

C:\DOCUME~1\CURT>
```

FIGURE 9.9   Tracert

NSLOOKUP

Nslookup is used to look up IP address to DNS mappings in a DNS database. Of course, this tool only works in domain environments where DNS is in use. You can gain the DNS server's name and IP address by simply typing **nslookup** at the command prompt. To see a listing of available switches, type **nslookup** so that the DNS server is found, then simply type **?** to see the options available to you.

SETTING UP A HOME OR OFFICE NETWORK

As an A+ technician, your first thought might be that home and small office networking is beneath your skills. However, don't assume things are that simple. How about a small office network with 50 Windows XP clients, a single Internet connection, and a network that spans several rooms? How about adding laptop computers to that mix that need to travel from room to room? Or what about a home network of five computers, each one running different versions of Windows and even using different types of networking components?

As networking has become more complex, so has home and small office networking, and it is not at all unusual for home users to hire extra help (like you!) to set it all up. Also, small businesses may use a workgroup rather than a domain, but still hire a full-time network and computer manager (you again). So the importance of home and small office networking in today's computing environment cannot be understated, and your skills in this area will surely be put to use at some time or another. The following sections explore the issues you should keep in mind when configuring home or small office networks with Windows XP.

HOME AND SMALL OFFICE HARDWARE

The networking hardware you need for a home or small office network is typically the same as you might see in larger networks, but much more scaled down and simplified, of course. The following bullet list gives you an overview of the hardware you'll need:

- **Network interface cards**   Regardless of the type of network you want, each computer must be outfitted with a NIC. The NIC gives the computer access to the network. Before purchasing NICs, you'll need to decide what kind of network you want to configure (which we'll explore in the next section).

- **Cabling**   You'll need the correct cabling to connect computers on a home or small office network. The exception, of course, is wireless networks, where no cabling is needed. We'll cover wireless networking later in this chapter.

- **Hub or access point**   A hub is a device in which all computers connect in a home or small office network. The hub routes traffic between computers; think of it as a central connection device. Hubs come in a number of different sizes that support different numbers of clients. Some hubs even provide DSL/cable connections and firewall functionality. An access point is like a hub, but is used for wireless networks.

- **Routers and residential gateways**   Depending on the needs of your network, you may need a router or residential gateway. A router or residential gateway manages traffic coming onto the network from the Internet as well as traffic flowing from the network to the Internet. You can think of a router or a residential gateway as a gatekeeper between the workgroup and the Internet. Routers and residential gateways often provide firewall services and even network address translation (NAT) functions as well. The purpose of this configuration is to keep all computers separated from the Internet. The router or residential gateway is the only device that connects to the Internet (on behalf of the network clients), and with the client management functions, it provides a great measure of security. Of course, you can use Internet Connection Firewall and Internet Connection Sharing to achieve this same purpose (see Chapter 13), but many people prefer the flexibility and additional security features provided by some routers and residential gateways.

TECH TALK

Understanding NAT

I mentioned that a number of routers and residential gateways provide network address translation (NAT). NAT is an industry standard service that hides the internal IP address of a LAN from the Internet or other destinations beyond the gateway. NAT translates all internal IP addresses of LAN clients into a different IP address range. These new addresses are then used on the Internet. If a hacker on the Internet attempts to break into a network computer using the IP address, guess what? He doesn't have the real IP address of the client, so the attack fails. In many cases, the router or residential gateway will use a translated address to act like one computer connecting to the Internet, when in fact all of the clients sit behind the router or residential gateway. This measure is very helpful when it comes to security. Routers and residential gateways typically cost from $100 to around $400, depending on what you want. You'll find them at most computer stores, and you can find them for sale on the Internet as well from a number of providers, such as NetGear (**www.netgear.com**). If you want to know more about the technical details of NAT, access RFC 1631 on the Internet.

CHOOSING A TYPE OF NETWORK

When working with home and small office networks, you have some flexibility when it comes to the type of network that you want to use. There are three primary options that are commonly supported (and for which you'll find plenty of hardware).

ETHERNET

Ethernet is a networking standard and the most popular kind of network in use today. When you think of a network with a typical wired configuration, you are generally thinking of Ethernet. Ethernet was introduced in the 1970s by Xerox, and it is defined by the Institute of Electrical and Electronics Engineers (IEEE) specification 802.3. This specification defines how hardware devices must function in order to conform to the Ethernet standard. For this reason, you can use a mixture of Ethernet NICs from different vendors with no compatibility problems. Ethernet NICs connect to RJ-45 cables (looks like a larger phone cable), and you'll need an Ethernet hub, router, or residential gateway, depending on your needs. Ethernet networks provide three different speeds, which must be supported by the NICs that you purchase:

- **10 Mbps**   The 10BaseT Ethernet standard defines 10 megabits per second (Mbps) transfer speed.

- **100 Mbps**   The 100BaseT (also called Fast Ethernet) standard supports up to 100 Mbps transfer speed.

- **Gigabit Ethernet**   Gigabit Ethernet is a standard that provides 1000 Mbps, or 1 Gbps. You must have Gigabit Ethernet NICs and hubs in order to get the speed, but you still use the same RJ-45 cabling.

NOTE   Since Ethernet is the most common type of home and small office network (not to mention larger networks as well), you'll find a plethora of NICs, routers, hubs, and residential gateways at any computer store.

HOMEPNA

HomePNA is another type of network topology that is designed for home use, but it works well in small offices too. HomePNA networks use typical PCI or USB NICs, but each NIC connects to a standard phone jack in the home or small office using standard RJ-11 phone cable. Rather than using a hub and having wiring running everywhere, you simply use the existing phone lines in the home as the network. Even though the computers are connected to the phone lines, you can still have voice conversations. This type of setup works great in homes where computers reside in different rooms, or in small offices with the same situation. You don't have to run additional cabling and you don't have to worry about a hub. If this sounds like a dream come true, it certainly does solve a number of problems. However, the problem with HomePNA is that you are limited to 10 Mbps. If you are only sharing files, printers, and accessing the Internet, but you need to run large multimedia files over the network or play network games, the speed is a little slow. For most users, though, the 10 Mbps speed is all you need to use the network and access a broadband Internet connection from a residential gateway or ICS host computer. Some small office networks even combine existing Ethernet networks with HomePNA networks for more flexibility. In this case, you'll need one Windows XP computer to act as a network bridge. See the "Network Bridges" section later in this chapter for details.

WIRELESS NETWORKS

Windows XP brings a lot of wireless networking capabilities to the table, making it easier for you to configure and use wireless networks than ever before. Since this is a newer kind of network and one that requires a little more thought, I've devoted an entire section to wireless networking later in this chapter.

SETTING UP A HOME OR SMALL OFFICE NETWORK

As you are preparing to create a home or small office network, you'll need to gather the hardware that you'll need and determine the kind of network that you want, such as Ethernet, HomePNA, or wireless. If you have an existing network and you want to create a different network using a different network type, such as Ethernet and HomePNA, you can use a Windows XP Professional computer as a network bridge, which is explored in the next section. Before you get started configuring Windows XP for networking, you'll need to complete the following tasks:

1. Install any necessary NICs and gather cables (if needed).

2. Arrange the physical topology of the computers and connect the network cabling (if needed) to the hub, router, or residential gateway. You should review any documentation and instructions that accompanied the hardware.

3. Once the computers are all connected, determine if you will use Internet Connection Sharing (see Chapter 13 for more information). If you will be using ICS, you need to start the configuration of the home or small office network with the computer that will host the ICS connection. Follow the steps provided here to configure the computer.

CONFIGURING THE FIRST WINDOWS XP COMPUTER ON THE HOME OR SMALL OFFICE NETWORK

1. Click Start | Control Panel | Network Connections. In the Network Tasks pane of the Network Connections window, click the Set Up a Home or Small Office Network link.

2. The Network Setup Wizard appears. Click Next on the Welcome page.

3. In the Before You Continue page, read the instructions and make sure that all network components are connected and working. If you want to set up the ICS host at this time, connect to the Internet.

4. In the Select a Connection Method page, shown here, select the first button option if the computer will function as the ICS host. If not, choose the second button option if there currently exists another ICS host. If neither of these options apply to you, click Other. Make a selection and click Next.

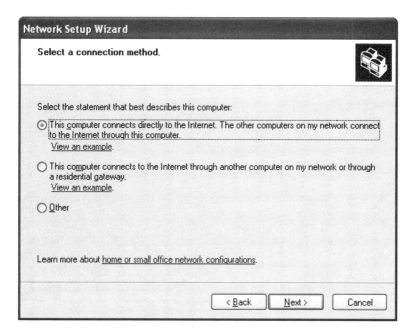

5. If you chose the Other option, the next page allows you to select one of the following:

- This computer connects to the Internet directory or though a network hub. Other computers on my network also connect to the Internet directly or through a hub.
- This computer connects directly to the Internet. I do not have a network yet.
- This computer belongs to a network that does not have an Internet connection.

6. In Step 4, if you determined that the computer should function as the ICS host, an Internet connection page appears, shown here. Select the Internet connection that you want to share and click Next.

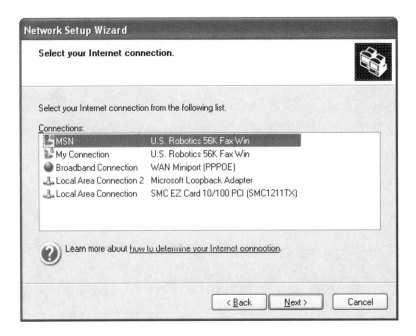

7. If you have multiple LAN connections installed on your computer, a page appears asking if you want to bridge those connections. You can choose to allow Windows XP to automatically bridge the connections by selecting the provided button option, or you can choose the button option so that you can choose your own bridge connections. Make a selection and click Next.

8. If you chose to select your own bridge connections, a page appears so that you can select the connections to bridge, shown next. Do not choose any Internet connections—you cannot bridge a LAN connection with an Internet connection, and doing so presents a serious security breach on your network! Make your selections and click Next.

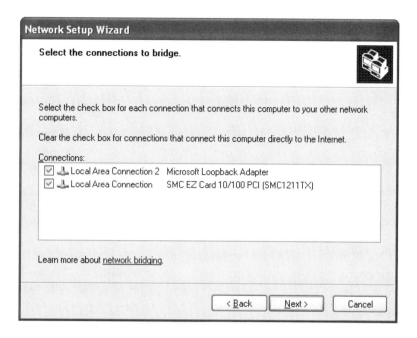

9. In the next page, give the computer a name and a description. The name you assign the computer should be a friendly name that is easily recognizable on your network. However, if you are using a broadband connection, your computer may have a required name (often true of cable modems). In that case, do not change the name if it is required by your ISP. See your ISP documentation for additional details. Click Next.

10. In the next page, assign a name for your network by typing it in the provided dialog box. By default, your workgroup is named MSHOME. However, you can change it to anything you like. The name should be friendly, and all computers on your network must use the same workgroup name. Click Next.

11. Review the settings you are about to apply on the next page. When you are sure they are correct, click Next. Use the Back button to make any necessary changes.

12. Windows XP configures the computer for networking, and you see a "waiting" page while the computer is configured.

13. When prompted, you can choose to create a network setup disk to use any downlevel clients. Make a selection if necessary and click Next.

14. Follow any additional instructions to create the network setup disk and click Finish. If all of the clients on your network are Windows XP clients, you will not need a network setup disk.

Once the first computer is installed, you are now ready to begin installing the other Windows XP computers. Simply follow these same steps to install the networking software on the additional client computers. If you are using ICS, keep in mind that the Network Setup Wizard will ask you to choose how the computer connects to the Internet. Select the option to connect "through another computer," and the Network Setup Wizard will locate the ICS host and proceed with setup from there.

Windows 98, Windows ME, Windows NT 4.0, and Windows 2000 clients can also natively function in your workgroup with your existing Windows XP clients. Windows 95, Windows 3.x, and earlier versions of Windows NT are not supported. These clients, collectively called down-level clients, can be configured manually for networking, or you can run the Network Setup Wizard on these clients as well. To use the Network Setup Wizard, you can either use the floppy disk that you created when you configured the Windows XP clients, or you can use the Windows XP installation CD-ROM to run the Network Setup Wizard.

INSTALLING DOWN-LEVEL CLIENTS

1. Insert the Windows XP CD-ROM into the down-level client's CD-ROM drive.

2. On the Welcome screen that appears, click the Perform Additional Tasks option.

3. In the next window, click the Set Up a Home or Small Office Network option.

4. Depending on the operating system version you are using, the Network Setup Wizard may need to copy some additional files to your computer and restart it. Click Yes to continue.

5. At this point, the Network Setup Wizard Welcome page appears. Click Next to continue. The remaining steps are the same. See the steps earlier in this section for instructions.

TECH TALK

Using Manual IP Addresses

When you run the Network Setup Wizard, APIPA is used to automatically assign IP addresses to network clients. Clients on your workgroup assign themselves an APIPA address in the 192.168 range. Each client on the network has a unique IP address, and a query method is used during setup to make sure that the IP address being assigned is unique.

If you want to manually assign different IP addresses to the clients on your workgroup, you can easily do so by accessing Internet Protocol properties from the General tab of the NIC's properties pages. APIPA is designed to service workgroups and was specifically developed for networks where no centralized DHCP server is in use. The fact is, manual IP address configuration can be complicated and problematic, so before making any static changes to the IP addressing scheme automatically used on your network, keep the following issues in mind. First, each client on your network must have a unique IP address in the same range and an appropriate subnet mask. You must manually change the IP addressing properties of each client on the network. If you use ICS, the default gateway assigned to your network clients must be the address of the ICS host.

NETWORK BRIDGES

Consider this scenario. You manage an office network. The network is an Ethernet network and contains 22 computers. Recently, your office bought the building next door, which consists of a number of cubicles. Management does not want to spend money on the network at this time, so they want to use HomePNA so that the existing phone lines can be used for networking, rather than running new cable. This way, the ten new employees in the new office can have a network with no additional wiring expenses to the company. Your task as the administrator is to connect the Ethernet network with the HomePNA network. Can it be done? The answer is yes, through a software feature in Windows XP called a bridge.

A *network bridge* is a piece of software or hardware that can connect two dissimilar networks or network segments. In our example, the Ethernet and HomePNA networks will not readily communicate with each other, but you can use a Windows XP computer to act as the bridge between the two networks.

All communication flowing from the Ethernet and HomePNA networks flows through the bridge, which acts as a translator. This process is invisible to users who do not have to be aware of the bridge at all.

 You don't need a bridge if you are using a wireless network and a wired Ethernet network. The wireless Access Point can connect into the wired hub so that the two networks can communicate.

If you need to configure a network bridge, the configuration in Windows XP is quick and easy. Select the desired Windows XP computer that will act as a bridge, then physically install a NIC from each network. For example, if I wanted to bridge an Ethernet network with a HomePNA network, I would install an Ethernet NIC and a HomePNA NIC. Connect the two NICs to their networks, and you are ready to configure the bridge.

NOTE   Never, never bridge a private network with a connection that has a public Internet address. This will open your private network to the Internet. Rather, use ICS to connect the computers to the Internet. Also, do not bridge local networks with VPN connections or dial-up connections.

CREATING A NETWORK BRIDGE

1. Log on with an administrative account.

2. Access the properties pages of both connections. Using the Advanced tab, turn off ICS or ICF if they are in use.

3. Open Network Connections. Hold down the CTRL key and click each of the LAN connections you want to bridge so they are both selected.

4. Release the CTRL key. Then right-click the selected adapters and select Bridge Connections.

5. Windows XP creates the network bridge. When the process is complete, the bridge appears in the Network Connections folder, along with the LAN connections that now appear under the Network Bridge category, shown in Figure 9-10.

NOTE   The computer that contains the bridge must be turned on at all times for the two network segments to be bridged. If the bridge is offline, the segments will not be connected.

You can add or remove connections to the bridge at any time by right-clicking the bridge icon and selecting Properties to open the Network Bridge Properties dialog box, shown in Figure 9-11. You can only have one bridge on a Windows XP

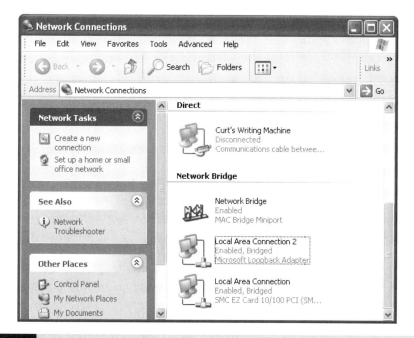

FIGURE 9.10   Network Bridge

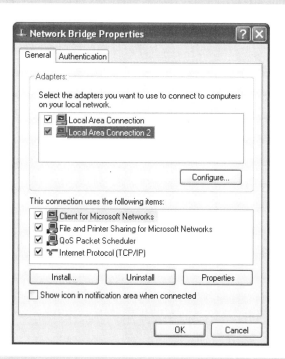

FIGURE 9.11   Network bridge properties

computer, but the bridge can support multiple connections (up to 64). You can easily add or remove connections from a bridge by right-clicking the bridge, and selecting the connection, and clicking Remove From Bridge or Add To Bridge.

CONNECTING TO A WINDOWS DOMAIN

Workgroup connections, such as those configured for home and small office use, do not provide any centralized administration or security. To use the network, you have to authenticate on a local machine using a local account configured on that computer. Because workgroups can be difficult to manage and rather difficult to secure, medium to larger environments typically use a domain.

In a domain environment, the domain controllers hold the local security database and network administrators manage user and computer accounts through the Active Directory from a Windows 2000 or Windows.NET server. A network administrator determines your username and password, and configures an account for you in the Active Directory. When a Windows logon dialog box appears, you enter that username and password. The username and password is sent to the domain controller for authentication. If granted access, you log on to Windows, and your computer and user account are active on the network. So you do not configure user accounts on a local computer, and you can log on to any workstation using your username and password, unlike a workgroup environment where user accounts are managed locally.

Domains, of course, are much more expensive than workgroups, since you have to provide Windows servers and administrators to manage those servers. Since Windows XP cannot be a domain controller, we'll focus on domain connectivity in this section, not the management of a domain from Windows 2000 or Windows.NET server. To join a Windows XP Professional computer to a Windows domain, you'll need a few things set up and ready before you can actually join:

- You must be using Windows XP Professional. Windows XP Home edition cannot join a Windows domain.

- A network administrator must create a computer account for the computer in the Active Directory.

- A network administrator must create a username and password for the user. You'll need this information, along with the name of the domain, when you configure your computer to join a domain.

- The computer's TCP/IP settings should be set to "obtain an IP address automatically" so that a DHCP server can provide a valid IP address for your computer.

- Your computer must be configured with a NIC and physically connected to the network.

- You can join a domain with wizard help, or you can do so manually. If you do not have a lot of experience using the manual approach, I recommend the wizard to get you started. The following steps show you how to join a domain using the Network Identification Wizard.

JOINING A DOMAIN

1. On Windows XP Professional, log on with an administrator account.
2. Click Start | Control Panel | System.
3. In the System Properties dialog box, click the Computer Name tab. As you can see here, the name tab gives you a computer description and Network ID and Change buttons.

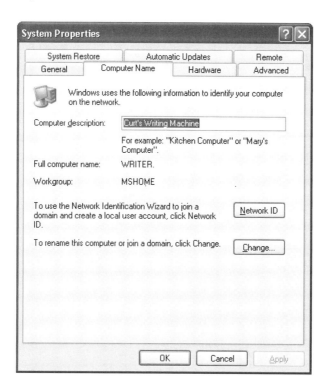

4. Click the Network ID button. This opens the Network Identification Wizard, which guides you through the rest of the process. Click Next on the Welcome page that appears.

5. The next page asks you if the computer will be a part of a business network (domain) or a home/small office computer (workgroup), as shown here. Select the business network option and click Next.

6. In the Connecting a Network page, select the My Company Uses a Network with a Domain option and click Next.

7. The next page tells you about the username, password, domain name, and possibly computer name information that you will need. Click Next when you have read the page.

8. On the User Account and Domain Information page, shown here, enter your username, password, and domain name. Keep in mind that the password is case sensitive. Click Next.

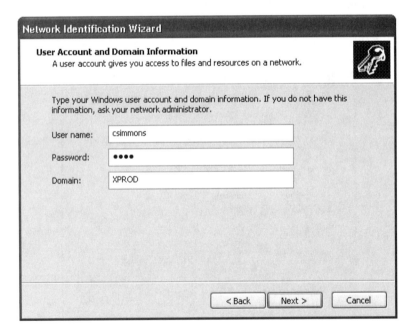

9. You may also be asked to verify the computer and the domain. If so, enter the information in the provided page and click Next.

10. In the User Account page, you can choose to add the domain user account to the local user accounts so the user can gain access to local system resources, as shown here. This feature enables you to limit what the user can do on the local machine or even make the user account a local administrator account.

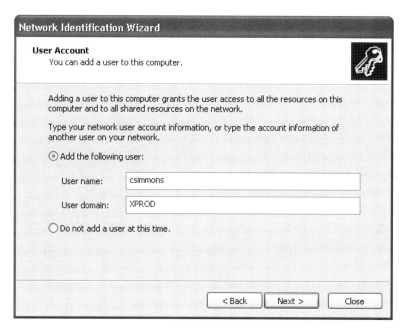

For example, I am logging on to a domain using my username, csimmons. However, I also want administrative control over my local computer. So I simply agree to add the new user account to the local computer. I can then log on locally with my administrative account and make this domain account a local administrator account. Now I have one login for the domain that allows me to completely manage my local computer as well. Make a selection and click Next.

11. If you chose to add the user, choose the level of access that you want to assign, as shown here, and click Next.

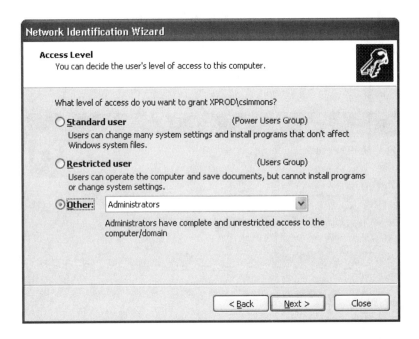

12. Click Finish. A prompt appears for you to restart your computer.

The Network Identification Wizard helps you walk through the steps of joining a domain, but you can do so more quickly simply by clicking the Change button on the Network Identification tab of System properties. This option basically distills the wizard pages to a single dialog box, shown in Figure 9-12, where you enter the computer name and (if necessary) click the option to log on to a Windows domain, and enter the domain name. Simply click OK to join the domain and enter the username and password for your domain account when prompted. You'll need to restart your computer once you complete the joining process.

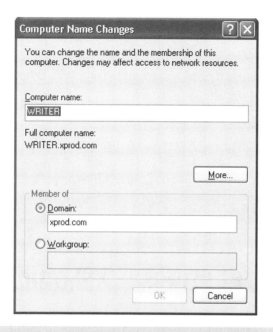

Computer Name Changes

TROUBLESHOOTING

Changes in Windows XP Professional After Joining a Domain

Once you join a Windows XP Professional computer to a domain, there are some changes and restrictions that take place on the operating system. You may hear complaints about some of these, and it's a good idea to get familiar with them so you'll know what is really a problem and what is simply normal behavior. After you join Windows XP Professional to a domain, you'll find

- Fast user switching will not work when you log onto a domain.

- There is no automatic logon.

- There are no password hints available, should you forget your password.

(continued)

- The Logoff and Shut Down screens appear differently (they do the same thing, but they look more like Windows 2000).

- No username icon appears on the Start menu.

- CTRL-ALT-DEL gives you the Windows security dialog box instead of Task Manager.

- There is no Internet Time tab found on Date and Time properties.

- Simple File Sharing is disabled.

OTHER IMPORTANT NETWORK CONNECTIONS

Aside from configuring workgroup and domain connections, there are a few other important networking connections that you might find useful. A major one, of course, is Internet connections, which you can learn more about in Chapter 12, but you may also find direct cable connections and even incoming connections helpful in a variety of situations. The following two sections show you how to configure these.

DIRECT CABLE CONNECTION

Let's say you have two computers that need to exchange information on a temporary basis. You do not want to install a network and you do not want to install NICs in those computers. Can you do it without having to use the floppy disk shuffle? Yes, you can easily create a connection between the two computers using a direct cable connection (DCC).

A DCC connection is a great temporary solution where one computer needs to share information with another. The DCC connection uses a null modem cable (connects to serial ports), a DirectParallel cable, or even two modems or ISDN devices. The transfer speed tends to be slow (usually around 24 Kbps to 50 Kbps), but the DCC gets the job done when no network is available or is not desired. The null modem or DirectParallel cable you'll need to connect the two computers is readily available at most computer stores.

You can create a DCC with Windows XP and another Windows XP computer, or even with Windows 95, Windows 98, Windows ME, or Windows 2000. During a DCC session, one computer acts as the host (the computer you are downloading files from) and one computer acts as the guest. The guest computer accesses information on the host, and the transfer is one way. In other words, the host cannot access information on the guest computer. As you can see, DCC isn't a true networking solution, but a way to get files from one computer to another. To create the DCC, simply connect the two computers together using the null modem cable, DirectParallel cable, or even two modems, then follow these steps.

CREATING A DIRECT CABLE CONNECTION

1. Log on to Windows XP with an administrator account. You cannot create a host direct cable configuration unless your account has administrative privileges.

2. Click Start | Control Panel | Network Connections.

3. In Network Tasks, click Create a New Connection. Click Next on the wizard's Welcome page.

4. In the Network Connection Type page, shown here, select the Set Up an Advanced Connection radio button and click Next.

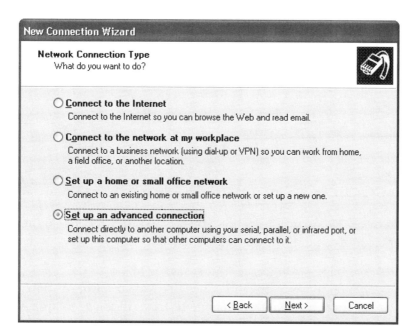

5. In the next page, choose the Connect Directly to Another Computer radio button option and click Next.

6. In the Host or Guest page, select the Host radio button and click Next.

7. In the Connection Device page, choose the port that you want to use for the connection (such as serial or parallel) from the drop-down menu. When you select the desired port, the port is configured for direct cable communication. You cannot use a port that currently has another device attached to it. Click Next.

8. In the User Permissions page, you can select which users are allowed to access the host computer through a direct cable connection. Notice that you can also create additional user accounts as needed directly from this window, as shown here. Make your selections and click Next.

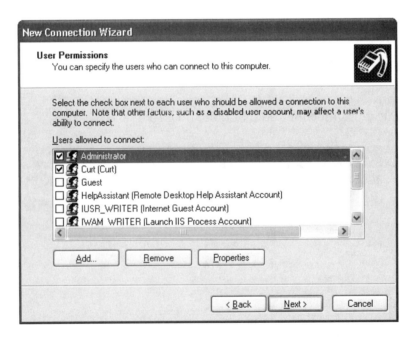

9. Click Finish. The new connection appears in the Network Connections folder under the label Incoming Connection.

Once you have the host set up, your next task is to set up the guest computer. For Windows XP computers, you simply use the Network Connections Wizard again and choose the Guest option instead of Host. If you are using another version of Windows as the guest, see that operating system's help files for setup instructions. In Windows XP, the connection on the client computer appears as Direct in Network Connections, as you can see in Figure 9-13. Simply double-click the icon to make the connection, then enter a valid username and password.

FIGURE 9.13   Direct connection

Keep in mind that you can create multiple direct cable connections to different computers as needed. Simply create the connections, enter the computer name that you want to connect to, and choose the appropriate port.

INCOMING CONNECTIONS

Let's say you have a lot of files on a certain Windows XP computer at your office. You access those files regularly when you travel with your laptop computer. Your network does not use a proxy server, so you need to configure a dial-up connection so that you can dial into the Windows XP computer and access files. Although you can accomplish this task using Remote Desktop (see Chapter 11), Windows XP also allows you to create a simple incoming connection. Connect the computer's modem to the desired phone line, then simply use a dial-up connection from the remote computer to dial the Windows XP computer in your office. You can determine what users can have dial-up access, and as you can see, this is an easy way to access your computer when you are away. This same principle is true if you want your computer to accept incoming virtual private network connections, which you can learn more about in the next section.

Setting up an incoming connection on a Windows XP computer is easy—just follow these steps.

SETTING UP AN INCOMING CONNECTION

1. Log on with an administrator account.

2. Click Start | Connect To | Show All Connections.

3. Click the Create a Connection link in the Network Tasks portion of the window.

4. Click Next on the Welcome page.

5. In the Network Connection Type page, choose the Set Up an Advanced Connection option. Click Next.

6. In the Advanced Connections Options page, click the Accept Incoming Connections option and click Next.

7. In the Devices for Connection page, select your modem and click Next.

8. In the next page, you can choose to allow VPN connections or not. If you choose to allow VPN connections, the wizard configures ICF for VPN connections. Make a selection and click Next.

9. In the User Permissions page, select the users that can connect using the incoming connection. You can create additional user accounts as needed by clicking the Add button. Click Next.

10. In the Networking Software page, you can choose to enable or disable any protocols or services that can be used on the connection. Make any necessary changes and click Next.

11. Click Finish. The incoming connection now appears in the Network Connections folder.

NOTE You can make changes to the connection, such as VPN support or user permissions, at any time by simply right-clicking the connection and selecting Properties.

VIRTUAL PRIVATE NETWORKS

Virtual private networks (VPNs) have become very popular during the past several years because they can give you the connection flexibility and security that is needed for remote connections—and you can use an existing network infrastructure, such as an intranet or even the Internet. VPN connections enable you to use an existing public network, such as the Internet, freely and in a way that is private. When a VPN connection is used, the actual network data that you are transferring is encapsulated in a Point to Point Tunneling Protocol packet (PPTP) or a Layer 2 Tunneling Protocol (L2TP) packet. The packet has the typical header destination that you might find on a typical PPP packet traveling the Internet. The PPTP or L2TP packet can traverse the Internet as a PPP packet. When the packet reaches the destination network, the PPTP or L2TP encapsulation is stripped away and the true data is revealed. The end result? You can connect to segments of your network using the Internet without paying WAN link charges. This feature works well for a company that has a satellite office where a few people need to send data over the VPN connection each day. Of course, the VPN connection is not designed for high levels of traffic, but in many connectivity cases, it is an easy and cost-efficient solution.

PPTP allows tunneled traffic through an IP network, such as the Internet. The second type of protocol is L2TP, which provides more functionality. For example, PPTP can only be used on IP networks, whereas L2TP encapsulates PPP frames to be sent over IP, X.25, frame relay, or ATM networks. Also, L2TP supports header compression and tunnel authentication, as well as the use of IP Security (IPSec). PPTP does support encryption, however, whereas L2TP only supports encryption when IPSec is used. The end result is that L2TP gives you more options and functionality than PPTP, but both are highly effective VPN protocols. However, if you are using Windows XP Professional to access a Windows NT VPN server, note that only PPTP is supported. You can use L2TP to connect to Windows 2000 VPN servers, or another Windows XP Professional computer acting as a VPN server.

You can configure Windows XP Professional to both make VPN connections and allow incoming VPN connections. The following steps show you the process of configuring Windows XP Professional to make VPN calls.

CONFIGURING VPN CONNECTIVITY

1. Click Start | Control Panel | Network Connections.

2. Start the New Connection Wizard and click Next on the Welcome page.

3. In the Network Connection Type page, click Connect to the Network at My Workplace and click Next.

4. In the Network Connection page, choose the Virtual Private Network Connection radio button and click Next.

5. In the Connection Name page, enter a friendly name for the connection and click Next.

6. In the Public Network page, choose which existing dial-up connection you want to dial so that the VPN tunnel can be established. For example, if you had a dial-up connection configured to access a RAS server, you could select that connection for the VPN server. Make your selection and click Next.

7. Enter the host name or IP address of the VPN server to which you are connecting.

8. Click Finish. The VPN connection is created and now appears in the Network Connections folder.

The VPN connection's properties pages are basically the same as a typical dial-up connection. You have the same security setting options, calling options, and so on. The General tab lists the host name or IP address of the destination and the dial-up connection that should be used to generate the VPN connection. If you want to accept incoming VPN connections, you can use the New Connection Wizard to create an incoming connection, and then allow VPN connections during the wizard steps. See the previous section for more information about creating incoming connections. Keep in mind that VPN connectivity can be managed with authentication protocols, just as a typical dial-up connection. This feature enables you to use VPN solutions without compromising network security standards.

WIRELESS NETWORKING

Wireless networking has been around for some time, but many people in the early days of wireless networking abandoned it due to compatibility problems and a general lack of reliability. Wireless networking has come a long way since then, and Windows XP Professional includes a number of features that support common wireless networking standards and hardware. In short, if you need a wireless network, Windows XP has what you need to create and configure it.

UNDERSTANDING WIRELESS NETWORKING

Just as there are different wired networks, such as Ethernet and HomePNA, there are also several different types of wireless networks. These different types of wireless networks define different standards that hardware manufacturers must adhere to when creating wireless networking components and devices. The following bullet list gives you the skinny on each of the major types:

- **Infrared**   Infrared wireless uses an infrared beam to transmit data from one device to the next, and is most often used in PC devices. For example, wireless keyboards, mice, printers, and game devices can connect with an infrared port on your computer. Additionally, laptops and PDAs can connect with a desktop computer for data transfer. Infrared is a great solution for device-to-PC connectivity, but in terms of an actual LAN, infrared is not a preferred connectivity method.

- **Wireless personal area networks (WPANs)**   A WPAN is a personal area network, meaning it resides in one generalized space, such as a room. In other words, a personal area space is the area surrounding a person. WPANs are useful for wireless network computing in one location, or wireless networking between PDAs, cell phones, laptop computers, and so on. WPANs can make use of infrared connections for objects that are very close, or you can use Bluetooth, which communicates through radio waves up to 30 feet. The IEEE has established a working group for the development of WPANs, numbered 802.15. You can learn more about the standard by simply searching for IEEE 802.15 on any search engine.

- **Wireless local area networks (WLANs)**   A WLAN is a wireless network that exists within one geographical location, such as in a home, office building, school, or other such structure. The IEEE 802.11 standard for WLANs defines transfer rates at 1–2 Mbps. As you can see, the 802.11 standard was rather slow. However, today, the new IEEE standard for WLAN networking is 802.11b, which defines data transfer rates of up to 11 Mbps using a 2.4 GHz frequency band. 802.11b is the popular standard today, which gives you speeds comparable to a typical Ethernet network.

- **Wireless metropolitan area networks (WMANs)**   WMANs allow communication between different locations within a single metropolitan area. For example, let's say your company resides in New York, but there are three offices in different locations in the city. Using wireless technologies, a WMAN could be created so that users between those different offices could connect.

- **Wireless wide area networks (WWANs)**   A WWAN connects WLANs that are separated over wide geographic areas. For example, if your company has offices in New York, Seattle, and Dallas, a WWAN could be used to wirelessly connect the different WAN network segments. WWAN technologies involve the use of satellite communications maintained by service providers, and use the same technologies used in cellular phones and wireless PDAs.

Both Windows XP Professional and Windows XP Home editions support infrared and 802.11b wireless networking. The 802.11b standard, which is also called Wi-Fi, is the most popular wireless networking standard in use today, providing transfer rates of around 11 Mbps. In a Wi-Fi network, you have a range of up to 300 feet from point to point, and it provides the best wireless security that is currently available. Since Wi-Fi is the most popular, you'll find plenty of wireless network devices at any computer store that are compatible with Windows XP.

NOTE If you are shopping for wireless devices, look for compatibility information right on the box. You should see an "802.11b standard" or "Wi-Fi standard" note on the box as well.

UNDERSTANDING INFRARED

Infrared technology uses a line-of-sight infrared beam to send data from one device to the next. It is the same principle as a grocery store scanner. Since this is a line-of-sight technology, the two infrared devices must be in range and aligned (pointing to each other). The single infrared beam then transfers the data. Because you have to line up the two infrared ports on the two computers or the device (such as a PDA) and the computer, infrared networking is not as practical as Wi-Fi.

UNDERSTANDING WI-FI

Wi-Fi networks provide two different topologies or modes. Wireless NICs can support either of the two modes, which are called infrastructure mode and ad hoc mode. In infrastructure mode, an existing wired LAN, such as Ethernet, extends to include wireless devices. The wireless devices use a hub, called an access point, that connects to the wired LAN's hub. In other words, the access point manages all of the traffic between the wired network and the wireless devices, just as a typical hub might do. Like a hub, the access point can support a certain number of wireless clients, depending on the model you purchase. You can also use several access points in a daisy chain fashion, if necessary.

The second kind of mode is ad hoc mode. Ad hoc mode allows one wireless computer to connect to another without the use of an access point. For example, let's say you have four wireless computers in the same room. Rather than using an access point, the computer's wireless NICs can be configured to use ad hoc mode. The four computers can communicate with each other, and since no interface is needed with a wired network, an access point is not necessary.

The good news is you can also use infrastructure mode and ad hoc mode at the same time, through a process called zero configuration. When in infrastructure mode, all wireless NICs look for an access point. If one is not found, the NICs switch to ad hoc mode so that communication with other computers within range can occur. Windows XP can automatically configure wireless NICs from infrastructure mode to ad hoc mode, and vice versa.

UNDERSTANDING WIRELESS SECURITY

Unless security is your passion, most of us would rather not spend our time thinking about or worrying about security. However, in an age of electronic theft and malicious networking attacks, security is an ever-important issue, and in fact, the problems with wireless security have kept many networks from implementing wireless features.

TECH TALK

Wireless Networking Hardware

So, what do you need to configure a wireless network? As with other types of networking, you'll need wireless NICs that are compatible with Windows XP and you'll need an access point, if you intend to use infrastructure mode. Of course, no cabling is necessary, with the exception of an RJ-45 cable to connect the access point to an Ethernet hub.

Wireless NICs are readily available as PCI internal NICs, USB external NICs, and PCMCIA cards for laptop computers. Generally, if you buy an internal PCI NIC, you must also buy the wireless PCMCIA card that plugs into the PCI NIC. In other words, most wireless PCI NICs simply provide a way to use the PCMCIA wireless radio NIC on the PC. Each wireless NIC has a miniature antenna for transmitting and receiving wireless data. As you might imagine, major NIC providers such as NetGear, Linksys, SMC, and other vendors provide wireless NICs. As a general rule, wireless NICs will cost you between $60 and $100, depending on the manufacturer and the type (PCMCIA costs more). They are a little more expensive than Ethernet or HomePNA NICs, but the price difference is not enough to prohibit you from using a wireless network. Make sure that any wireless NIC you buy is compatible with 802.11b.

The access point looks somewhat like a wired hub (except there are no ports for cable connections) with a small antenna. You connect the access point to the Ethernet or HomePNA network with an RJ-11 or RJ-45 cable as needed. Wireless clients connect to the access point and then the wired network. Access points generally cost around $150–500, depending on what you want and the brand. As with hubs, there are many options to choose from, and some wireless access points also function as a router for a DSL or cable connection, in the event that you want a completely wireless network.

The good news is Windows XP supports the major wireless security features that you may need to implement. 802.11b contains a basic security feature for access points called the Service Set Identifier (SSID). An SSID is a known security identifier taken from the NIC on each computer. The access point is aware of the SSID, and once it is taken from the NIC, an association with the NIC and the SSID is made on the access point. However, the SSID is not encrypted, which makes it available for theft during transit. As you can see, the 802.11b security standard really isn't that secure.

However, there is another security standard that is commonly supported by wireless hardware called the Wired Equivalent Privacy (WEP). This security standard provides a 60-bit encryption scheme. The encryption scheme prevents theft of data that is airborne, and this built-in standard provides a great measure of security, especially for home and small office wireless networks. Along with WEP, many wireless NICs also support a standard called 802.1x. The 802.1x standard provides authentication for access to Ethernet networks over a wireless access point. Using 802.1x, the access point authenticates users in conjunction with server software on the Windows network. Most major brands of wireless NICs support both the WEP and 802.1x standards, so make sure you read the box before purchasing any particular brand of wireless NIC. Although you may not be worried about security or need these standards, it is good to know that your NICs support them.

SETTING UP AN INFRARED NETWORK

As I mentioned earlier, an infrared network is a great way to exchange data between a few computers, or between a computer and some device, such as a PDA, printer, mouse, game device, and so forth. In Windows XP, infrared networking technology is implemented by the Infrared Data Association's standards (IrDA), which provide fast data transfer over an infrared beam of light. In order to communicate, the computer must be outfitted with an infrared port. Most laptop computers ship with an infrared port, and if you need one on a PC, you can purchase an infrared port device that connects to the computer via USB. As always, check the Microsoft HCL before purchasing an infrared device. Once you install an infrared device, you'll see a wireless link icon in the Control Panel. If you double-click the wireless link icon, the Wireless Link dialog box opens, which contains a few configuration tabs. On the Infrared tab, shown in Figure 9-14, you have the following options:

- **Display an Icon on the Taskbar Indicating Infrared Activity**   This option will allow you to see when you are connected to an infrared link and when another computer or device is within your infrared range.

- **Play Sound When Infrared Device Is Near By**   A tone is played when a device first comes into range of your infrared port.

- **Allow Others to Send Files to Your Computer Using Infrared Communications**   If you want to let other devices send files to your computer over the infrared link, make sure this item is selected. Otherwise, users will receive an error message stating that access is denied.

- **Notify Me When Receiving Files**   When this item is selected, a transfer status dialog box appears when files are being received.

- **Default Location to Receive Files**   If you choose to receive files, you can configure a default location where those files are stored. Click the Browse button to select the location.

On the Image Transfer tab, you can choose to use the wireless link to transfer images from a digital camera to your computer, which is a popular application

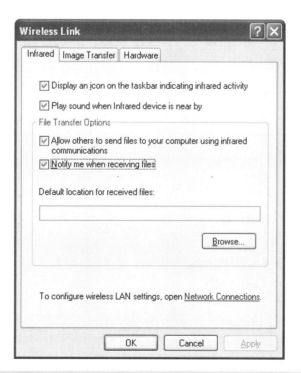

FIGURE 9.14   Infrared tab

of infrared technology. You can enable the option and choose a default storage location for the picture files as they arrive. Also notice the Explore Location After Receiving Pictures option. If you choose this option, the folder in which the pictures are stored will automatically open after you have received the files.

The Hardware tab simply lists the infrared device that is installed. You can see basic information about the device, such as the manufacturer, COM port location, and the current device status. If you select the device in the window and click the Properties button, Device Manager properties for the device open. You'll see the standard General and Driver tabs, but there is also an IrDA Settings tab that may come in handy. This tab, shown in Figure 9-15, allows you to set the maximum connection rate as well as the COM port. If you are having problems with communications with a certain device, try lowering this value.

Once you have the infrared port up and working, there are two different connections that you can establish using Windows XP. The first is an infrared link, which allows the computer to communicate with another computer or device over an infrared link. You can connect with another Windows XP computer, a Windows 2000 computer, a Windows 98 computer, or other devices such as PDAs and digital cameras. This kind of link connection allows you to transfer files from one computer/device to the other computer/device.

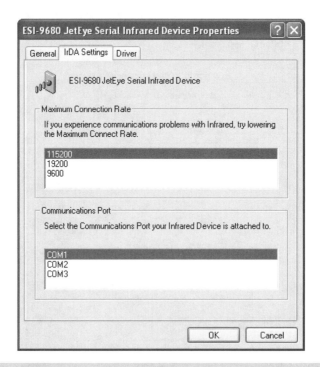

FIGURE 9.15   IrDA Settings tab

CREATING AN INFRARED LINK

1. Move the infrared computers or devices so that the infrared receivers are facing each other and are within one meter of each other.

2. When the infrared device is detected, an icon appears in your Notification Area and the Wireless Link icon appears on the desktop.

3. Right-click the Wireless link icon and select Connect. The connection is made and data can now be transferred.

The second kind of connection is an infrared network connection. An infrared network connection provides a direct connection between two infrared computers where the two computers can communicate with each other over the network connection. One computer acts as the host and one computer acts as the guest, whereas the guest computer primarily accesses shared resources on the host computer. As you can see, this works basically like a direct cable connection. The guest computer provides a username and password, and then can access shared information on the host computer. The guest computer can even map to shared drives and folders. To set up an infrared network connection between two computers, just walk through the following steps.

SETTING UP AN INFRARED NETWORK CONNECTION

1. On the host computer, create a user account for the guest computer if necessary.

2. Align the two computers so that the infrared transceivers are within one meter of each other and are pointing at each other.

3. The infrared icon appears in the Notification Area and the Wireless Link icon appears on the desktop.

4. To establish the network connection, open Network Connections and click Create a New Connection.

5. Click Next on the Welcome page.

6. In the Network Connection Type page, choose Set Up an Advanced Connection. Click Next.

7. On the Advanced Connection Options page, choose Connect Directly to Another Computer and click Next.

8. Choose the role of the computer, which is the Host computer in this example. Click Next.

9. On the Connection Device page, choose the infrared port as the connection device. Click Next.

10. In the User Permissions page, choose the accounts that can connect over the infrared port. Click Add if you need to add additional accounts. Click Next.

11. Click Finish. The connection now appears in Network Connections as Incoming Connection.

12. On the Guest computer, repeat this same process, but choose the Guest option. When the wizard is complete, both computers can open the connection in the Network Connections folder and click File | Connect to start the infrared network session.

SETTING UP AN 802.11B NETWORK

Before setting up an 802.11b network, you'll need to decide if you'll use infrastructure mode or ad hoc mode. If you have a few wireless computers that only need to communicate with each other, an access point is not necessary (infrastructure mode). However, if you have security concerns, you'll need an access point to use the security features wireless networks bring to the table. As you are shopping for hardware, also keep in mind that some access points can also act as routers or residential gateways for Internet access. Once you install 802.11b NICs, Windows XP configures the NICs automatically to look for an access point. If no access point is found, Windows XP reconfigures the NICs to use ad hoc mode. When the connection to the wireless network is attempted after the NIC is installed, a Connect to Wireless Network dialog box appears, shown in Figure 9-16, where you can choose the

FIGURE 9.16 Connect to Wireless Network

wireless network you want to the connect to and provide the WEP key, if required by the network.

In most cases, Windows XP does a good job of automatically managing the wireless network connections and configuration. However, you can also access the NIC's properties pages and manually configure some settings, if necessary. The following steps show the options.

MANUALLY CONFIGURING WIRELESS SETTINGS

1. Open Network Connections and right-click the wireless connection. Select Properties.

2. On the Wireless Networks tab, shown here, notice that by default, Windows configures the wireless network settings for you. You see the available networks and the preferred networks. If you need to configure an available network that you want to connect to, select the option in the Available Networks list and click Configure.

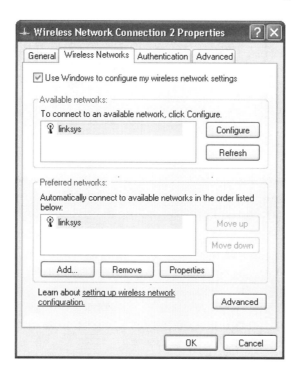

3. The Wireless Network Properties dialog box appears, shown next. By default, the wireless network key and network authentication are enabled.

If you need to enter the network key manually, do so in this dialog box and configure any necessary options. Check the NIC's documentation for details. Under most circumstances, the key is provided automatically and the options here are grayed out. Notice also that if you are using ad hoc mode, you can disable the settings on this tab by choosing This Is a Computer-to-Computer Network; Wireless Access Points Are Not Used.

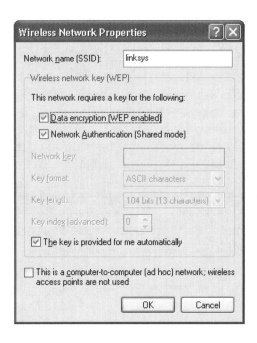

4. You can reorganize the Preferred Networks list if you have more than one network by using the Move Up and Move Down buttons. Place the network that you use most often at the top of the list to speed up your initial access to that network.

5. If you only want to connect to access point networks or you only want to connect to ad hoc networks, click the Advanced button at the bottom of the Wireless Networks tab. You see an Advanced dialog box, shown here. By default, Any Available Network (Access Point Preferred) is selected. If you want to restrict the connection to only access points or ad hoc networks, choose the desired option.

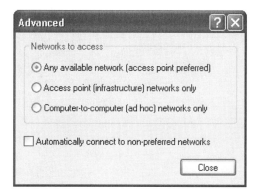

WRAPPING UP

Windows XP brings a lot of networking features and functions to the table. Using Windows XP Professional, you can create home and small office networks and you can configure Windows XP for domain networking. Aside from standard LAN features, you can also create direct cable connections, virtual private network connections, and even wireless networks. Now that you have taken a look at Windows XP's networking features, the next chapter explores preventative maintenance.

PREVENTATIVE MAINTENANCE

10

As with most things in life, preventing problems is much easier than solving them. The same statement can be applied to computer operating systems, including Windows XP. The concept of "preventative maintenance" simply means that you perform various checks on Windows XP to maintain the operating system. Maintenance helps you avoid problems before they occur and it helps you find performance problems that may be developing. You can think of preventative maintenance both in terms of preventing problems from occurring as well as optimization. As you work with Windows XP in your network environment, it is important for you to understand and use the features Windows XP gives you that can help you optimize, monitor, and prevent problems. Using these tools, you can keep the operating system running at its peak, and certainly make your job easier. In this chapter, you'll...

- Optimize desktop settings
- Manage Windows XP performance
- Use scheduled tasks
- Work with power options

OPTIMIZING DESKTOP SETTINGS

As you have already seen at this point, Windows XP is a more graphic operating system than we have seen in the past. There are more colors, icons, interactive graphics—in fact, the entire default interface is actually a theme, which can even be modified and changed. How important is all of this to your job? That depends.

Let's say that money is a little tight in your network. Previous operating systems ran Windows ME, which worked fine. After the upgrade to Windows XP, users often complain that the computers work more slowly than they did under Windows ME. A quick check of processor speeds and RAM probably tells you that the computers barely met the minimum recommended installation requirements. If this scenario describes your situation, don't be surprised. It is not at all uncommon for management to spend money on new operating systems, while trying to save money on the hardware side of things. In the end, this approach often costs more because the hardware simply does not keep up well with the needs of the operating system. Regardless, you may be faced with the task of optimizing the operating system in order to make the best of what you have to work with. In this case, there are a few things you can do that can help optimize the desktop, which simply reduces some of the graphical features of Windows XP in order to conserve RAM and CPU cycles. The tasks are easy, but I recommend that you keep these in mind when faced with this common performance situation.

GOING BACK TO THE PREVIOUS LOOK

Windows XP gives users a new, sleek look and a more graphical interface, but Windows XP is also rather forgiving, and you do not have to use this interface if you don't want. Simply put, you make the computer look like earlier versions of Windows, such as Windows ME and Windows 2000. This reduces the use of graphics and stops the use of the default Windows XP theme. This reduction can save you processor cycles and RAM usage, which can then be used for more important tasks.

If you open the Display applet in Control Panel and click the Themes tab, you see that, by default, Windows XP uses the Windows XP theme, shown in Figure 10-1.

If you want to save some system resources, use the drop-down menu provided on the Themes tab and choose the Windows Classic option. This will make the computer look like earlier versions of Windows. Sure, you lose the cool Windows XP interface, but if you are scrambling to free up system

FIGURE 10.1   Themes tab

resources, losing the XP theme can help. When you choose this option, the graphics look like earlier versions of Windows; however, the operating system remains the same. Your Start menu is still the same Windows XP Start menu and everything in the operating system still resides in the same place.

MANAGING GRAPHICS USE

If you want to keep using the Windows XP theme, but remove some of the resource-eating graphics and interactive items, you can without having to completely turn off the Windows XP theme, which may be a better option for you. In Control Panel, select System, then click the Advanced tab. Under the Performance heading, click the Settings button. This opens the Performance Options dialog box, where you see a Visual Effects tab, shown in Figure 10-2.

You have four options:

- **Let Windows choose what's best for my computer**   This option allows Windows XP to perform a balancing act between visual effects and system resources. If resources are low, Windows XP will automatically turn off

TECH TALK

Moving Backwards

You may have users who are resistant to working with a new operating system such as Windows XP. In short, they want their old Windows back. You can't completely make Windows XP look and act like previous versions of Windows (not that you would want to anyway), but you can change the Start menu from Windows XP to Classic. Just right-click on the Start menu and select Properties, then click the Classic Start Menu button. This will give you the same Start menu you saw in previous versions of Windows and will place My Computer, My Documents, and My Network Places icons back on the desktop. Change can be painful, so if you are in a situation where the old look is simply better, don't hesitate to use the Classic option.

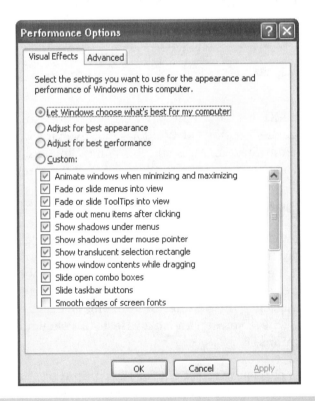

FIGURE 10.2 Visual Effects tab

some of the more animated features in an effort to save system resources. Under most conditions this setting is best—it gives you the best look with the best performance.

■ **Adjust for best appearance**   If you select this option, Windows XP uses all visual effects at all times, regardless of the drain the effects put on computer resources. If a computer has plenty of RAM and a fast processor, this setting is fine, but as a general rule, the "Let Windows choose what's best for my computer" setting is your best option.

■ **Adjust for best performance**   In a case where the computer is barely limping along, this is your best setting. All Windows XP visual features are removed and you basically end up, once again, with the Classic Windows look.

■ **Custom**   You can customize the balance between visual effects and performance. This lets you keep the features that you really want to see, but removes those that are not important. If you click the Custom option, you can then clear the various check box options that appear. For example, you can stop Windows from giving you the fade features or from showing contents in Windows while dragging, along with a number of other options. Just clear the check boxes next to the features you do not want to use.

Keep in mind that Group Policy, both on the local computer and in a Windows domain setting, can also be used to control the appearance of the Windows XP desktop. If you can't make changes to these features, there is probably a Group Policy in place.

WORKING WITH MEMORY USAGE

You already know the drill: add more RAM. If memory is a problem on a computer system, the only true solution to the problem is to either stop using so much or add more. To stop using so much RAM, you have to stop using the computer in the same manner, which generally means using fewer applications or not as many applications at the same time. A good starting place for Windows XP is 256MB. You can use less RAM, but you'll often find that applications run more slowly, and if you are using graphics applications, you'll probably find that you need more than 256MB for the best optimization.

Like previous versions of Windows, Windows XP also uses virtual memory. Virtual memory allows the operating system to use a portion of the computer's hard disk to write memory data while it is not in use. For example, let's say you are using three applications. One of the applications is minimized. When you are not using this application, data in RAM can be written to the hard disk. When it is needed, it can be read back into RAM. This frees up more real memory, but allows you to keep more applications open without getting an "out of memory" error. The problem, though, is that virtual memory can be costly in terms of performance. In essence, virtual memory causes the computer to have to juggle items from memory to the hard disk and back again. This may not give you a readily noticeable performance hit, but once again, the old truth comes back: install more physical RAM.

You can adjust the size of the paging file, which holds the data written to the disk. However, Windows XP does a good job of managing its own virtual memory settings. You can experiment with them, but don't expect any real performance gains, and you might even cause more performance problems by trying to adjust the settings. Still, you can work with the virtual memory settings to see if manual adjustment is helpful to you, by using the following steps.

ADJUSTING VIRTUAL MEMORY SETTINGS

1. Click Start | Control Panel | System.

2. On the Advanced tab, click the Settings button found under the Performance heading.

3. In the Performance Options dialog box, click the Advanced tab, then click the Change button under Virtual Memory.

4. The Virtual Memory dialog box appears, as shown in Figure 10-3. Select the desired drive and enter a desired initial size in MB and a maximum size for the page file. You can also enable the System to manage virtual memory on its own by selecting the radio button, or you can choose to use no paging file at all (which is not recommended). The recommended settings appear at the bottom of the dialog box. If you want to try to get a little more power out of the paging file, try increasing its initial size, but make sure you have enough free space on the hard disk to accommodate the size you select. Click OK when you are done.

By default, the paging file minimum size that is recommended on the Virtual Memory tab is 1.5 times the amount of physical RAM installed on your computer. This should be the least amount that you use. If you have two drives installed, consider assigning the page file to the faster drive for a performance tweak. In fact, try to always install the page file on a different physical disk whenever possible, and always try to avoid placing the page file on the same drive as the operating system.

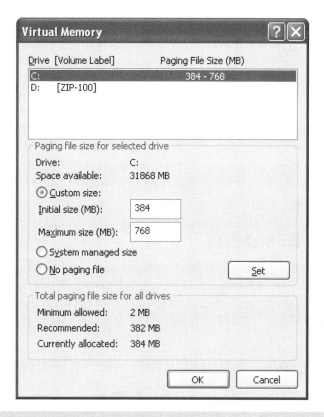

FIGURE 10.3   Virtual memory

WINDOWS XP PERFORMANCE

Aside from the performance of the Windows XP desktop and memory, there are a few other performance issues and tools that you can use. As you work with Windows XP, keep in mind that you can apply the principles discussed in the following sections and the tools we explore so you can keep Windows XP running at its peak and avoid potential problems.

ENVIRONMENT VARIABLES

Environment variables are made up of a list of information about your computer. The information is used to determine how Windows runs and where temporary files and folders are located. Environment variables are connected with each user's account, and they can be edited and even deleted if necessary. In terms of performance and management, you typically do not need to do anything with environment variables, but if a user seems to be having problems, you can inspect the paths and file locations to make sure they are correct. To make environment variable changes to an account other than yours, you must be logged on to Windows XP with an administrative account.

You can access the Environment Variables dialog box (shown in Figure 10-4) by clicking the Environment Variables button on the Advanced tab of System Properties. If you select a variable and click the Edit button, you can change the path of the variable. As I mentioned, you typically do not need to change any of these, but you can check them out if users seem to have problems with files from within their accounts.

PERFORMANCE MONITORING

Performance, which used to be called Performance Monitor, is an older tool that has been around since the days of Windows NT. Using Performance, you can gain real-time data about the performance of different system components and

TECH TALK

Stopping Error Reporting

You have probably noticed that when an error occurs in Windows XP, such as an application hang or lockup, a dialog box appears asking if you want to report the information to Microsoft. This reporting feature allows the computer to connect to a server at Microsoft.com and send the information to that server, where it is stored in a database. This essentially gives Microsoft more information about application problems as well as other Windows XP difficulties that Microsoft can use to look for trends, which could result in software patches and fixes. Of course, sending this information is completely voluntary, so if you don't want this dialog box appearing every time there is a problem, you can stop it, as follows:

1. Open System Properties and click the Advanced tab.

2. On the Advanced tab, click the Error Reporting button.

3. In the Error Reporting dialog box that appears, click the Disable Error Reporting button. You can continue to be informed of critical errors when they occur if you like. Click OK.

FIGURE 10.4   Environment variables

identify potential bottlenecks. Performance can provide you with information in a chart, report, or histogram format. You can also log data to a log file and configure administrative alerts. Administrative alerts can be sent by creating an entry to the application event log, broadcasting a network message, starting a performance data log, or running a program.

The purpose of performance monitoring is to gain information about the performance of various system components and hardware, such as memory and processor utilization. Typically, performance monitoring is best used with a baseline of performance. This means that you use Performance over a period of time during peak and non-peak times to determine the baseline the component functions under. You'll see high and low peaks of performance, and you can effectively determine what is normal and satisfactory operation for that component. With the baseline, you can later use Performance to see if the component is functioning within normal parameters. If it is not, you know that either a problem exists with the component or the load placed on the component has increased. Either way, you can effectively identify what component is not able to keep up with the demand placed on it, which is commonly called a *bottleneck*.

For example, let's say that a Windows XP Professional computer has 128MB of RAM. During initial testing, the 128MB was enough to meet the demands placed on it by the operating system and applications. With a baseline established, you are aware of what the memory can handle on a daily basis. However, several custom applications have recently been added to the system, which are used extensively throughout the work day. Now the user complains that the system is running slowly. You use Performance to check the performance of memory and see that it is consistently running high. This simply means that the 128MB of RAM is now not enough to keep up with operating system and application demands. The memory has become a bottleneck because it cannot handle the demands placed on it by the operating system and applications in a timely manner. Your action: install more RAM or reduce the load on the system.

Although this example may not seem that complicated, you'll certainly run into performance problems that are not so easily identifiable. The trick, once again, is to have baselines of performance established. With those baselines, you can then begin using Performance to find bottlenecks that need to be corrected.

In Performance, *objects* represent certain performance categories, such as memory, physical disk, processor, and related categories of system components and hardware that can be monitored by the Performance tool. Under each object, there are specific counters that you can monitor. Counters represent what you are actually monitoring under that object, such as bytes per second. Some objects have only a few counters, depending on what can be monitored, while others may have ten or more. The idea is to provide you with specific counters so that you can monitor specific actions of the object. For example, you can monitor the "memory" object, you could monitor the "available bytes" counter and the "pages/sec" counter to gain information about memory availability and current usage, or you could use a combination of a number of other memory counters. If there is more than one application of the counter, you'll see an Instances option to select as well. For example, if you are monitoring a hard drive using a counter, you'll need to choose the instance (which hard drive) you want to monitor.

If you click Start | Control Panel | Administrative Tools | Performance, the Performance tool opens, as shown in Figure 10-5.

As you can see, Performance is a basic MMC interface. The left console pane contains the System Monitor node and the Performance Logs and Alerts node. However, you primarily interact with Performance by using the right console pane. There are three basic divisions of this pane, starting at the top, which are

■ **Toolbar** The toolbar contains icons you will use regularly to generate the types of charts and information that you want. The toolbar contains

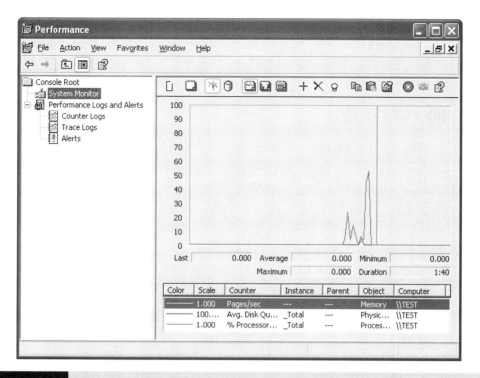

FIGURE 10.5   Performance tool

the following button options, which are seen from left to right in the
following illustration. They are New Counter Set, Clear Display, View
Current Activity, View Log Data, View Chart, View Histogram, View
Report, Add Counter, Delete, Highlight, Copy Properties, Paste Counter
List, Properties, Freeze Display, Update Data, and Help.

- **Information area**   The information area contains the chart, histogram,
  or report that you want to view. Just click the desired button on the
  toolbar to view counter information in the desired format.

- **Counter list**   The bottom portion of the window contains a counter list.
  All of the counters displayed in the list are currently being reported in the
  information area. You can easily remove or add counters to the list using
  the toolbar. Each counter in the counter list is given a different color for
  charting and histogram purposes.

The primary functionality of Performance rests in objects and counters. You choose the counters that you want to monitor and then view those counters in either a chart, histogram, or report format. The following steps show you how to add counters to the Performance interface.

CREATING A NEW CHART

1. Click Start | Control Panel | Administrative Tools. Open Performance.

2. In the Performance MMC, click the New Counter Set button on the toolbar. Then click the Add button on the toolbar.

3. In the Add Counters window, shown here, use the drop-down menu to choose a Performance object. For this exercise, I have chosen the PhysicalDisk counter.

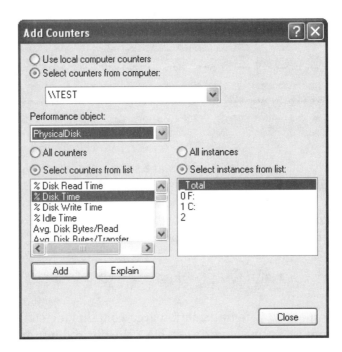

4. Next, you can choose to monitor all counters under the object you selected, or you can choose individual counters. To select individual counters, simply select the counter and click the Add button. Notice that the Instances of the dialog box may be active, depending on your selection. The Instances dialog box allows you to choose certain instances, if they are available. For example, as you can see in the previous illustration,

I have three physical disks on the computer. I can monitor all disks or a selected one if I choose.

5. Repeat the counter add process until you have added all desired counters, then simply click Close.

6. You can see that the counters you added are being monitored, as shown here. You can change the chart/histogram/report view by simply clicking a different option button on the toolbar. As you can see here, I am currently using the Report feature.

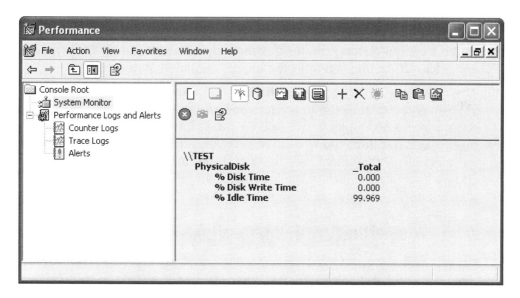

As you monitor various counters, you can gain information about the performance of the system processes and components that you selected. Generally, consistently high readings mean that the component or hardware is not able to meet the burden placed on it by the operating system's processes. Although high spikes are normal, consistently high readings on counters usually mean that a problem exists. This is, of course, where your baseline data is important. Using the baseline, you can tell if a component has higher readings than normal and what those readings might mean for system performance.

NOTE   While the chart view helps you see readings in a graphical format, be sure to experiment with the report view, from which you can often gain more specific data.

So, if it's important to establish baseline performance, how can you gain that data without sitting in front of a screen all day? Or, if a particular object seems to be causing problems, how can you monitor that object during an entire day's operations without physically watching the screen? Using Performance, you can sample performance data for the desired object(s) and counter(s) over a period of time, and record the data in a log file. You can then use the log file to examine the data at a time that is convenient for you. The following steps show you how to create a log file.

CREATING PERFORMANCE LOGS

1. In Performance, expand Performance Logs and Alerts in the left pane. Right-click Counter Logs and select New Log Settings.

2. In the New Log Settings dialog box that appears, give the log file a name and click OK (in this example, the log file is named Memory).

3. The settings window for the log appears. On the General tab, shown here, you can change the default log file name and storage location if you like. Next, use the Add Objects and Add Counters buttons to add the desired objects and counters you want to log. As you can see in the illustration, I am logging several memory counters. Under the sample data heading, choose how often you want the log file to sample data. In the following illustration, I am sampling memory data every 15 seconds.

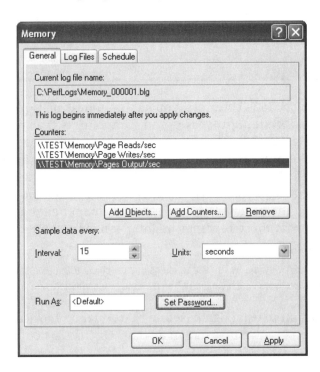

4. On the Log Files tab, shown here, you can choose the type of log file that you want to produce, which is a binary file by default. You can use the drop-down menu to configure a text file, binary circular file, or even an SQL database file. You can use the rest of the tab to adjust the file naming scheme.

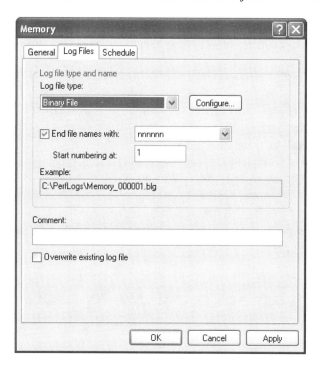

5. The Schedule tab allows you to configure how the log file is started or stopped. The settings here are self-explanatory. When you are done with all of the settings for the log file, just click OK.

Let's say that you are using a Windows XP Professional computer for certain network tasks. In order to make sure that the computer if functioning at its peak, you want to be notified when a certain performance object falls below the baseline of performance. Performance can provide you with this information though an alert. An alert is simply an action that Performance carries out when "triggered." The trigger occurs when an object or counter falls below a certain baseline of performance. You configure the alert to carry out a particular action, such as sending a network message or recording an event to the event log, when the alert is triggered. This is a great way to keep track of objects that fall below baseline standards, and in critical scenarios, to find out about the baseline failures as they occur. Like log files, alerts are rather easy to configure, as you can see in the following steps.

CREATING A PERFORMANCE ALERT

1. In Performance, expand Performance Logs and Alerts in the left pane. Right-click Alerts and select New Alert Settings.

2. Give the new alert setting a name in the dialog box that appears and click OK.

3. On the General tab that appears, shown here, add counters to the alert, just as you do for a log file. When the counters are added to the list, choose a baseline limit and a data sample rate.

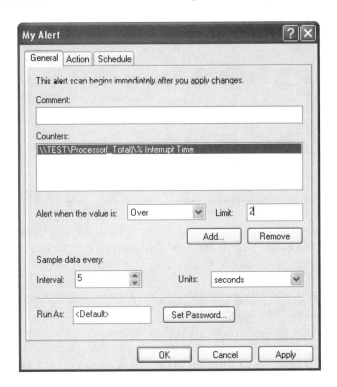

4. On the Action tab, shown next, choose an action that occurs when the event is triggered.

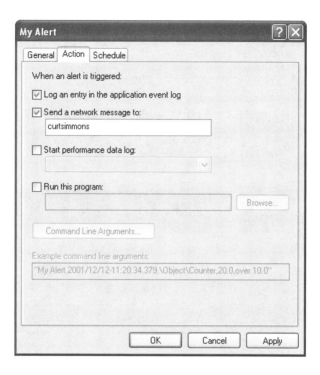

5. On the Schedule tab, you can configure a schedule as desired. This is the same schedule tab you see when configuring a log file.

QUICK PERFORMANCE CHECK WITH TASK MANAGER

Although Performance gives you detailed information about many different performance objects in Windows XP, you also get a quick look at processor and page file performance, along with a few other related items, through Task Manager. Simply open Windows Task Manager by clicking CTRL-ALT-DEL, then click the Performance tab, as shown in Figure 10-6. Here you can quickly see how the CPU and page file are doing. If you are running applications or processes and things seem to be moving slowly, you can quickly open this graph and see what is happening. Obviously, this feature doesn't give you any additional options and there is nothing you can configure here, but it is a good feature to keep in mind when you need a quick performance check.

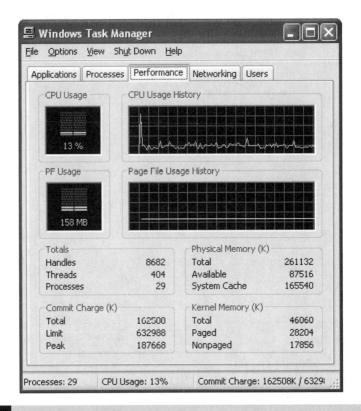

FIGURE 10.6 Task Manager Performance tab

OPTIMIZING APPLICATION PERFORMANCE

In a nutshell, the application performance in Windows XP is determined by a few simple things:

- **Compatibility** Sure, you can try to run applications that are not written for Windows XP, and you may have some success, but the best way to avoid application problems is to simply use programs updated for Windows XP. If you need to use custom applications that were written for a previous version of Windows, try using Windows XP's Program Compatibility feature, which you can learn more about in Chapter 5.

- **Memory**   Like system processes, applications require physical memory in order to function—and they must have enough of it. Before installing and running applications, be sure to check the requirements and see if the computer meets them. Keep in mind that multimedia applications consume a lot of RAM and will not perform well without it.

- **CPU**   Like memory, the processor must be powerful enough to handle the needs of the application. If not, the application will run very slowly.

NOTE   Remember to check out Chapter 5, which is devoted to application usage and performance, for additional tips and information.

USING SCHEDULED TASKS

Disk tools and other utilities, such as Disk Defragmenter, need to be run periodically to keep Windows XP working at its peak. You may also have custom applications that you would like to run at inconvenient times, such as 2:00 in the morning. Scheduled tasks give you a way to schedule certain tools and utilities to run at certain times so you can automate the process of keeping Windows XP functioning at its peak, as well as running desired applications at specified intervals. Scheduled tasks are straightforward and easy to configure with the help of the Add Scheduled Task Wizard. The following steps walk you through the process of adding a scheduled task.

NOTE   Make sure that the date and time on the computer's clock are accurate so that scheduled tasks will actually run when you want them to.

CREATING A SCHEDULED TASK

1. Click Start | All Programs | Accessories | System Tools | Scheduled Tasks.
2. In the Scheduled Tasks folder, double-click the Add Scheduled Task Wizard.
3. Click Next on the Welcome page.

4. In the Scheduled Task page, select the task that you want to schedule, as shown here. You can also browse for other programs if necessary. Click Next.

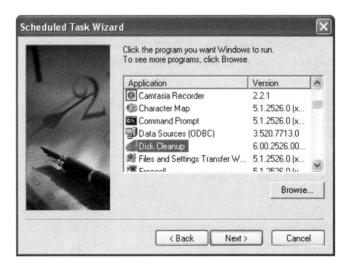

5. In the next page, give the task a name and choose when you want to run the program (daily, weekly, monthly, when you log on, and so on). Click Next.

6. Depending on your selection, an additional page may appear where you can configure the time and day of the week, as shown here. Make any necessary selections and click Next.

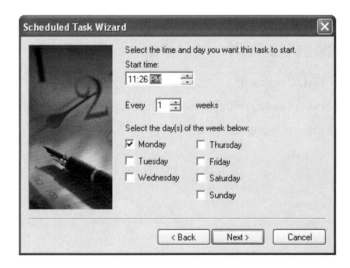

7. Your username is listed in the next page. Enter your password, if required for your account. Note that scheduled tasks are configured for a certain user; multiple users on the same computer can have different scheduled tasks configured. Click Next.

8. Review your settings and click Finish. If you want to see advanced properties for the scheduled task, click the check box before clicking Finish.

9. If you chose to view advanced properties, the properties pages for the task appear. The Task and Schedule tabs allow you to make changes to the values you configured when using the wizard. However, the Settings tab, shown in Figure 10-7, enables some additional configuration options, which are

- **Delete the task if it is not scheduled to run again**   If the task is only scheduled to run one time, this option deletes the task once it has run.

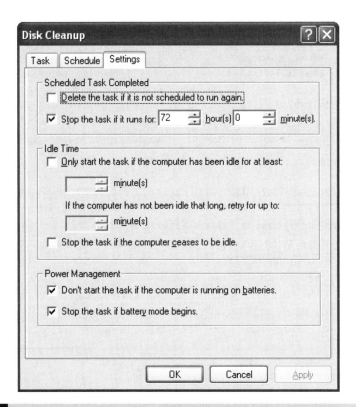

| FIGURE 10.7 | Scheduled task configuration options |

■ **Stop the task if it runs for *X* number of hours and *X* minutes**   This is a safety feature that stops a task that is taking too long to complete.

■ **Idle Time**   You can choose to start the task only if the computer has been idle for *X* number of minutes and you can stop the task if the computer ceases to be idle.

■ **Power Management**   You can choose not to start the task if the computer is running on batteries and to stop the task if the computer enters battery mode.

Once you create a scheduled task, it appears in the Scheduled Tasks folder. You can right-click the task and run it manually if desired, delete it, or change its properties.

NOTE Scheduled tasks run at the time they are configured to run, even if the user who created the scheduled task is not logged on to the computer. In this case, the scheduled task runs but is invisible to the currently logged-on user.

MANAGING SERVICES

When you start Windows XP, a number of services also start by default. These services give Windows XP the functionality that you want to see from the operating system, and a general rule, they do not need to be managed—they automatically start and run at bootup. However, it is important to remember that any background service also consumes system resources, so if performance is an issue for you, you should certainly inspect the services that are running and make sure they are needed. Of course, you have to be careful that you do not turn off any service that Windows XP actually needs.

You can view the services that are running through the Computer Management console. Expand the Services and Applications node, and select Services. The services appear in the right console pane, as shown in Figure 10-8.

Notice that the console tells you if a service is running or not. Some services start automatically, while others start if they are needed. If you double-click a service in the right console pane, the properties dialog box for that service appears.

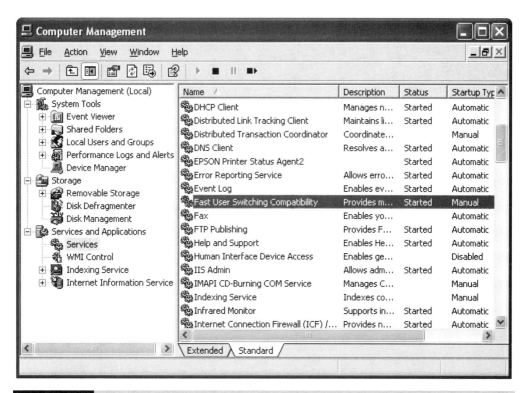

FIGURE 10.8   Computer Management services

On the General tab, shown in Figure 10-9, you see the name, description, path, and startup type of the service. If some services are starting automatically but are typically not needed, you can change the service startup to manual by using the drop-down menu.

The Log On tab shows you how a service is started by logon. For most services, the service is started by the Local System account, but you can tie a particular service to a designated account if necessary, such as if you want a particular service to only start when a certain user logs on. For most services, which should start regardless of the user, the "local system account" option should stay selected.

FIGURE 10.9 Service general properties

The Recovery tab, shown in Figure 10-10, specifies how recovery should work if a service fails to start. The options are Take No Action, Restart The Services, Run A Program, or Restart The Computer.

The Dependencies tab, shown in Figure 10-11, is one you should watch carefully if you are considering disabling a service. Services often do not work independently of each other, so before disabling a service, you should consider

FIGURE 10.10   Recovery tab

what other services will not run if the service is disabled. For example, as shown in the figure, if you disable the Network Connections service, the ICS and ICF services will not run, since they are dependent on the Network Connections service. Keep in mind that services often work together, and check this tab so you will know what additional services will not function when you disable one.

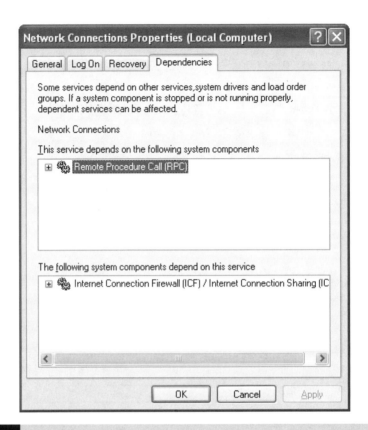

FIGURE 10.11   Dependencies tab

TROUBLESHOOTING

Services

What should you do if some components of Windows XP simply do not seem to work? You guessed it: check the Services portion of the Computer Management console. Services may fail to start for a variety of reasons, and when they do fail to start, they often affect other dependent services. This can result in several different components not working at the same time. In some cases, there are underlying operating system problems that can cause a service to not start, but if you identify a portion of Windows XP that does not seem to work, always check Computer Management to see if there are any problems with the service.

MANAGING POWER OPTIONS

Power options can be very important in Windows XP, especially if users are running laptop computers. It is highly possible that you are working in an environment where a number of laptop computers are in use. In fact, you may be in an environment where laptop computers are favored over desktop computers, since this gives users much more mobility. As corporate computer users have become more mobile, the importance of mobile optimization for laptop computers is as important as ever. In many networking environments, laptop computers are the desktop and mobile systems of choice, so it is important that laptop computers perform well both when connected to the network and on the road.

System performance for mobile users is primarily concerned with hardware and power management. In terms of hardware, you may consider creating different hardware profiles for the laptop computer, one of which can be used when the computer is docked and one when the computer is not docked. This feature tells the laptop computer what hardware is available under docked or undocked conditions. The best way to manage battery power is to disable the hardware features that are not needed when the computer is mobile. You can learn more about creating hardware profiles in Chapter 4.

Beyond the hardware profile option, you should also keep the following settings in mind for laptop computers. First, in the Performance Options window, on the Visual Effects tab, consider choosing the "adjust for best performance" setting option. This will remove a lot of Windows XP's graphical features, but will help conserve power. On the Advanced tab, be sure that Programs are selected for Processor and Memory usage.

Aside from these basic settings, you should take a look at power settings in order to make the best use of battery power when the laptop computer is running off batteries. In Control Panel, open Power Options. You'll see the Power Options properties tabs, shown in Figure 10-12.

On the Power Schemes tab, you can choose a power scheme that is appropriate for the laptop computer, such as the Portable/Laptop option. By default, this option turns off the monitor after 15 minutes and the hard disks after 30 minutes, but you can adjust these settings to create your own specific scheme. If you have enabled hibernation, you'll also see a hibernation scheme option here as well, which is set by default to hibernate after three hours of inactivity.

Speaking of hibernation, Windows XP supports the hibernation feature that enables the computer to write current memory data to the hard disk and then effectively shut down. When you reboot the computer, the data stored on the disk is loaded back into memory so that your computer appears just as you left it. This is a great energy-saving feature. You can enable hibernation by clicking

Power options

the check box option on the Hibernate tab, but the computer's BIOS must support ACPI or APM 1.2 for it to work.

WRAPPING UP

Managing Windows XP performance can be difficult, especially if the computer you are working on barely meets the hardware requirements of Windows XP. You can avoid many performance problems by ensuring that processors and memory can meet the needs of Windows XP, as well as any applications that need to function on the computer. As you are working with Windows XP, keep in mind the optimization and monitoring tools that are available to you, and make use of those tools as necessary.

Now that we have taken a look at preventative maintenance, let's look at Remote Desktop and Remote Assistance in the next chapter.

REMOTE DESKTOP AND REMOTE ASSISTANCE

11

Windows XP brings two new remote networking features to your environment: Remote Desktop and Remote Assistance. For the A+ technician who supports Windows XP, these tools can be a great help. How would you like to access your work computer easily from your home computer? How about remotely controlling a user's desktop in order to fix problems, without ever leaving your desk? Both of these options are readily available in Windows XP Professional, and in this chapter we'll take a look at these features and learn how to configure and use them. In this chapter, you'll…

- Set up and use Remote Desktop
- Set up and use Remote Assistance

CONFIGURING AND USING REMOTE DESKTOP

Over the past several years, workers have become more mobile. Rather than sit at a computer for eight hours a day, many people find themselves moving between offices and even working from home periodically. Because of this mobility, administrators of networking environments spend a lot of time configuring remote access services, and many organizations even spend a lot of money on remote devices such as the BlackBerry or Palm.

Realizing that remote access is very important in today's workplace, Microsoft has added a new feature called Remote Desktop Sharing, or more simply Remote Desktop, to Windows XP Professional. Suppose that you have a computer at your office, as well as a laptop computer or even a home computer. Using Remote Desktop, you can connect to your office computer from another computer and access the office computer, just as if you were actually sitting in front of the office computer. Using Remote Desktop, a terminal window appears and you simply use your office computer from your home or remote computer. If this sounds vaguely familiar, you guessed it: Remote Desktop is built on Windows 2000 Terminal Services, which allow you create terminal sessions with remote machines. Through the terminal window that appears, you can open files, launch programs, configure system changes, browse folders—basically anything you might do if you were sitting at the computer locally. As you can imagine, this feature has a lot of possibilities since your desktop PC no longer needs to be a local resource. Simply use another computer in a remote location to connect, and you can work from where ever you might be.

Remote Desktop is generally easy to use and set up, but depending on the needed configuration, you might need to work through a few networking snags. However, keep in mind the following important points and restrictions:

■ Windows XP Professional can function as a Remote Desktop host in that other computers can connect to it. You can connect to a Windows XP Professional computer and manage it remotely by using Windows XP Home Edition, or by installing the Remote Desktop Connection software on Windows 2000, Windows NT 4, Windows Me, Windows 98, and Windows 95.

■ Remote Desktop allows multiple users to connect to the same computer so that different users can access different resources and run different applications as needed.

■ When a remote user connects to the Remote Desktop host, the local desktop is locked. This prevents anyone from using the computer while you are logged on remotely.

■ Each client accessing the Remote Desktop host must have a direct connection to the host. You can accomplish this using a local area network (LAN) or wide area network (WAN) connection, a dial-up connection, or a Virtual Private Network (VPN) connection, or you can do it over the Internet if the Remote Desktop host has a public IP address.

TURNING ON REMOTE DESKTOP

In order to use Remote Desktop, you must first turn on the Remote Desktop service on a Windows XP Professional computer that you want to function as the remote host. Keep in mind that only Windows XP Professional computers can be Remote Desktop hosts, but you can connect to the Remote Desktop using other computer systems that run the Remote Desktop Connection software. To turn on Remote Desktop on a Windows XP Professional computer, follow these steps:

1. Log on to the Windows XP Professional computer as a member of the Administrators group. You cannot enable Remote Desktop without an administrator account.

2. Click Start | Control Panel | System. On the System Properties dialog box, shown here, click the Remote tab.

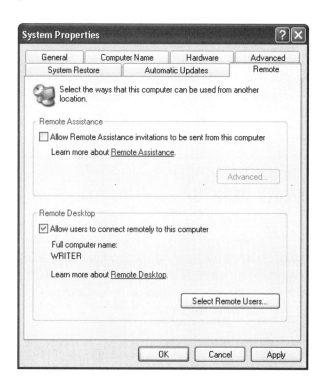

3. Select the Allow Users to Connect Remotely to This Computer check box in order to enable Remote Desktop. Once the setting is enabled, the current

user and any member of the Administrators or Remote Desktop groups can access the computer using Remote Desktop. However, you might want to change the default settings to allow or prevent users from accessing Remote Desktop. However, any user who attempts to use Remote Desktop must have a password. Remote Desktop connections do not allow blank passwords. To manage the users who can access the Remote Desktop, click the Select Remote Users button.

4. In the Remote Desktop Users dialog box, shown here, you can click the Add button to add users to the Remote Desktop group, or use the Remove button to remove users from that group. Keep in mind that local administrators automatically have access. When you are done, click OK.

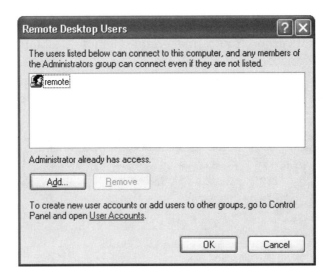

CONNECTING REMOTE DESKTOP

In order for Remote Desktop to work, you must be able to connect to the host computer from the client computer. That sounds simple enough, but if you have spent any time working with networks, you know that *simple* is not often a word that accompanies the concept of networking. So, before configuring your client computers, you must determine how clients will connect to the Remote Desktop host. The following sections explore your options.

CONNECTING OVER A LAN/WAN

Connecting to a Remote Desktop host over a LAN or WAN is the easiest way to connect. The client computer uses the host computer's IP address to make a direct connection. You need not make any additional configuration.

CONNECTING USING A DIAL-UP CONNECTION

You can connect to a Remote Desktop host through a dial-up connection to that host. For example, suppose that your work computer resides in a small office. The computer has a modem and is connected to the phone line. To access your work computer from a home computer, you first use the Create a New Connection Wizard on your work computer to configure the computer to accept incoming calls. Then, from your home computer, configure a dial-up connection to dial the work computer's number. You can then dial the work computer directly and create a Remote Desktop session.

CONNECTING USING THE INTERNET

You can connect to a Remote Desktop host over the Internet, but the process is a bit more complicated. When a computer is connected to the Internet, the Internet service provider (ISP) assigns the computer an IP address. You must use this public IP address to make the Remote Desktop connection. The problem, however, is that public IP addresses change frequently. For example, if you are using a modem to connect to the Internet, each time you connect, you are usually given a new dynamic IP address. Even with broadband connections, such as cable and DSL, the IP addresses may frequently change. There is now direct workaround for this issue. To find the public IP address, connect to the Internet, then double-click the connection in Network Connections. Click the Details tab, and you'll see the current public IP address. You can then use this IP address to connect to the host from the client computer. If you are using a dial-up connection, you must leave the host computer connected to the Internet in order to make the Remote Desktop connection.

Another difficulty concerning Remote Desktop connections over the Internet is firewalls. Most firewalls will not, by default, allow Remote Desktop traffic. If you need to connect to a Remote Desktop host that resides behind a firewall, keep these points in mind:

- If you are using Internet Connection Firewall on the host computer, you need to access the Advanced Settings dialog box and enable Remote Desktop traffic. This will allow Remote Desktop traffic to pass through the firewall, once the service is enabled. See Chapter 12 to learn more about using Internet Connection Firewall.

- If the host computer resides on a LAN that is protected by a firewall, or if another individual firewall product is used, you'll need to ask an administrator to configure the firewall to allow incoming access on TCP port 3389. Remote Desktop uses TCP port 3389, and the connection will fail if the firewall is not configured to allow incoming access on this port.

CONNECTING THROUGH A REMOTE ACCESS SERVER

If you need to connect to a Remote Desktop host over the Internet and through a Remote Access server, you should use a VPN connection. This will give you the highest security when using the Remote Desktop host over the Internet. An administrator must configure the Remote Access Server (RAS) server to allow VPN traffic. Once you connect to the network, you can start the Remote Desktop session with the host by simply connecting to it using the host's IP address.

CONFIGURING THE REMOTE DESKTOP CLIENT

Once you have enabled the Remote Desktop host and you have determined how the client(s) will connect to the host, you can configure the Remote Desktop client. In Windows XP, the client software is known as Remote Desktop Connection, which was called Terminal Services Client in previous versions of Windows. The Remote Desktop Connection software enables a client to generate a Terminal Services connection with the host. If you are using Windows XP Professional or Windows XP Home Edition, there is nothing you need to configure. The Remote Desktop Connection software is already installed and configured on the system. Simply click Start | All Programs | Accessories | Communications | Remote Desktop Connection. If you are using Windows 2000, Windows NT 4.0, Windows Me, Windows 98, or Windows 95, you must install the Remote Desktop Connection software on those computers. You can find this software on the Windows XP CD-ROM. Insert the CD-ROM in the desired client, choose the Perform Additional Tasks option, then choose the Remote Desktop Connection option. This will install the software. If you do not have a Windows XP CD-ROM available, you can also download the software from Microsoft's web site at **www.microsoft.com/ windowsxp/pro/downloads/rdclientdl.asp**. Follow the simple setup instructions that appear.

ESTABLISHING A REMOTE DESKTOP CONNECTION

Once the host and client are configured as needed, you can establish a Remote Desktop connection. To start the connection from a Windows XP client, click Start | All Programs | Accessories | Communications | Remote Desktop Connection. If you are connecting from a down-level client, click Start | Programs | Accessories | Communications | Remote Desktop Connection. The Remote Desktop Connection dialog box appears, as shown next.

If you are connecting a host that resides on your LAN or WAN, simply enter the computer's name or IP address. If you are connecting through a VPN connection or over the Internet, use the IP address of the remote host. Once you have entered the name or IP address, just click Connect. Once the connection is made, the screen turns black, then you see a Log on to Windows dialog box, as shown in Figure 11-1. Enter a username and password for a user who is a member of the Remote Desktop group or for a user who has administrative privileges. Then click OK.

NOTE   Remember that blank passwords cannot be used. You must use an account that has a password.

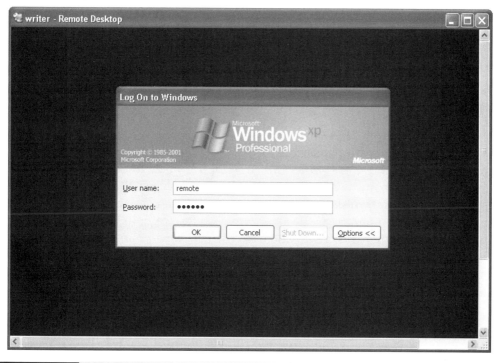

FIGURE 11.1   Enter a valid username and password

FIGURE 11.2 Remote Desktop session

Once the username and password have been accepted, the terminal window provides your Remote Desktop, as shown in Figure 11-2. You can maximize and minimize the terminal window as needed and can simply use the remote computer through the terminal window, just as you would if you were sitting locally at the computer. Keep in mind as you are working with the Remote Desktop that you can open applications and create and save files. However, the files you create, edit, and save are saved on the remote computer; the terminal window simply shows you what is happening on the remote computer. For this reason, you cannot save files to your local client desktop and you cannot drag and drop items from the terminal window (the host computer) to your local computer (the client computer). You can also use the terminal window to access network files remotely, but keep in mind that the remote account you are using must have permissions to access items on the network.

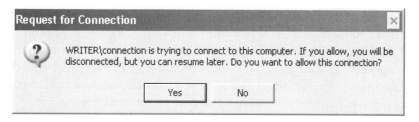

FIGURE 11.3   The local user sees this message

WORKING WITH MULTIPLE USERS

When you are using Remote Desktop, you can easily connect to the remote computer and use a terminal window. However, what happens if another user is accessing the computer locally? For example, suppose that you have a Remote Desktop account to access a computer from your home office. However, sometimes other administrators use the Windows XP Professional computer at the office when you are not there. In this case, one of two things can happen:

■ If Fast User Switching is enabled on the remote computer, the remote user sees a message, shown in Figure 11-3. You will see the message shown in Figure 11-4. The user sitting at the computer locally has the ability to reject

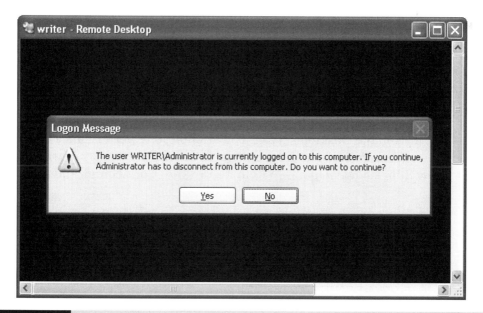

FIGURE 11.4   The remote user sees this message

your message and keep you from logging on by clicking the No button. If no one is actually sitting at the computer (but is logged on), then the local user is logged off because there has been no response. However, the local user's session actually remains logged on because Fast User Switching is enabled, so all applications and all open files remain open. However, the local user will not be able to use the computer until you log off.

■ If Fast User Switching is not enabled on the remote computer, then you have the option to log the local user off the computer forcefully. The problem, though, is that the local user will not have the option to save any open files. For this reason, it is best to use Fast User Switching with Remote Desktop so that any local users accessing the computer will not lose data. On the other hand, in this same scenario, a local administrator can forcefully log on, disconnecting the remote user, or if the same account is used by more than one person, the local user can always disconnect the remote user. As you can see, you should put some thought into the management of users when multiple people use the same machine. The best practice if you are working with Remote Desktop is to give each user a different account and ensure that Fast User Switching is enabled.

MANAGING REMOTE DESKTOP PERFORMANCE

As with all networking connectivity, Remote Desktop performance can be an issue. If you are using Remote Desktop to connect to a remote desktop over the LAN or WAN, performance will probably not be an issue since there is plenty of available bandwidth. However, what if you need to connect to a remote desktop using a dial-up or VPN connection, or over the Internet? In this case, the amount of graphics that must be downloaded and displayed on your computer can slow down Remote Desktop's performance.

For this reason, Windows XP gives you some performance options that can help speed up Remote Desktop service. For example, one performance option enables you to remove some of the graphical interface, the display of which can tend to slow things down. Open the Remote Desktop Connection, and in the

TECH TALK

Logging on Automatically

As an A+ technician, you may face the task of supporting users who use Remote Desktop. To make Remote Desktop even easier to use, you can configure users' computers to log on to Remote Desktop automatically. For example, suppose that a user accesses her Windows XP Professional computer at work from a Windows XP Home computer most evenings. You can configure automatic logon to make the process quicker and easier. To configure the automatic logon option, follow these steps:

1. Click Start | All Programs | Accessories | Communications | Remote Desktop Connection.

2. On the Remote Desktop Connection dialog box, click the Option button.

3. On the General tab that appears, enter the computer to which you want to connect, then enter the username, password, and domain (if necessary). Click the Save My Password check box.

4. Click the Save As button. By default, the settings are saved in an .RDP file in My Documents with a filename of Default. If you want the settings you entered to be your default settings, simply click Save. If not, give a different name to the logon settings.

5. Click Connect to make the connection. From now on, you'll not be asked to provide the username and password when you make the Remote Desktop connection.

Remote Desktop Connection dialog box, click the Options button. You see several available tabs. Click the Experience tab, shown in Figure 11-5.

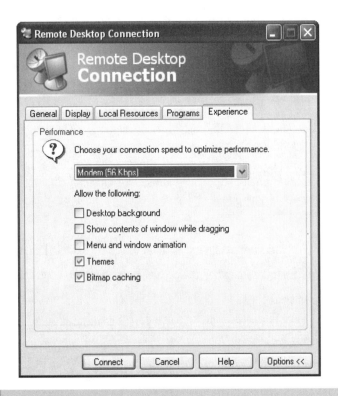

FIGURE 11.5 Experience tab

Use the drop-down menu to select your connection speed, then use the check boxes to specify further connection options. As you can see, using fewer features, such as Display Background, can reduce the amount of bandwidth required to transmit the images to your remote computer. You can adjust these settings as needed until you find the performance level that meets your needs.

NOTE Leave the bitmap caching option enabled. Bitmap caching allows your computer to store bitmap images locally on your remote computer so that they do not have to be downloaded each time they need to be displayed; this actually speeds up the performance of the connection.

You can also click the Display tab, shown in Figure 11-6, which will modify how Windows handles the remote session in the terminal window. You can specify the resolution of the terminal window and also the color depth. Again, lower settings help conserve bandwidth—they may result in a less attractive interface, but you will see performance gains.

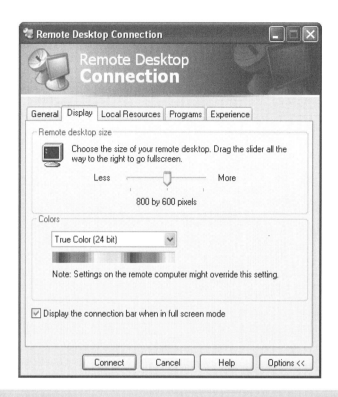

FIGURE 11.6   Display tab

The Local Resources tab, shown in Figure 11-7, gives you some configuration options that can also help performance. This tab features three categories: Sound, Keyboard, and Local Resources. You can choose to download and play sounds

TROUBLESHOOTING

Remote Desktop and Group Policy

Suppose that you adjust the Experience settings but fail to improve performance. What can cause the Experience settings not to work? The answer is Group Policy. The Windows XP Professional computer that functions as the remote host may have local as well as site, domain, and organizational unit (OU) policies that prevent changing the Experience settings. If this is the case, talk to a network administrator about changing the Group Policy settings so that they are more lenient and allow the configuration of performance options.

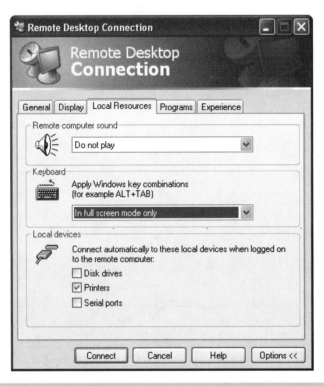

FIGURE 11.7 Local Resources

locally, such as in the case of Windows events, but this option does consume more bandwidth.

NOTE Sound files are transmitted using User Datagram Protocol (UDP), which some firewalls block. If you decide to use sounds and you still cannot hear them, this may be the problem.

The Keyboard option allows you to use special key combinations that will operate when the remote session is open. The options you'll find here are self-explanatory. Finally, Local Resources enables you to map client disk drives, printers, serial ports, and smart card devices to the remote host. This option allows you to map drives from the remote host to your local computer. For example, suppose that you are working on the remote computer, but you want to print the document on your home computer (the remote client). This feature allows you to do that, or even access information on your local drives from within the terminal window.

USING REMOTE DESKTOP WITH INTERNET EXPLORER

If you travel with a laptop and you frequently use Remote Desktop over the Internet, you can choose to use Internet Explorer to launch Remote Desktop sessions rather than using the Remote Desktop Connection software. If you want to access Windows XP Professional Remote Desktop connections using Internet Explorer, you have to configure Internet Information Services (IIS) on Windows XP Professional to allow the connection. After configuring IIS, you can then generate a terminal session using Internet Explorer 4.0 or later.

To configure the Windows XP Professional host to allow web connections, you must first install IIS. Use the Add/Remove Programs and Add/Remove Windows Components options in Control Panel to install IIS. Then you can configure IIS to allow Remote Desktop, which runs the Remote Desktop Web Connection software. Follow these steps:

1. Click Add/Remove Programs in Control Panel.

2. Click Add/Remove Windows Components.

3. In the Windows Components Wizard page, select Internet Information Services (IIS) and click the Details button.

4. In the Internet Information Services dialog box, select the World Wide Web Service and click Details.

5. In the World Wide Web Service dialog box, select Remote Desktop Web Connection and click OK, as shown here. Click OK again, and then again, and complete the wizard.

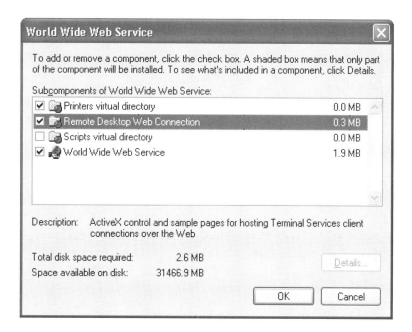

After installing the Remote Desktop Web Connection component, you need to set the permissions. Follow these steps:

1. Click Start | Control Panel | Administrative Tools | Internet Information Services.

2. Expand the computer name, then navigate to Web Sites, then to Default Web Site, then to tsweb, as shown here.

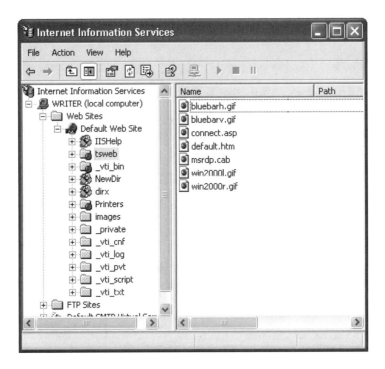

3. Right-click the tsweb container and click Properties.

4. Click the Directory Security tab and click Anonymous Access and Authentication Control | Edit.

5. On the Authentication Methods dialog box, shown next, ensure that the Anonymous Access check box is selected and click OK. Anonymous access gives a remote user access only to the IIS directory. Once connected, Remote Desktop will still require a username and password.

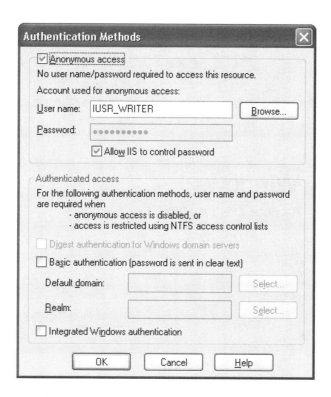

After configuring the remote computer to allow Web access to Remote Desktop, you can use your client computer to connect. Keep these important points in mind:

- You must be using Internet Explorer 4 or later.

- If you are connecting over the Internet to the remote computer, use the computer's public IP address to connect.

- If you are connecting through a RAS server, make the connection and use the name or IP address of the remote desktop to generate the connection.

To connect to the remote desktop using Internet Explorer, open Internet Explorer and type the default address, which is **http://*server*/tsweb**. Again, if you are connecting over the Internet, use the public IP address to connect, as in **http://*ipaddress*/tsweb**. You'll see a Remote Desktop Web Connection screen, shown in Figure 11-8.

FIGURE 11.8   Remote Desktop Web Connection screen

When you can connect to the remote computer through IIS, the process consumes less bandwidth, which helps speed up the connection. Also, the full screen will take up the entire computer screen; other options give you a resizable window. When you first connect, you'll probably see a security warning (depending on your Internet Explorer configuration). Remote Desktop installs an ActiveX control on your computer, so just click Yes in response to the security warning (if you do not, Remote Desktop will not work). You'll see the same logon dialog box. Enter your username and password and click OK. The Remote Desktop sessions open in Internet Explorer or in full-screen mode, depending on your selection.

TECH TALK

Remote Desktop Web Connection Logon

Concerning logon, when you arrive at the Remote Desktop Web Connection window in Internet Explorer, you can select the Send Logon Information for This Connection check box. This provides you the Username and Domain dialog boxes. However, a better workaround is simply to add the remote desktop to your Favorites menu. Log in first, and after you see the desktop, click the Favorites menu and add the favorite. This saves your server name, screen size, and username in a URL so that you can connect automatically by simply clicking the Favorites option. Although you'll still have to enter your password, this method is much faster. Note that to make this work, you must select the Send Logon Information for This Connection check box and enter your username and domain in the provided dialog boxes on the Remote Desktop Web Connection screen.

CONFIGURING AND USING REMOTE ASSISTANCE

Because supporting users (and enabling users to support each other) continues to be such an important issue, Windows XP provides a new and very helpful tool called Remote Assistance (RA). Suppose that as an A+ technician you support Windows XP in a large LAN environment. One of your users, who resides in a remote office across town, is having problems with his Windows XP computer. Sure, you can talk to the user on the phone, which is often unfruitful and aggravating, or you can drive to the user's site and work on the computer. Or, you can use Remote Assistance and remotely see and control the computer and fix it from your office. Which alternative sounds best?

As you can see, Remote Assistance has far-reaching implications for support situations, or even for two users communicating over the Internet. I live about five hours away from my sister, who also uses Windows XP. If she has a problem, she can just send me a Remote Assistance invitation, and I can connect to her computer and control it remotely, just as I would using Remote Desktop.

When you use Remote Assistance, one user is termed the *expert* while the user who needs help is called the *novice*. When the novice properly authorizes the expert to do so, the expert can connect to the novice's computer and see what is going on. If the novice gives the expert full control, the expert can make configuration changes on the remote computer. For Remote Assistance to work, the following must be true:

■ Both users must be connected to the same network or the Internet at the same time.

■ Both must be using Windows XP Professional or Home editions (sorry, no down-level systems are supported on either side of the connection).

■ The novice user must be an administrator on the local computer. Limited users cannot send Remote Assistance invitation.

UNDERSTANDING HOW REMOTE ASSISTANCE WORKS

Remote Assistance works with "invitations." The novice user sends an invitation for Remote Assistance to the expert user through e-mail or through Windows Messenger. The expert user then accepts the invitation, which opens a terminal window showing the novice user's desktop. Using Windows Messenger, the novice user and the expert user can even communicate with messages as the session is taking place. The novice user can allow the expert user simply to "see" the computer, or the novice user can give the expert full control.

The Remote Assistance invitation is made up of eXtensible Markup Language (XML) fields, containing data and the IP address of the novice user. The expert's computer connects to this IP address and uses TCP port 3389 for the terminal session. All of these details are hidden from the user, so the connection seems easy, immediate, and transparent.

TURNING ON REMOTE ASSISTANCE

In order to use Remote Assistance, you must first turn on the feature. Open Control Panel, then the System applet. Click the Remote tab and select the

TROUBLESHOOTING

Firewalls and Remote Assistance

As with Remote Desktop, Remote Assistance can give you some problems when connecting through a firewall. Internet Connection Firewall (ICF) works transparently with Remote Assistance, automatically opening TCP port 3389 for the connection. So, if either (or both) the novice and expert user(s) are running ICF, there is nothing you need to configure; Remote Assistance will work automatically.

If you are using Windows Messenger to make the connection, you shouldn't have any problems with firewalls. Windows Messenger is configured to work around the port issue, so if the firewall allows Windows Messenger traffic, you should still be able to use Remote Assistance without any problems.

Any router or residential gateway you may be using needs to support Universal Plug and Play (UPnP). UPnP is a standard that allows devices to communicate with each other over a network. If only one Remote Assistance computer is behind a Network Address Translation (NAT)-based firewall, Remote Assistance should still work; however, if both are behind a NAT firewall, the connection cannot be established. The lesson here is that routers and residential gateways should support UPnP to allow Remote Assistance to function. If you are about to purchase a router or residential gateway for your network, make sure it supports UPnP so that you can work around this problem.

option Allow Remote Assistance Invitations to Be Sent from This Computer, shown in Figure 11-9.

After turning on Remote Assistance, click the Advanced button. This opens the Remote Assistance Settings dialog box, shown next, which allows the novice to give the expert full control of the computer if desired, and to set a time limit

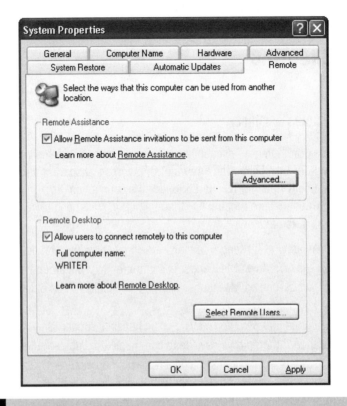

FIGURE 11.9 Turn on Remote Assistance

for the invitation to expire. If you select the default, the invitation is good for 30 days. After the time expires, the expert can no longer connect to the novice using the invitation. You can adjust this expiration value as needed.

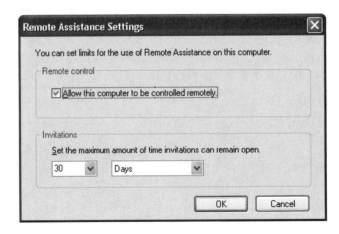

REQUESTING HELP FROM AN EXPERT

After turning on Remote Assistance on the novice computer, the novice user can easily request help from an expert. This can be done in a few different ways:

- The Remote Assistance invitation can be sent through e-mail.

- The Remote Assistance invitation can be sent using Windows Messenger.

- The Remote Assistance invitation can be sent manually by copying the RA ticket to a floppy disk and hand-delivering it to the expert.

When the novice is ready to request help from the expert, the novice uses the Windows XP Help and Support Center to generate the ticket. The process is easy, and the following steps guide you through it.

Remember that if you are using Remote Assistance over the Internet and a dial-up connection is in use on the novice computer, you must connect to the Internet before creating the invitation so that the correct public IP address can be used. Since you typically receive a different IP address each time you connect, you must connect and stay connected for the duration of the invitation and the session. Otherwise, you'll have to cancel the invitation and send another one, since the expert will not receive the correct IP address if a disconnect occurs. Aggravating, but true.

REQUESTING REMOTE ASSISTANCE

1. Click Start | Help and Support.

2. In the middle-to-upper-right portion of the window that appears (the Help and Support Center), notice there is a section labeled Ask for Assistance. Click on the green square labeled Invite a Friend to Connect to Your Computer with Remote Assistance.

3. Now the Remote Assistance portion of the Help and Support Center should be open. Click the check box Invite Someone to Help You, shown in Figure 11-10.

After you click the Invite Someone to Help You check box, there are as many as three possible methods for sending a request from a novice to an expert:

- **Windows Messenger**   Click the Sign In button in the Windows XP Help and Support Center. Once you are signed in to Windows Messenger, choose a name and click Invite This Person. The expert receives the request in

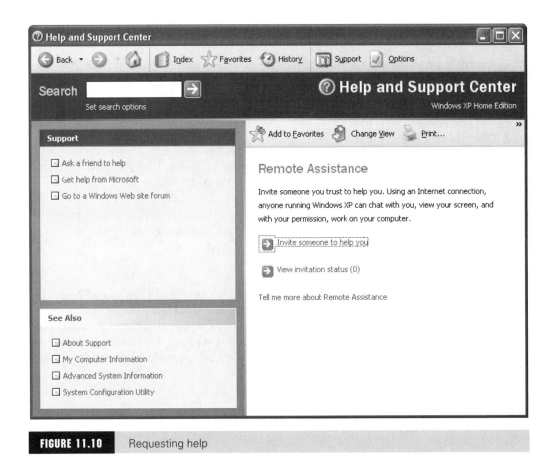

FIGURE 11.10   Requesting help

Windows Messenger and can accept your invitation. If you want to use Windows Messenger, you can also bypass the Windows XP Help and Support Center and request help directly through Windows Messenger by clicking Actions | Ask for Remote Assistance from the Windows Messenger toolbar.

■ **E-mail**   You can send the invitation via e-mail by entering the e-mail address in the Windows XP Help and Support Center and clicking Invite This Person. In the next window that appears, enter your name and a message, then click Continue. In the next window, specify a duration for the invitation and enter a password that the user must enter to access your computer. Click Send Invitation. The message is entered in your default mail client (such as Outlook Express). As you can see in Figure 11-11, the e-mail message contains instructions and a file called rcBuddy.MsRcIncident. When the user receives the file, he or she can double-click it to start the Remote Assistance session.

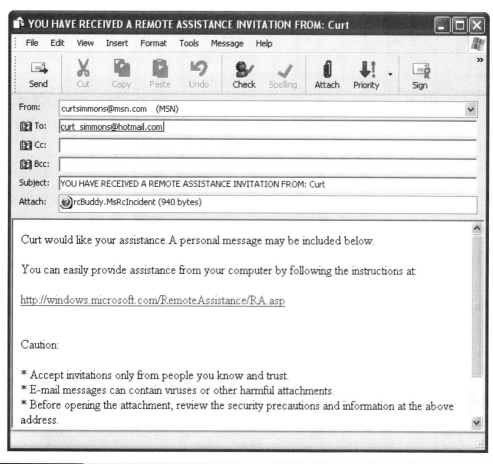

FIGURE 11.11   E-mail invitation

- **Invitation file**   If you cannot e-mail the invitation or use Windows Messenger, you can save the invitation as a file, which can then be hand-delivered to the desired recipient. Using this option, you can also enter a duration for the invitation and a password. The file is saved as RAInvitation. You can then transfer the file by hand, in an e-mail message, or via a network share.

USING THE REMOTE ASSISTANCE SESSION

Once the expert accepts the invitation and the connection takes place, the terminal session begins. The novice user receives a message that the invitation has been accepted. A terminal window appears on both the novice and expert users' computers, and a chat panel appears so that the two users can talk to each other during the session, as shown in Figure 11-12. The session appears in real time, and depending on network conditions, can be somewhat slow at times. If the novice has given the expert the option to "take control," then the expert can simply click the Take Control button that appears in the Remote Assistance terminal window. At any time during the session, the novice can get control of the session and end it by clicking the Stop Control button or by pressing ESC or CTRL-C.

NOTE   In addition to the control features mentioned, other self-explanatory features are readily available, such as chat, file transfers, and other helpful communication options.

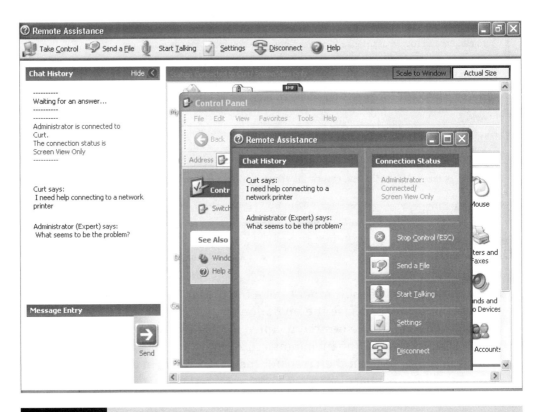

FIGURE 11.12   Remote Assistance session

WRAPPING UP

Remote Desktop and Remote Assistance are both great tools for remote networking. Using Remote Desktop, you can connect to a remote computer and use the computer as if you were actually sitting in front of it. This option opens a number of helpful doors that conventional networking has not provided. Similarly, you can support users from your desk using Remote Assistance. With Remote Assistance, you can even control a remote user's computer and quickly and easily fix problems that might be occurring. Connections for Remote Desktop and Remote Assistance are typically easy, as long as you keep the basic IP rules in mind and work around any firewall issues.

Now that you have taken a look at these remote networking features, let's turn our attention to Internet Connection Sharing, Internet Connection Firewall, and network bridging in Chapter 12.

MANAGING INTERNET CONNECTIONS

12

Internet connections provide access to the Internet. Without some kind of Internet connection, a computer residing at a home, at an office, or even in a Windows domain cannot access the Internet. Windows XP gives you several options to configure Internet connections. In today's complex networking environments, you are likely to face a number of Internet connection issues and even problems that you, as the A+ technician, will be asked to solve. The good news is Internet connection configuration and management is easier in Windows XP than it has been in previous versions of Windows, and in this chapter, you'll explore the features and tasks that you need to know. In this chapter, you'll…

- ■ Choose an Internet connection
- ■ Configure a broadband and dial-up connection
- ■ Manage dial-up connection properties

CREATING INTERNET CONNECTIONS

An Internet connection is simply software that is designed to use some kind of connection hardware, such as a modem or broadband hardware, in order to connect to a remote server. The Internet itself is a free network, but users and companies must pay an Internet service provider (ISP) for the access. To create an Internet connection on a computer, you need a few items:

- **Hardware** The computer has to be outfitted with some kind of connection hardware, such as a dial-up modem, Digital Subscriber Line (DSL) modem, cable modem, satellite connections, or other types of broadband hardware that are available. The Internet connection uses the hardware to connect to the ISP.

- **Account** To connect to an ISP, you must have an account with that ISP. The account includes a username and password that the connection software requires to validate your identity and give you Internet access.

- **Connection** Once you have the necessary hardware and the account with an ISP, you must use Windows XP to create a connection that can use the hardware and the account to connect to the ISP.

Aside from providing basic connectivity, most ISPs provide you with an e-mail account, a certain amount of web space for a home page, technical support, as well as other service features. If you are faced with the task of finding and signing up with an ISP, you should certainly shop around. Some ISPs cost more than others, so you want to make sure you know what you are getting before parting with your hard-earned money. Also, some ISPs offer broadband service, whereas others do not. The important point, as with most things in life, is simply to shop around and make sure that your ISP provides the services and features that you need.

TYPES OF CONNECTIONS

Several different types of connections to the Internet may be available, depending on the area where you live. For a small office network, you may need to choose a type of Internet connection that can service the needs of the network. For such networks, you can make use of Internet Connection Sharing (ICS) so that a single connection to the Internet can be used, and you can also use Internet Connection Firewall (ICF) to protect the connection from hacker attacks. See Chapter 13 to learn more about ICS and ICF.

TECH TALK

Corporate Internet Access

Corporate access to the Internet generally works the same way as a small office's or an individual's access to the Internet: An account with an ISP is necessary. The difference is that the ISP allows many connections from the clients within the corporate network at the same time, and some kind of backbone connection is typically made (such as a T1 or T3 link) from the corporate office to the ISP. These accounts, which often cost thousands of dollars per month, are designed to service the needs of many users. Often, a proxy server handles service within the corporate network, managing all of the connections to the ISP. Client computers connect to the ISP on the network, and the ISP handles all access to the Internet. This process provides faster service to network clients and greater, centralized security.

If you are faced with the task of choosing a connection type, you'll find the following types of connections and service plans available, depending on your area:

- **Dial-Up**   Most areas of the world have some type of dial-up service. Dial-up service requires a modem and a phone line, where your computer dials a phone number to connect to an ISP server. Dial-up connections are the most common type of Internet connections used today. Most dial-up connections cost around $20 per month for unlimited use. The greatest problem is that all modem connections are slow by today's standards. Phone line limits restrict modems to 56Kbps transfer, but dial-up connections are actually capable of about 45Kbps transfer. Considering the multimedia nature of the Internet, this speed is rather slow and you'll spend a lot of time waiting for pages to load. Additionally, streaming media and even Internet radio are difficult to use with a dial-up connection. If you need Internet access for a small office, all computers will share the dial-up connection, which will further reduce the amount of available bandwidth.

NOTE   See Chapter 4 to learn more about installing and configuring modems.

- **DSL** DSL is a broadband technology that has become very popular during the past few years. DSL provides broadband throughput, with speeds often between 400Kbps and 800Kbps. However, newer versions of DSL now support up to 8Mbps for downloading and up to 1Mbps for uploading. Also, DSL is an "always-on" technology. The computer is always connected to the Internet and there is no need to dial a connection. DSL also works with public telephone lines, but different channels are used to transmit high-speed data. This feature allows DSL always to be connected, but subscribers can also make voice calls over the line at the same time. DSL requires a special DSL modem that connects to your computer, which is often included for free when you sign up for service. DSL service typically costs around $40 per month, but it is, unfortunately, not available in all areas.

- **Cable** Cable Internet connections are another form of broadband connection, and a direct competitor with DSL. Cable Internet uses a typical coaxial cable attached to your computer, just as you would use a coaxial cable with your television. Access to the Internet is performed over the cable connection, and your cable company or service provider provides an always-on service, just as you would receive with cable television. In the past, cable connections worked well, but often did not have the bandwidth of DSL. However, with new cable implementations, the cable access speed is just as fast as DSL, and sometimes faster. As with DSL, you can expect to pay around $40 a month for cable Internet.

- **Satellite** Two-way satellite connections are new in the Internet market and are the least popular type of Internet connectivity available. However, for people who cannot get other types of broadband connections, satellite connectivity is a good broadband solution, providing on average 300Kbps transfer. However, it is not as fast as DSL and cable, and costs considerably more. The satellite disk equipment generally costs around $500, and monthly unlimited access is around $70. Still, for users who cannot get other types of broadband, satellite may be a great solution. See **www.starband.com** to learn more.

NOTE DSL, cable, and satellite modems typically connect to a USB port on the computer or an Ethernet card. See the ISP's documentation for installation and setup instructions.

CREATING AN INTERNET CONNECTION

Once you have the hardware installed on the computer and the account information from the ISP, you are ready to create the Internet connection that Windows XP can use to access the Internet. Some ISPs give you an installation disk and specific setup instructions for your computer, which are often necessary for broadband connections. You should follow the ISP's instructions for creating the Internet connection. However, if you need to create a connection without ISP software, Windows XP can help you create that connection with the New Connection Wizard. The following steps show you how to create an Internet connection.

CREATING AN INTERNET CONNECTION

1. Click Start | Control Panel, then open the Network Connections folder.

2. In the Network Tasks dialog box, click the Create a New Connection link.

3. The New Connection Wizard appears. Click Next.

4. In the Network Connection Type window, you can choose the kind of connection that you want to create. Select the Connect to the Internet radio button, then click Next.

5. In the Getting Ready window, you can choose from a list of ISPs if you do not have an account. This process opens a connection to a referral service so that you can sign up with available service providers on the Internet. If you have an installation CD, you can also choose the option to run setup from the CD. Finally, you can choose the manual setup option. This setup option is described in the rest of the wizard steps here.

6. In the Internet Connection window, choose the type of connection that you are using, such as a dial-up, broadband that is always on, or broadband that requires a username and password. Make your selection and click Next. Since you are most likely to use the New Connection Wizard to set up modem connections, the rest of the steps focus on that option.

7. In the Connection Name window, enter a name for the connection and click Next. The name should be something user-friendly that distinguishes the connection from other connections.

8. In the Phone Number window, enter the phone number required to dial the ISP. Then click Next.

9. In the Internet Account Information window, shown next, enter your username and password and click the check box options that you want to use. Note that you can specify that anyone using your computer can access the account. You can also make the connection the default connection, and you can turn on the Internet Connection Firewall. See Chapter 13 to learn

more about Internet Connection Firewall. Make your entries and selections and click Next.

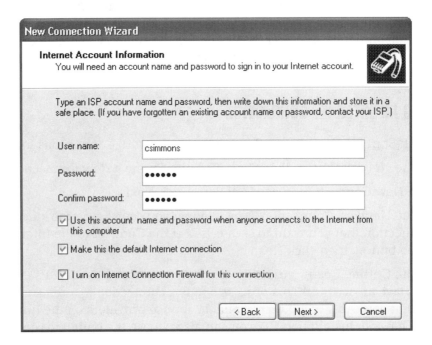

10. Click Finish. The new connection now appears in the Network Connections folder.

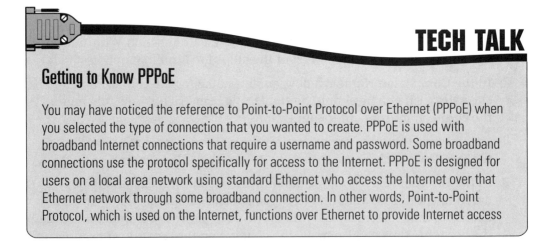

TECH TALK

Getting to Know PPPoE

You may have noticed the reference to Point-to-Point Protocol over Ethernet (PPPoE) when you selected the type of connection that you wanted to create. PPPoE is used with broadband Internet connections that require a username and password. Some broadband connections use the protocol specifically for access to the Internet. PPPoE is designed for users on a local area network using standard Ethernet who access the Internet over that Ethernet network through some broadband connection. In other words, Point-to-Point Protocol, which is used on the Internet, functions over Ethernet to provide Internet access

(continued)

to these users. With PPPoE, each user can have a different access configuration, even though all the users reside on the same LAN. ISPs also use PPPoE to control the use of static IP addresses. You can learn more about PPPoE by accessing Requests for Comments (RFC) 2516 on the Internet.

LAUNCHING A CONNECTION

Broadband connections are typically "always on, always connected." This means that you do not have to dial a connection or worry about disconnects. You simply launch a browser or your e-mail client to connect. However, if you are using a dial-up connection, you must establish a connection to the ISP each time that you want to connect to the Internet. To launch the connection, you can use the connection icon that appears in the Network Connections folder, now that you have created the connection. Internet connections appear in Network Connections, which is available by clicking Start | Control Panel | Network, and is displayed in the folder as Dial-Up or LAN or High-Speed Internet, as shown in Figure 12-1.

You can easily launch the connection from within Network Connections simply by double-clicking the connection icon, or by right-clicking the connection icon and clicking Connect. The Connect dialog box appears, as shown in Figure 12-2.

Enter your username and password for the ISP. Notice that you can choose to save the username and password so that you do not have to retype it each time you want to connect. You can save the password for Me Only, which will allow the connection to be used only with your user account, or you can choose to allow anyone who uses the computer to use the Internet connection. The phone number you entered appears by default. Simply click Dial to make the connection.

NOTE   If you use the Me Only option, you are the only user who can launch the connection. However, if you leave the computer unattended, anyone who sits at the computer while you are logged on can launch the connection. If you want to make certain that no one else can ever use the connection, simply leave the Save This User Name and Password for the Following Users check box disabled, which will disable both suboptions. This way, you'll have to supply the username and password each time you connect.

FIGURE 12.1 Network Connections dialog box

CONFIGURING DIAL-UP CONNECTION PROPERTIES

If you right-click an Internet connection in the Network Connections folder, you can click Properties, which opens the Properties sheets that manage that particular Internet connection. The Properties sheets have a number of settings that determine how the connection operates, so you'll take a look at those in the following sections.

Connect dialog box

GENERAL TAB

On the General tab of the connection's Properties sheet, shown in Figure 12-3, you have a few different items:

- **Modem Configuration**   If you click the Configure button, you can access the modem's Properties sheet and make configuration changes as desired. See Chapter 4 to learn more about modem configuration.

- **Phone Numbers**   You can configure alternative phone numbers that can be used with the connection, and you can configure dialing rules.

■ **Notification**   Use the Show Icon in Notification Area When Connected check box at the bottom of the page to display an icon in the Notification Area when connected.

Concerning phone numbers and dialing rules, it is important that you understand the options and features that dialing rules bring to the table, since you may be required to support dial-up configurations in your network. Dialing rules simply tell Windows XP how to handle area codes, long distance calls, and even calling cards. In other words, area code rules help Windows XP know what calls are "local," which ones are "long distance," and which special treatment to give to certain phone numbers. The following steps show you how to set up and configure dialing rules.

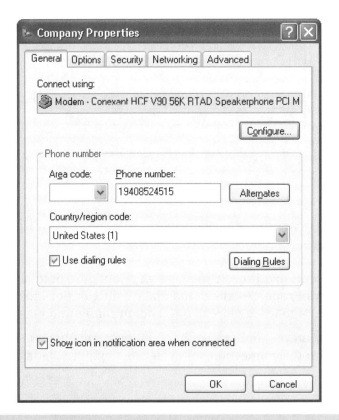

FIGURE 12.3   General tab of the connection's Properties sheet

CONFIGURING DIALING RULES

1. On the General tab, click the Use Dialing Rules check box, then click the Dialing Rules button.

2. The Phone and Modem Options dialog box appears, as shown next. On the Dialing Rules tab, you see the current location that is configured. You can choose to edit the existing location by clicking the Edit button or create a new one by clicking the New button. Whether you choose to edit a current location or create a new one, a similar configuration dialog box appears — either New Location or Edit Location.

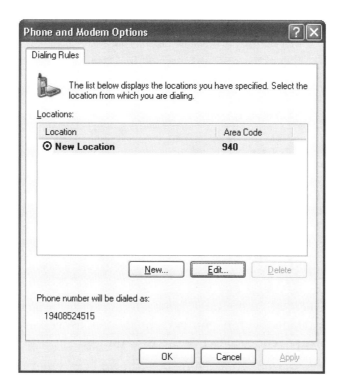

3. In the New Location or Edit Location dialog box that appears, you see a General tab, shown next, with several setting options. On this tab, type a location name, then enter the area code and the country/region of the area code, then use the Dialing Rules text boxes to determine the rules for the

use of the area code. You can also choose to disable call waiting and choose tone or pulse dialing.

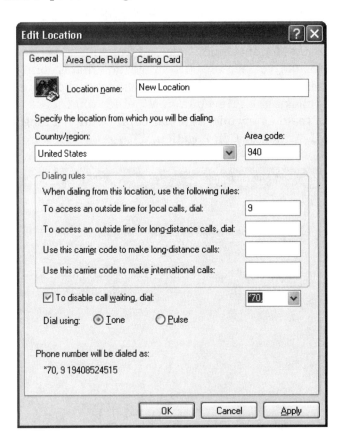

4. Click the Area Code Rules tab. Area code rules determine how phone numbers are dialed within your current location as well as other locations. To create an area code rule, click the New button.

5. In the New Area Code Rule dialog box, shown next, enter the area code to which this rule applies. Then you can enter a list of prefixes that can be used with the area code, or accept the default that all prefixes you use can work with the area code.

For example, suppose that the area code is 214. You want to use only 555 prefixes with the area code. In this case, click the Include Only button and click Add to enter that prefix. If you do not place any prefix restrictions, then Windows XP will assume that any prefix you dial can be used with the area code. At the bottom of the dialog box, use the check boxes to determine whether a 1 should be dialed when using the area code, and whether the area code should be dialed when using the entered prefixes. For example, if a dial-out number is 214-555-1234, and the area code is required each time you dial the number, then click the Include the Area Code check box. Click OK.

6. The new area code rule now appears in the Area Code Rules tab, shown next. You can create new area codes and edit existing ones at any time on this tab.

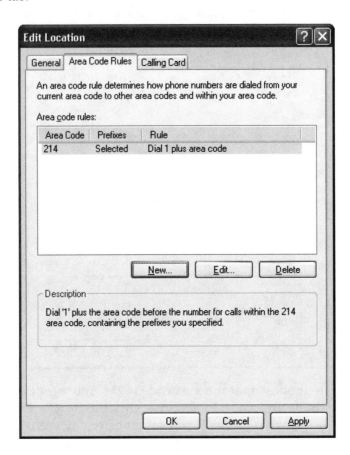

7. Click the Calling Card tab. If you need to use a calling card to make the connection, such as in the case of dialing a long distance number when you are traveling with a laptop, enter your card information as necessary on the Calling Card tab, shown next. Click OK to save your changes.

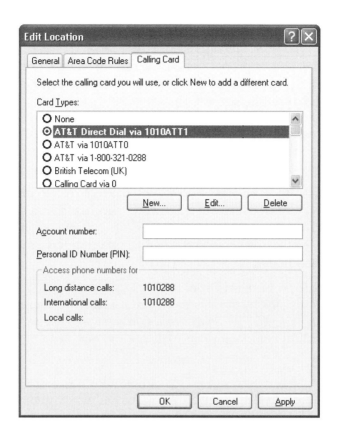

Area Code Rules

Area Code Rules give you just about every option you might need in any kind of environment. You can use multiple locations, calling cards, along with other options. Of course, the more options there are, the more likely you are to experience problems. Once again, your best bet is to keep the configuration as simple and streamlined as possible. Make sure the feature is necessary before you enable it—this will help keep your troubleshooting time to a minimum.

OPTIONS TAB

Once you leave the default properties for the dial-up connection, you return to the connection's Properties sheet. The Options tab, shown in Figure 12-4, gives you a few dialing and redialing options:

- **Display Progress While Connecting**   If you want to see the progress of the connection as it is being made, click this check box. If it is cleared, you'll not see any progress information during the connection process.

- **Prompt for Name and Password, Certificate, Etc.**   If you want to be prompted for the username, password, certificate, and so on during the connection, check this option. If this information is entered in the connection Properties sheet and you don't want to have to reenter it each time, do not use this option.

- **Include Windows Logon Domain**   This option, which can be used only with the Prompt for Name and Password, Certificate, Etc. option, requests the use of the Windows domain for logon purposes. Generally, when dialing to an ISP, you do not need this option, but it can be used in some proxy connections.

- **Prompt for Phone Number**   This option allows you to see, modify, and select the phone number that will be used when dialing the connection. If you use only one phone number, you can simply clear this check box option.

- **Redial Attempts**   If the first dial connection attempt fails, Windows can automatically redial the number. Use the selection box to determine how many times Windows will redial the number before stopping. The default is 3.

- **Time between Redial Attempts**   By default, Windows XP waits one minute between each redial attempt. You can change this value if desired.

- **Idle Time before Hanging Up**   If you want the connection to disconnect automatically after a certain period of idle time, enter the value here. Select Never as your value if you do not want the connection to disconnect automatically.

- **Redial If Line Is Dropped**   If you lose the connection, this option will have Windows XP automatically try to redial the connection.

■ **X.25**   If you are logging on to an X.25 network, click the X.25 button and enter the X.25 network provider and the remote server information as required.

SECURITY TAB

The Security tab, shown in Figure 12-5, provides security settings for the dial-up connection. By default, the Typical connection options are used. These options validate your username and password with the ISP's server. Notice that the Security tab also provides advanced connection options, but these options are generally used for dial-up connections to corporate networks, not to ISP servers. Do not change any of the settings on this tab unless your ISP explicitly instructs you to do so. Incorrectly changing these settings will stop your computer from successfully logging on to the ISP.

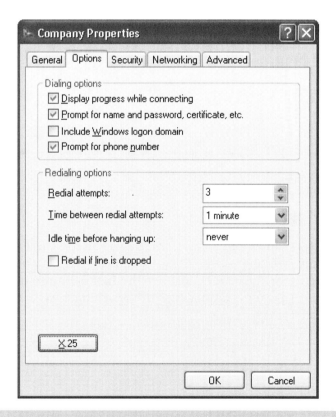

| FIGURE 12.4 | Options tab |

FIGURE 12.5   Security tab

NETWORKING TAB

The Networking tab, shown in Figure 12-6, shows you the current networking services and protocols that are used for the connection. If you need additional services or protocols for the connection, use the Install button to add them. For most ISP connections, you need not configure anything here.

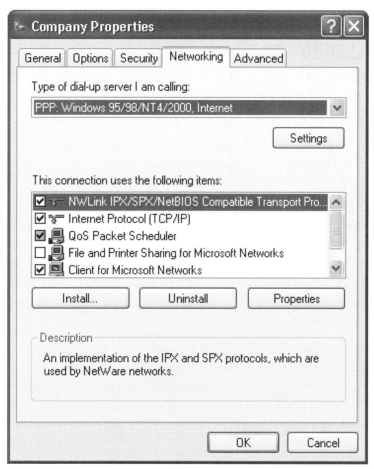

FIGURE 12.6   Networking tab

ADVANCED TAB

The Advanced tab enables you to turn on Internet Connection Firewall and
Internet Connection Sharing. See Chapter 13 to learn more about ICF and ICS.

TROUBLESHOOTING

Common Connection Problems

Due to the nature of dial-up connections, users may experience dial-up problems from time to time, and as you might guess, your job will most likely include examining and solving some of these problems. The following list gives you a number of common dial-up problems and their solutions:

- **Connections drop.** Due to problems with phone line noise and/or problems with the ISP, connections can be dropped. Generally, there isn't anything you can do except simply redial the number. Keep in mind that the Options tab enables Windows XP to redial automatically if the connection is dropped, so you might want to make sure this option is enabled. If the drops occur often, you should call technical support at your ISP for assistance, or contact your phone company.

- **Users' connections automatically disconnect.** As a safety measure to keep connections from staying connected when not in use, the Options tab has an autodisconnect option. After the connection is idle for a certain period of time, the connection is disconnected automatically. If you do not want to use this option, however, simply disable it on the Options tab.

- **Connections are slow.** Slow connections can occur for a number of reasons, most of which are outside of your control. Modem speeds at your ISP, phone line congestion, and even phone line noise can contribute to this problem. If the modem always seems to connect at a low speed, make sure you have the correct modem driver installed. Otherwise, call the ISP for support.

- **The user is prompted for name and password at each dial-up session.** Keep in mind that you can have Windows XP prompt you for the username and password, and even the phone number, each time a connection is made to the ISP. If you do not want to use these options, turn them off on the Options tab.

- **A 1 is always dialed when dialing phone numbers.** If a 1 is always dialed, you need to edit the area code rules properties from the General tab.

Common Connection Problems (continued)

■ **The logon fails each time during authentication.**   If the logon fails during authentication, make sure you are using an appropriate username and password for the connection. Also, check the Security tab and make sure you are using settings that are compatible with the ISP. If all seems to be in order, contact the ISP for assistance.

WRAPPING UP

Internet connections do not have to be a terrible part of your job, and Windows XP gives you a number of dial-up and broadband support solutions that can certainly make configuration easier. If you are working with dial-up connections, be sure to check the Properties sheets for different settings that can cause dial-up failure or certain problems with your service.

Now that you have taken a look at Internet connections, Chapter 13 explores Internet Connection Firewall and Internet Connection Sharing.

ICS, ICF, AND NETWORK BRIDGING

13

In corporate environments where Windows domains are used, Windows 2000 Server computers running various types of software provide Internet access and firewall protection from malicious Internet users. However, in many networking environments, Windows 2000 Server is not practical or available. In fact, you may work in such an environment. In home networks and most small office networks, 20 or more computers may be in use without a centralized server. For this reason, Windows XP includes software that enables Windows computers to use a single Internet connection, and such networks can employ the new Internet Connection Firewall (ICF) to help keep the network safe from possible threats from the Internet. In this chapter, you'll...

- Configure and use Internet Connection Sharing (ICS)
- Configure and use Internet Connection Firewall
- Configure a network bridge

USING INTERNET CONNECTION SHARING

Internet Connection Sharing, or ICS, first introduced with Windows 98, enables you to connect one computer to the Internet and set up all other computers on the network to share the Internet connection. This feature is specifically designed for home networks or small office networks that do not have a centralized server.

NOTE With ICS, you need only one Internet connection and one piece of hardware; each computer does not need a modem or broadband hardware, such as a cable modem or DSL modem. Through sharing, you save money and aggravation because you don't have to configure each computer to use the Internet.

If you decide that ICS is right for your networking environment, you must first ensure that your network is up and running. ICS will work with any kind of networking hardware, such as Ethernet, HomePNA, or even wireless networks. HomePNA is a networking technology that uses a home or office's existing phone lines as the network cabling, without interfering with voice conversations. This technology makes home and small office networking a real snap, and HomePNA kits are available at most computer stores, often for under $70.

Next, you determine which Windows XP computer will function as the host computer. This computer is the only computer connected to the Internet; all other computers, called the client computers, will access the Internet through the host computer. ICS is supported on Windows 98, Windows Me, Windows NT 4.0, Windows 2000, and Windows XP computers. You cannot use ICS with Windows 95 or earlier versions or other operating systems, such as Macintosh.

NOTE ICS is designed for use with broadband Internet access (ISDN, DSL, cable, satellite, and so on). Although you can use ICS with a 56KB modem, your modem will operate very slowly if several people are trying to use the Internet connection at the same time. This is due to the fact that a 56KB modem does not have enough bandwidth to perform at a desirable speed. However, if users on your network do not access the Internet at the same time, the 56KB modem shared connection will be fine.

HOW ICS WORKS

When you use ICS, your Windows XP computer should be the *ICS host*. All other computers on your network, called *ICS clients,* access the host to get information from the Internet. Using this setup, your host computer has a connection to the Internet and a connection to your home network. All of the client computers only need a network adapter so they can connect to the host.

(Again, Windows 95 clients are not compatible.) Under this setup, it appears as though only one computer is accessing the Internet. You don't have to use the Windows XP computer as the host; you can use a different computer, such as Windows Me. However, you will have fewer operational problems if the Windows XP computer is the ICS host.

ICS does not work with some versions of AOL. Check with AOL to see whether ICS supports your version of AOL. It is also possible, although unlikely, that your ISP will charge you for multiple computer connections to the Internet. Check with your ISP to make certain that you will not incur additional charges.

When you set up the ICS host, the local area connection for your internal NIC is configured as 192.168.0.1 with a subnet mask of 255.255.255.0. If the ICS host has more than one NIC for your workgroup, such as in the case of a multisegment network, you need to bridge those connections so that both network segments can use ICS. The DHCP Allocator service is configured on the ICS host. When additional network clients are added to the network, the DHCP Allocator assigns those clients IP addresses, ranging from 192.168.0.2 through 192.168.0.254, with a subnet mask of 255.255.255.0. A DNS proxy is also used so that no additional DNS servers are required on your network. These services run automatically and in the background and require no additional configuration from you. If a modem connection is used on the ICS host, autodial is turned on by default so that the connection is automatically dialed when an ICS client makes a request to the Internet. Also, ICF is automatically used on the shared connection, which you can learn more about later in this chapter.

RUNNING THE HOME NETWORKING WIZARD

Once you have all of your hardware and your computers are connected to each other, you can run the Home Networking Wizard, which will set up home networking on your computers and configure the ICS host. The following steps walk you through the wizard steps to set up the ICS host.

SETTING UP THE ICS HOST

1. Turn on all computers on your home network so they are all booted and operational.

2. On the Windows XP computer that will be the ICS host, click Start | All Programs | Accessories | Communications | Network Setup Wizard.

3. Read the information on the Welcome screen and click Next.

4. The next window gives you more information about home networking. Make sure you have completed the preparation tasks listed, then click Next.

5. The Select a Communication Method window appears. Essentially, the radio button options here ask you to describe how the Windows XP computer connects to the Internet. For this exercise, assume that the Windows XP computers connect to the Internet and that the other computers on your network will connect to the Windows XP computer. Select the desired radio button, then click Next.

6. The Internet Connection window appears. In the provided box (which lists all entries in your Network Connections folder), select your connection to the Internet, then click Next.

7. If you're using a dial-up connection, then the wizard will prompt you to dial a connection to the Internet. Accept the prompt and connect.

8. In the provided window, enter a description for your computer and a computer name. If you are using a cable broadband connection to the Internet, you should probably not change the name of your computer because the Internet service provider (ISP) may require a particular name.

9. Review the changes that will be made to your computer and click Next. Windows XP automatically configures all of your computer's software and hardware components for networking, according to the selections you made when running the wizard.

10. Click Finish. You will need to restart the computer for the new changes to take effect.

Once you have run the Home Networking Wizard on the Windows XP computer, you need to run the wizard on each computer that you want to include in the home network. If you need to configure down-level clients, such as Windows 2000, Windows Me, Windows 98, and so on, use the Windows XP installation CD-ROM. You'll find that the Network Setup Wizard appears in the Other Tasks category. Or, you can choose the option to create the network setup disks; this option appears at the end of the Network Setup Wizard. You can then run the wizard on your client computers. When you run the wizard on the client computers, choose the option to connect to another computer or a residential gateway, as shown in Figure 13-1. The wizard will then locate the ICS host and configure the client computer to access the Internet through the ICS host.

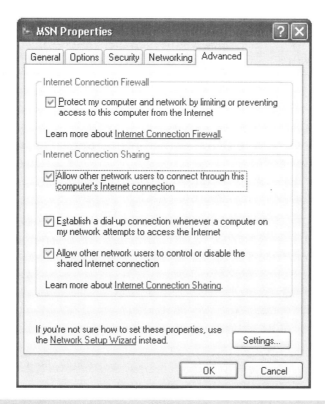

FIGURE 13.1   Advanced tab

ICS only works with Internet Explorer 5.0. Users in your network may try to use Netscape or Opera, but these browsers will not work with ICS. Also, if you are using down-level clients, make sure they have at least IE 5.0 installed.

MANAGING ICS

After ICS is set up and configured on the host computer and the client computers, the software is designed to be trouble-free as well as hands-off. There isn't a lot of configuration that you will need to do with ICS, and for the most part, users will not need to come to you for help. However, the following sections explore a few important issues that you should note.

ICS HOST CONFIGURATION

The Network Setup Wizard configures everything you need on the ICS host so that the ICS works the way it is supposed to. There are only a few settings for

ICS that you can access, and you can find these on the shared Internet connection by opening Network Connections. Right-click the shared Internet connection (which appears with a hand under it), then click Properties. On the Properties dialog box, click the Advanced tab.

On the Advanced tab, shown in Figure 13-1, are three check box options concerning ICS:

- **Allow Other Network Users to Connect through This Computer's Internet Connection**   This option essentially turns ICS on or off. If you want to stop sharing the connection, clear the check box, which automatically turns off the other check box options.

- **Establish a Dial-Up Connection Whenever Another Computer on My Network Attempts to Access the Internet**   If the shared connection is a dial-up connection, this option allows Windows XP to dial the connection automatically when another client attempts to use the Internet. If this selection is cleared, ICS clients will be able to use the Internet only when you manually connect the ICS host computer to the Internet. Under most circumstances, this auto-dial setting is best.

- **Allow Other Network Users to Control or Disable the Shared Internet Connection**   This feature, which is new in Windows XP, essentially allows the ICS clients to control the connection. In a small home or office network, this setting may work well. Users can manage the shared connection as though it were physically located on their computers.

ICS CLIENT MANAGEMENT

As the previous section mentioned, a new feature in Windows XP's ICS is client management. By default, clients on an ICS network can manage the Internet connection. This includes connecting to and disconnecting from the ISP as well as accessing connection statistics. As the ICS host administrator, you can stop clients from controlling the Internet connection and accessing information; to do so, simply clear the Allow Other Users to Control or Disable the Connection check box found on the Advanced tab. However, if you allow clients to manage the connection, which is often the best choice in busy networking environments, clients will see an Internet Gateway icon in the Network Connections folder, representing the ICS host, as shown in Figure 13-2.

FIGURE 13.2   Internet Gateway icon

ICS clients can also have their own connections to the Internet. For example, some of your client computers may have a modem connection to the Internet for backup purposes. Likewise, you might provide an Internet connection for a laptop computer that the user can use when the computer is not connected to the network.

If you double-click the icon, you see a status dialog box, shown in Figure 13-3. You can view the status, duration speed, and activity of the connection using the dialog box. Notice also that you can disconnect the connection simply by clicking the Disconnect button. If other users are accessing the Internet at the time, they are disconnected as well.

Click the Properties button. A simple window appears telling you what connection you are using. Click the Settings button. The Services tab appears, as shown in Figure 13-4. These services work with ICF to allow certain kinds of Internet traffic that would otherwise not be allowed. See the next section to learn more about ICF.

Internet Gateway status box

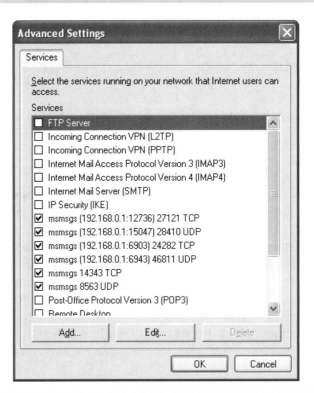

Services tab

TECH TALK

Changing the ICS Host

You can easily add new client computers to the network by running the Network Setup Wizard so that the new clients access the ICS host for Internet access. However, what if you need to change the computer that is acting as the ICS host? Windows XP will not allow another computer on the network to become the ICS host until you remove ICS sharing on the original host. If you try to enable another computer as the ICS host, you'll receive an IP address conflict error message, as shown here.

So, to change the ICS host to another computer, you need to follow these steps:

1. Disable the ICS host computer by clearing the ICS option on the Advanced tab of the Internet connection's Properties sheets. This will clear the former ICS host's IP address.

2. On the new ICS host computer, run the Network Setup Wizard again and choose the option to share the Internet connection.

3. Once the setup of the ICS host is complete, rerun the Network Setup Wizard on the client computers so that they will be configured to use the new ICS host.

USING INTERNET CONNECTION FIREWALL

In networks, a firewall is any piece of computer software or hardware that protects a network from intruders. For example, suppose that you own a small company that uses 200 computers. Each user needs to access the Internet every day, so there is a primary Internet link going from your company to an ISP. Although you want to use the Internet each day, you do not want Internet users to get inside of your private network and steal information from you. What to do? The answer is a firewall.

Firewalls use various kinds of tactics to check traffic as it flows in and out of the network. Using rules that are configured by system administrators, certain kinds of traffic are allowed or not allowed, and some kinds of traffic can even be seen as threatening. In short, the firewall acts as a traffic cop who makes certain that no one gets inside of the private network. Firewalls are nothing new; they have been around for years, and most larger, private networks today use some kind of firewall technology. In addition, a number of server products provide firewall and caching services.

However, because of threats from the Internet, home PCs and small office environments also need firewall protection. Indeed, firewalls are not limited to protecting large networking environments. Windows XP includes its own firewall to help protect your computer from malicious users when you're on the Internet. You can think of the firewall found in Windows XP as a "personal firewall," and indeed, other companies even produce firewalls for the typical home or small office user. An example of such a product is Norton Internet Security.

NOTE Although the Windows XP firewall provides basic firewall protection, it does not have the flexibility and caching services provided by other third-party firewall products. Depending on your needs, you might consider a third-party firewall product for Windows XP instead of ICF. Of course, ICF is already built into Windows XP and it is free, so it is more convenient to use.

Whenever you are using the Internet, your computer is open for potential attacks. With a dial-up connection, the attacks are limited because you are not connected to the Internet all of the time. However, with the explosive growth of broadband connections (DSL, cable, satellite), the need for a firewall becomes very important because computers with such connections are always connected to the Internet, and therefore always exposed to danger. In a network situation where ICS is used, the entire network is open to attacks from the Internet since all computers connect to the Internet through the ICS host. For this reason, ICF is included with Windows XP and is available for your use.

UNDERSTANDING HOW ICF WORKS

ICF is a software solution in Windows XP. This means that ICF uses code built into the Windows XP operating system to monitor and manage traffic. ICF is considered a *stateful* firewall. This simply means that ICF works with your

Internet connection to examine traffic as it is passing through the firewall both to and from your computer or network.

Because ICF is stateful, it examines Internet traffic in terms of its live use. If something attempts to enter the firewall that is not allowed, ICF simply steps in and blocks the traffic from entering. In other words, IP packets that are not allowed are simply dropped at the firewall. Thus no unallowed traffic ever enters the firewall. To use stateful inspection, ICF examines the destination of every piece of traffic coming from your computer or from computers on your network. Whenever something is sent to the Internet (such as a URL request), ICF keeps a routing table to track your requests. When data comes to the firewall, ICF inspects it to see whether it matches up with requests found in the routing table. If so, IFC passes the data onto your computer or the requesting computer on your network. If not, IFC simply blocks the data from entering the firewall. The end result is that any traffic you want from the Internet can enter the firewall, and anything you have not requested is blocked.

NOTE Dropped communication is done automatically without any intervention from you. In fact, ICF doesn't even tell you when communication from the Internet has been dropped.

As you might imagine, ICF control is very helpful, but it can be a problem with some applications and services. Fortunately, you can configure to meet your specific needs.

TROUBLESHOOTING

ICF and Virus Protection

ICF is a method for protecting your computer against attacks from the Internet, but it does not provide any protection against computer viruses or Trojan horses. Windows XP does not provide any software to protect against these very real and common threats, so it is imperative that you install antivirus software on all computers on your network and keep that software up to date at all times. I have had to solve countless virus-related problems on users' computers simply because those computers did not have antivirus software installed. The moral to this story is simply this: ICF provides you with protection against hacker attacks, but you must use antivirus software to protect against computer viruses. Be safe, rather than sorry!

ISSUES WITH ICF

Before getting into more detail about ICF configuration, you need to understand a few issues concerning ICF's default behavior. You should keep these in mind as you are setting up Internet connections and home or small office networks.

- ICF should be enabled on any shared Internet connection in your home or small office network. You do not have to use a home or small office network to use ICF; if you have only one computer and you want the additional protection, ICF works great on one computer too.

- ICF works on a per connection basis. For example, suppose that your computer has a DSL connection and a modem connection. You use the modem connection in the event that the DSL connection goes down. You need to enable ICF on both the DSL and modem connections to have full protection. ICF is per connection—not per computer.

- In a small network setting using Internet Connection Sharing (ICS), you should certainly enable ICF on the ICS connection. However, if other computers on the network have other ways to connect to the Internet (such as through modems), you need to enable ICF on each of those connections as well. Again, ICF is only good on a per-connection basis.

- Any configuration changes that you make to ICF are only for that particular connection; they do not transfer from connection to connection. For example, if you have two connections and ICF is enabled on each of them, you must individually configure each connection as needed.

- Outlook Express will work with ICF and will continue to check for and download mail automatically. Microsoft Office applications such as Outlook 2000 will not be able to check mail automatically when Microsoft Exchange Server is in use because Remote Procedure Calls (RPCs) are used with the mail server. The mail server must be able to contact the Outlook client—but ICF will block this kind of communication. If you are using Outlook 2000 to connect to ISP mail, you'll not have any problems.

- ICF should not be enabled on any computer's network adapter card that is used to connect to local computers. Doing so will prevent connectivity. ICF should be used only for connections to the Internet—not connections between computers on your private network.

NOTE ICF, like ICS, is a home and small office solution. In environments where Windows XP is used with Microsoft DNS or DHCP and other large-scale networking services, ICF should not be used.

TURNING ON ICF

You can enable ICF through the Internet connection's Properties sheets, or when you run the Network Setup Wizard. If you have configured ICS, then you were prompted to enable ICF as well. If you right-click any Internet connection found in the Network Connections folder and click Properties, you will see the Properties sheets for that connection. Click the Advanced tab, and you see the ICF check box, as you saw in Figure 13-1.

ICF is designed to work with ICS in order to protect your shared Internet connection, therefore protecting the computers on your network. In most circumstances, the check box option that enables ICF is all you need to click in order to protect your network. However, there are some additional configuration options that you can use if necessary, and the next section takes a look at those settings.

CONFIGURING ICF SETTINGS

If you click the Settings button on the Advanced tab, you see advanced settings that govern how ICF works and what kinds of applications and services it allows. Again, you typically do not need to configure anything here if you are simply using the Internet and accessing Internet mail. However, if you are using certain applications or you are providing certain types of content to the Internet, then you may need to configure some of these settings.

The first tab is the Services tab. The Services tab provides you a list of check box options concerning services that are running on your computer or network that you are allowing Internet users to access. For example, suppose that you are running a web server on your Windows XP Professional computer. If ICF is in use, you need to check the Web Server (HTTP) and possibly the Secure Web Server (HTTPS) check boxes so that Internet users can access content on your web server. When you click these check boxes and click OK, ICF basically reconfigures itself to allow certain kinds of content to pass through the firewall in order to meet these needs. Or, suppose for example that you want to use Remote Desktop Sharing with someone on the Internet. By default, ICF will not allow this kind of communication, but if you enable it here, ICF understands that Remote Desktop Sharing should allow it.

If you want to enable one of the services listed on the Services tab, just click the desired check box. A Service Settings dialog box, shown in Figure 13-5, then appears where you must enter the name or IP address of the computer on your network that runs the service. Under most circumstances, you do not need to change any of the port information because Windows XP configures this

FIGURE 13.5 Service Settings dialog box

information on its own. The computer name or IP address tells Windows XP which computer runs the service so that only that computer receives the service traffic—not other computers on your network. As you can see, this is an additional security feature that keeps service traffic from entering computers that do not offer the service.

You can also configure services that are listed by default. Click the Add button and enter the service name and TCP/IP port numbers on which the service communicates. This is an advanced configuration, but the option is provided for networks that use custom applications or those who want to provide custom services to Internet users.

NOTE ICF is designed to keep your computer and network secure, but it can do its job only if you keep it enabled and configured effectively. For this reason, you should never make any changes to the Services tab that you do not clearly understand. For example, suppose that you enable the Web Server feature. This setting tells ICF that your computer is a web server and that it should allow web server request messages to pass through the firewall. However, if your computer is not really a web server, then you have opened the door for intruders to get into your computer or network. ICF is one of those great features where less is more. Do not enable anything extra unless absolutely necessary.

The next tab is Security Logging. The Security Logging tab enables you to log unsuccessful inbound connections, unsuccessful outbound connections, or both.

Keep in mind that ICF does not tell you when inbound communication is dropped from the firewall. However, if you are naturally curious or you believe there are regular Internet attacks on your computer, you can turn on the logging feature, then check out the log file periodically to see what is going on.

By default, the security log is stored in C:\Windows\pfirewall.log, but you can click the Browse button on the Security Logging tab, shown in Figure 13-6, to change the location. Also notice that the log file has a default maximum size of 4,096KB (4MB). You can increase or decrease this space if you like, but this is plenty of room. To enable logging for unsuccessful inbound or outbound connections, just click the applicable check boxes.

If you want to check out the log file, just browse to the location of the file and open it (it will open with Notepad). As you can see in Figure 13-7, the log file contains TCP addressing and port information and is not exactly easy to read. However, you can see how many firewall drops occurred over a period of time.

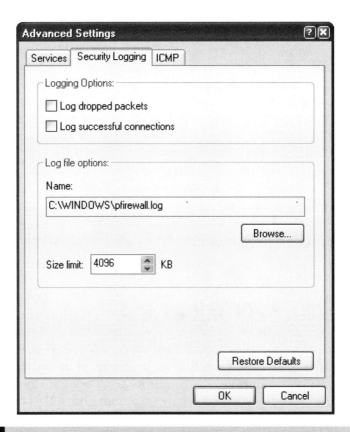

FIGURE 13.6   Security Logging tab

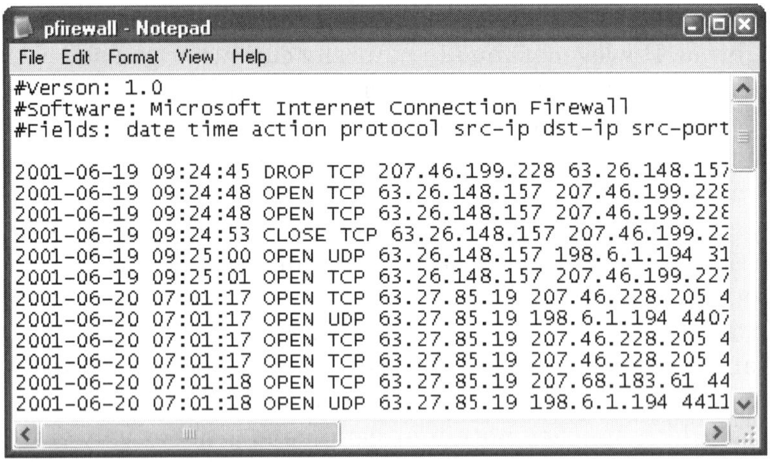

```
pfirewall - Notepad

File  Edit  Format  View  Help

#verson: 1.0
#Software: Microsoft Internet Connection Firewall
#Fields: date time action protocol src-ip dst-ip src-port

2001-06-19 09:24:45 DROP TCP 207.46.199.228 63.26.148.157
2001-06-19 09:24:48 OPEN TCP 63.26.148.157 207.46.199.228
2001-06-19 09:24:48 OPEN TCP 63.26.148.157 207.46.199.228
2001-06-19 09:24:53 CLOSE TCP 63.26.148.157 207.46.199.22
2001-06-19 09:25:00 OPEN UDP 63.26.148.157 198.6.1.194 31
2001-06-19 09:25:01 OPEN TCP 63.26.148.157 207.46.199.227
2001-06-20 07:01:17 OPEN TCP 63.27.85.19 207.46.228.205 4
2001-06-20 07:01:17 OPEN UDP 63.27.85.19 198.6.1.194 4407
2001-06-20 07:01:17 OPEN TCP 63.27.85.19 207.46.228.205 4
2001-06-20 07:01:17 OPEN TCP 63.27.85.19 207.46.228.205 4
2001-06-20 07:01:18 OPEN TCP 63.27.85.19 207.68.183.61 44
2001-06-20 07:01:18 OPEN UDP 63.27.85.19 198.6.1.194 4411
```

FIGURE 13.7 Firewall log

The final tab is the ICMP tab, shown in Figure 13-8. ICMP (Internet Control Message Protocol) is a protocol used on the Internet that enables computers to send information to and from each other about network problems or transmissions problems. For example, if one computer is sending information to another computer and an error occurs, that computer can use ICMP to tell the other what has happened. ICMP is a commonly used protocol and can be very helpful to computers on the Internet.

However, some attacks from the Internet act like ICMP messages, so by default, no ICMP messages are allowed on your network. Depending on your needs, however, you may want to enable some (or all) of these ICMP message types. Just click the check boxes on the ICMP tab, shown in Figure 13-8, and you can select a message type and read more about it in the Description portion of the window.

CONFIGURING A NETWORK BRIDGE

Windows XP includes a new networking feature called a *network bridge*. The bridge feature is designed to solve particular problems in home and small office networks when two dissimilar types of networks are used. For example, suppose that you work in an office that uses Windows XP computers. Part of your office is a standard Ethernet network, whereas another part of the office uses HomePNA. The two network types cannot connect and communicate, so you are faced with

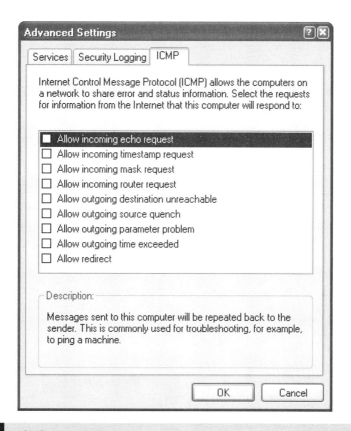

FIGURE 13.8   ICMP tab

two dissimilar network segments. Rather than converting the HomePNA network to Ethernet, or vice versa, you can save money and time by using Windows XP's network bridge feature. When you use a network bridge, one Windows XP computer is outfitted with a network interface card (NIC) from each network segment. This computer then acts as a bridge that connects the two networks. In the previous example, the Windows XP computer can be outfitted with an Ethernet NIC and a HomePNA NIC. You then bridge the connections and computers on each side of the segment, so that users on one side of the segment can then communicate with users on the opposite segment.

NOTE   You can bridge different kinds of connections together, but you cannot bridge a local area connection with a Virtual Private Network (VPN) or dial-up connection. Also, never bridge a private network with a connection that has a public Internet address. This opens your private network to the Internet, which poses many potential security threats.

CREATING A NETWORK BRIDGE

1. Log on with an administrative account.

2. Access the Properties sheets of both connections. Using the Advanced tab, turn off ICS or ICF if they are in use.

3. Open the Network Connections folder. Hold down CTRL and click each of the LAN connections that you want to bridge so that they are both selected.

4. Release CTRL. Then right-click the selected adapters and click Bridge Connections. Windows XP creates the network bridge. When the process is complete, the bridge appears in the Network Connections folder, along with the LAN connections that now appear under the Bridge category, as shown here.

NOTE The computer that contains the bridge must be turned on at all times for the two network segments to be bridged. If the bridge is offline, the segments will not be connected.

WRAPPING UP

Windows XP provides ICS and ICF for home and small office networks so that Internet connections can be shared and firewalled. These features give you the connectivity flexibility that you need, as well as protection from attacks from the Internet. Keep in mind that one Windows XP computer acts as the host computer on an ICS network, and Windows XP will automatically assign the appropriate IP address and subnet mask. When using ICF, ensure that all connections to the Internet have ICF enabled, and consider enabling additional services as needed. To handle dissimilar network segments, Windows XP provides a network bridge feature.

In the next chapter, you'll turn your attention to Windows XP and multimedia.

CONFIGURING INTERNET EXPLORER

14

Internet Explorer (IE) is Microsoft's answer to Internet surfing and all things pertaining to the Web. It is the default browser available in Windows XP and Internet Explorer is essentially tied to the Windows XP operating system, as it has been in previous versions of Windows. The good news for A+ technicians is that Internet Explorer 6 is the best version of IE that Microsoft has produced to date. It is more flexible and provides more configuration options, including additional security controls. If you think configuring IE is a simple, end-user task—think again. There are numerous settings and features that you may be called upon to support. After all, intranet and Internet connectivity in corporate networks is very important, and you can bet that IE will play a big part in serving those needs. In this chapter, you'll…

- Configure IE connectivity
- Work with general settings
- Configure security settings and options
- Configure the IE interface

CONNECTING WITH INTERNET EXPLORER

Internet Explorer 6 is designed to be a flexible piece of software that you can use to connect to intranet and Internet web sites. As such, it is designed to work with local area network (LAN) connections, modems, broadband connections to the Internet, and just about any other type of remote network connectivity that is available. In most cases, IE's connectivity options are readily configured and available. In other words, IE is good at determining what Internet connections are available on your computer and using those connections.

However, what if you need to configure IE's dial-up actions or even broadband connections? What if your environment uses a proxy server that IE must access in order to access the Internet? IE gives you a simple location that you can use to configure connectivity options when necessary. Open Internet Explorer, then click Tools | Internet Options. This opens several Internet Options tabs where you can configure a number of features, which you will explore throughout this chapter. If you click the Connections tab, shown in Figure 14-1, you see

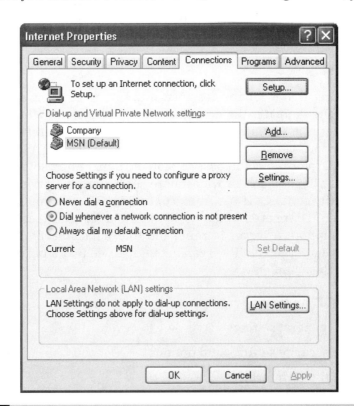

| **FIGURE 14.1** | Connections tab |

that you can manage dial-up and broadband connections, and you can even configure IE for proxy server access.

In the first panel of the Connections tab, you can configure dial-up and Virtual Private Network (VPN) connections. Note that this panel simply lists the existing dial-up or VPN connections that are configured on your computer, which in this example consist of Company and MSN. If you need to create a dial-up or VPN connection, you should use the Network Connections folder to first create the connection (see Chapter 12). You can also create a new connection by clicking the Add button, or you can also click the Setup button at the top of the tab to configure a connection.

The Add and Remove buttons simply allow you to manage the connections that are available for IE to use. Since the Connections tab lists them all by default, you usually do not have to do anything here. However, suppose that you have two Internet connections—one of which is used by a custom application. If you don't want IE to use a certain connection, simply select it and click Remove. This removes the connection from IE's availability, but leaves the connection configured in the Network Connections folder so that it can be used for other purposes.

In other instances, you may need to connect to a proxy server in order to access a dial-up or VPN connection. In this case, you can click the Settings button and enter the proxy server contact information in the Settings dialog box, shown in Figure 14-2. This dialog box, however, is used only for dial-up and VPN connections that must be made through a proxy server. Do not use this option when you need to connect via a typical LAN proxy server or with a broadband connection. Instead, use the LAN Settings button at the bottom of the Connections tab, which you'll explore later in this section.

You can use the Bypass Proxy Server for Local Addresses check box on the Settings dialog box to access local resources on your network without accessing the proxy server. This typically speeds up access and resolves connectivity problems. If users are having problems accessing local resources using IE, you may need to enable this setting when a proxy server is in use.

The Connections tab also gives you three radio button options that allow you to manage how the dial-up/VPN connection functions:

- **Never Dial a Connection**   This option prevents IE from automatically dialing a connection when it is launched. If you choose this option, before you can use IE you must first manually connect to the dial-up/VPN connection using the Network Connections folder. If clients complain

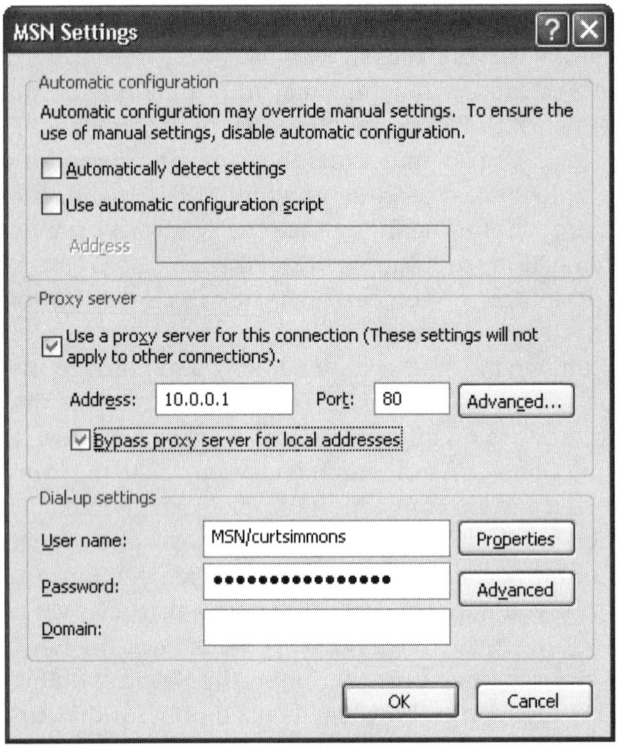

FIGURE 14.2   Proxy Settings dialog box

that IE never connects to a dial-up/VPN connection when it is first opened, check this setting and disable it.

- **Dial Whenever a Network Connection Is Not Present**   This setting, which usually is the optimal setting, simply tells IE to dial the default connection when no existing Internet connection is available. In other words, when you launch IE, it will launch the default Internet connection if the computer is not currently connected.

- **Always Dial My Default Connection**   If you do not want IE to use any Internet connection, choose this option. If you open IE and there is a current connection to the Internet, IE will still try to dial the default connection.

TROUBLESHOOTING

Problems with Automatic Disconnects

If you are connecting to a proxy server or VPN server for dial-up Internet access, you may run into a problem where IE automatically disconnects after a certain period of idle time. You can easily stop this behavior by clicking the Advanced button on the Settings dialog box of the proxy dial-up/VPN connection. If you click the Advanced button, you see a simple Advanced Dial-Up dialog box, shown here. Simply clear the Disconnect If Idle For check box to stop the automatic disconnect behavior.

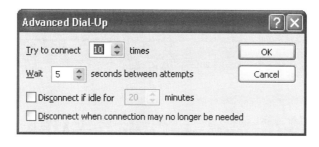

In the lower portion of the tab, you see the LAN Settings button. If you need to connect to a proxy server for Internet connectivity, or if you are using a broadband connection, click the LAN Settings button. This opens the Local Area Network Settings dialog box, shown in Figure 14-3. You can configure access to a specific proxy server by IP address or through automatic discovery. When automatic discovery is used, IE uses broadcast messages to "discover" a network proxy server. You need to check with a network administrator to determine how you should configure these settings. If you are using broadband hardware, check the hardware documentation for details concerning the configuration of these settings. Also, note that in a Windows domain, you can also use Group Policy to configure these settings automatically on Windows XP computers.

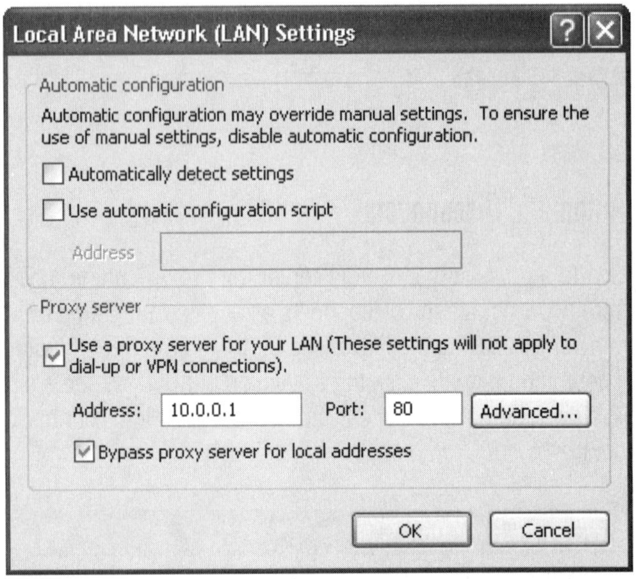

Local Area Network (LAN) Settings

Automatic configuration

Automatic configuration may override manual settings. To ensure the use of manual settings, disable automatic configuration.

☐ Automatically detect settings

☐ Use automatic configuration script

   Address   [   ]

Proxy server

☑ Use a proxy server for your LAN (These settings will not apply to dial-up or VPN connections).

   Address: [10.0.0.1]   Port: [80]   [Advanced...]

   ☑ Bypass proxy server for local addresses

[OK]   [Cancel]

FIGURE 14.3   Local Area Network Settings dialog box

CONFIGURING INTERNET EXPLORER SETTINGS

Several important Internet Explorer settings determine the way that IE responds and behaves when it is used. For the most part, these settings are easy and straightforward, but you should be familiar with them since users may complain of different issues related to these settings. The following section explores these settings.

CONFIGURING GENERAL SETTINGS

If you access Internet Options, you'll see a General tab where you can configure several standard IE settings. The General tab, shown in Figure 14-4, contains settings for the home page, temporary Internet files, and history, as well as some other basic settings.

The home page starts Internet Explorer with the URL that is entered in the Address text box. In other words, each time the user opens IE, the browser connects to the specified page. You can put any valid URL in the Address text box. You can also just leave the text box blank if you do not want to use a home page, in which case IE doesn't open anything until you enter a URL in the Address text box.

TECH TALK

Using Other Web Browsers on Windows XP

Of course, browsers other than Internet Explorer are available, and you may prefer to use alternatives such as Netscape and Opera with Windows XP. That's fine—you and the users you support are not locked into using IE on Windows XP. You can simply install and use another browser if you like. If you want to remove Internet Explorer icons and shortcuts from the Windows XP taskbar and Start Menu, open Add/Remove Programs in Control Panel, then click the Add/Remove Windows Components button. This opens the Windows Components Wizard. Simply clear the check box next to Internet Explorer to remove the icons and shortcuts, as shown here.

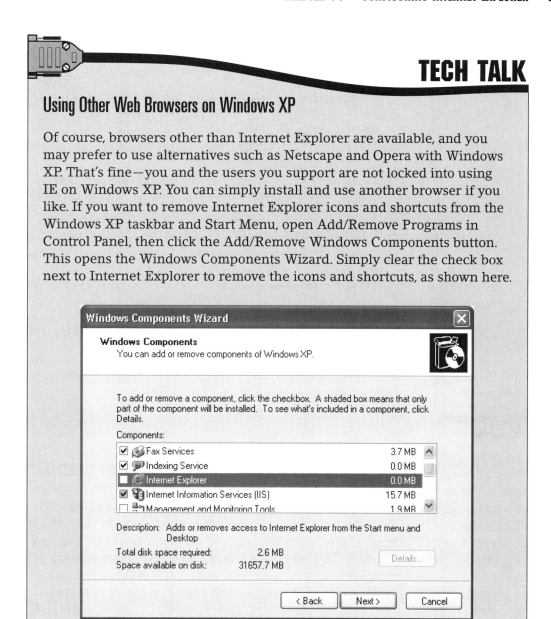

The Temporary Internet Files panel lists web page files and graphics that Internet Explorer caches in an attempt to make web surfing faster. If IE caches files and objects, there is less information to download each time the user connects

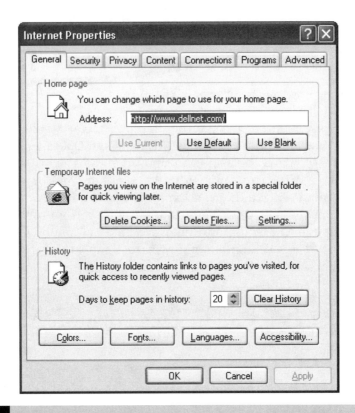

FIGURE 14.4　General tab

to that particular page, fostering the illusion that the Internet is working faster than it actually is. You can choose to delete all temporary files and cookies from this location by simply using the Delete buttons. You normally do not have to do this since IE does a good job of managing its own cached content. However, if IE seems to be performing slowly, consider using the Delete option so that IE can rebuild the cache. If you click the Settings button, a Settings dialog box, shown in Figure 14-5, appears that allows you to configure how the cache is managed.

By default, IE checks for new pages automatically, but you can change this behavior by choosing a different radio button so that IE checks for pages more often, or even never. The Settings dialog box also displays the amount of disk space that is used for temporary Internet files, and provides buttons that enable you to view the files and to move the temporary Internet files folder to a different location.

On the General tab, you can also manage the history. Internet Explorer keeps track of all web pages that the user visits, and this history makes it easy for the

FIGURE 14.5   Caching Settings dialog box

user to return quickly to previously viewed pages, which are simply stored as links. By default, the history is maintained for 14 days, but you can adjust this setting on the General tab, and you can manually delete the history as well.

Finally, the General tab gives you several easy-to-use buttons that adjust how web pages are displayed. The Colors, Fonts, Languages, and Accessibility buttons all open simple dialog boxes that allow you to adjust these features on web pages.

MANAGING CONTENT

The Content tab of Internet Options, shown in Figure 14-6, contains three panels—Content Advisor, Certificates, and Personal Information—that can help you manage content. The following sections explore these features.

USING CONTENT ADVISOR

Content Advisor is used to control different kinds of questionable or objectionable content in Internet Explorer. Typically, the Content Advisor is thought of as a "home" feature that is used to protect children, but in fact, many professional environments use this feature to help block inappropriate content in the workplace.

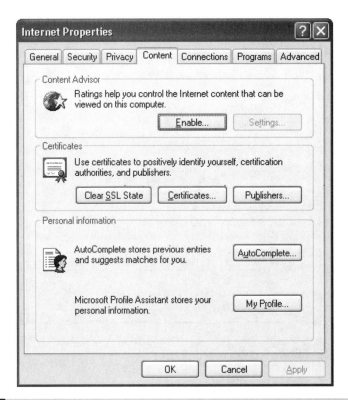

FIGURE 14.6   Content tab

Content Advisor works through voluntary site ratings. Web site administrators complete a form provided by the Internet Content Rating Association (ICRA). This association evaluates the web site administrator's responses to the questionnaire, then determines a content rating for the site. IE then examines the content rating of the site, which is found in the site's HTTP header information, then determines whether or not to block the site. ICRA is not a censor, but simply provides a method for rating web sites based on the site's feedback about itself. In other words, the effectiveness of the Content Advisor feature depends on the truthful data given by the web site. So, while Content Advisor can help control objectionable material, it is not foolproof. If you are working with children, you may consider using additional third-party products to help control content. Examples of such products are Net Nanny, found at **www.netnanny.com**, or CyberSitter, found at **www.cybersitter.com**.

ICRA ratings are based on language, nudity, sexual content, and violence. Using IE, you simply enable Content Advisor to adjust the level of content you want to make available (or unavailable). The following steps show you how to configure the feature.

CONFIGURING CONTENT SETTINGS

1. Choose Tools | Internet Options, then select the Content tab. Click the Enable button.

2. The Content Advisor dialog box appears with four configuration tabs. On the Ratings tab, shown here, you see a listing of rating categories. Select a desired category, and then move the slider bar to the desired level of content you want users to be able to see. Note that each category defaults at Level 0, which is the least offensive setting. Adjust the categories as desired, then click the Approved Sites tab.

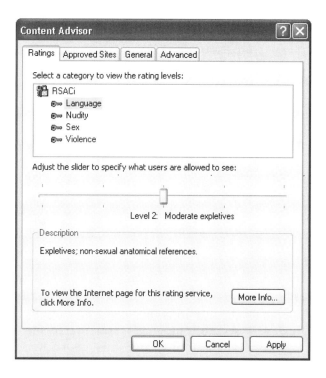

3. On the Approved Sites tab, you can override the settings that you configured on the Ratings tab by entering a desired web site address and clicking the Always or Never button. The Never setting will always prompt the user for an administrator password in order to see the site, and the Always setting will allow anyone to see the site without an administrator password.

4. Click the General tab. This tab presents a few different configuration options, as shown here.

First, you see two important check boxes that allow users to see unrated sites and to override a supervisor's settings. You should not use the Users Can See Sites That Have No Rating option if you are trying to secure the computer from harmful content. Some sites with inappropriate content do not have a rating, so to secure computers from unrated sites, Content Advisor will display a prompt. The administrator must override this prompt. This may cause some surfing difficulty, but it is the safest setting. You should always keep the supervisor setting selected so that you can override any Content Advisor prompts. If you need to change your supervisor password or find rating systems used by other companies, you can use the additional options found on the General tab. Keep in mind that the administrator password that you assign is used to control and even turn off Content Advisor, so make sure that you remember the password.

 If you should forget your password, you can override it with a Registry edit. Navigate to KHLM\Software\Microsoft\Windows\CurrentVersion\Policies\Ratings and delete the key value that you see. If you are worried about other people deleting the key value to gain access to content management settings, you can use Group Policy to prohibit access to the Registry or you can even use Registry permissions (available from the Edit menu) to control access to the key value.

5. Click the Advanced tab. This tab includes the option to locate and use a ratings bureau and use PICSRules. A ratings bureau is an Internet site that can check a rating of a site if the site is not rated by ICRA. This option, however, can seriously slow down browsing time. You can also import PICSRules, which are labels that can also help you determine whether sites can be viewed or not. No default rules are configured, but you can import them.

NOTE If you decide that you no longer want to use Content Advisor after you have configured it, you can always return to the Content tab and click the Disable button. You'll need to provide your administrator password to turn off the feature.

USING CERTIFICATES

Internet Explorer allows the use of digital certificates for identification purposes. For example, suppose that your network contains a secure Internet site. Users on the network must be able to access the secure site, which requires a digital certificate. The certificate is an authentication tool that allows the user to prove his or her identity before granting access to the site. In cases where certificates are used, a user can obtain a digital certificate from a certificate authority, such as VeriSign. The certificate then can be imported into Internet Explorer using the Certificates option on this tab. Then, when the user attempts to access the secure site, Internet Explorer can provide the user's certificate to the web site.

USING AUTOCOMPLETE

AutoComplete is a simple feature that allows Internet Explorer to remember information that you have entered when using the Internet, such as URLs, names, passwords, e-mail addresses, and other information that you might have typed into web forms. IE remembers this information, then tries to identify and complete it automatically for you when you are entering the same information later. The idea is to reduce the amount of time required to type URLs and data on web forms.

On the Content tab, you can click the AutoComplete button. The AutoComplete Settings dialog box, shown in Figure 14-7, then appears. In this dialog box,

AutoComplete Settings dialog box

enable or clear the check boxes to determine the kinds of information that you want Internet Explorer to remember and to adjust how AutoComplete works.

NOTE Although AutoComplete can remember passwords that you enter on web sites, the passwords will also be available to anyone else who uses the computer. If this is a possible security issue for you, just click the User Names and Passwords on Forms check box.

SETTING DEFAULT PROGRAMS

Internet Explorer's Internet Options gives you the Programs tab, shown in Figure 14-8, so that you can set default programs that Internet Explorer should use. For example, although Outlook Express is Internet Explorer's default e-mail program and newsgroup reader, you may be using Eudora or some other e-mail program. In this case, you can use the Programs tab to select the alternative program that you want to use. Just use the drop-down menus to change the default programs to the programs that you want.

Two other important settings here are the Reset Web Settings option and the Internet Explorer Should Check to See Whether It Is the Default Browser check box. Neither of these settings has anything to do with programs per se. The Reset Web Settings button simply resets the default home page and search pages.

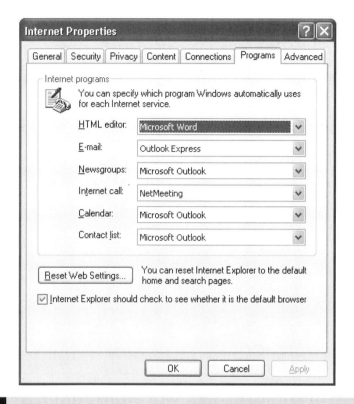

FIGURE 14.8   Programs tab

If users have changed these settings, use this button to restore the defaults easily. Also, if other browsers are in use, you can stop IE from giving you that aggravating "Is IE the default browser?" message that will appear each time you open Internet Explorer. Just clear the Internet Explorer Should Check to See Whether It Is The Default Browser check box to stop this action.

WORKING WITH ADVANCED SETTINGS

Internet Explorer gives you a number of different advanced settings, organized by category, which you can access on the Advanced tab of Internet Options, shown in Figure 14-9.

The default settings here are typically all you need, but the options can solve particular problems or give IE some additional functionality if needed. You can

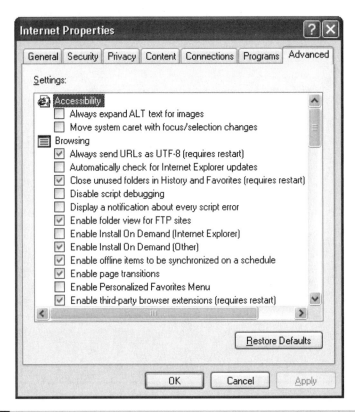

FIGURE 14.9 Advanced tab

browse these to get familiar with them. The following bullet list points out a few of the interesting ones that you might consider taking a look at.

- Under Browsing, the Automatically Check for Internet Explorer Updates check box is not selected by default. If you have a broadband or network connection to the Internet, consider enabling this setting so that Internet Explorer can periodically check **Microsoft.com** for updates.

- Under Browsing, consider disabling the Enable Page Transitions check box if you are using a slow Internet connection. Some web sites have page transitions configured so that one page fades into another. While visually attractive, these transitions waste your bandwidth and time, so disable this feature if your connection is slow.

- Under Browsing, consider enabling the Enable Personalized Favorites Menu check box. If you use Favorites a lot, the list can become long and cluttered. The Personalized Favorites menu hides the favorites you haven't used in a while so that the list is easier to see and use.

- Under Browsing, if you want Internet Explorer to help you automatically complete web addresses that you have used before, click the AutoComplete check box option.

- Under Multimedia, consider clearing the Play Animations in Web Pages, Play Sounds in Web Pages, and Play Videos in Web Pages check boxes if you have a slow Internet connection. This will help speed up your browsing experience so you will not have to wait so long when downloading multimedia content.

- Under Security, consider using the Empty Temporary Internet Files Folder When Browser Is Closed check box option if you want to keep Internet Explorer clean and cookies deleted.

MANAGING INTERNET EXPLORER SECURITY

Internet Explorer 6 provides a number of security features that manage how Internet Explorer uses different sites and how IE uses and manages cookies. These features, in a further attempt to control online piracy and privacy invasion, give you a number of controls that can be very important in a home or office situation. As an A+ technician, you should be well versed in these options both to configure IE and to solve potential security problems.

NOTE   Internet Explorer does not provide antivirus software or firewall protection. To make certain that a computer is always safe when using the Internet, third-party antivirus software should always be running and you should also enable the Internet Connection Firewall to prevent hacker attacks. See Chapter 13 to learn more about Internet Connection Firewall.

CONFIGURING INTERNET EXPLORER ZONES

Internet Explorer uses four different security zones, which you can access on the Security tab of Internet Options, shown in Figure 14-10. On the Security tab, you see the Internet, Local Intranet, Trusted Sites, and Restricted Sites zones. If you select a zone, you can see the current security level of the zone in the lower portion of the window.

You can select from four preconfigured levels of security for each zone by simply moving the slider bar. The levels are as follows:

- **High**   This setting disables all features that are less secure. This is the safest way to use the Internet, but it provides you with the least amount of functionality. The setting disables all ActiveX content along with all

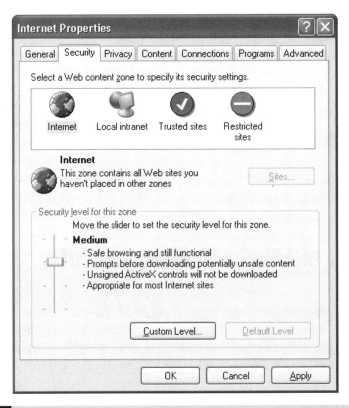

FIGURE 14.10   Security tab

downloads. Additionally, there are a number of restrictions on accessing data and requesting data.

■ **Medium**   The Medium setting does not allow the downloading of unsigned ActiveX controls, and you see the familiar prompt before downloading potentially unsafe content. Browsing is safe, yet functional, under this setting, and in most cases, this is the best setting to use.

■ **Medium-Low**   The Medium-Low setting will run most content without prompts, but still does not allow unsigned ActiveX controls. This setting is safe for intranet use.

■ **Low**   The Low setting provides basic warnings and few safeguards. All active content can run. This setting is not recommended unless the site is one you completely trust.

You can configure different settings for each zone by simply selecting the zone and moving the slider bar. However, you can also customize the settings

TECH TALK

Understanding Security Threats

What exactly are the potential security issues and threats that Internet usage tends to bring to your network? There are a few important ones that you should keep mind as you are thinking about and configuring security:

- **Active Content**   Active content from a web site, such as ActiveX controls, scripts, Java applets, and such, give the Internet its vast multimedia appeal. However, this active content can also harbor viruses and other malicious code. The problem with active content is that an antivirus program cannot scan this content because it is run when downloaded (you can't download it and then run it). So, the problem comes down to trust: Is the content what it seems to be, or is it really malicious? Internet Explorer attempts to alleviate some of that problem with Authenticode, which is a digital signature technology. Authenticode enables Internet Explorer to verify that active content has arrived to you without being changed in transit. In other words, the content is from the place that it says it is from. If the content is signed, that is still not a guarantee that it is safe—but more than likely, it is. Beyond that, the use of active content still comes down to trust. Users should be familiar with any web site from which they are downloading information.

- **Downloads**   Downloads can also contain viruses and other malicious code. The good news about downloads is that you can download the package to your computer and use an antivirus program to scan it for viruses before installing it on your computer. To be safe, always download the content first and install it after scanning it with antivirus software.

- **Data Management**   A lesser, but still important, security issue concerns user data and interaction with web sites. Internet Explorer can prevent a number of potentially risky actions, such as submitting form data over nonencrypted connections.

by clicking the Custom Level button. This opens the Security Settings dialog box, as shown in Figure 14-11. You can scroll through the list of settings and choose the Disable, Enable, or Prompt option for each security setting. This enables you to create a custom security setting that invokes the features that

FIGURE 14.11　Security Settings dialog box

you want instead of the default options. If you want to see what settings are used under one of the default options (such as High, Medium, and so on), click the Reset To drop-down menu at the bottom of the Security Settings dialog box and click Reset. You can then see how each of the custom settings is applied under one of the default security options, and then customize the settings as you wish.

WORKING WITH ZONES

As you can see, IE's security features work with different zones so that you can configure different security settings according to those zones. The settings you choose for each zone will depend on the security needs of your network, but there are some basic words of advice that you should heed.

For the Internet zone, the Medium setting is the best. It provides the best browsing functionality, but still has enough controls in place to keep the computer reasonably protected. You can, of course, customize the settings as needed, but as you are working with the Internet zone, it is a good idea to keep the highest security settings possible, but maintain good usage features. Low security settings may make browsing easier, but you are asking for problems.

The opposite is also true: Settings that are too high are very secure, but they hinder browsing capabilities.

The default setting for the Local Intranet zone is Medium-Low. This setting allows you to use the intranet basically as you wish, but prohibits the use of unsigned ActiveX controls. In some cases, you may even want to use the Low setting, if you are certain all of the content on your intranet is safe. If it is, then the Low setting will not prevent any active content from running. If you select the Local Intranet icon on the Security tab, you can also click the Sites button and select or deselect a few other options, as shown here.

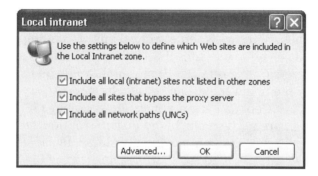

You can choose to include all local sites not listed in other zones, including all sites that bypass the proxy server and all network paths. The default setting enables all three of these options, and you should usually leave these enabled. You can also click the Advanced button and add web sites to this zone as well.

If you use a particular site often and you know that content from the site is safe, you can add the site to your Trusted Sites zone. The Trusted Sites zone is made up of sites that you deem trustworthy. When a site is added to the Trusted Sites list, then the Low security setting is used when that site is accessed. This allows you to use the site freely without any security restrictions. Of course, you should make absolutely certain that a site is trustworthy before adding it to your Trusted Sites zone; otherwise, you have no security protection from that site.

The Restricted Sites zone works like the Trusted Sites zone—except in reverse. Sites listed in the Restricted Sites zone are given the High security level in order to protect the computer from harmful content. You can select the Restricted Sites zone and click the Sites button in order to add sites to the zone that might expose harmful content.

WORKING WITH PRIVACY SETTINGS

Privacy settings, which are a new feature in Internet Explorer 6, give you a way to manage cookies that are used by Internet Explorer. A *cookie* is a text file that is exchanged between your browser and a web site. Cookies contain personal information about you, such as your name, e-mail address, and even your surfing and access habits. Cookies are a great feature because they allow a web site to recognize you, remember what you have done at the site in the past, and in the case of online stores, remember what you have bought. The problem, though, comes back to security. If the cookie information gets in the wrong hands, you have just given someone personal information about you. That's where the problem comes in—cookies personally identify you, and on the Internet, that can be a bad thing. Cookies account for many different kinds of privacy invasions, including a lot of the spam you probably receive in your e-mail inbox.

Internet Explorer 6 provides a collection of settings that can restrict and control cookies. These settings, when effectively used, can help safeguard your information but allow you to use sites that manage cookies in an appropriate manner. Previous versions of Internet Explorer allowed you to block all cookies or be prompted by them, but the use of these features is really impractical. If you activate the Block Cookie feature, you cannot even log on to some web sites, and because cookies are used so much, the Prompts option can drive your users to call you for help. Rather than employing the simple block feature, Internet Explorer 6 uses a standard called the Platform for Privacy Preferences (P3P), which enables Internet Explorer to inspect cookies, determine how they will be used, and then decide what to do about them. The feature is not perfect, but it does help control cookie usage and the user's privacy. Before you configure privacy settings, there are a couple of concepts with which you should be familiar:

- **Compact Privacy Statement** A compact privacy statement tells how cookies are used on the site and how long a particular cookie is used. When you access a web site, the compact privacy statement is contained in the HTTP header of the web site. Internet Explorer can read the compact privacy statement when you first access the site.

- **First-Party Cookie** A first-party cookie is a cookie that is generated and used by the site you are currently viewing. First-party cookies contain information about you and your browser, and are commonly used to tailor site content to your needs. First-party cookies are commonly used on online store sites.

- **Third-Party Cookie** A third-party cookie is used by a site other than the one that you are currently accessing, such as a banner advertisement. Third-party cookies can be a problem because you do not really know who is using them or what they will do with the personal information contained in the cookie.

- **Session Cookie** A session cookie is generated during a single session with a web site, and then deleted once the session has ended. In many cases, you cannot use a web site unless a session cookie can be generated.

- **Implicit and Explicit Consent** Implicit consent means that you have not blocked a site from using a cookie—in other words, you have not granted permission, but you have not denied it either. On the other hand, explicit consent means that you have acted to allow a web site to use or gain personal information about you.

Privacy settings are managed on the Privacy tab, shown in Figure 14-12. A slider bar option enables you to select a desired privacy setting.

The standard privacy setting options that are available are as follows:

- **Block All Cookies** All cookies are blocked. Web sites cannot generate any new cookies, and no existing cookies can be read. This setting will prevent access to some web sites.

- **High** No cookies that use personally identifiable information can be generated without your explicit consent. Web sites that do not have a compact privacy statement cannot generate cookies.

- **Medium-High** First-party cookies that use personally identifiable information, which is information that identifies the user, are blocked without your implicit consent. Cookies are blocked from third-party web sites that do not have a compact privacy statement. Also, third-party cookies that use personally identifiable information are blocked without your explicit consent.

- **Medium** First-party cookies that use personally identifiable information without your implicit consent are allowed, but they are deleted when you close Internet Explorer. Third-party cookies that use personally identifiable information without your implicit consent are blocked, as well as third-party cookies that do not have a compact privacy statement. The Medium setting is the default Internet Explorer setting.

- **Low** The Low setting accepts all first-party cookies. Third-party cookies are blocked from sites that do not have a compact privacy statement. However, third-party cookies that use personally identifiable information are allowed without your implicit consent, but the cookies are deleted when you close Internet Explorer.

- **Accept All Cookies** All new cookies are allowed, and all web sites can read existing cookies.

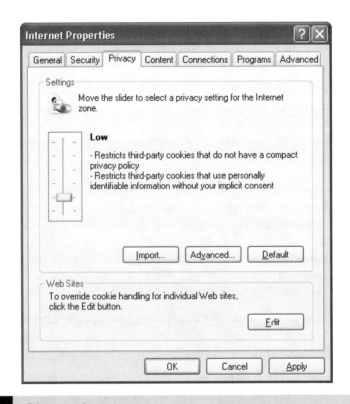

FIGURE 14.12 Privacy settings

Clicking the Advanced button opens the Advanced Privacy Settings dialog box, shown in Figure 14-13. The Advanced Privacy Settings dialog box essentially allows you to override how cookies are handled for this particular zone. As you can see, you can choose to accept, block, or prompt for first- and third-party cookies, and you can also always allow session cookies. For some users, the automatic cookie-handling settings do not provide the right support. In this case, you can override these settings and choose how you want to handle all first- and third- party cookies at all sites, regardless of the compact privacy statement.

You usually should allow session cookies to be generated so that the web site can keep up with your surfing selections while you are there. Session cookies are typically harmless, and you may find that web surfing is hindered without them. You can try these advanced settings and see if they work for you.

FIGURE 14.13   Advanced Privacy Settings dialog box

If you choose to use automatic cookie handling, you can override the privacy settings for certain web sites. For example, suppose that a site that you regularly use contains first- and third-party cookies. However, the site does not have a compact privacy policy, and your current cookie settings prohibit the use of first-party cookies on sites with no compact privacy policy. Rather than changing your entire policy, you can simply create an exception for the web site.

On the Privacy tab, click the Edit button. The Per Site Privacy Actions dialog box, shown in Figure 14-14, appears. Simply enter the URL of the web site and click the Block or Allow button. Web sites that you have added appear in the Managed Web Sites list, which you can edit and change at any time.

PAINFUL LESSONS I'VE LEARNED

Keeping Things Simple

As with most things in the networking world, simplicity is the best option. Although cookie security is great and can be useful in a number of situations, be wary of configuring too many restrictions. Cookies are common and necessary on the Internet, and too many restrictions can cause many browsing problems for your users—which sends them screaming to you for help!

FIGURE 14.14   Per Site Privacy Actions dialog box

CONFIGURING THE INTERNET EXPLORER INTERFACE

The Internet Explorer interface gives you several configuration options that can make IE easier to use, or at least customize IE to suit the user's needs. As an A+ technician, why do you need to know about IE's interface? The answer is simple: Because you are a part of support in your organization and are often the organization's problem solver, users may frequently ask for help with IE's interface. You may also need to configure some options within IE to meet the needs of certain users. In any case, it's a good idea to spend a few minutes working with IE's interface options to make sure your skills are adequate.

CUSTOMIZING THE INTERNET EXPLORER TOOLBAR

The Internet Explorer toolbar provides users with easy usability features and access to related programs and functions, such as e-mail and searching capabilities.

The toolbars are easily customizable, and you can easily choose what toolbars you want to display by clicking the View menu and choosing the desired options on the Toolbars and Explorer Bar submenus. You can even move the toolbars around so they are placed in different locations within the Internet Explorer interface. In addition, you can separate toolbars on the top and bottom of the screen, or you can even combine them into one long toolbar in order to save more screen space. By selecting the button items that appear, you can also customize the Internet Explorer toolbar. To customize the toolbar, just click View | Toolbars | Customize. On the Customize Toolbar dialog box, shown in Figure 14-15, you can see the toolbar buttons that are available to you as well as the current toolbar buttons. Simply move the items you want displayed to the current toolbar area, and remove items that you do not want displayed.

SECRET

If you cannot move your toolbars, click View | Toolbars and clear the check next to Lock the Toolbars. The toolbar handles now appear on the left side of the toolbars and you can drag and drop them.

HISTORY OPTIONS

Internet Explorer keeps track of the web sites that you or anyone using your computer accesses. The sites are listed by URL in the History folder and are kept for 20 days by default (you can change the default setting on the General

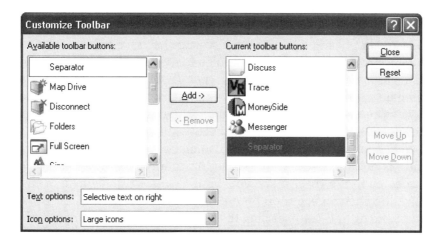

FIGURE 14.15   Toolbar options

tab of Internet Options). The idea behind the History feature is to enable you to find web sites you have accessed, but cannot seem to find a second time. You can view the history by clicking the History button on the toolbar. By expanding the day and week categories, you can see the sites that have been accessed on those days. Overall, the History feature is simple to use, but there are few important usage points you should keep in mind:

- Use the View drop-down menu on the History bar to view the history listing in several different organizational formats.

- You can delete history items individually by right-clicking them and clicking Delete. You can remove the history from an entire day or week by right-clicking the category and clicking Delete. You also delete all history items by clicking the Clear History button on the General tab of Internet Options.

- Even though you can delete the Today category, it will pop back into place when you use the Internet or access the History folder. In other words, you cannot permanently delete the Today category or the items that it holds. You can, however, delete items individually from the Today list.

- If you change the Days to Keep History Value setting to 0 on the General tab of Internet Options, the current day's history is still recorded anyway.

WORKING WITH FAVORITES

The Favorites feature in Internet Explorer provides you with a quick and easy way to keep track of your favorite web sites. Rather than remember individual URLs, you can simply add sites to your Favorites list, give them a user-friendly name, and click the option in Favorites to go to the site.

To add a site to your Favorites list, just click Favorites | Add to Favorites. A small dialog box appears. You can change the name to whatever you want and click OK. To store the favorite in a particular folder available under the Favorites menu, click the Details button and select the folder.

When you choose a favorite, you can also make the favorite available offline. This feature is helpful if you want to read information on a web site without being connected to the Internet. If you want to make the favorite available offline, click the check box option on the Add Favorite window, and if you want to customize the offline feature, click the Customize button. A wizard appears that enables you to customize how the offline web site is handled.

IMPORTING AND EXPORTING

Internet Explorer enables you to import and export certain data. For example, you could export your Favorites list so that your favorites can be used on another computer, or you can even import and export cookies. The good thing about importing and exporting is that you can import and export to a file so that you can share information with Netscape or even print Favorites lists easily. The following steps walk you through the import and export feature.

IMPORTING AND EXPORTING ITEMS

1. To import or export an item, click File | Import and Export.
2. Click Next on the Import/Export Wizard Welcome screen.
3. In the Import/Export Selection window, shown here, choose what you want to do. For this example, you will export your Favorites list. Make a selection and click Next.

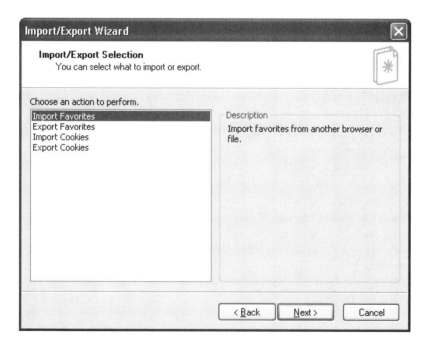

4. In the source folder, you can choose to export everything or a subfolder. Make a selection and click Next.

5. You can choose to export to another browser on your computer or to a file. For this example, you will export the Favorites list to a file. Make a selection and click Next.

6. Click Finish.

USING ENCODING FEATURES

Internet Explorer supports a number of different languages that allow you to view web sites in languages other than English. This process, called *encoding,* uses HTML information from the web page to determine the language in which the web page is written. This tells Internet Explorer what character set to use to display the web page correctly. If the web page does not tell Internet Explorer the language, Internet Explorer can usually figure the language out anyway, if you have the Auto-Select feature turned on. To make sure Auto-Select is turned on, click View | Encoding | Auto-Select.

If Auto-Select still does not display the language correctly, you can specify the language that is in use. Click View | Encoding | More, and then select the language that you want to use with the web site. In some cases, you may be prompted to download a language pack so that the web site can be displayed correctly.

WRAPPING UP

Internet Explorer 6, which is included in Windows XP as the default browser, gives you many configuration options that can enhance and customize a user's web browsing experience, including new security features that help protect data. As you are working with Internet Explorer in your environment, it is important to keep all of these features in mind as you configure users' computers and solve Internet usage problems.

In the next chapter, you'll take a look at working with digital media.

WORKING WITH DIGITAL MEDIA

15

Windows XP provides better support than ever for digital media and devices that use digital media. In fact, digital media has become very popular, both in the workplace and for entertainment purposes. CD-RW drives, streaming media, Internet radio, and even movie editing are just a few of the features that are available to users. In this chapter, you'll explore all Windows XP has to offer. In this chapter, you'll…

- Manage scanners and cameras
- Work with CD drives
- Use Windows Media Player
- Use Windows Movie Maker

WORKING WITH SCANNERS AND CAMERAS

Windows XP supports many different scanners and digital cameras, most of which you can simply plug into Windows XP and begin using. Gone are the days of difficult scanner configurations and digital cameras that will not work under Windows. As with many peripheral devices, you should ensure that the product is compatible with Windows XP before you buy it. As always, when you install any hardware device, be sure to read the manufacturer's instructions. If you are having problems installing a scanner or a camera, Windows XP gives you a wizard that can help, as demonstrated in the following steps.

NOTE You should not have to use this wizard unless you are having problems with installation. Generally, you can just plug the scanner and camera into the correct port and begin using it.

INSTALLING A CAMERA OR A SCANNER

1. Click Start | Control Panel | Scanners and Cameras.

2. The Scanners and Cameras dialog box appears, shown here. Any currently installed scanners or cameras appear in this dialog box. To install a troublesome scanner or camera, click the Add an Imaging Device link under Imaging Tasks.

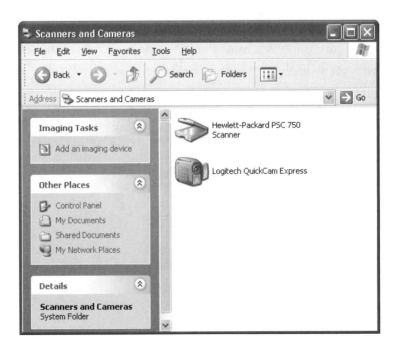

3. The Camera and Scanner Installation Wizard appears. Click Next on the Welcome screen.

4. In the selection screen, shown here, select the model and make of the scanner or camera that you want to install. Use the Have Disk button if you have an installation disk or CD-ROM. Click Next.

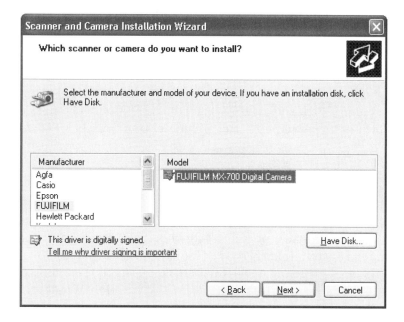

5. In the detection screen, you can choose automatic detection or you can assign the port on which the device is connected. As a general rule, automatic detection is the best selection option. Make a selection and click Next.

6. Provide a name for the device and click Next.

7. Click Finish.

NOTE Some cameras use a memory stick that will show up as an additional hard drive. To copy pictures to the computer, simply open the drive and copy the files.

IMPORTING PICTURES

Once the digital camera is installed and connected, you can easily move pictures from the digital camera by simply opening the camera icon in the Scanners and Cameras dialog box, or you can simply right-click the camera and click Get

Pictures. By default, pictures are stored in the My Pictures folder. However, users in your environment may wish to save pictures in an alternative location. You can easily configure this option by selecting a different folder in which to save the pictures. The following steps show you how.

LINKING THE CAMERA TO A FOLDER

1. Right-click the camera, and then click Properties.

2. On the Events tab, in the Select an Event control, click the event for which you want to initiate an action.

3. In the Actions window, click the Save All Pictures to This Folder option. All the pictures you select will be saved to the folder you specify when the event occurs. To search for a specific folder or drive, click Browse.

4. When you are done, just click OK.

SCANNING ITEMS

Once the scanner is installed, you can easily scan items by simply right-clicking the scanner's icon in the Scanners and Cameras dialog box and clicking Scan. See the scanner's documentation for additional configuration options and instructions as needed. One noteworthy item concerns the scanning of pictures. Rather than just treating pictures like any kind of scan job, Windows XP gives you the Get Picture Using Scanner Wizard option when you right-click the scanner icon. This easy-to-use wizard can help you scan pictures at any resolution you might need. See the following steps for details.

SCANNING PICTURES

1. In the Scanners and Cameras dialog box, right-click the scanner icon and click Get Picture Using Scanner Wizard.

2. The Scanner and Camera Wizard appears. Click Next on the Welcome screen.

3. In the Choose Scanning Preferences window, shown here, choose the kind of picture that you want to scan, such as color, grayscale, and so on. If you click the Custom Settings button, you can choose the resolution, color, brightness, and more. Make your selections and click Next.

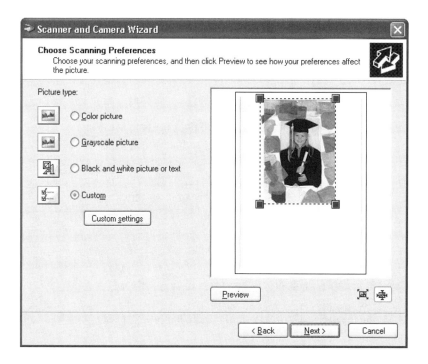

4. In the next window, choose a name for the picture, the file format, and the place where the picture will be saved. Click Next.

5. The picture is now scanned. A window appears asking whether you want to publish the picture, order copies, or do nothing else. Make a selection and click Next to complete the wizard.

WORKING WITH CD/DVD-ROM DRIVES

CD-ROM and DVD-ROM drives basically work like any other hardware device in Windows XP, so we'll not spend a lot of time dwelling on them. Depending on your environment, client computers may be equipped with simple CD-ROM drives, but they may also have CD-RW drives as well as DVD-ROM drives. The key point to remember is that all of these drives must be compatible with Windows XP and have a proper driver. You can use Device Manager to manage them, just as you would any other device.

If you open My Computer and right-click the desired CD or CD-RW drive, you can access the Properties sheets. Notice on the AutoPlay tab that Windows can try to open the media found on the CD for you, primarily using Windows

TECH TALK

Printing Pictures

If you work in a multimedia environment, picture printing may be a common task that users face. Thus, to support your environment's users, you may have to solve their picture printing problems, even though photography may not be your first job choice. There are entire books on photography and print output, and Windows XP can help you as well. However, here are a few quick pointers. First, resolution is very important. To print quality pictures, you'll need .TIF or .BMP file types at around 300 dpi (dots per inch, the standard by which resolutions are measured). Higher resolution results in higher print quality. The second rule of printing is to use photo quality paper—this is a must, since standard copier paper will not provide quality results. For other problems, Windows XP gives you a Photo Printer Wizard that can help, as described in the following steps:

1. Right-click the desired picture and click Print. Windows XP opens the Photo Printing Wizard. Click Next on the Welcome screen.

2. The wizard's next window gives you several photo-printing options. Just select the picture(s) that you want to print and click Next.

3. In the Printing Options window, choose the printer that you want to use. Click the Printing Preferences button to select the paper quality. Click Next.

4. In the Layout Selection window, choose the layout that you want to use, and click Next.

5. The picture is printed. Click Finish.

Media Player. However, Windows XP may also prompt you for an action. If users are complaining that Windows Media Player always opens when they put a CD in the CD drive, select the Prompt Me Each Time to Choose an Action radio button option, as shown in Figure 15-1.

NOTE Depending on your CD device, you may see additional Properties sheets with different options. Check your CD drive documentation for details about these additional tabs.

Also, if you are using CD-RW drives, Windows XP includes a new feature that enables you to write directly to the drive without having to use the CD-RW

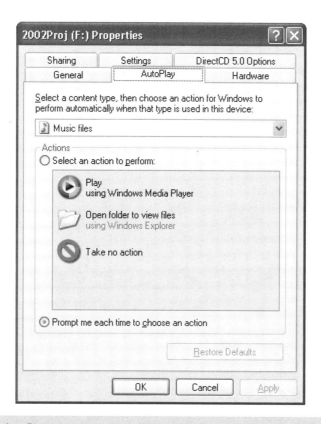

FIGURE 15.1   AutoPlay tab

software. Typically, you can simply right-click a file or folder, point to Send To, then click the CD-RW drive to copy data to the CD-RW drive, just as you would with a floppy disk or Zip disk.

USING WINDOWS MEDIA PLAYER

Windows Media Player is the default Windows player for audio and video. Although you can use other media players, such as Real Player, Windows Media Player is the preferred player for Windows. Now, if you are thinking that working with Media Player is a little beneath your job skills, you are probably right. However, you are often asked to solve all kinds of problems and support all kinds of operating system features, and Media Player no exception. In fact, if a lot of multimedia content is used in your network, you can expect to get some questions and problems with Media Player, so it's a good idea to use this section as a configuration and problem solving guide.

You can find Windows Media Player by clicking Start | All Programs | Accessories | Entertainment | Windows Media Player. Depending on your system configuration, you may also have a shortcut to Media Player on your desktop or on your taskbar.

When you open Media Player, you see a default interface. You can consider this interface the default because you can completely change the interface using a variety of skins, which you'll learn about later in this chapter. As you can see in Figure 15-2, the default interface provides you with a primary media area, a list of buttons on the left side of the Media Player (called *features*), and a standard toolbar. When you first open Media Player, it attempts to connect with **www.windowsmedia.com**.

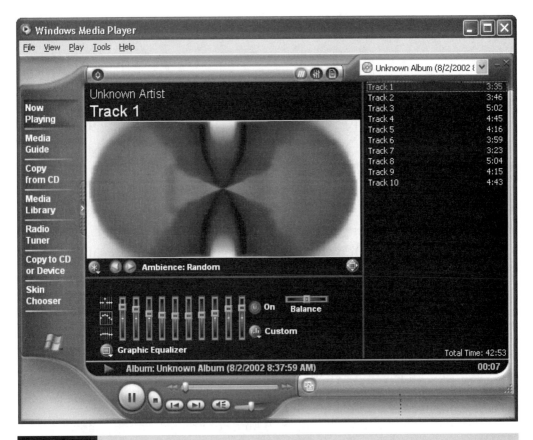

FIGURE 15.2   Default Windows Media Player interface

You use Media Player by accessing one of the features on the left side of the Media Player interface. By default, Media Player always opens to Media Guide, which gives you the Internet page found at **windowsmedia.com**. Each feature does something different, of course, and the following sections explore those primary features

NOW PLAYING

Now Playing is the primary interface area that you will use with Media Player. It lists or shows whatever type of media you are currently playing. Most types of media will automatically launch Windows Media Player. For example, suppose that you want to listen to your favorite CD. All you need to do is put the CD into the CD-ROM drive. Windows XP scans the CD, recognizes it as an audio CD, and launches Window Media Player. Media Player then begins playing the CD, which shows up in the Now Playing area. If you decide to watch a movie clip, it also appears in the Now Playing area.

So, what can you change and configure on the Now Playing interface? The primary purpose of Now Playing is simply to provide a convenient area in which to see and hear all multimedia. Although you do not have specific configuration options for the media, you can adjust what is displayed in the Now Playing area and how Media Player displays it to you.

First, in the upper-right corner of the Media Player interface, you see three buttons:

- **Show/Hide Equalizer Settings**   This button lets you either show or hide the equalizer settings in the Now Playing window.

- **Show/Hide Playlist**   This shows or hides the playlist in the Now Playing window. For example, if you are listening to a music CD, the Now Playing window displays the songs on the CD if this option is enabled.

- **Shuffle**   This button shuffles your current playlist. This feature is cool if you want to play a music CD and not hear the songs in the same old order.

NOTE   Get familiar with these button options. Users often have problems using this interface, so you may be expected to provide some help.

Use the standard buttons at the bottom of the Media Player to play the media, stop playing the media, adjust the volume, and use related stereo/video controls. You can find these same controls in the Play menu at the top of the interface.

The little boxes with an arrow through them that you see in the bottom-right of the interface enable you to shrink the interface to a compact mode or enlarge it back to full-screen mode.

Aside from configuring the immediate options on the interface, you can use the View menu to change a number of items concerning the Now Playing interface. The following bullet list tells you what options are available to you and what they do:

- **Full Mode** The default display is shown to you in Full Mode. If you switch to SkinMode, use this option to return to Full Mode.

- **SkinMode** This option gives you a smaller interface. You have the same options, but some of them appear as pop-out menus. This option takes up less room on your desktop. If you are in Full Mode, click this option to move to a more compact mode.

- **Now Playing Tools** This option provides a pop-out menu where you can choose to perform the following actions:

  - **Show Playlist** This is the same option as the button found directly on the interface.

  - **Show Titles** This option displays title information about the media, such as the artist and songs, name of the video, and so on.

  - **Show Visualizations** Windows Media Player can give you visualizations in the Now Playing window. Visualizations are just interesting graphics files. You'll learn more about visualizations later in this list.

  - **Show Equalizer and Settings** This option gives you an equalizer and related video settings on the Now Playing area. You can use these controls to adjust playback quality. If you choose the Show Equalizer and Settings option, Media Player displays controls for such features as SRS WOW Effects, Graphic Equalizer, Video Settings, Media Information, Captions, and DVD Controls. Your choice here depends on the type of media that you want to play. If you choose to use the Show Equalizer and Settings option, a small drop-down menu is available on the Now Playing interface so you can easily switch controls as needed.

  - **Show Resize Bars** Resize bars appear between the different options that you elect to show in the Now Playing area. The resize bars enable you to adjust the size of the components.

- **Visualizations** As mentioned earlier, visualizations give you a graphical view while you are playing audio-only media. For example, when you play a CD, the Visualizations option displays interesting graphical patterns that move to the beat of the music. If you like this feature, the pop-out menu that appears here allows you to select the type of visualization you want to use.

You can also change the visualization directly from the Now Playing area by clicking the arrow buttons found under the graphical visualization window. You can also easily manage the visualization available to you by clicking Tools | Options, then selecting the Visualizations tab. You'll find a simple interface where you can add and remove visualization files.

NOTE   Additional visualizations can be downloaded from the Windows Media Player web site at **http://windowsmedia.com/mg/visualizations.asp?**.

- **DVD Features**   The DVD Features controls enable you to manage playback quality if you are currently playing a DVD disk. A number of control options are available, such as playing in slow or fast motion, playing one frame at a time, and so on. If you're not playing a DVD disk, this option is grayed out, and of course, the features are only available if you have a DVD drive.

- **File Markers**   When playing video, you can use this option to view the different markers within the video file. This feature enables you to skip to different areas of the video.

- **Statistics**   When playing videos, access this option to view statistics about the video transmission quality. The statistics window may be particularly helpful when troubleshooting problems with streaming media.

- **Full Screen, Refresh, and Zoom**   The final options in the View menu provide basic viewing capabilities that are self-explanatory.

MEDIA GUIDE

The next feature in Media Player is the Media Guide, as mentioned earlier in this chapter. This option connects you to **windowsmedia.com**, where you can download all kinds of music and movie files.

Firewalls and proxy servers may prevent the downloading of streaming media. If users in your network complain that streaming media from the Internet does not work, a corporate firewall or proxy server may very well be the culprit.

COPY FROM CD AUDIO

The CD Audio feature, shown in Figure 15-3, gives you information about the music CD to which you are currently listening. CD music shows up as "unknown album" and "unknown artist" as you saw in Figure 15-2. However, if you click Get Names, Media Player retrieves the album, artist, and song names from the Internet.

In the upper-right corner of the interface, you see an Album Details button. When you click this button, sometimes you get additional information from the Internet about the album, depending on how the album is listed. You may also be able to purchase the CD online from this interface.

The Get Names button on the interface takes you back into the additional album information downloaded from the Web. This simply gives you the names of the songs, which are typically available within the primary interface anyway.

Next, you see a Copy Music button. You can copy any music track from a music CD so the track is stored on your hard drive. This feature has two benefits. First, you can store songs you really like directly on your hard disk so that Media Player can play them without the music CD. Also, you can generate your own

FIGURE 15.3   Use the CD Audio feature to manage and save songs on your music CDs

collection of favorites and create a playlist (which you learn about later in this chapter). The following steps tell you how to copy and configure copies of songs.

COPYING A CD

1. In Media Player, click the CD Audio feature button.

2. In the list of songs, clear the check boxes next to the song(s) you do not want to copy. In other words, any songs with the check box enabled will be copied to your hard disk.

3. Click the Copy Music button. Depending on your configuration, you may be able to hear the song while it is being copied. The right window pane shows you the progress of the copy as it occurs.

4. Once the copy is complete, the song is placed in your Media Library, which you will explore in the next section.

You can manage how songs are recorded and managed by clicking Tools | Options in Media Player. Then click the Copy Music tab, shown in Figure 15-4.

Under most circumstances, the default options configured on this tab are all you need, but there may be instances where you will want to change the default behavior. The following list explains the options found on this tab:

■ **Copy Music to This Location**   By default, the location is C:\My Documents\My Music. If you want to change this default location, simply click the Change button and select a different folder on your computer's hard drive.

■ **Copy Settings**   You can choose to copy music in either the Windows Media format or MP3—the choice is yours. The Protect Content check box simply means that Windows Media Player is keeping a license for you to copy the content and play it on your computer. It is illegal for you to e-mail copies of music to other people, however. Finally, you can choose a Copy Music at This Quality setting by adjusting the slider bar. The higher quality that you copy, the more hard drive space is consumed. Even at a lower quality, several megabytes of storage space will be needed to copy only a few songs.

NOTE   Music copies are automatically compressed to help save disk space. This is an internal feature that does not affect playback.

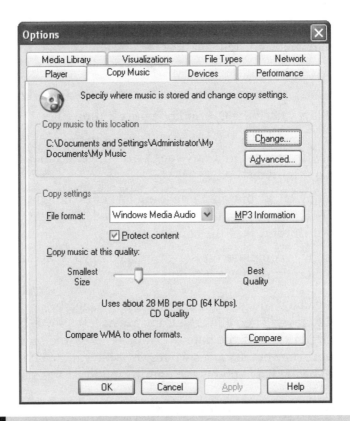

FIGURE 15.4   Use the CD Audio tab to configure how music is copied

TECH TALK

Copying Music and Copyright Law

Musicians, singers, and all kinds of other content creators (including writers!) make money from selling copies of their work. Copyright law enables the publisher of the work to make copies and sell those copies to consumers like you and me. The creator of the work, such as the artist, receives royalties on each copy sold. The copyright protects the producer and the artist, and prohibits other people from making copies and selling or even giving them away.

When you make a copy with Windows Media Player, Media Player handles a license for you. This means you are licensed to copy the music from a CD and play it on your computer. However, it is illegal for you to give that music away to anyone else (or sell it, of course). This includes putting the music on a disk or CD, or even e-mailing it to another person.

MEDIA LIBRARY

The Media Library feature is simply a library of media. All of your saved music and video files are stored in the library under different categories so you can easily access them, as shown in Figure 15-5.

In the left side of the interface, you see various categories with plus boxes next to them. Click on a category, and you can see the songs and/or videos in your library for that category. For example, when you expand Album, you can select an album and then in the right pane see a list of songs that you have copied to your computer from that album. Just double-click on a song or video clip to hear or see it.

Keep in mind that the library's purpose is to help you keep track of files that you want. Media Library is able to detect the type of multimedia you are using and add it to the appropriate location in the library. You can search your library

FIGURE 15.5   Media Library keeps track of all your multimedia files

by clicking the Search button at the top of the interface and perform standard add, remove, and delete functions. If you delete items, they are stored in the Deleted Items folder until you empty this folder by right-clicking on it and selecting the Delete option. This helps ensure that you do not accidentally delete a file that you want to keep.

You can also use Media Library to create a playlist of your favorite tunes or videos. The following sections show you how to use these options.

ADDING AN ITEM TO MEDIA LIBRARY

To add a new item to Media Library, just click the Add button (the plus sign) on the interface. A submenu pops out that enables you to add a track that is currently being played, a file, or other media found on the Internet. If you want to add a file, a typical browse window appears that you can use to locate the file that you want to add. If you want to add something from the Web, a window appears where you can enter the URL of the media item.

USING PLAYLIST

You can copy different songs, store them on the computer's hard drive, and then create a playlist so that each song is played directly from the hard drive in the order you want. The following steps show you how to create a playlist.

CREATING A PLAYLIST

1. In Media Library, click the New Playlist button.

2. Enter a name for the new playlist in the dialog box that appears, then click OK.

3. In Media Library, expand the Playlists category to see your new playlist.

NOTE   You can also import and export playlists in and out of Media Player. Just click the File menu and use either the Import or Export option.

ADDING FILES TO A PLAYLIST

Once you have created a playlist, you need to add the items to the playlist. Just follow these steps.

MANAGING THE PLAYLIST

1. In Media Library, find the item you want to add to the playlist, then select it in the right pane.

2. Click the Add to Playlist button. A selection menu pops out so you can determine the playlist to which to add the file (if you have more than one playlist).

3. Continue this process until you have added to your playlist all of the files that you want.

Once you have created your playlist, you can easily adjust the order of the items on the playlist. Simply select an item and use the up and down buttons to move it around in the list, as shown in Figure 15-6. This feature enables you to adjust the order in which the songs are played. You can return to this screen at any time and adjust the order as desired.

FIGURE 15.6   Use the up and down arrows to adjust the playlist order

You can also delete any item in the playlist by right-clicking the item and clicking Delete, or by just clicking the Delete icon on the interface. This action moves the file to the Deleted Items folder. To restore a deleted item later, just open the Deleted Items folder, right-click the file you want to get back, and click Restore. To play your playlist, just select it in the left pane and click the Play button (or right-click it and click Play).

RADIO TUNER

The Radio Tuner feature, shown in Figure 15-7, brings Internet radio to Media Player. With a good Internet connection, you can listen to radio stations all over the world that stream data over the Internet.

FIGURE 15.7   Use Radio Tuner to listen to Internet radio stations

As you can see in Figure 15-7, the Radio Tuner has two basic portions of the interface: Presets and Station Finder. The following two sections show you how to use each.

NOTE   As I mentioned, the Radio Tuner feature uses streaming media. If you're using a dial-up connection, you may find that radio listening is somewhat choppy and unpredictable. This problem is caused by a slow modem connection, and there isn't much you can do about it. Like many Internet features today, Internet radio simply works better with a broadband connection.

USING PRESETS

In the Presets section of the interface, you see a drop-down menu where you can select a Preset option. Windows Media Player gives you a list of a few popular Internet radio sites from which you can choose. If you want to reach one of these, just double-click the name in the list to connect to the site. You can create your own preset radio stations by changing the drop-down window to My Presets. You can create your own preset stations much like a playlist so you can easily access radio stations that you like. Use the Edit, Add, and Remove buttons to manage your Presets list. As you can see, you can't add any stations to the Presets list until you have located one using the Station Finder pane, which is explained in the next section.

USING STATION FINDER

You locate Internet radio stations using the Station Finder pane. To find a station, you can use the Search drop-down menu to find a particular station, or you can find a station by category (such as rock, jazz, and so on). When you find a station you want, just double-click it in the list to connect to and listen to the station. If you click the station, click the Add button in the Presets list to add the station to your presets, as shown in Figure 15-8.

COPY TO CD

The Copy to CD feature, shown in Figure 15-9, provides you with an easy way to copy files from your Media Library to a compact disk or other portable device.

As you can see, the interface is very simple. Use the drop-down menu to select the device to which you want to copy the items, then select the items you want to copy. Then click the Copy Music button. Your specified items are copied and you can now use them on your portable device.

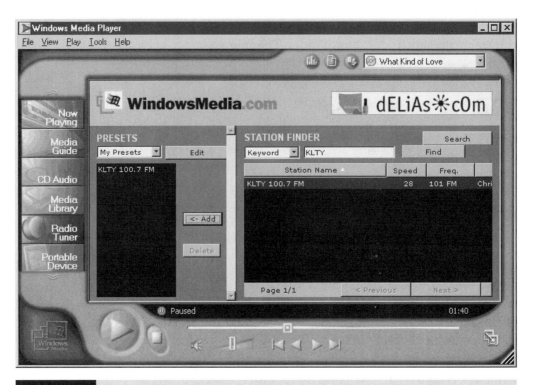

FIGURE 15.8 You can play radio stations you like and add them to your Presets list

SKIN CHOOSER

Media Player includes a number of different *skins*—or interface overlays—that you can apply to Media Player. These skins give Media Player a completely different look, which you may find very appealing or very aggravating, depending on your taste. For example, you can choose a skin that looks like the inside of someone's head, one that looks like a heart, and a number of other interesting options. As you can see, these are just for fun; you still have the same functionality in Media Player, regardless of what skin you choose to use. To use a skin, just select the one you want and click the Apply button. You can also click More Skins to connect to the Media Player web site, where you can download other skins; you'll find several others available on this site.

FIGURE 15.9   Use the Copy to CD feature to copy items to a compact disk or other portable device

MEDIA PLAYER CONFIGURATION OPTIONS

Aside from enjoying all the fun and frills of Media Player, you can click Tools | Options to perform a few worthwhile tricks. As an A+ technician supporting Media Player, you'll probably need to employ these options from time to time.

You see several different tabs that each offer a number of options. The default options are typically all you need, so this is not an interface where you need to wade around and make configuration changes. However, there may be instances where you need to use these options. The following bullet list tells you what is available on each tab.

- **Player**   This tab contains a number of basic check boxes. By default, your Media Player checks the Media Player web site for updates to Media

Codecs

Notice on the Player tab the Download Codecs Automatically check box, which is selected by default. A codec is a compressor/decompressor mathematical algorithm that is used for audio, video, and image files. The codec allows the file to be compressed, then uncompressed so that it can be read. Media must have codecs to be able to play files. If a codec is used to compress a file, then the same codec is used to decompress it. If Media Player does not have the correct codec, it will attempt to download it for you automatically. If you clear this check box option, Media Player will not be able to get the codecs it needs—so leave this check box selected!

Player on a monthly basis. This setting is all you need. By default, Media Player opens and starts the Media Player Guide. You can change that behavior by clearing the check box on this tab.

- **Copy Music**   This tab enables you to adjust settings that control the copying of CD music. See the "Copy from CD Audio" section for details.

- **Devices**   This tab simply lists all devices found on your computer that can be used for media playback, such as your CD/DVD drive. If you select your CD/DVD drive and click Properties, a simple window appears, as shown in Figure 15-10. This window allows you to choose whether to use analog or digital playback and copy. Typically, the Digital radio button is selected, but if you're having problems, you can try the Analog radio button. The error correction feature, available only with digital playback, allows Windows to attempt to resolve problems found in the digital media. You can select the Use Error Correction check box, but you may notice a performance decrease in your system. Thus, you should leave this check box unchecked unless you're having problems with digital media.

- **Performance**   These settings affect how Media Player uses your Internet connection. You should not need to configure anything here. However, by default, Windows Media Player can detect your connection speed to the Internet. This allows Media Player to determine how best to handle media downloads. Make sure you leave this setting as is because Media Player will perform better if it can detect your Internet connection speeds. See Chapter 9 to learn more about Internet connections.

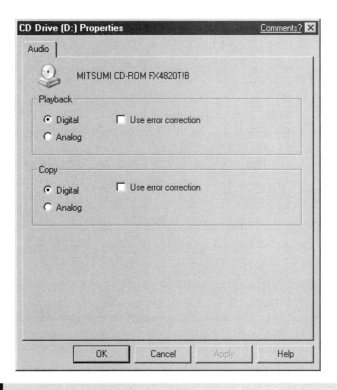

FIGURE 15.10   Drive Properties sheet

- **Media Library**   By default, Media Library gives other applications that access Media Library full control, read-only access, and no access to anyone on the Internet. You should leave these settings alone.

- **Visualizations**   Use this tab to add and remove visualizations. Remember that you can also download new visualizations quickly and easily from the Tools menu.

- **File Types**   This tab lists the file formats that Media Player uses. You don't need to change anything on this tab. All of the options you see here are selected and they should remain that way so that Media Player can work with your devices and all file types. Clearing any of these check boxes will prevent some types of media from working in Media Player.

- **DVD**   The DVD tab gives you management options if you are using a DVD drive. The first option is parental control. Suppose that you have some R-rated DVDs, but you don't want your kids sneaking to the computer to watch them. Aside from locking up the DVDs, you can also use the DVD tab to enable parental control. Click the check box option, then use the drop-down menu to select the highest rating that is allowed with a user name and password. For example, if you select PG-13, then your children can watch G, PG, and PG-13 DVDs without entering a user name and password. You must have Windows accounts set up on your computer for this feature to work, so see Chapter 6 to learn more about user accounts in Windows XP. The second section of the DVD tab allows you to select language settings for subtitles, audio, and menu. Just use the drop-down menus to select the desired language, or you can just leave these as "title default," which uses the DVD's default settings.

■ **Network**   This tab contains protocol usage settings and proxy server enabler settings. You don't need to change anything here unless your computer is on a network that uses a proxy server. Unless a network administrator instructs you to make changes, leave this tab alone.

NOTE   From time to time, you should check the Media Player web site for updates that need to be made to Media Player. You can easily check for updates by clicking Help | Check For Player Updates. This menu selection connects you to the Internet and opens an installation options window where you can choose what new features you want to download and install.

MANAGING MOVIE MAKER

Like Windows Media Player, Movie Maker is another tool included in Windows XP that allows you to edit and create home movies. With any luck, you won't be caught in a support trap with this tool. However, if your environment has a lot of multimedia needs, you may have to help a user who is trying to put something together with Movie Maker. This section points out the major issues you might face.

Windows Movie Maker is a free application included with your XP system. Video editing software is not Microsoft's main focus, so as you might guess, Windows Movie Maker is a basic video editing package. It is not an advanced application. Overall, the software is very intuitive and easy to use.

There is one caveat for Windows Movie Maker, however: When you create movies in Movie Maker, you are forced to save those movies as a Windows Media Video (.WMV) file. You do not have the option to use other standard video formats, such as .AVI or .MPEG. Windows Movie Maker can read these types of files, but you can't save your work using one of these file types. Therefore, to be able to play these files, you will need a Windows computer that has Windows Media Player installed. That may not be a big deal unless you want to play the video on a system that does not have Windows Media Player, such as a Macintosh, in which case you may have some compatibility problems.

When you use Movie Maker, you simply gather video or pictures for use within the program. First, if you are using a digital camera or camcorder, you should not run into any problems. Because the media is already digital, you simply connect your camera or camcorder into your computer and follow the manufacturer's instructions for saving the digital content to your hard disk.

For the best performance, your computer needs an IEEE 1394 card so you can import movies from a digital camcorder into your computer. This card is particularly necessary if you'll be using any streaming media devices. This type of card provides fast transfer from the camcorder to the computer and is highly recommended by Microsoft. You will need to do a little investigative work to determine whether your computer has this card, whether your digital camcorder supports it, and whether this transfer card is right for you. Refer to your computer and camcorder documentation for more information.

Windows Movie Maker can recognize all kinds of graphics files, from .AVI and .MPEG to basic web files such as .JPEG and .GIF. Once the files are loaded and saved on your hard disk, you can then use Windows Movie Maker to import the files and begin working with them.

But what about still pictures or analog video? What about a song you have written that you want to use as background music? Once you move out of the native digital arena, you then must use capture devices to move the analog information into your computer, where it is converted to digital information and saved. The capture device that you choose thus must be capable of importing the data to your computer. A *capture device* is a video card that has video and audio input ports, and a sound card that has an audio input port. You use these cards to connect your analog camcorder or VCR to the sound and video cards. The cards can then receive the analog data from the camcorder or VCR and convert it to a digital format for use on your computer. In the same manner, your sound card can use data from a different device to record music and voice into a digital format so it can be used on your computer.

You may already have a video card and sound card that support this process. If not, you can purchase new cards at your local computer store. They're not terribly expensive, generally anywhere from $100 to $200, but make sure that your choice is compatible with Windows XP; check the Windows XP web site (**www.microsoft.com/windowsxp**) for constantly updated information about compatible hardware. Also, if you previously owned one of these cards under Windows 98/Me/2000, you may need to download new drivers from the card's manufacturer for it to work correctly with Windows XP. Check out the manufacturer's web site to see whether there is an update.

Once you connect your analog device to the capture devices, you can start the video on the analog device, then use Windows Movie Maker to view and capture it—in a perfect world, anyway. Unfortunately, depending on your hardware, you might experience problems. Due to the variety of hardware that you might pick, it is impossible to solve all potential problems here. But here's one big tip that might save you some headaches: Usually, the capture device will ship with a CD-ROM containing the card's drivers and a program or two to help you capture video. Use the card's capture program and save the video in a common file format, such as .AVI or .MPG. You can then import the file into Movie Maker and use it there (see the next section for information about importing).

Many capture devices save video files in their own default format, which may include compression not supported by Windows XP. When you start to save video using the card's program, make sure you are saving it in a format that is supported by Windows Movie Maker.

Before you get started using Movie Maker, you'll need to take a few moments to familiarize yourself with the Movie Maker interface. Fortunately, the Movie Maker interface follows the typical Windows program interface, so it will not seem completely foreign to you. You can find Windows Movie Maker by clicking Start | Programs | Accessories | Windows Movie Maker. The basic interface, shown in Figure 15-11, appears.

There are four major parts of the Windows Movie Maker interface:

- **Toolbars** At the top of the interface are the Windows Movie Maker toolbars. First are the menu options, such as File, Edit, View, Clip, and so on. The menu options contain typical Windows menu features plus those specific to Windows Movie Maker. You'll be using these throughout this section. Also under the menus is the standard toolbar, which presents typical toolbar options. Finally, a third toolbar called the Collections/Locations toolbar is used to manage the video collections that you are working on at the moment. Collections are simply file folders used to hold portions of video or pictures—a simple way to organize your files.

- **Collections** The middle-left side of the interface is called the Collections area. This area is used to view and manage collections of data and view clips that you are working on at the moment. Clips are pieces of video or pictures, and you'll learn about those in a moment.

- **Monitor** The middle-right side of the interface is called the Monitor. When you are working with video or still shots, the picture appears here.

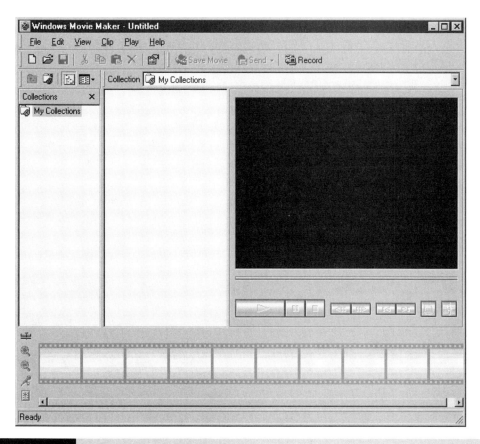

FIGURE 15.11   Windows Movie Maker interface

The Monitor also provides standard start and stop buttons (along with others) to control your viewing of the video.

■ **Workspace**   The bottom portion of the interface is called the Workspace. You use this area to edit video and/or combine still shots. You'll learn how to use the Workspace in the "Using the Workspace" section.

RECORDING AND IMPORTING VIDEO

Now that you have taken a look at the interface setup, you are ready to begin recording or importing video. To record video, you stream it live into your computer. For example, with your digital camcorder, analog camcorder, or other device, such as a DVD player or VCR, you can begin the streaming process, which appears in the Monitor in Windows Movie Maker. To record the video as it appears, just follow the steps described in the following section.

RECORDING VIDEO

1. Begin playing the video from the desired device into your computer.

2. Click Start | All Programs | Accessories | Windows Movie Maker to open the interface.

3. The video appears in the Monitor. Click the Record button on your toolbar. A window appears where you can change the default recording options. Make sure the Create Clips check box is selected, then click the Record button again.

4. The video is recorded by Windows Movie Maker, as shown in Figure 15-12. Notice that clips are being created and appear in the Collections area.

5. When you are finished recording, press the Stop button in the Monitor.

FIGURE 15.12 Windows Movie Maker records the video

6. Press the Save button on the toolbar, or click File | Save Project As.

7. The Save As window appears. By default, the project is saved in the My Videos folder found in My Documents. You can select an alternative location if you want. The file is saved as a Windows Movie file (.mswmm).

Aside from recording video, you can import multimedia files as well. This includes both video and audio (as well as still pictures). In many cases, you will choose to use the Import feature simply because you can work with previously saved files. To import a file that has been previously saved, just follow the steps described in the next section.

IMPORTING A FILE

1. In Windows Movie Maker, click File | Import.

2. The File Import window opens. By default, the Import feature looks in My Videos for a file to import, so you may have to navigate to another location on your computer where the file is stored. Windows Movie Maker looks for all kinds of media files; just select the one you want and click Open. Leave the Create Clips for Video Files check box enabled.

3. The file is imported into Windows Movie Maker. You can now work with it or save it as a project.

ASSEMBLING MOVIES

Using Windows Movie Maker, you record or import the clips you want to use, organize them into collections, edit them as desired, then save the project. You are now ready to begin editing your video and still shot clips. Keep in mind that you can combine video and still shots into one collection and blend them together as desired. You can also import background music and narrate a movie by recording your voice.

Windows Movie Maker creates clips for you; however, you may need to split those clips into more manageable pieces. You can perform this option by using the Split Clip command. The following easy steps show you how.

SPLITTING CLIPS

1. Select the clip that you want to split in Collections area.

2. In the Monitor, click the Play button.

3. When the clip reaches the point where you want to split it, click the Split Clip button in the Monitor. You can also click Clip Menu | Split or simply press CTRL-SHIFT-S on your keyboard. In the Collections area, the clip is split into two parts. The first part of the clip retains its original name, whereas the second clip contains the original name followed by *1*, as shown in Figure 15-13. You can change the name as desired.

Just as you can split a clip so that you have two or more additional clips, you can also combine clips as needed. If you want to combine two or more clips, just follow the steps described in the next section.

COMBINING CLIPS

1. In the Collections area, select the clips that you want. Select the first clip, then hold down SHIFT, then select the remaining clips that you want to combine.

2. Click Clip | Combine. The clips are combined using the first clip's name.

USING THE WORKSPACE

The Workspace area at the bottom of the interface is where you edit and assemble movies. On the left side of the interface, shown here, are a few buttons that correspond to areas on the Workspace.

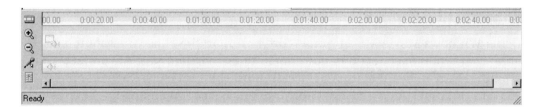

The areas on the Workspace are as follows:

- **Timeline**   Click the Timeline icon to make a timeline appear. You'll use the timeline to assemble and edit video clips.

- **Video/Audio Area**   You see zoom-in and zoom-out icons and an area to place video clips.

- **Audio Clips**   At the bottom of the Workspace is an area where you can place audio clips. You use this area to add sound to a movie.

FIGURE 15.13 Split existing clips into more manageable pieces

To create a storyboard, or to sequence your clips, use the Workspace. Drag clips onto the Workspace area to create the storyboard. You can then edit them as desired to create transitions. Begin by dragging the first clip in your movie to the video area of the Workspace. Once the clip is in position, you see the first frame of the video displayed and a gray area indicating the rest of the clip. Notice in the timeline that the time of the clip is displayed. This corresponds to the grayed, or blocked out, area in the video frame. By using the timeline, you can connect pieces of clips together while keeping a watch over the timeframe of the movie, as shown here.

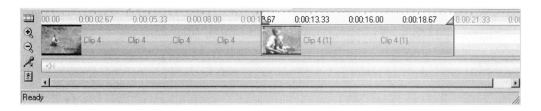

CREATING TRANSITIONS

Windows Movie Maker provides a default fade transition that you can use between clips. For example, suppose that your movie contains clips of your vacation in Hawaii. You can use Movie Maker to assemble the clips and place a transition between them so the flow from clip to clip is more natural and less choppy.

You can easily create transitions by using the Workspace. Follow the steps described in the next section.

CREATING TRANSITIONS

1. In the Workspace, make certain that the timeline view is enabled.
2. Between the two clips where you want to make the transition, select the bar separating the clips, then drag a portion of the right clip over the left clip. The overlapping area is the transition. From the first clip, the screen will fade into the next clip. You can make the transition as long or short as you like (but it can't exceed the entire length of the clip).
3. Experiment with the transitions by altering the amount of overlap. Remove the transition by moving the clip back to its original position.

ADDING AUDIO TO A MOVIE

At the bottom of the Workspace area is the audio portion of the storyboard. To record your voice or some background music or sounds, you click the microphone icon. You should have your computer microphone, or the other sound input device that you want to use to record the audio, connected and tested. If you have an existing audio file you want to use, just use the Import feature to import the audio file into your existing collection, then drag the audio file to the audio portion of the Workspace area.

RECORDING AN AUDIO FILE

1. In the Workspace area, click the microphone icon.
2. The Record Narration Track dialog box appears listing the sound device that you will use to record the audio, as shown next. If you have more than one sound device installed on your computer, click the Change button and

use the drop-down menu to select a different device as desired. When you are ready, click the Record button. If you do not want to hear the existing video soundtrack while you are recording your narration, just click the Mute Video Soundtrack check box.

3. Give the file a name and save it. The file now appears in your Collections area.

NOTE   Recording narration or other background music and sounds does not erase the original video soundtrack; it simply adds another stream of sound to the existing movie.

Once you add audio to your movie, you can adjust the audio level as needed. This is particularly helpful if you have two streams of audio—for example, a primary audio stream, such as voice, and a secondary audio stream, such as background music. By default, Movie Maker sets both streams to the same audio level, so you'll need to adjust them for your movie. To adjust audio levels, just follow the steps described in the next section.

ADJUSTING AUDIO LEVELS

1. In Windows Movie Maker, click Edit | Audio Levels.

2. Move the slider on the slider bar as needed. The video track contains your primary audio, and the audio track contains the secondary audio.

WRAPPING UP

Windows XP gives you a number of features that allow you to manage and use digital media. From easy CD-RW usage to Windows Media Player and Movie Maker, Windows XP is designed to meet the needs of our multimedia age. As an A+ technician, you can expect to support some of these features in your network environment. In Chapter 16, you'll turn your attention to diagnosing and troubleshooting problems in Windows XP.

GATHERING INFORMATION AND SOLVING PROBLEMS

16

Windows XP is the easiest operating system that Microsoft has produced to date for information gathering and troubleshooting. So, does that mean you'll not have any problems? No, of course not. Even though Windows XP is built on the Windows 2000 code and is a rock-solid operating system, you will certainly run into problems from time to time. As an A+ technician, you will need to handle instances where a user reports that his or her computer will not start, or some error message keeps popping up. Regardless of the problem, your job is to fix that problem and get the user back to work. Armed with the tools and features you'll learn about in this chapter, you'll have few problems handling this job. In this chapter, you'll…

- Use System Information
- Solve common problems
- Use Windows Help
- Work with System Restore
- Use the Recovery Console

USING SYSTEM INFORMATION

System Information is a Windows XP tool that can give you a lot information about your system's configuration and the software installed. First introduced in Windows 98, System Information is a powerful tool that includes some additional tools that can fix problems on your system, as you can see in Figure 16-1. You can open System Information by clicking Start | All Programs | Accessories | System Tools, or you can more simply type **MSINFO32** in the Run line. Either way, System Information, which is actually a part of the Help and Support Center, opens.

If you take a look at the left pane, you see a list of information categories. If you click the plus sign (+) next to each category, you can select specific topics for which you want to gather information. You cannot use System Information to actually configure or "do" anything, unless you use its troubleshooting tools. Instead, System Information is designed to give you information that can help you troubleshoot a problem. On a more practical note, System Information is very useful for telephoning support personnel who you may need to call in the event of a problem you can't solve. Of course, it is always best if you can solve your own PC problems, so the next several sections tell you all about the information you can gain in each major category, and I'll point out some tips for you along the way.

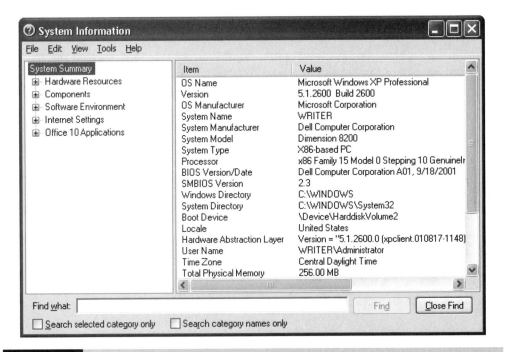

FIGURE 16.1 System Information

SYSTEM SUMMARY

When you first open System Information, the default view is the System Summary. This view just gives you an overview of your computer. You see everything from the operating system to the total amount of RAM installed on your computer. This page is excellent to access if you want a quick report about the basics found on your computer. You can easily print this page as well.

HARDWARE RESOURCES

The Hardware Resources category of System Information gives you a complete look at the hardware on your computer. This section, shown in Figure 16-2, is an excellent way to see exactly what is installed, what's working and what's not, and whether there are any conflicts.

Should there be any conflicts, you'll see warning messages in yellow and conflict or error messages in red. This helps you quickly identify problems if they exist. By expanding Hardware Resources in the left pane, you see the following categories that you can select and view:

- **Conflicts/Sharing**   This option tells whether there are any hardware conflicts between devices. In some cases, hardware devices share certain computer resources, and this section tells you about those as well.

- **DMA (Direct Memory Access)**   This option tells you what devices have direct access to memory resources.

- **Forced Hardware**   If you have problems installing a device and it has been "forced" onto your system using manual settings, the device will be listed here.

- **I/O (Input/Output System)**   This category reports information about input/output operations. Technical support personnel may find this information useful.

- **IRQs (Interrupt Request Lines)**   Each device uses an IRQ to access your computer's processor. This category tells you which device is using which IRQ.

- **Memory**   This category provides a list of memory resource assignment per device.

COMPONENTS

The Components category provides a list of components installed and used on your system. Some of the component options listed here have additional pop-out menus as well, as shown in Figure 16-3. As a reminder, System Information will display problems in yellow and red lettering so you can easily identify them.

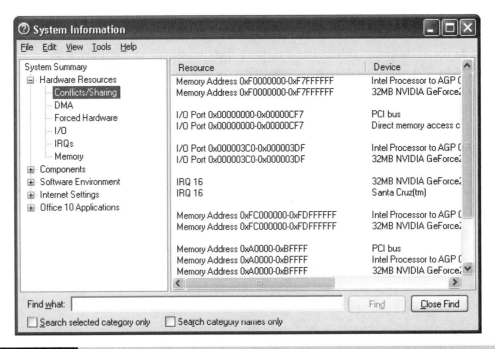

FIGURE 16.2 Hardware Resources in System Information

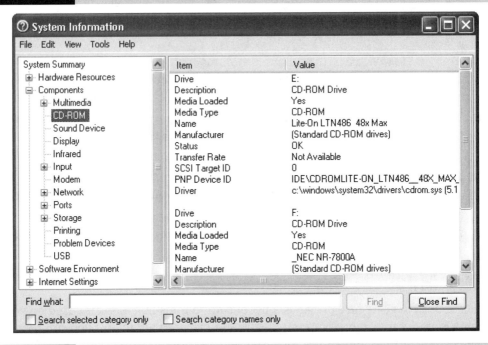

FIGURE 16.3 Components category

You gain information about the following:

- **Multimedia** This category gives you information about your audio and video configuration.

- **CD-ROM** Information is listed here about your CD-ROM drive.

- **Sound Device** This category lists information about your sound card.

- **Display** Information about your display appears here.

- **Infrared** If you are using any infrared devices, they are listed here.

- **Input** Get information about your keyboard, mouse, or other pointing device here.

- **Modem** Modem information is listed here

- **Network** This category provides information about network adapters, protocols, and WinSock.

- **Ports** Get information about ports on your computer, such as serial and parallel ports.

- **Storage** This category lists information about the drives on your computer.

- **Printing** Find out about print and print drivers here.

- **Problem Devices** If any devices are not working correctly, they are listed here. This category is very useful for quickly finding troublesome devices.

- **USB (Universal Serial Bus)** USB configuration and devices are listed here.

SOFTWARE ENVIRONMENT

The Software Environment category, shown in Figure 16-4, gives you information about the software configuration of Windows XP. If there are any problems or errors, you'll see them appear in red or yellow. This category can be very helpful to technical support personnel who are helping you solve a problem with Windows XP.

You see the following information in this category:

- **System Drivers** This section lists the drivers that manage your computer's software environment.

- **Signed Drivers** This section provides a list of installed drivers that are certified by Microsoft.

- **Environment Variables** This section list such items as your TEMP file that is used for temporary files and other variables in the software environment.

- **Print Jobs**   This option gives you the information found in your print queue.

- **Network Connections**   All network connections currently held by your computer are listed here.

- **Running Tasks**   This option lists all of the tasks on your computer that are currently running.

- **Loaded Modules**   This option lists all software modules currently loaded.

- **Services**   This section list the services—such as automatic updates, fax, and much more—that are currently installed on your computer.

- **Program Groups**   This option lists all program groups currently configured on your computer.

- **Startup Programs**   This option lists all programs that are configured to run automatically when your computer starts up.

- **OLE (Object Linking and Embedding) Registration**   Windows XP uses OLE so that various system components and programs can communicate with each other. OLE information is listed here.

- **Windows Error Reporting**   This section provides a listing of software errors reported by the system.

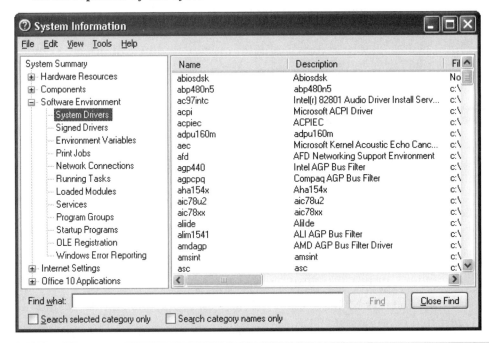

FIGURE 16.4   Software Environment category

NOTE The Windows Error Reporting section, which is new in Windows XP, is a great feature because it lists all of the application lock-ups and related service problems. If you are having trouble, this can be a great place to find the culprit!

INTERNET SETTINGS

The Internet Settings category, shown in Figure 16-5, provides you information about the configuration of Internet Explorer.

You'll find the following information in this category:

- **Summary** Access this option for a quick summary of IE's configuration.
- **File Versions** This option lists all files and file versions used by IE.
- **Connectivity** Access this page to see a quick review of IE's connectivity configuration. This consists of the settings that you configure in Internet Options in IE.
- **Cache** IE uses a cache to store temporary Internet files. Access this option to learn more about the cache size and to view a list of objects in the cache.
- **Content** Examine security and content settings here.
- **Security** View the zone security configuration here.

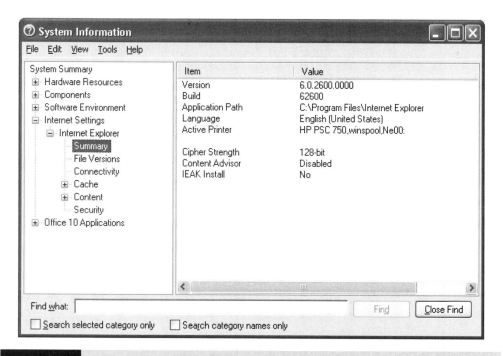

FIGURE 16.5   Internet Settings category

APPLICATIONS

Any applications that are installed on your computer are listed in the Applications category. Click the plus sign (+) next to each listed application to learn about configuration specific to that application. This is a useful option to find out about problems and conflicts with any installed applications.

NOTE   If you are having problems finding the information that you need, try the Find What quick search utility that appears at the bottom of the System Information window.

SYSTEM INFORMATION TOOLS

System Information also gives you a Tools menu that provides easy access to some features and tools in Windows XP. If you check out this menu, you see right away that you can access the Backup tool, the Network Connections folder, the Hardware Wizard, and a Disk Cleanup utility. However, you can also access three additional tools not yet discussed in this book, and the next three sections explore these tools and show you how they can help you.

FILE SIGNATURE VERIFICATION UTILITY

To protect and ensure Windows XP's compatibility and security, Microsoft signs files that the operation system uses. You can use the Signature Verification Utility, shown here, to make certain that no unsigned files are in use on your system.

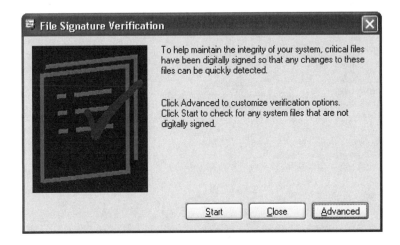

By default, Windows XP displays a warning message before you install unsigned files. You can use this tool to gather information about any unsigned files on your system. When you open Signature Verification, just click the Start button to run the verification scan.

Once the scan is complete, you see a report showing all of the unsigned files on your system. Generally, you shouldn't have to use this tool. However, if you have installed some programs on your computer that are giving you problems, you can run this utility to check for signatures. If you need to use the tool, you can specify a few options by clicking the Advanced button. This opens an Advanced properties dialog box, which includes a Search tab and a Logging tab.

On the Search tab, shown in Figure 16-6, you can specify search parameters to look for system or other files that are not signed. For example, if you want to look for all .DLL files that are not signed, you can perform that search here. You can also choose to search in a particular folder.

On the Logging tab, shown in Figure 16-7, you can choose to log the results of the scan. With each scan, you can either append the data to the existing log or overwrite the log each time. By default, the log file is named sigverif.txt.

DIRECTX DIAGNOSTIC TOOL

DirectX is a graphics technology that enables you to play three-dimensional (3-D) games and use other multimedia software. However, you can have problems with various versions of DirectX and its operation with your system components. The DirectX Diagnostic Tool gives you an easy interface with a bunch of tabs, shown in Figure 16-8.

FIGURE 16.6   Search tab

FIGURE 16.7 Logging tab

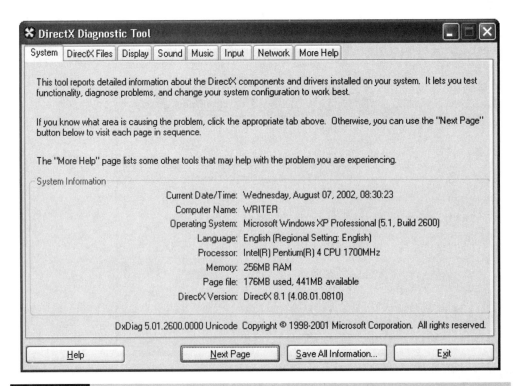

FIGURE 16.8 Use the DirectX Diagnostic Tool to solve compatibility problems with DirectX

The DirectX files, media files, and drivers tabs of this tool report a variety of information to you. The Display, Sound, Music, Input, and Network tabs give you information about how DirectX is interacting with these system resources. Each of these tabs also contains a test button so you can directly test how DirectX is interacting with the hardware. This is a great tool that can help you identify exactly what incompatibilities are occurring with DirectX and your hardware.

DR. WATSON

Dr. Watson is a Windows tool that can inspect your system and generate a detailed report after a system fault has occurred. Dr. Watson can tell you what went wrong and sometimes suggest what can be done to fix the problem. Should you ever need to contact technical support, the staff may have you run Dr. Watson in order to take a "snapshot" of your system. Once the snapshot is taken, the report may be helpful in solving the problem.

NOTE   You can run this tool yourself, of course. The results are usually easy to understand. If you see a particular application or device listed, you may need to retry reinstalling the application or device in question—or just remove it from Windows XP altogether.

SOLVING PROBLEMS

No one likes to hear the word *problem,* but as an A+ technician supporting Windows XP, you'll certainly hear this word from time to time. In fact, the main focus of your job may be to solve problems that occur with users' Windows XP computers. Problem solving is always a process—a task that you should carefully and logically approach in order to find a solution. As you are troubleshooting problems with Windows XP, remember to do the following:

- **Gather**   Find out as much information as you can. Quiz the user about the problem, when it happened, and under what conditions. The more information you have, the better able you will be to troubleshoot the problem.

- **Analyze**   After you have gathered information, analyze it. Determine what is probably important and what is not.

- **Act**   Using the information you have gathered and analyzed, plan a course of action. Determine what you need to do, then systematically take that course of action until you solve the problem.

Along the way, Windows XP gives you several tools that can help you solve problems and even get control of the operating system or boot it when such failures occur. The following sections explore these features.

USING CTRL-ALT-DEL

Although you will not experience the system lock-up problems that you did in previous versions of Windows, you may have an application that stops responding from time to time. In Windows 9x, this would often bring your entire system to a standstill, but that is typically not the case in Windows XP. A system lock-up occurs when an application tries to do something that the operating system does not allow. The application can interfere with Windows XP functionality and cause the application to lock. This means that you can't click any buttons or do anything with the application. In some cases, two applications that are open can interfere with each other and cause them both to lock.

In the case of a system lock, you should press CTRL-ALT-DEL one time. This action will open the Windows Task Manager dialog box. where you can select the name of the program and click End Task on the Applications tab, or you can end a process on the Processes tab, as shown in Figure 16-9. This action forces the task to end so you can get control of your computer. If you have any unsaved data in your application at the time it locked up, you unfortunately will lose that data (you should save data frequently when working, to avoid loss). While you're

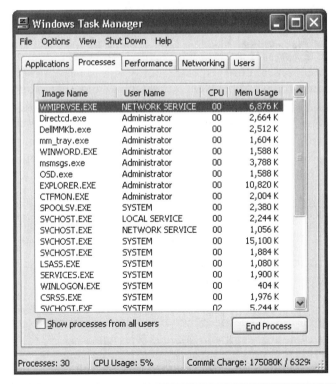

FIGURE 16.9 Windows Task Manager dialog box

looking at the Task Manager, you can also explore the Processes, Performance, Networking, and User tabs to find out current system information.

NOTE If you are in a domain environment, pressing CTRL-ATL-DEL opens the Windows Security dialog box instead of Task Manager. In this case, you can access Task Manager from the Computer Management console.

In some cases, pressing CTRL-ALT-DEL will not give you control of the computer. You might experience this problem when errors occur within Windows XP, possibly resulting from an application causing the operating system to hard lock. In this case, pressing CTRL-ATL-DEL doesn't do anything. In fact, your keyboard and your mouse are essentially disabled in such a situation. The only way to get control of Windows XP in such instances is to turn off the computer using your computer's power switch. ScanDisk will automatically run during the reboot, and you should let it finish so it can to check for file system errors. Again, a complete hard lock is not common in Windows XP, but you may experience the problem just the same.

USING WINDOWS HELP

Windows XP has the best Help files that have ever been produced by Microsoft. They are easier to use, are more attractive, and contain a wealth of information both locally on your machine and on the Internet. You can easily access Windows Help by clicking Start | Help and Support. The Windows Help interface appears, as shown in Figure 16-10.

There are several major parts of the Windows Help program. Aside from using these different sections, you can also perform text searches to find the information you want and need. The following sections address these issues.

TECH TALK

Panicky Users

In the case of lock-ups, users sometimes get panicky. It is important that computer users in your environment have at least a little training so they will know what to do when the computer locks. Many users randomly press keys or power down the computer at times when they should not. As an A+ technician, try to be a teacher along the way and help users learn about their computers as well as troubleshooting techniques. The more your users know, the more time you will save!

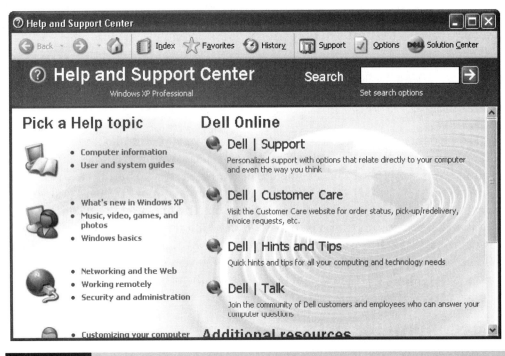

FIGURE 16.10 Windows Help and Support Center dialog box

HELP HOME

When you first open the Help files, you find yourself in the Home section, shown in Figure 16-11. Home is the starting point of accessing Help, and as you can probably guess, Home mimics a web page because the Windows Help files are HTML-based, just like a web page. As you use Help, you'll notice hyperlinks that enable you to jump from the Help files to an additional help resource on the Internet. Depending on your computer manufacturer, you may also see additional links to information provided by the manufacturer.

On the left side of the Home window are some generic categories that can help you get moving in the right direction, such as Networking, Games, Sound, Video, and so on. You also see sections where you can fix a problem or find more resources.

INDEX

The Index option in Help, shown in Figure 16-11, is just like any other index— the only difference is that this index grabs the information for you instead of requiring that you look it up.

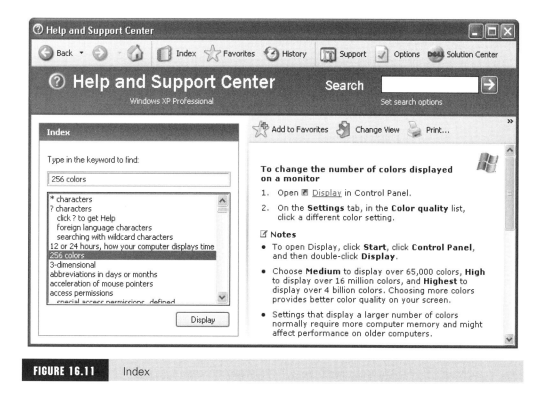

FIGURE 16.11   Index

The left side of the window displays the entire index in alphabetical order. Just use the scroll bar to locate a topic you want, select it, then click the Display button. The information about that topic appears in the right pane. You can read the information, click the Print icon to print a copy, and can even reorganize the window by clicking the Change View icon.

NOTE   If you don't want to scroll down the list of index topics, you can just type something you want in the Search text box above the index. The closest matches to your search request will appear.

FAVORITES

The Favorites option works a lot like Favorites in Internet Explorer. Whenever you find a help page that you want to visit again, just click Add to Favorites button and the page will be added to a Favorites list. Whenever you want to see that list, just click the Favorites menu option at the top of the window.

HISTORY

Just like Internet Explorer, History keeps track of all of the pages you have visited on the Internet from the Help and Support Center dialog box. You can check out the History and revisit any of these pages by double-clicking the link that appears in the History list.

OPTIONS

The Options section allows you to change the interface of Help and Support Center and even share help with others. The options presented here are very easy and self-explanatory.

SUPPORT

If you are having serious problems with Windows XP that you can't seem to resolve, you can access the Support option of Windows Help, shown in Figure 16-12, so you can get help from one of two different places: from MSN, or directly from Microsoft.

First, you see that you can use the Internet to complete an "incident" report that is sent directly to Microsoft. The Windows XP web response team receives your report and will attempt to communicate with you via the Web in order to resolve your problem. When you click the Support option in the Support Help feature, an Internet connection is launched and Microsoft's support site appears in the Help

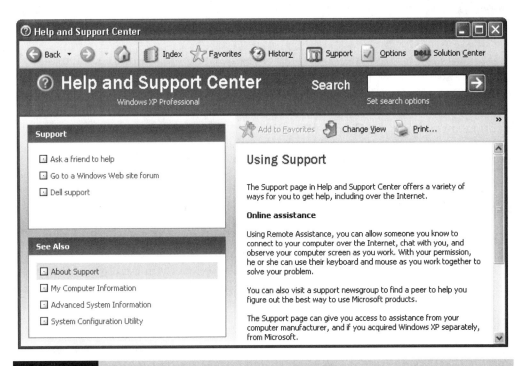

FIGURE 16.12   Support

and Support Center dialog box, where you can begin filling out information to get help from Microsoft. Your second option is to get help from MSN's forums and discussion boards. These options are obviously not the only possible solutions, but you might be surprised by the answers you can gain from these sites. You learn all about problems other people have experienced as well as the solutions they have tried, and you may find the answer to your problem before your eyes!

SEARCHING WINDOWS HELP

One of the primary ways you will use Windows Help is to search for topics. You use the Search text box to find information about a certain topic or troubleshoot a problem you are having. The Windows Help files support text searches, which simply means you can type a keyword or keywords into the Search text box that appears in the upper-right corner of the Help and Support Center dialog box. Then click the Go button. Windows XP Help will then return all possible matches for your subject.

USING WINDOWS TROUBLESHOOTERS

Within the Windows Help and Support Center interface, you can access a very helpful component called the troubleshooter. The troubleshooter is an HTML interface that appears on the Help and Support Center dialog box. The troubleshooter asks you a series of questions and suggests different actions you can try to resolve a problem you are having. Many troubleshooters are available in the Help files, and they are very easy to use. Just follow the steps in the following section.

USING A TROUBLESHOOTER

1. Click Start | Help.

2. In the Help and Support dialog box's Search text box, type the kind of troubleshooter you want. For example, you might type **modem troubleshooter**, **ICS troubleshooter**, **sound card troubleshooter**, and so forth. To see a full list, just type **troubleshooter**.

NOTE Obviously, a troubleshooter does not exist for every possible problem that you might experience with Windows, but there are troubleshooters for most hardware devices.

3. Begin the troubleshooter by clicking an appropriate radio button under What Problem Are You Having?, as shown in Figure 16-13. Then click the Next button to continue.

4. Continue following the troubleshooter to attempt to solve the problem.

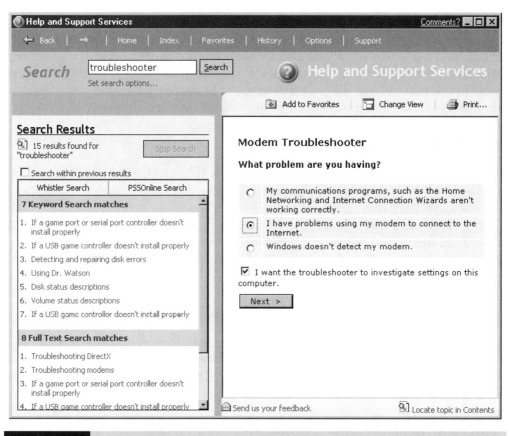

FIGURE 16.13 Answer the troubleshooter's question and click Next

USING SAFE MODE

Safe Mode is a Windows XP feature that enables you to start Windows with a minimal number of drivers. Safe Mode is used in instances where you cannot start Windows normally. You can use Safe Mode to fix problems with your system—it essentially gets Windows up and running, but that's about it. Most major Windows XP features do not work in Safe Mode.

So, why would you use Safe Mode? Let's consider an example. Suppose that you have installed a new video card and the driver for the card. When you restart Windows XP, it boots, but then you get a "fatal exception" blue screen just before your desktop appears. You try this over and over and get the same result. More than likely, the video card's driver is not working correctly with Windows XP. If you boot the computer into Safe Mode, Windows will load a basic VGA driver to use with the card. Once the computer is booted, you can use Device Manager to remove or update the bad driver.

A number of other repair tools require you to boot your computer into Safe Mode in order to work. Before you see how to boot into Safe Mode, you should be aware of some other boot options that you can choose along with Safe Mode. You can access all of these options by using the Windows Startup menu, which you'll see if you hold down CTRL when you turn on your computer. (If holding down CTRL doesn't seem to work, try pressing F8 when you start the computer.) You'll see a Startup menu that allows you to choose Safe Mode, Safe Mode with Networking, and some other options. When your computer boots into Safe Mode, you can access the tools and try to solve the problem. When you're done, just reboot the computer and it will boot into normal mode. The following Safe Mode options are available:

- **Safe Mode**   Use Safe Mode when the computer will not start normally. Once you boot into Safe Mode, you can start and stop services, change computer settings, uninstall hardware or drivers, and launch System Restore.

- **Last Known Good Configuration**   This option starts Windows with the last known good Registry saved. If you make some configuration changes and restart Windows, but the restart fails, use the Last Known Good Configuration option. This setting is particularly helpful if you have installed a new driver that does not work correctly. The Last Known Good Configuration boot will use the last saved Registry, using the driver(s) that originally started correctly.

- **Enable VGA Mode**   This option starts the computer with a standard VGA driver. If you are sure that a video card driver has caused the problem, use VGA mode.

- **Safe Mode with Command Prompt**   This option boots you to a command prompt where you can run command-line utilities.

- **Safe Mode with Networking**   This option keeps the computer configured with networking capabilities, which would typically not be available in standard Safe Mode.

- **Directory Services Restore Mode**   This option actually doesn't do anything; it is a leftover from Windows 2000 domain controllers.

- **Debugging Mode**   This choice starts Windows XP so that kernel debugging occurs. Typically, this mode is not used, since the data provided in Debugging Mode is not particularly helpful unless you are a programmer.

■ **Enable Boot Logging**   This option creates a log file of the boot process that you can review.

■ **Start Windows Normally**   With this option selected, Windows starts normally without using any Safe Mode options.

USING SYSTEM RESTORE

System Restore is a great feature of Windows XP that can get you out of all sorts of trouble. What if your computer won't start? What if you install a bad application that wrecks your computer? If you have ever worked with Windows, you know that bad configuration problems can become a serious troubleshooting problem. System Restore makes this concern a thing of the past because you can easily restore your computer to a previous state. The following sections show you how to use System Restore.

SYSTEM RESTORE REQUIREMENTS

System Restore is automatically installed and configured on Windows XP if your computer has at least 200MB of free disk space after Windows XP is installed. If your computer does not have 200MB of free disk space, System Restore is installed, but it is not set up to run. System Restore functions by saving information about your system so that it can be restored in the event of problem. To function correctly, System Restore requires 200MB of free disk space, and actually may need much more. Fortunately, if you are using a newer computer, you most likely have plenty of free disk space, and System Restore is already operational on your computer.

MAKING SYSTEM RESTORE AVAILABLE

If your computer did not have 200MB of free disk space upon initial installation, but you have made 200MB or more of free disk space available, you can enable System Restore so that it begins functioning on your Windows XP computer. To enable System Restore, just follow the steps described in the next section.

ENABLING SYSTEM RESTORE

1. In Control Panel, double-click System, or just right-click My Computer and click Properties.

2. Click the System Restore tab.

3. You can click the Enable System Restore check box, shown here, to turn off System Restore on all drives on your computer. If this check box is selected, just click to clear it so that System Restore is enabled.

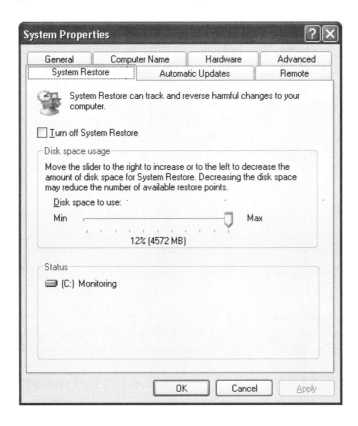

4. Click OK, then click OK again on the System Properties window.

NOTE   System Restore is set on a per-drive basis. If you are using multiple drivers, you must access the System Restore tab on each drive's Properties sheet to configure the option.

USING RESTORE POINTS

System Restore functions by creating restore points. A *restore point* is a "snapshot" of your computer's configuration that is stored on your hard disk. If you launch System Restore, System Restore accesses a restore point to reconfigure your computer. This brings your computer back to a stable state—a place where it was when the system was stable.

TROUBLESHOOTING

Adjusting System Restore Disk Usage

By default, System Restore is given 12 percent of your hard disk space when you install Windows XP, assuming that 12 percent is at least 200MB. If you access the System Properties sheet and click the System Restore tab, then click the Settings button, you see a slider bar on the Hard Disk tab indicating the total amount of disk space that System Restore is allowed to use. You can lower this amount by moving the slider bar. However, keep in mind that System Restore must have at least 200MB, and if you want System Restore to function really well, you should leave this 12 percent setting at its default level.

NOTE System Restore restores your operating system and applications only; it does not save and restore any files. For example, if you accidentally delete a Word document, you cannot use System Restore to get the document back. Also, System Restore does not affect other files, such as e-mail messages and web pages.

System Restore automatically creates restore points for you, so usually you need not create a restore point manually. However, what if you are about to try some configuration option or configure a software program that you know may be risky or that has caused you problems in the past? You can then manually create a restore point so you can restore your system to the exact present state. To create a restore point, just follow the easy steps described in the next section.

CREATING A RESTORE POINT

1. Click Start | All Programs | Accessories | System Tools | System Restore.

2. In the System Restore window, shown in Figure 16-14, click the Create a Restore Point radio button, then click Next.

3. In the window that appears, enter a description. You may want to include information that will help you distinguish this new restore point from others. The date and time of the restore point are added automatically, so you don't need to include those. Click Next.

4. The restore point is created. Click OK and you're done.

FIGURE 16.14   Click the Create a Restore Point radio button, then click Next

RUNNING SYSTEM RESTORE

The eventful day finally arrives, and someone has done something improper to a computer in your environment. Now it doesn't boot or it acts erratically. Whatever the problem, you can use System Restore to bring your computer back to an earlier time when it was functioning appropriately. The following steps show you how to use System Restore.

RESTORING THE SYSTEM IF YOU CAN BOOT WINDOWS

1. Click Start | All Programs | Accessories | System Tools | System Restore.
2. Click the Restore My Computer to an Earlier Time radio button, then click Next.

3. A calendar and a selection list are presented to you, as shown in Figure 16-15. You can select different days to find a desired restore point. If you did not create a restore point, you should choose to use the latest one available. The latest one will be listed first in the current or previous day window. Select a restore point and click Next.

4. A message appears telling you to save all files and close all open applications. Do so, then click the Next button.

5. Restoration takes place on your computer, and your computer automatically reboots once the restoration is complete. Click OK to the restoration message that appears once you reboot.

RESTORING THE SYSTEM IF YOU CANNOT BOOT WINDOWS

1. Turn on your computer and hold down CTRL or F8 until you see the Startup menu options.

2. Choose Safe Mode, then press ENTER.

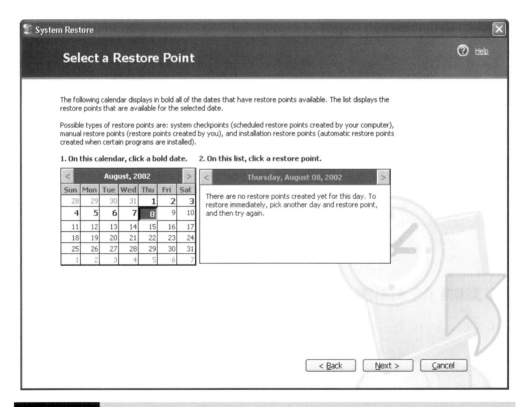

FIGURE 16.15 Select a restore point and click Next

3. Once Windows boots, a screen appears asking whether you want to do a diagnostic check of the system. Click No. System Restore will automatically start.

4. Click the Restore My Computer to an Earlier Time radio button, then click Next.

5. A calendar and a selection list are presented to you. You can select different days to find a desired restore point. If you did not create a restore point, you should choose to use the latest one available. The latest one will be listed first in the current or previous day window. Select a restore point and click Next.

6. A message appears telling you to save all files and close all open applications. Do so, then click the Next button.

7. Your computer automatically reboots once the restoration is complete. Click OK in response to the restoration message that appears after booting has taken place.

A restoration does not affect current documents, files, e-mail messages, and so on. However, if you installed an application after the last restore point was made, you will need to reinstall that application.

UNDOING A RESTORATION

What happens if the restore doesn't go so well? What if there is a problem with the restore that leaves Windows XP in worse shape, or even unbootable? Good news: Restoration is completely reversible, and the following two sections show you how to reverse a restoration.

REVERSING A RESTORATION IF YOU CAN BOOT YOUR COMPUTER

1. Click Start | All Programs | Accessories | System Tools | System Restore.

2. In the System Restore window, click the Undo My Last Restoration radio button, then click Next.

NOTE The Undo My Last Restoration option does not appear unless you have previously run a restoration.

3. Close any open files or applications, click OK, then click Next.

4. The previous restoration is removed and your computer reboots. Click OK in response to the restoration message that appears after the reboot.

UNDOING A RESTORATION IF YOU CANNOT BOOT INTO WINDOWS

1. Turn on your computer and hold down CTRL or F8 until you see the Startup menu options.

2. Choose Safe Mode, then press ENTER.

3. Once Windows boots, the Help screen that appears gives you the option to restore your computer. Click the System Restore link.

4. Click the Undo My Last Restoration radio button, then click Next.

5. A message appears telling you to save all files and close all open applications. Do so, then click the Next button. Your computer is rebooted once the restoration has been removed.

WORKING WITH THE RECOVERY CONSOLE

Windows XP includes an advanced command-line tool called the Recovery Console. The Recovery Console is designed to provide just what the name implies: You can try to fix Windows XP in the event that Windows will not start. The preferred method for fixing Windows when it will not start is to use Safe Mode. However, in some circumstances, using Safe Mode will not work either. In this case, you can turn to the Recovery Console for assistance. The primary advantage of the Recovery Console is that it works independently of Windows system files, so if files are corrupted, you can still use the Recovery Console to repair them

The Recovery Console is a powerful tool and one that you should spend some time working with in order to become adept. You can do lots of things—create and format drives, repair system files, repair the system boot sector or Master Boot Record, enable or disable services and devices, copy new Windows system files and folders, just to name a few.

If you need to use the Recovery Console, you can start it directly from the Windows CD-ROM. Just start the computer with the CD and follow the prompts to load the Windows startup files. At the Welcome to Setup screen that appears, press **R** to start the Recovery Console. You'll need to type the administrator password on Windows XP Professional computers (it's blank on Windows XP Home Edition). When the command prompt appears, you can begin entering Recovery Console commands.

The command prompt that you see works with Recovery Console commands only; it does not work with other typical command prompt commands.

Once you have started the Recovery Console, you type **Help** to see a list of the available commands. Once you see the list of commands, type **Help** *commandname* to learn more about that particular command. Table 16-1 lists and explains the most common commands that you can use.

Command	Explanation
Attrib	For a single file or folder, this command sets or clears the attributes, such as Read Only, Hidden, and System.
Batch	Executes commands from a text file.
Bootcfg	Scans all disks for Windows installations, then solves any existing problems in Boot.ini.
CD (Chdir)	Changes folders.
Chkdsk	Scans the disk and finds back sectors. The command can repair a drive and recover readable information.
Cls	Clears the screen.
Copy	Copies a file.
Del (Delete)	Deletes a file.
Dir	Shows the contents of a folder, including any system or hidden files.
Disable	Disables a service or a driver.
Diskpart	Manages partitions on basic disks. It should not be used on dynamic volumes.
Enable	Enables a service or driver.
Exit	Closes the Recovery Console.
Expand	Extracts a file from a .cab (compressed) file on the local disk or Windows CD.
Fixboot	Creates a new partition boot sector on the partition you specify when using the command.
Fixmbr	Fixes the Master Boot Record on the disk you specify when using the command.
Format	Formats a partition, drive, or volume.
Help	Shows Help menu and information.
Listsvc	Lists all available services and drives and their current start types.
Logon	Shows all detected installations of Windows XP, 2000, and NT so that you can choose the installation to which you will log on.
Map	Shows all drive letters, file system types, partition sizes, and the mappings to physical devices. This command works only with basic disks and may provide inaccurate information if you try to use it on dynamic disks.
Md or Mkdir	Creates a new folder or subfolder in the desired location.
More	Shows more information, such as when there is a text break on the screen.
Net Use	Allows you to connect to a network resource.
Rd (Rmdir)	Removes a folder.
Ren (Rename)	Renames a file.

TABLE 16.1   Recovery Console Commands

Set	Displays and modifies Recovery Console environment variables.
Systemroot	Sets the current folder to the %SystemRoot% folder.
Type	Shows a text file.

TABLE 16.1   Recovery Console Commands *(continued)*

TROUBLESHOOTING WINDOWS STOP ERRORS

Have you ever seen the "Blue Screen of Death?" The Blue Screen of Death, as it is lovingly called, occurs when some kind of error prevents Windows from running. A "stop" page occurs with a blue background, and often a bunch of cryptic data about why the failure occurred. Any unsaved data is lost at this point, and the only thing you can do is shut down the computer and restart Windows.

Stop errors, though, are not an anomaly; they occur because some problem arose with Windows, an application, or the hardware. Stop errors contain the stop error name, often some troubleshooting recommendations, and error numbers and/or parameters. Some stop messages also contain driver information as well.

So, as an A+ technician, what can you do if stop errors continue to occur on a certain computer? In some cases, you can discover the cause of the problem and solve it; in other cases, you'll need to get some help from technical support. However, in many cases, you can simply follow the troubleshooting information and get the help you need. Also, if you know what the stop message means, you stand a better chance of figuring the problem out. The following bullet list gives you many of the most common stop error labels and what they mean. Use this list as a quick reference the next time you run into stop error problems:

- **Stop 0x00000024 NTFS_FILE_SYSTEM**   This error occurs when a problem with the NTFS file system driver causes the system to stop. Typically, a hardware failure, such as a failed disk or disk controller, causes this error. Make sure all disks are working and check the disk controllers. You should run the chkdsk *drive*: /f command.

- **Stop 0x0000002E DATA_BUS_ERROR**   This error occurs due to failed physical RAM. A corrupted hard disk or a motherboard failure can also produce this error. Check RAM, hard disks, and the motherboard for problems.

- **Stop 0x0000000A IRQL_NOT_LESS_OR_EQUAL**   This is a common error that occurs when a driver has tried to access a memory space that is not allowed. Usually, this error results from a problem with a piece of hardware or software or an incorrect driver. Check the stop message to see whether the name of the driver appears; then you can troubleshoot the driver from there.

- **Stop 0x0000001E KMODE_EXCEPTION_NOT_HANDLED**   This is also a common error that can occur when an illegal or unknown processor instruction occurs. Faulty drivers or hardware can also cause this error. Check the stop message to see whether the problematic driver is listed, then troubleshoot the driver from there.

- **Stop 0x00000079. MISMATCHED_HAL**   This error occurs when there is a mismatch in the hardware abstraction layer (HAL) and the Windows XP system files. This message often has to do with Advanced Configuration and Power Interface (ACPI) BIOSs. You may have to disable some or all of the ACPI BIOS features and reinstall Windows if the problem continues.

- **Stop 0x00000050 PAGE_FAULT_IN_NONPAGED_AREA**   This error occurs when a hardware device or driver calls for data that is not in memory. Physical memory can also cause this error, but the culprit is sometimes antivirus software. Make sure that the antivirus software is up to date and that the correct driver for Windows XP is in use. A number of other causes are possible, so check the error message for clues.

- **Stop 0x0000007B INACCESSIBLE_BOOT_DEVICE**   This error occurs when Windows XP cannot locate the system partition or the boot volume during startup. Generally, the problem occurs after upgrades or changes to the disk configuration have been made and boot.ini no longer points to the correct boot partition. You can use the Recovery Console to fix boot.ini.

- **Stop 0x000000D1 DRIVER_IRQL_NOT_LESS_OR_EQUAL**   This is a common stop message that occurs when a driver attempts to access an illegal memory address. You may have unsigned drivers or drivers that are not compatible with Windows XP. Check your hardware, and also check antivirus programs as well as any disk or backup programs for correct drivers.

- **Stop 0x0000007F UNEXPECTED_KERNEL_MODE_TRAP**   A hardware failure of some kind typically causes this error. You'll need to check RAM, the CPU, the motherboard, and the power supply.

TROUBLESHOOTING

Stopping Automatic Restart

When a stop error occurs, Windows XP is configured to restart the computer automatically. However, if want to give yourself time to study the stop message so that you can look for a solution, you can stop the automatic restart behavior easily. Just follow these steps:

1. Click Start | Control Panel | System.

2. Click the Advanced tab and click the Settings button under Startup and Recovery.

3. In the Startup and Recovery dialog box that appears, shown here, clear the Automatically Restart check box and click OK.

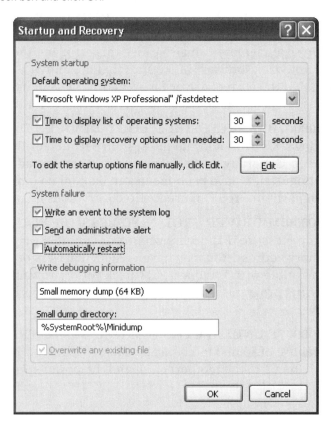

USING MSCONFIG

MSCONFIG, or System Configuration Utility, is a tool that you can use to manage system components, startup, as well as several services. You can open MSCONFIG by clicking Start | Run and typing **msconfig** in the provided dialog box. Click OK. The MSCONFIG utility opens and gives you several tabs, which are explained in the following sections.

GENERAL TAB

On the General tab, shown in Figure 16-16, you can choose how you want Windows to start. Normal Startup is the typical selection, but you can choose Diagnostic Startup, where only basic drivers and services are started, or Selective Startup, where you determine what processes and services to load. These features are all helpful if you need to troubleshoot startup.

SYSTEM.INI AND WIN.INI TABS

The System.ini tab, shown in Figure 16-17, and Win.ini tab allow you to modify the contents of system.ini and win.ini respectively. You can adjust the order of the file, disable and enable items, and create new time settings. Before making changes to these files, make sure you have specific troubleshooting goals in mind, and see the Windows Help and Support Center for more information about the files.

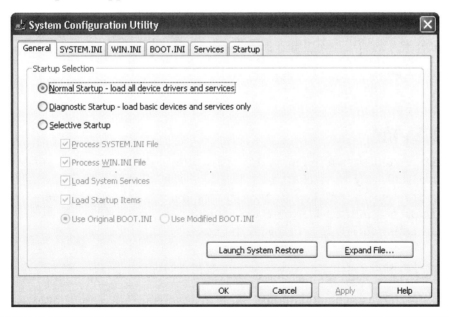

FIGURE 16.16   General tab

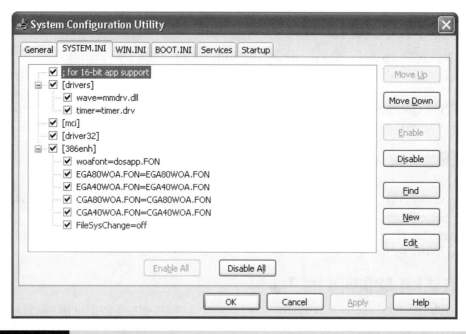

FIGURE 16.17 System.ini tab

BOOT.INI TAB

The Boot.ini tab, shown in Figure 6-18, shows you the contents of the boot.ini file, so this tab is basically a graphical interface to adjust this file. You can invoke different boot options, and you also check all of the boot paths. There are also advanced options so that you can manage memory usage and debug. The boot options are simply your Safe Mode options.

SERVICES TAB

The Services tab, shown in Figure 16-19, lists the services that start at startup. You can disable any services that are not necessary or that you believe are causing problems, but make sure you understand what the service does and how it impacts other services before disabling it. Again, this can be a great troubleshooting tool to solve boot problems.

STARTUP TAB

The Startup tab lists the commands that run at startup. You can disable any that are not necessary, but as with the Services tab, make sure you have a specific troubleshooting plan in mind before you disable any of them.

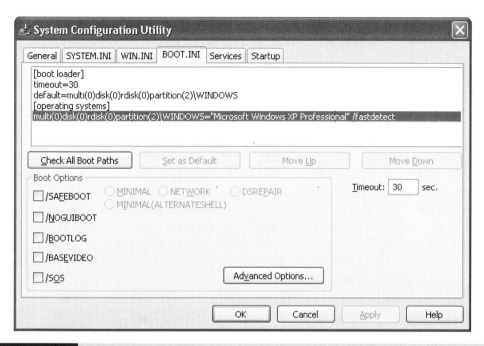

FIGURE 16.18   Boot.ini tab

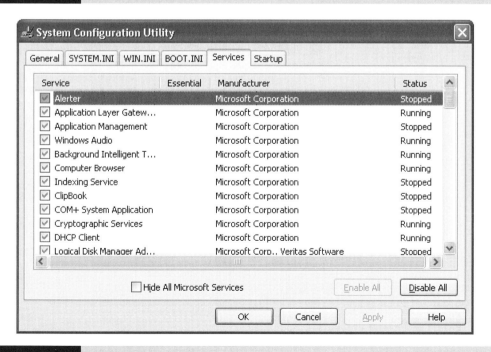

FIGURE 16.19   Services tab

CHECKING EVENT VIEWER

If you are having problems with Windows XP, always check the Event Viewer for additional information that may be available to. Event Viewer, which is available in Start | Control Panel | Administrative Tools | Computer Management, gives you an easy way to review system events and problems that have occurred. You can view application events, system events, and security events. Simply click the file you want to view, then double-click the event in the right console pane for details. For example, in Figure 16-20, you can see that an application hang has occurred, as noted in the right console pane.

If you double-click the event, you can read more information about the application hang and discover which application was running when the problem occurred, as shown in Figure 16-21. Event Viewer is rather intuitive and easy to use, so make sure you don't forget about it when you are trying to sort through problems; it can be a great source of information.

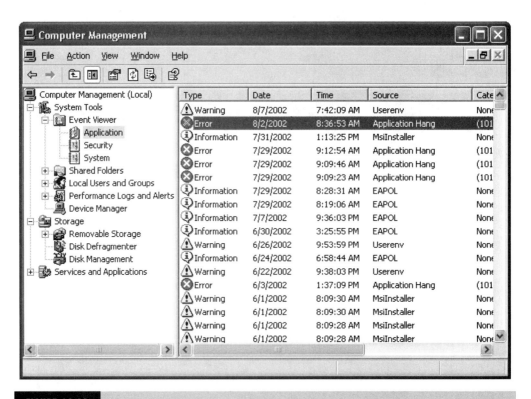

FIGURE 16.20 Event Viewer

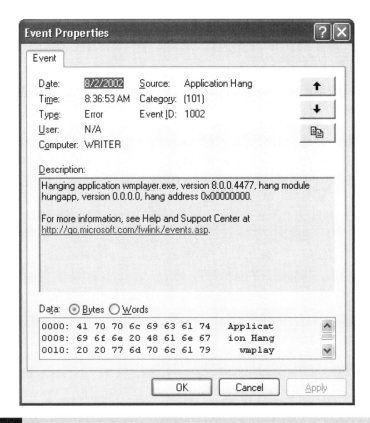

FIGURE 16.21   Event description

GETTING HELP ONLINE

If you are having difficulty solving a problem, which you most certainly will from time to time, keep in mind that you can get help from Microsoft using the Help and Support Center. However, you can also go directly to **support.microsoft.com** and enter a search query about the problem. You'll probably find information and even troubleshooting help at this site. Also, check out **windows-help.net/windowsxp** and **winsupersite.com** for additional troubleshooting help.

WRAPPING UP

Getting information and solving problems with Windows XP can be a real chore, as you are probably already aware. However, as you are working with Windows XP and troubleshooting the system, keep in mind that Windows XP can give you a lot of information and troubleshooting support, directly from the operating system. Make sure you get familiar with the tools and features you explored in this chapter—doing so can greatly reduce troubleshooting time and make your work with Windows XP a lot easier!

TOP 25 WINDOWS XP PROFESSIONAL PROBLEMS AND SOLUTIONS

A

This book has focused on Windows XP configurations and solutions that you can put to work in your networking environment. As you can imagine, there are a number of issues and problems that you are likely to run into as you work with Windows XP. However, there is a collection of common problems that tend to cause difficulty for users and support personnel on a regular basis. This appendix explores the 25 most common problems you are likely to encounter, and gives you quick and fast steps to resolve those problems as well. Use this appendix as a quick reference guide for quick troubleshooting!

A HARDWARE DEVICE DOES NOT WORK

Hardware devices and drivers must be compatible to work under Windows XP. If you ensure that the hardware and the drivers you are installing are compatible with Windows XP, you are not likely to have many hardware installation difficulties. However, this does not mean that hardware devices will always be easy to install and configure. As an A+ technician, you should approach hardware troubleshooting from a logical, point-to-point view. In other words, start with the obvious and work down from there. Follow these general steps as a quick help guide to resolve hardware device problems.

SOLVING HARDWARE DEVICE PROBLEMS

1. Ensure that the device and the driver are compatible with Windows XP. If a Windows XP device driver is not available, try to use a Windows 2000 driver.

2. Make sure that the hardware is physically connected to the correct port or installed correctly in the internal slot.

3. Restart the computer. This ensures that Windows XP's plug and play has the full opportunity to detect the devices. You can also use the Scan for Hardware Changes option within Device Manager.

4. Use the Add Hardware Wizard, shown here. Work through the wizard steps until you reach the device selection window, where you can choose the manufacturer and model of the device you are trying to install. Or, use the Have Disk option.

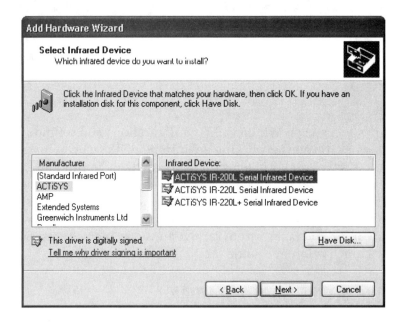

NOTE Remember to check the manufacturer's web site for additional troubleshooting information.

WINDOWS XP CRASHES AFTER A HARDWARE INSTALLATION

If after you install hardware Windows XP crashes or the system begins to behave erratically, the problem is almost always with the driver. Once again, device drivers must be compatible with Windows XP. If a device driver worked with a previous version of Windows, that certainly does not mean that the device driver will work with Windows XP.

If you are having problems with performance after a new piece of hardware is installed, you'll need to visit the manufacturer's web site and see whether you can get a new driver that is compatible with Windows XP. If the driver you are using is a Windows XP driver, the driver may be corrupted, in which case you need to reinstall the driver. Follow these steps.

SOLVING HARDWARE DRIVER PROBLEMS

1. Boot the computer using Safe Mode.

2. Once the computer is booted, open Device Manager, then open the Properties sheet for the device in question.

3. On the Driver tab, choose the Update Driver option and follow the wizard steps that appear.

USERS COMPLAIN OF PERMISSIONS MESSAGES

Depending on your networking environment (workgroup or domain), users have certain privileges, but are also denied certain privileges as well. As you are working with Windows XP, it is important to keep in mind that local administrator accounts have full access to the system. Limited accounts, however, do not have the ability to add or remove hardware or even to install some applications. For the most part, limited users can only change Windows XP configuration options that apply directly to their user accounts, such as desktop wallpaper and the screensaver. Only administrator accounts can make systemwide changes.

As you respond to user complaints about permissions and access, it is important to determine whether the problem is a local problem or a network problem. From a networking point of view, the user may need access to certain resources, but the user's account may not have been granted access to those resources. As an A+ technician, you'll then have to decide whether the user actually should have access to those resources and who should configure access to those resources. Concerning the local computer, users will simply have to be educated about the restrictions placed on them by the limited account, if it is in use.

WINDOWS XP WILL NOT BOOT

In the case of a boot failure, you should stop and ask yourself, "What has changed?" In most cases, a hardware installation or some other configuration has caused the computer to stop booting. In this case, if you can determine what has changed, you usually can figure out what you need to do. However, there are a few important tips to keep in mind:

- Try booting into Safe Mode or the Last Known Good Configuration.

- If Safe Mode does not work, take note of the boot failure message that appears. The message can often give you clues about what the problem might be.

- If there are problems with files, such as boot.ini or Ntdetect.com, you can use the Recovery Console to copy new files and fix related problems that should return the computer to a bootable state.

- In cases where you can boot the computer using Safe Mode, but you are not sure what is causing the boot failure, try using System Restore.

WINDOWS XP RUNS SLOWLY

Windows XP requires a processor and enough RAM to meet the needs of the operating system. If you upgraded from a previous version of Windows that barely supported Windows 98 or Windows Me, performance problems are likely. To resolve the performance problems, consider upgrading the hardware. If this is not practical, you can optimize the Windows XP interface for performance. This will give you a more basic Windows XP graphical interface, but may give you a little more power. To adjust the setting, follow these steps.

ADJUST THE VISUAL PERFORMANCE SETTINGS

1. Click Start | Control Panel | System.
2. Click the Advanced tab and click the Settings button under Performance.
3. Choose the Adjust for Best Performance radio button, and click OK. This setting removes many of Windows XP's visual effects.

Applications and Memory

You may also have to help users understand that applications use a lot of memory. The more applications that are open, the slower the computer will tend to run, especially if graphics applications are in use. You may have to become a teacher of sorts and help users understand that they must close unused applications in order to boost system performance.

APPLICATIONS DO NOT WORK OR DO NOT WORK CORRECTLY

All software, including applications and games, must be compatible with Windows XP in order to work. If you are having problems with older applications or games when working with Windows XP, you can try using the Program Compatibility Wizard to configure a compatibility mode. If this does not work, your only option is to upgrade the software to a version that supports Windows XP. You should never use antivirus programs or disk management programs that are not explicitly written for Windows XP. If you upgraded from a previous version of Windows, you should upgrade these programs as well. Check the program manufacturers' web sites for details.

INDIVIDUAL NTFS PERMISSIONS ARE NOT AVAILABLE

Simple File Sharing is used by default on Windows XP, but you can change the setting so that you can configure NTFS permissions. Once you turn off Simple File Sharing, the typical Security tab appears on shares so that you can configure NTFS permissions. Note that you cannot turn off Simple File Sharing on Windows XP Home Edition. To turn off Simple File Sharing on Windows XP Professional, follow these steps.

TURNING OFF SIMPLE FILE SHARING

1. Click Start | Control Panel | Folder Options.

2. Click the View tab, shown here. Scroll to the bottom of the window and clear the Use Simple File Sharing check box. Click OK.

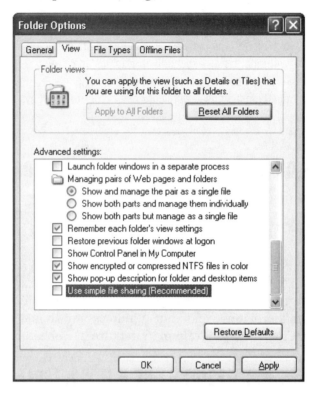

WINDOWS MEDIA PLAYER DOES NOT PLAY CD MUSIC

If Media Player does not seem to play a CD-ROM drive, then the drive probably needs to be configured to play CD music. If you are having problems putting CD music in the Media Library, keep in mind that you must first copy that CD music to your hard drive before you can place it in the Media Library. To configure the CD-ROM drive to play CD music, follow these steps.

CONFIGURING THE CD-ROM DRIVE FOR MUSIC

1. First, check your CD-ROM drive. Click Start | My Computer.

2. In the My Computer window, right-click your CD-ROM drive and click Properties.

3. Click the AutoPlay tab. Under Actions, choose the Select an Action to Perform button and choose Play Using Windows Media Player, as shown here, and click OK.

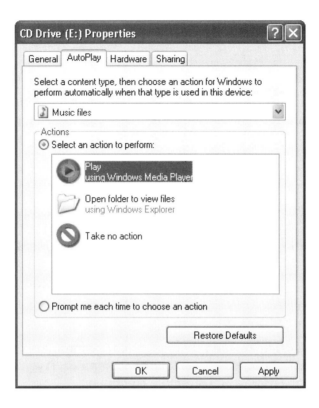

4. Next, you want to make sure the device is configured to play CD music. Click Start | Control Panel | System.

5. Click the Hardware tab and then click the Device Manager button.

6. Expand the DVD/CD-ROM drives category, and then right-click the CD-ROM and click Properties.

7. Click the Properties tab. Set the CD Player Volume slider bar to High. If the Enable Digital CD Audio for This CD-ROM Drive check box is selected, leave it selected. If not, select the check box and click OK. Close Device Manager.

8. Now open Windows Media Player. Click Tools | Options.

9. Click the Devices tab. Make sure that your audio CD drive appears in this window. If it does not, try clicking the Refresh button.

10. If the CD-ROM drive still will not play CDs, then go back to the Device Manager CD-ROM Properties sheet (see steps 4 through 7) and clear the Enable Digital CD Audio for This CD-ROM Drive check box. Then click OK.

A COMPUTER IS HAVING NETWORK ACCESS PROBLEMS

If a computer residing on a network is having problems accessing the network, you'll need to troubleshoot a few different items. The following list gives you some quick tips:

- Use Device Manager and make sure the computer's network adapter card is functioning and is connected to the network.

- Access the TCP/IP properties and make sure the computer is configured as needed for your network (dynamic or static IP address configuration). Also, check the default gateway and make sure a correct DNS server is specified.

- Use the Ipconfig.exe command to determine the IP address and subnet mask of the computer. Ensure that the IP address and subnet mask are valid for your network.

- Use the ping command and try to ping other computers. Also try to ping the problematic computer from another computer. Try pinging a local computer, the gateway, and a remote computer.

- In a domain environment, ensure that the user/computer has a domain account and is logged on to the domain.

A MODEM DISCONNECTS WHEN THERE IS IDLE TIME

Both modem and dial-up account configuration can hang up an Internet connection if a certain period of idle time passes. However, you can stop this behavior. To stop the autodisconnect feature, follow these steps.

STOPPING IDLE DISCONNECT BEHAVIOR

1. Click Start | Control Panel | Phone and Modem Options.

2. Click the Modems tab. Select your modem in the list and click Properties.

3. Click the Advanced tab, and then click the Change Default Preferences button.

4. On the General tab, shown here, clear the Disconnect a Call If Idle for *X* Mins check box, or change the value if desired. Click OK, then click OK again.

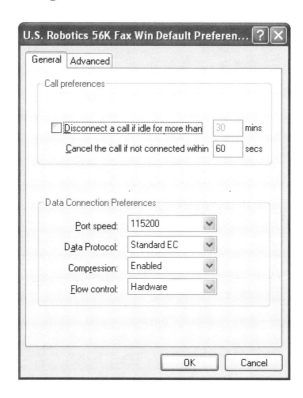

5. To check the connection properties, click Start | Connect To | Show All Connections.

6. Right-click the Internet connection and click Properties.

7. In the Options tab, change the Idle Time before Hanging Up setting to Never, as shown here. Click OK.

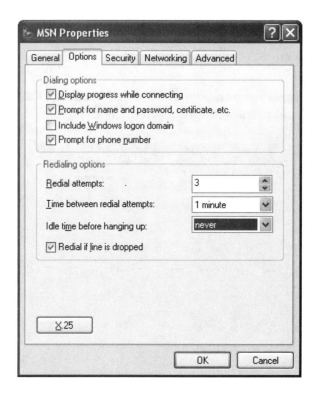

INTERNET CONNECTIVITY IS SLOW

Internet connectivity is one of those aggravating issues that you'll need to support in workgroup situations where a proxy server does not handle Internet connectivity. There are a few basic guidelines to follow:

■ The speed of your connection often depends on your Internet service provider (ISP). If you believe you should have better speeds than what you are getting, you can talk with technical support for your ISP, who may have some suggestions.

■ Keep in mind that peak usage times during the day will be slower. Web servers are busy and often are quite congested. Late at night or early in the morning are always the best times to surf—even with broadband connections.

- If Internet Explorer seems to have slowed down over time, you can dump all of the temporary Internet files and cookies. Doing so sometimes helps IE work faster. Click Start | Control Panel | Internet Options. On the General tab, click the Delete Files button under Temporary Internet Files.

- If you are using ICS, traffic among ICS clients can slow down Internet connectivity, especially if you are not using a broadband connection. Either the users have to stop using the Internet as much, or you will have to upgrade the connection on the ICS host.

INTERNET EXPLORER BLOCKS CERTAIN SITES, OR SITES ARE NOT ACCESSIBLE

If Internet Explorer blocks certain web sites, or some sites do not seem accessible, you probably need to adjust security and/or privacy settings. The security settings can be set too high so that IE blocks certain web sites that the user wants to visit. Or, privacy settings may be set to block all cookies—some web sites simply will not work with IE unless temporary cookies can be exchanged.

To remedy this problem, access Internet Options in Control Panel and adjust the settings found on the Security and Privacy tabs.

ICS USERS DISCONNECT A DIAL-UP ICS CONNECTION

In Windows XP, your ICS clients can control the Internet connection, if allowed to do so from the ICS host. This feature is new in Windows XP and can be useful in a number of scenarios. When the option is turned on, users can connect, disconnect, and even reconfigure the connection. If you do not want users to manage the Internet connection, however, you can disable this feature. To stop ICS clients from managing the Internet connection, follow these steps.

RESTRICTING ICS CLIENTS FROM MANAGING THE INTERNET CONNECTION

1. On the ICS host computer, click Start | Connect To | Show All Connections.
2. Right-click the Internet connection and click Properties.

3. Click the Advanced tab, as shown here. Clear the check box option Allow Other Users to Control or Disable the Shared Internet Connection and click OK.

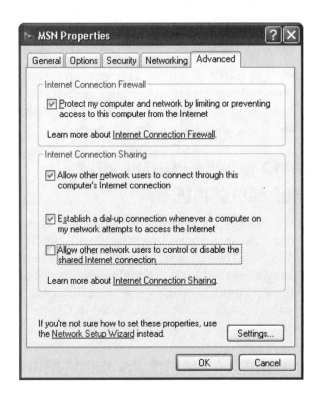

A USER CANNOT ENCRYPT A COMPRESSED FILE

In Windows XP, encryption and compression do not work together. You can either encrypt a file or compress it, but you cannot do both. In this case, once again, user education is required. To encrypt the file, access the file's Properties sheet and choose to encrypt the file. However, doing so will automatically uncompress the file.

NOTE Keep in mind that Windows XP Home Edition does not support encryption. Windows XP Home Edition also does not support other features found in Windows XP Professional, such as Remote Desktop hosting features, NTFS permissions, or even the backup tool. However, the backup tool is available on the Windows XP Home Edition CD-ROM (in the ValueAdd folder). You can install it from this location and use it on the Home Edition.

A USER COMPLAINS THAT WINDOWS XP TURNS ITSELF OFF

If your computer hardware supports it, Windows XP provides a hibernation feature. After a period of inactivity, Windows XP can save to the hard disk all of the data held in RAM, and then shut itself down. When you reboot, the data is read off the hard disk and back into RAM so that your computer is in the same state as you left it. No data is lost on any open applications using hibernation. However, you can disable hibernation if you want.

TURNING OFF HIBERNATION

1. Click Start | Control Panel | Display.

2. Click the Screen Saver tab and then click the Power button.

3. On the Power Schemes tab, as shown here, change the System Hibernates option to Never. Click OK.

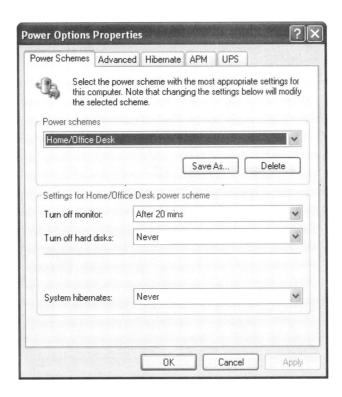

WINDOWS XP AUTOMATICALLY CONNECTS TO THE INTERNET

Windows Update is a feature that allows Windows XP to check for operating system updates and automatically download them so that you can install them. This feature works great, especially if you are on a broadband connection, but if you are not, it can be a real pain because it will try to dial your connection. You can change this automatic feature, however, if you don't want to use it. To change the Windows Update feature, follow these steps.

DISABLING AUTOMATIC UPDATE

1. Log on as an administrator.
2. Click Start | Control Panel | System.
3. Click the Automatic Updates tab, as shown here. Choose the Turn Off Automatic Updating option and click OK.

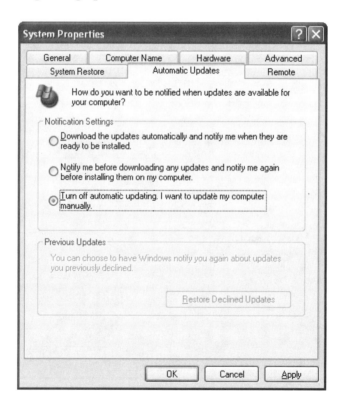

NTFS FEATURES ARE NOT AVAILABLE

Windows XP works best with NTFS, but is completely compatible with FAT32. If your drive is currently FAT32, you can convert it to NTFS without any problems. However, you should make certain that the conversion is really necessary. NTFS drives provide you with compression capabilities and security features, but depending on your use of Windows XP, you may not need any of these features. See the Windows XP help files for comparisons and more information about using NTFS or FAT32. If you decide that you want to use NTFS, you can convert your FAT32 drive easily and without any loss of data by following these steps.

CONVERTING A DRIVE TO NTFS

1. Log on as an administrator.

2. Back up your data, just to be safe.

3. Click Start | Run. Type **cmd** and click OK.

4. At the command prompt, type **convert** *driveletter*: **/FS:NTFS**, where *driveletter* is the letter of the drive that you want to convert. For example, if you wanted to convert your C drive, the command would be **convert C: /FS:NTFS**, as you can see here.

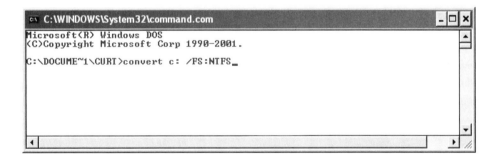

A USER HAS FORGOTTEN HIS OR HER LOCAL PASSWORD

Windows XP ties certain user information directly to the account and password. If a user forgets his or her password, you can choose to reset the password. However, you will lose data if you do so. Specifically, user certificates and web-related passwords, along with basic computer settings, will be lost once the password is reset. There is no workaround for this problem once the password has been forgotten, but you can prevent the loss of data and the reset problems by creating a Password Reset Disk. To reset a password without a Password Reset Disk, follow these steps.

RESETTING A PASSWORD WITHOUT A PASSWORD RESET DISK

1. Log on with an administrator account.
2. Click Start | Control Panel | User Accounts.
3. Select the account that you want to reset.
4. Click the Create a Password option.
5. On the Create a Password page, create a new password for the user. The user will lose personal certificates and stored passwords for web sites and network resources.

To create a Password Reset Disk so that manual resetting and loss of data does not occur, follow these steps.

RESETTING A PASSWORD WITH A PASSWORD RESET DISK

1. Log on with the desired account.
2. Open User Accounts in Control Panel.
3. In the Related Tasks box that appears in the left pane, select the user account and click the Prevent a Forgotten Password option.

NOTE You cannot create a Password Reset Disk for another user. You can only create the Password Reset Disk for the account that you used to log on. If you try to create it for someone else, the option does not appear in the Related Tasks box.

4. The Forgotten Password Wizard appears. Click Next on the Welcome screen.
5. Choose the drive (such as your floppy drive) where you want to create the Password Reset Disk. Then click Next.
6. Enter the current user account password and click Next.
7. The Password Reset Disk is created. Click Next and then click Finish.

If you need to use the Password Reset Disk, follow these steps.

USING THE PASSWORD RESET DISK

1. On the Welcome screen, click the question mark button next to your user account.

2. The "Did you forget your password?" message appears. Click the Use Your Password Reset Disk option and follow the instructions that appear.

ACCOUNT LOCKOUT AND OTHER ACCOUNT FEATURES ARE NOT AVAILABLE

Windows XP Professional provides you with some additional account management features that you can implement if you want fine control over user account logons. However, these options are not intuitive because you configure them through local Group Policy.

Group Policy is a feature that allows an XP administrator to configure all kinds of settings and account options that are applied to all users. Users cannot override the settings and are forced to live with what you configure. Group Policy provides uniformity and enables you to apply standards to all user accounts that you want to enforce. You can control much with Group Policy, including account configuration options. To use Group Policy to configure account restrictions, follow these steps.

CONFIGURING ACCOUNT RESTRICTIONS

1. Click Start | Run.

2. Type **gpedit.msc** and click OK. Keep in mind that this command will work only on Windows XP Professional computers. The Group Policy console opens, as you can see here.

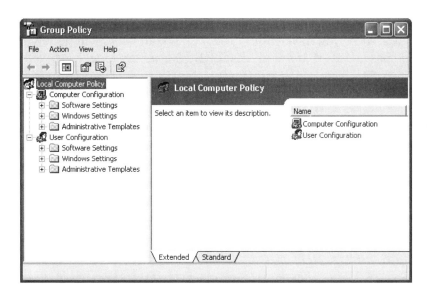

3. Under Computer Configuration, expand Windows Settings. Then expand Security Settings and select Account Policies.

4. In the right pane, you see containers for Password Policy and Account Lockout Policy. You can double-click a container and see the policy options available. For example, as shown here, you see the options to configure minimum and maximum ages, complexity requirements, and other settings.

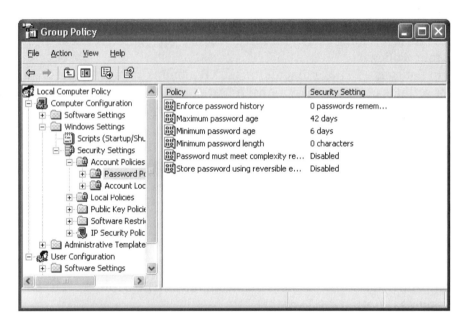

5. To configure a policy, double-click it. A policy configuration window appears. After you have configured a policy, all users will be forced to use passwords that are at least eight characters long.

6. Once you are done, click OK and exit Group Policy.

INTERNET EXPLORER DOES NOT ALLOW YOU TO DOWNLOAD A DRIVER

Internet Explorer 6, which is included with Windows XP, has some security features that try to help you avoid downloading unsigned drivers, and thus prevent you from downloading viruses and other malicious code. Normally, Internet Explorer will prompt you before downloading an unsigned driver, but if the setting has been configured to Block, then you will not be able to download the driver.

To enable Internet Explorer to prompt you for driver download action, follow these steps.

SETTING UP A PROMPT TO APPEAR WHEN DOWNLOADING UNSIGNED DRIVERS

1. Log on with an administrator account.

2. Click Start | Control Panel | System.

3. Click the Hardware tab and click the Driver Signing button.

4. In the Driver Signing Options dialog box that appears, click the Warn radio button so that IE will warn you before downloading unsigned driver files, rather than blocking the downloading. If you want this setting to apply to all users on the computer, click the Make This Action the System Default check box, as shown here. Click OK.

A HARD DISK READS AND WRITES DATA VERY SLOWLY

Over time, your hard disk may become fragmented. As files are saved and opened, Windows XP may have to store pieces of the files in different places on the disk, which in turn requires more time to save and open them. Fragmentation is a normal result of excessive disk use. The primary signs of fragmentation are slow reading and writing—you double-click a file and it takes a little too long to open it, or you save a file and it takes a little too long to save it. The good news is that Windows XP gives you a tool to defragment the hard disk and resolve the fragmentation problem. To defragment the drive, follow these steps.

DEFRAGMENTING A DRIVE

1. Click Start | My Computer. Right-click the drive letter and click Properties.

2. Click the Tools tab, and click the Defragment Now button.

3. In the Disk Defragmenter dialog box, shown here, click the Analyze button to see whether the disk needs to be defragmented.

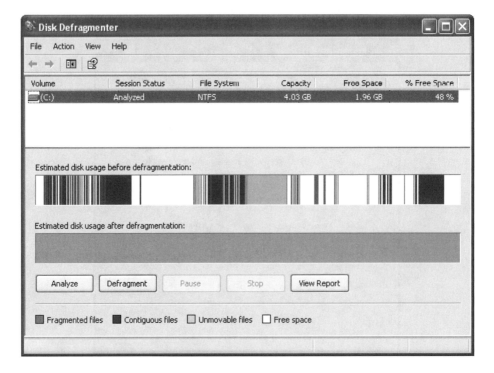

4. A message appears telling you whether or not you should defragment the volume. Click Defragment to continue. The defragmentation process begins and may take some time (possibly several hours), depending on the size of the hard disk.

WINDOWS XP STOPS RESPONDING WHEN A PRINT JOB IS SENT TO THE PRINTER

A utility called the Windows spooler should handle print jobs. The spooler processes and holds print jobs until they are printed. This frees up the computer so that you can continue to work and play while the printer is working. If the spooler is not used, however, the computer will not respond until the print job is finished. To make sure you are using the spooler, follow these steps:

ENSURING THAT THE SPOOLER IS IN USE

1. Click Start | Control Panel | Printers and Faxes.

2. Right-click the desired printer icon and click Properties.

3. Click the Advanced tab, shown here. Make sure that the Spool Print Documents So Program Finishes Printing Faster option is selected— *not* the Print Directly to the Printer option.

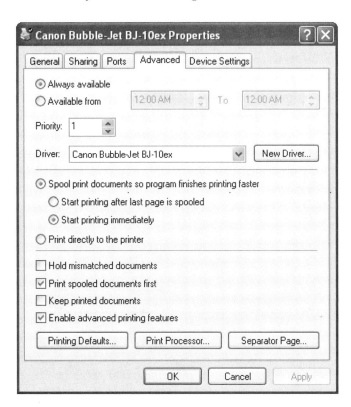

REMOTE DESKTOP DOES NOT WORK WITH ICF

By default, ICF does not allow incoming traffic that is not explicitly requested by a local user, and thus drops Remote Desktop traffic. However, you can configure ICF to allow Remote Desktop traffic. To configure ICF to allow Remote Desktop traffic, follow these steps.

CONFIGURING ICF FOR REMOTE DESKTOP TRAFFIC

1. Click Start | Network Connections. Right-click the Internet connection and click Properties.

2. Click the Advanced tab and click the Settings button.

3. In the Advanced Settings window, shown here, click the Remote Desktop check box on the Services tab, click OK, then click OK again.

A WINDOWS XP COMPUTER BOOTS SLOWLY

If your computer boots slowly, the problem may be that a number of applications or services are configured to begin at startup. This can cause the computer to take longer to boot because all of these extra features have to be loaded. Also, if your processor and RAM are barely meeting the requirements, then you can expect the computer to boot more slowly. To check the items that are configured to start when the computer boots, follow these steps.

CHECKING ITEMS CONFIGURED TO START ON BOOTUP

1. Click Start | Run. Type **msconfig** and click OK. This opens the System Configuration utility.

2. On the Services tab, you see a list of items that are configured to start when the computer starts. You can remove items simply by clearing the check box next to them. However, you should be careful; many items are needed for Windows XP to run properly. A good way to use this tab is to look in the manufacturer column for manufacturers other than Microsoft; among these manufacturers you might find a number of programs that you really do not use or even need. Check your computer documentation for details, and don't hesitate to contact technical support for help.

WINDOWS XP RUNS A LAPTOP COMPUTER'S BATTERY POWER DOWN QUICKLY

If your battery power runs down quickly, there are a few things you can do that will help:

■ First, check your laptop's documentation about the battery. A new battery may be all that you need to solve your problems.

■ Use Power Options System Standby features and hibernation in order to conserve power when you are not using the computer.

■ If you have multiple PC cards, consider creating a hardware profile that disables everything that you are not using when you are mobile. These resources consume valuable battery power, even when you are not directly using them.

■ Unless you are using the CD-ROM, take any CD out of the drive; the spinning CD consumes battery power resources.

INDEX

INTERNATIONAL CONTACT INFORMATION

AUSTRALIA
McGraw-Hill Book Company Australia Pty. Ltd.
TEL +61-2-9900-1800
FAX +61-2-9878-8881
http://www.mcgraw-hill.com.au
books-it_sydney@mcgraw-hill.com

CANADA
McGraw-Hill Ryerson Ltd.
TEL +905-430-5000
FAX +905-430-5020
http://www.mcgraw-hill.ca

GREECE, MIDDLE EAST, & AFRICA
(Excluding South Africa)
McGraw-Hill Hellas
TEL +30-210-6560-990
TEL +30-210-6560-993
TEL +30-210-6560-994
FAX +30-210-6545-525

MEXICO (Also serving Latin America)
McGraw-Hill Interamericana Editores S.A. de C.V.
TEL +525-117-1583
FAX +525-117-1589
http://www.mcgraw-hill.com.mx
fernando_castellanos@mcgraw-hill.com

SINGAPORE (Serving Asia)
McGraw-Hill Book Company
TEL +65-863-1580
FAX +65-862-3354
http://www.mcgraw-hill.com.sg
mghasia@mcgraw-hill.com

SOUTH AFRICA
McGraw-Hill South Africa
TEL +27-11-622-7512
FAX +27-11-622-9045
robyn_swanepoel@mcgraw-hill.com

SPAIN
McGraw-Hill/Interamericana de España, S.A.U.
TEL +34-91-180-3000
FAX +34-91-372-8513
http://www.mcgraw-hill.es
professional@mcgraw-hill.es

UNITED KINGDOM, NORTHERN,
EASTERN, & CENTRAL EUROPE
McGraw-Hill Education Europe
TEL +44-1-628-502500
FAX +44-1-628-770224
http://www.mcgraw-hill.co.uk
computing_neurope@mcgraw-hill.com

ALL OTHER INQUIRIES Contact:
Osborne/McGraw-Hill
TEL +1-510-549-6600
FAX +1-510-883-7600
http://www.osborne.com
omg_international@mcgraw-hill.com